German - English

Your

GERMAN

Dictionary

Second edition

al Levick

lenise Radford

lasdair McKeane

ACKNOWLEDGEMENTS

We are grateful to Anne, Mick and John for editorial, moral, typographical and technical support, to Claire, Jonathan, John, Andrew and James for their tolerance of the whole process of writing and publishing this book, and to Mike Nightingale and Gail Wilson for proof-reading.

Published by Malvern Language Guides
PO Box 76
Malvern
WR14 2YP
UK
Tel: 01684 893756 (for price enquiries only)
01684 577433 (for other enquiries)

Further copies can be obtained by completing the order form at the back of the book.

© Val Levick, Alasdair McKeane & Glenise Radford 1998

Typeset by Malvern Language Guides

Printed by Aldine Press Ltd
Barnards Green Road
Malvern
WR14 3NB
UK
Tel: 01684 562786

ISBN: 1 898219 72 9

Revised using Duden Rechtschreibung 21. Ausgabe and associated publications

CONTENTS

HOW TO USE A DICTIONARY

All learners of a foreign language will find knowing how to use a dictionary a really useful skill. From 1998 onwards dictionaries will be permitted in some parts of the GCSE exam, so it is sensible to learn how to look up words and to understand the abbreviations.

Alphabetical order

Dictionaries are arranged in alphabetical order. So all words beginning with the letter *a* come before all those beginning with the letter *b*, and so on. Within the section for each letter, the same applies. So the words which start with the letters *ab* come before those starting *ac*, and so on. In the same way, words starting *aba* come before those starting *abb*. If you are not totally sure of your alphabet, write it on a bookmark which you keep with your dictionary.

In German, the Umlaut does not affect the alphabetical order.

Abbreviations

All dictionaries contain abbreviations for convenience. However, they are only convenient if you know what they mean! In this dictionary there are reminders of the most frequent abbreviations at the foot of each page. The full list of abbreviations we have used is given on page xi.

Looking up a German word

When you look up a **German** word, it is possible that you may find a number of English translations given, listed with the most common first. You will then need to work out which meaning is most likely in the context.

You may find that a word is not listed. This may mean that it is a past participle, or some other part of an irregular verb. Check the verb table on page 210.

Adjectives and Adverbs

In German adjectives can usually be used as adverbs. Therefore in this dictionary most adverbs are listed as adjectives only.

Nouns

Nouns are identified as masculine, feminine or neuter.

Example: **man** – Mann (Männer) *nm*

                    woman – Frau (-en) *nf*

                    girl – Mädchen (-) *nnt*

Some nouns can be either masculine or feminine.

Example: **adult** – Erwachsene *nmf* ‡

Some masculine nouns and *das Herz* are irregular (weak). They are identified as *nm wk*.

Example: **boy** – Junge (-n) *nm wk*

German nouns have a number of ways of forming the plural. In each case where there is a plural form in common use we have listed the modification which needs to be made to form the plural.

Example: **girl** – Mädchen (-) *nnt*   Plural: Mädchen (no change)

                    woman – Frau (-en) *nf*   Plural: Frauen

                    fish – Fisch (-e) *nm*   Plural: Fische

                    face – Gesicht (-er) *nnt*   Plural: Gesichter

                    man – Mann (Männer) *nm*   Plural: Männer

                    car – Auto (-s) *nnt*   Plural: Autos

Verbs

Verbs are classified as regular (*v reg*), irregular (*v irreg*), reflexive (*v refl*) and as verbs with slight variations (†). Additionally, verbs of all kinds can be separable *(sep)* or inseparable *(insep)*.

Regular verbs are verbs which follow a regular pattern in all tenses. They form the past participle by adding **ge** before the stem of the verb and adding **t** to the stem.

Example: spielen   **ge**spiel**t**

These are identified as *v reg.*

Irregular verbs are verbs which just have to be learned individually. They may be regular in the present tense but may not follow the pattern of regular verbs in other tenses.

Example: trinken, fahren, schreiben

These are identified as *v irreg.* Look in the verb table on page 210 for help with these verbs. To find the changes in irregular verbs with a prefix, first remove the prefix and then look for the verb. Remember that * is the symbol used to show that a verb takes **sein** in the perfect and other compound tenses.

Reflexive verbs are verbs with an extra pronoun.

    Example: sich waschen

They are identified as *v reg refl* if they are regular, as *v irreg refl* if they are irregular and as *v reg refl* † if they are verbs with variations.
A small number of reflexive verbs require a dative reflexive pronoun. These are identified as *v irreg dat refl*.

You will not find every irregular reflexive verb listed in the verb table. If you cannot find the one you want, remove any prefix and look it up without **sich**.

Verbs with variations are verbs which broadly follow the regular pattern with some variations:

    Example: arbeiten   er arbeitet, sie hat gearbeitet
                   reparieren   ich habe repariert
                   besuchen   er hat besucht

These are identified as *v reg* †. Look at page 229 for help with these verbs.

Separable verbs are verbs with prefixes which often separate from the verb and move to the end of the sentence or clause. The past participle of a separable verb is formed by fitting the **ge** between the prefix and the main part of the verb.

    Example: **abfahren**   sie fährt **ab**   sie ist **ab**gefahren

These are identified as *v reg sep, v irreg sep,* or *v reg sep* †.

Inseparable verbs are verbs with prefixes which do not separate from the main part of the verb.

    Example: **unter**suchen   sie **unter**sucht   sie hat **unter**sucht

These are identified as *v reg insep, v irreg insep,* or *v reg insep* †.

Looking up an English word

When you look up an **English** word to find the German equivalent, it is important to know if you are looking for an adjective, a noun, a verb, an adverb, etc. (Adjectives, nouns and verbs are all identified in both parts of the dictionary. See page vi if you are unsure of any of these terms.) When you have found the German word, look that up in the German-English section. You should get the same English word you started with in the English-German section, or a word which means the same in the same situation.

In the English-German section of the dictionary, words which could be misleading have an explanation in brackets to clarify the meaning.

Example: **square** – (in town)

                 square – (on paper)

                 square – (shape)

What else is in the dictionary?

There is a **table of German irregular verbs** at the end of the dictionary. If a verb is described as *v irreg*, you will find it in the verb table on page 210. To save space, verbs which are compounds are not given.

So **ausgehen** will behave in exactly the same way as **gehen**.

There is information about **how to write letters**, both formal and informal, on page 231.

There is a **list of instructions** in German which you might see in text books, together with translations of these instructions. These will be found on page 235.

This dictionary also contains **simple explanations of grammatical terms**, with examples on pages vi - x, and a reminder of **simple grammar points** on pages 216 - 230.

GRAMMATICAL TERMS EXPLAINED

acc   Accusative (Akkusativ)

The accusative case is most common for direct objects and after certain prepositions.

adj   Adjectives (Adjektive)

These are words which describe or tell you more about a noun.
There are many kinds of adjectives:
     Example: **big** – groß *adj*
                  green – grün *adj*
                  intelligent – intelligent *adj*
                  German – deutsch *adj*
but they all serve to give extra information about their noun. If the adjective comes between an article and the noun the adjective almost always adds an ending.

adv   Adverbs (Adverbien)

These are words which are added to a verb, adjective or another adverb to tell you how, when, where a thing was done:
     Example: **quickly** – schnell *adv*
                  soon – bald *adv*
                  there – dort *adv*
In German adverbs are usually identical to adjectives. Adverbs are therefore only listed where the adverb is distinct or has no equivalent adjective.

art   Articles (Artikel)

There are two kinds of articles mentioned in this dictionary:
     def art: definite (bestimmt)   **the** – der, die, das, die
     indef art: indefinite (unbestimmt)   **a, an** – ein, eine, ein

coll   Colloquial (Umgangssprachlich)

These are words used in spoken German but which are perhaps not always suitable for written German.

co-ord conj   Co-ordinating Conjunctions (Nebenordnende Konjunktionen)

These are words used to join sentences and clauses, which do not affect word order at all.
     Example: **and** – und *co-ord conj*

dat   Dative (Dativ)

The dative case is used for the indirect object and after certain prepositions and verbs.

dem pron   Demonstrative Pronouns (Demonstrativpronomen)

These words are used to establish contrast between two things or people:
Example   **this one** – dieser *dem pron*

excl   Exclamations (Ausrufe)

These are phrases and words which are often used with an exclamation mark:
Example: **help!** – Hilfe! *excl*

gen   Genitive (Genitiv)

The genitive case is used to denote possession and after certain prepositions.
An **-s** (or **-es** for one syllable nouns) is added to masculine and neuter nouns.

inv   Invariable (Unflektiert)

These nouns or adjectives do not change their spelling or take any endings.
Example: **pink** – rosa *adj inv*

nm, nf, nnt, nmf, npl, nmf ‡, nm wk, nnt wk   Nouns (Substantive)

These are names of people, places or things. There are three genders in German:
masculine *nm*, feminine *nf* and neuter *nnt*. All nouns fit into one of these
categories. Plural forms are shown in brackets.
Example: **spoon** – Löffel (-) *nm*
               fork – Gabel (-n) *nf*
               knife – Messer (-) *nnt*
Some nouns are not found in the singular. They are listed as *npl*
Example: **sore throat** – Halsschmerzen *npl*

Some adjectival nouns can be either feminine or masculine. Information about them
can be found on page 220.
Example: **adult** – Erwachsene   *nmf ‡*

Weak nouns are shown as *wk*. Information about them can be found on page 221.
Example: **boy** – Junge (-n) *nm wk*

nom   Nominative (Nominativ)

The nominative case is used for the subject of the sentence or clause.

pers pron   **Personal Pronouns (Personalpronomen)**

This is the general name given to subject, direct object and reflexive pronouns:

Example: **he** – er *pers pron*

him – ihn *pers pron*

himself –sich *pers pron*

pl   **Plural (Plural)**

Nouns can be singular or plural. Plural forms of singular nouns are shown in brackets after the noun

Example: **boy** – Junge (-n) *nm wk*

holidays – Ferien *npl*

town – Stadt (Städte) nf

Some nouns have no plural and are shown as *no pl*

Example: **vegetables** – Gemüse *nnt, no pl*

poss adj   **Possessives (Possessivum)**

These adjectives show ownership.

Example: **my** – mein *poss adj*

pref   **Prefix (Präfix)**

A prefix is a syllable on the front of a word which alters its meaning.

Example: **anti~** – *pref* anti

prep   **Prepositions (Präpositionen)**

These are words placed in front of nouns and pronouns to show position and other relationships:

Example: **with** – mit (+ dat) *prep*

before – vor (+ acc/dat) *prep*

pron   **Pronouns (Pronomen)**

Pronouns are short words used to stand in the place of a noun to avoid repeating it. In German they must agree with the gender of the noun they are standing for:

Example: **he** – er *pron*

rel pron   **Relative Pronouns (Relativpronomen)**

These are words which join two phrases or ideas which are linked by meaning:

Example: **which** – der, die, das, die *rel pron*

*The book **which** is on the table is interesting*

Das Buch, **das** auf dem Tisch liegt, ist interessant

sub conj   **Subordinating Conjunctions (Unterordende Konjunktionen)**

Subordinating conjunctions introduce a subordinate clause. The verb is placed at the end of the clause. Further information can be found on page 220.

Example: **if** – wenn *sub conj*

v reg, v reg †, v irreg, v refl, v sep, v insep   **Verbs (Verben)**

A verb will tell you the actions and events in a sentence.

Example: *I am playing football*   Ich **spiele** Fußball

The form of the verb which is listed in this dictionary and verb table is called the infinitive. It means "to ..."

Example: **sehen** – see *v irreg*

v reg   **Regular Verbs (Regelmäßige Verben) (also called Weak Verbs)**

Many verbs belong to this group and they are identified as *v reg* in the dictionary.

v reg †   **Regular Verbs † (Regelmäßige Verben †)**

These regular verbs have slight variations. Further information about these verbs can be found on pages 229.

v irreg   **Irregular Verbs (Unregelmäßige Verben) (also called Strong Verbs)**

These verbs, which do not follow the regular pattern in all tenses, are set out for you in the verb table on page 210. They are verbs which are frequently used and which you **must** know. They are listed as *v irreg*

Example: **eat** – essen *v irreg*

be able to – können *v irreg*

come – kommen* *v irreg*

* is the symbol used to show that a verb takes **sein** in the perfect and other compound tenses.

v refl   **Reflexive Verbs (Reflexive Verben)**

These are verbs which have an extra pronoun. You must remember to use the correct reflexive pronoun.

Example: *I wash myself* – Ich wasche **mich**

She gets dressed – Sie zieht **sich** an

v dat refl   **Reflexive Verbs (Reflexive Verben)**

A reflexive verb where the pronoun is in the dative case is marked *v dat refl*

Example: *I wash my hair* – Ich wasche **mir** die Haare

v sep   **Separable Verbs (Trennbare Verben)**

Separable verbs have a prefix which often separates from its verb and moves to the end of the clause. More information about them can be found on page 228.

Example: **depart** – abfahren *v irreg sep*

v insep   **Inseparable Verbs (Untrennbare Verben)**

Inseparable verbs have a prefix but this prefix never separates from its verb.

Example: **examine** – untersuchen *v reg insep*

More details about Grammar can be found on pages 216 - 230.

LIST OF ABBREVIATIONS

*	verb takes *sein* in perfect tense (page 228)	*no pl*	no plural
†	regular verb with variations (page 229)	*npl*	noun found only in the plural
acc	accusative	*nt*	neuter
adj	adjective	*nm/nnt wk*	weak noun (page 221)
adv	adverb	*o.s.*	oneself
art	article	*pers pron*	personal pronoun
coll	colloquial	*pl*	plural
co-ord conj	co-ordinating conjunction	*poss adj*	possessive adjective
dat	dative	*pref*	prefix
def	definite	*prep*	preposition
dem pron	demonstrative pronoun	*pron*	pronoun
excl	exclamation	*rel pron*	relative pronoun
f	feminine	*sing*	singular
gen	genitive	*s.o.*	someone
indef	indefinite	*sthg*	something
inv	invariable	*sub conj*	subordinating conjunction
jdm	jemandem (dative)	*v dat refl*	verb, reflexive with dative pronoun
m	masculine	*v insep*	verb, inseparable
n ‡	adjectival noun (see page 220)	*v irreg*	verb, irregular; details in the verb table (page 210)
nf	noun, feminine	*v refl*	verb, reflexive
nm	noun, masculine	*v reg*	verb, regular
nnt	noun, neuter	*v sep*	verb, separable
nom	nominative		

A

ab (+ dat) – *prep* from (date, prices)
  ab und zu – *adv* from time to time
  ab morgen – from tomorrow
abbauen – *v reg sep* to take down
  ein Zelt abbauen – *v reg sep* take down a tent
abbiegen – *v irreg sep* turn (off road)
Abend (-e) – *nm* evening
  Bis heute Abend! – See you this evening!
  jeden Abend – every evening
  Guten Abend! – *excl* Good evening!
  Einen schönen Abend! – *excl* Have a nice evening!
  gestern Abend – last night, yesterday evening
Abendbrot (-e) – *nnt* evening meal, tea (cold)
Abendessen (-) – *nnt* dinner, evening meal
abends – *adv* in the evening
Abenteuer (-) – *nnt* adventure
Abenteuerfilm (-e) – *nm* adventure film
Abenteuerroman (-e) – *nm* adventure story
aber – *co-ord conj* but
abfahren* – *v irreg sep* depart, go, leave
Abfahrt (-en) – *nf* departure
  vor der Abfahrt – before leaving
Abfahrtsplan (-pläne) – *nm* departure board
Abfahrtszeit (-en) – *nf* departure time
Abfall – *nm* litter, rubbish
Abfalleimer (-) – *nm* rubbish bin
abfliegen* – *v irreg sep* to depart (plane)

Abflug (Abflüge) – *nm* flight departure
Abgase – *npl* exhaust fumes
abgeben – *v irreg sep* hand in (book, ticket)
Abgemacht! – *excl* Agreed!
abhängen von (+ dat) – *v irreg sep* depend on
abhauen – *v reg sep coll* go away
  Hau ab! – *excl coll* Clear off!
abholen – *v reg sep* meet, pick up
Abitur – *nnt* A level (-s)
Abiturient (-en) – *nm wk* Upper Sixth form student
Abiturientin (-nen) – *nf* Upper Sixth form student
Abkürzung (-en) – *nf* abbreviation
ablegen – *v reg sep* put aside
ablehnen – *v reg sep* decline, refuse
abnehmen – *v irreg sep* lose weight
  den Hörer abnehmen – *v irreg sep* pick up phone
Abonnement (-s) – *nnt* subscription
abräumen – *v reg sep* clear away
Abreise (-n) – *nf* departure
abreisen* – *v reg sep* depart
Absatz (sätze) – *nm* paragraph; heel
abschicken – *v reg sep* send away
abschleppen – *v reg sep* tow away
Abschleppwagen (-) – *nm* breakdown lorry
abschließen – *v irreg sep* lock
Abschlussprüfung (-en) – *nf* final exam
Abs./Absender (-) – *nm* sender (letter)
Absicht (-en) – *nf* purpose, intention
absichtlich – *adv* on purpose
abstauben – *v reg sep* dust
Abstellplatz (-plätze) – *nm* parking space
absurd – *adj* absurd

---

adj - adjective	*v reg* - verb regular	*v sep* - verb separable	† - see verb info
prep - preposition	*v irreg* - verb irregular	*v refl* - verb reflexive	* - takes sein

Abtei (-en) – *nf* abbey

Abteil (-e) – *nnt* compartment

Abteilung (-en) – *nf* department

abtrocknen – *v reg sep* † dry dishes

abwaschen – *v irreg sep* wash up

abwesend – *adj* absent

Abwesenheit (-en) – *nf* absence

Abzeichen (-) – *nnt* badge

Ach! – *excl* Oh!

acht – *adj* eight

achte – *adj* eighth

Achterbahn (-en) – *nf* rollercoaster

achten (auf + acc) – *v reg* † pay attention (to)

Achtung! – *excl* Look out! Attention!

achtzehn – *adj* eighteen

achtzig – *adj* eighty

ADAC – vehicle breakdown service

addieren – *v reg* † add up

Adjektiv (-e) – *nnt* adjective

adoptieren – *v reg* † adopt

Adoptiv~ – *pref* adopted

Adresse (-n) – *nf* address

Aerobic – *nnt, no pl* aerobics

Affe (-n) – *nm wk* monkey

Afrika – *nnt* Africa

afrikanisch – *adj* African

Agentur (-en) – *nf* agency

aggressiv – *adj* aggressive

ähneln (+ dat) – *v reg* resemble

ähnlich – *adj* similar, like

Ahnung (-en) – *nf* idea, knowledge

  Keine Ahnung! – *excl* No idea!

Aktentasche (-n) – *nf* briefcase

aktiv – *adj* active

aktuell – *adj* current, up to date

Akzent (-e) – *nm* accent

akzeptieren – *v reg* † accept, agree

albern – *adj* foolish

Album (Alben) – *nnt* album

Algebra – *nf* algebra

Alkohol (-e) – *nm* alcohol

alkoholfrei – *adj* alcohol free

  ein alkoholfreies Getränk – *nnt* a soft drink

All – *nnt* space (universe)

alle – all, everybody

  wir alle – all of us

  es ist alle – it's all gone

Allee (-n) – *nf* avenue

allein – *adv* alone

Alleinerziehende – *nmf* ‡ single parent

allergisch gegen (+ acc) – *adj* allergic to

allerlei – all sorts of

alles – everything

  alles in allem – all in all

  Alles Gute – love from, Yours

allgemein – *adj* general

  im Allgemeinen – in general

Alltag – *nm* daily routine, weekday

alltäglich – *adj* everyday

Alltagsleben – *nnt* everyday life

Alpen – *npl* Alps

Alphabet (-e) – *nnt* alphabet

Alptraum (-träume) – *nm* nightmare

als – *sub conj* than

als – *sub conj* when (in past)

als ob – *sub conj* as if

also – *adv* so, therefore

Also! – *excl* Right!

alt – *adj* old, elderly

  ich bin 16 (Jahre alt) – I am 16 (years old)

Alter (-) – *nnt* age, old age

  mittleren Alters – middle aged

älter – *adj* elder

älteste – *adj* eldest

altmodisch – *adj* old fashioned

Altpapier – *nnt* paper for recycling

am – (= an dem) on the

  am besten – *adv* best

  am Freitag – *adv* on Friday

---

nm - noun masculine	*nf* - noun feminine	*nnt* - noun neuter	*npl* - noun plural
nom- nominative	*acc* - accusative	*gen* - genitive	*dat* - dative

am liebsten – *adv* best of all
am Rhein – by the Rhine
Amerika – *nnt* America
Amerikaner (-) – *nm* American
Amerikanerin (-nen) – *nf* American
amerikanisch – *adj* American
Ampel (-n) – *nf* traffic lights
Amt (Ämter) – *nnt* office, position
sich amüsieren – *v reg refl* † enjoy oneself, have a good time
an (+ acc/dat) – *prep* at, on (vertical)
an (+ dat) ... vorbei – *prep* past
an Bord – on board
an der Themse – by the Thames
Ananas (-) – *nf* pineapple
anbauen – *v reg sep* grow (plants)
anbieten – *v irreg sep* offer
andauernd – *adv* continually
anbinden – *v irreg sep* tie
Andenken (-) – *nnt* souvenir
andere – *adj* other, another
andererseits – *adv* on the other hand
ändern – *v reg* change, alter
anders – *adv* differently
anderthalb – one and a half
Änderung (-en) – *nf* change
andrehen – *v reg sep* turn on (tap)
anfahren – *v irreg sep* knock s.o. over (car)
Anfang (Anfänge) – *nm* beginning
am Anfang – at the beginning
anfangen – *v irreg sep* begin
wieder von vorne anfangen – *v irreg sep* begin again
Anfänger (-) – *nm* beginner
Anfängerin (-nen) – *nf* beginner
Anführungszeichen – *npl* speech marks („...")
angeben – *v irreg sep* boast
Angeber (-) – *nm* show-off
Angeberin (-nen) – *nf* show-off

Angebot (-e) – *nnt* offer
angehen – *v irreg sep* concern
was mich angeht – as for me
Angeln – *nnt* angling
angeln gehen* – *v irreg* go angling
Angelrute (-n) – *nf* fishing rod
angenehm – *adj* pleasant, enjoyable
Angenehm! – *excl* Pleased to meet you!
angestellt sein* – *v irreg* be on the staff
Angestellte – *nmf* ‡ employee
angreifen – *v irreg sep* attack
Angriff (-e) – *nm* attack
Angst haben vor (+ dat) – *v irreg* be frightened of
große Angst haben – *v irreg* be terrified
Keine Angst! – *excl* Don't worry!
ängstlich – *adj* worried, anxious
anhaben – *v irreg sep* have on (clothes)
anhalten* – *v irreg sep* stop, halt
Anhänger (-) – *nm* trailer; pendant
anklagen – *v reg sep* accuse
ankommen* – *v irreg sep* arrive
ankreuzen – *v reg sep* tick (✓)
ankündigen – *v reg sep* announce
Ankunft (-en) – *nf* arrival
anlassen – *v irreg sep* start up (turn key)
anlegen – *v reg sep* dock
Anlieger frei – access only (road sign)
anmachen – *v reg sep* put on, turn on (light)
anmelden – *v reg sep* † register
sich anmelden – *v reg refl sep* † sign in
Anmeldung (-en) – *nf* registration
Anmeldungsformular (-e) – *nnt* registration form
annehmbar – *adj* acceptable
annehmen – *v irreg sep* accept, take
Annonce (-n) – *nf* small ad
Anorak (-s) – *nm* anorak

| adj - adjective | v reg - verb regular | v sep - verb separable | † - see verb info |
| prep - preposition | v irreg - verb irregular | v refl - verb reflexive | * - takes sein |

anprobieren – *v reg sep* † try on (clothes)

Anrichte (-n) – *nf* sideboard

Anruf (-e) – *nm* phone call

Anrufbeantworter (-) – *nm* answering machine

anrufen – *v irreg sep* ring up, phone

Ansager (-) – *nm* announcer

Ansagerin (-nen) – *nf* announcer

anschauen – *v reg sep* look at

sich anschauen – *v reg dat refl sep* take a look at

Anschlagbrett (-er) – *nnt* notice board

anschließen – *v irreg sep* plug in

anschließend – *adv* after that

Anschluss (-üsse) – *nm* connection

sich anschnallen – *v reg refl sep* fasten one's seat-belt

Anschrift (-en) – *nf* address

ansehen – *v irreg sep* look at

Ansichtskarte (-n) – *nf* picture postcard

ansprechen – *v irreg sep* address

anspringen* – *v irreg sep* start (vehicle)

anständig – *adj* decent

anstatt – *conj* instead of

anstellen – *v reg sep* employ

Anstreicher (-) – *nm* painter, decorator

Antenne (-n) – *nf* aerial

Anti~ – *pref* anti~

Antibiotikum (-ka) – *nnt* antibiotic

antibiotisch – *adj* antibiotic

Antiseptikum (-ka) – *nnt* antiseptic

antiseptisch – *adj* antiseptic

Antragsformular (-e) – *nnt* application form

Antwort (-en) – *nf* answer

die richtige Antwort – the right answer

antworten – *v reg* † answer

Anweisung (-en) – *nf* instruction

anwesend – *adj* present, not absent

anwesend sein* – *v irreg* be present, attend

Anwesenheit (-en) – *nf* presence

die Anwesenheit feststellen – *v reg sep* call the register

Anzahlung (-en) – *nf* deposit

Anzeige (-n) – *nf* advertisement

anziehen – *v irreg sep* put on clothes; attract

sich anziehen – *v irreg refl sep* get dressed

Anzug (-züge) – *nm* suit

anzünden – *v reg sep* † switch on, light

AOK – health insurance scheme

Aperitif (-s) – *nm* aperitif

Apfel (Äpfel) – *nm* apple

Apfelbaum (-bäume) – *nm* apple tree

Apfelkuchen (-) – *nm* apple cake

Apfelsaft – *nm* apple juice

Apfelsine (-n) – *nf* orange

Apfelstrudel (-) – *nm* apple strudel

Apfelwein (-e) – *nm* cider

Apotheke (-n) – *nf* chemist's shop

an der Apotheke – at the chemist's

Apotheker (-) – *nm* chemist

Apothekerin (-nen) – *nf* chemist

Apparat (e) – *nm* device, camera, phone

Anne am Apparat – This is Anne speaking

Bleiben Sie am Apparat, bitte! – *excl* Hold the line please!

Appetit (-e) – *nm* appetite

Guten Appetit! – *excl* Enjoy your meal!

Aprikose (-n) – *nf* apricot

April – *nm* April

im April – in April

Arbeit (-en) – *nf* work

---

arbeiten – *v reg* † work
halbtags arbeiten – *v reg* † work
part-time
Arbeiter (-) – *nm* worker
Arbeiterin (-nen) – *nf* worker
Arbeitgeber (-) – *nm* employer
Arbeitgeberin (-nen) – *nf* employer
Arbeitsbogen (-bögen) – *nm*
worksheet
Arbeitnehmer (-) – *nm* employee
Arbeitnehmerin (-nen) – *nf*
employee
arbeitslos – *adj* out of work
Arbeitslose – *nmf* ‡ unemployed
person
Arbeitslosigkeit – *nf* unemployment
Arbeitspraktikum (-en) – *nnt* work
experience
Arbeitszimmer (-) – *nnt* study
Architekt (-en) – *nm wk* architect
Architektin (-nen) – *nf* architect
Ärger – *nm* hassle
ärgerlich – *adj* annoying
ärgern – *v reg* annoy
sich ärgern – *v reg refl* be angry
Argument – *nnt* argument, discussion
Arm (-e) – *nm* arm
arm – *adj* poor
Armband (-bänder) – *nnt* bracelet
Armbanduhr (-en) – *nf* wrist watch
Armee (-n) – *nf* army
Ärmel (-) – *nm* sleeve
arrangieren – *v reg* † arrange
Art (-en) – *nf* way, sort of
auf diese Art und Weise – in
this manner
artig – *adj* well-behaved
Artikel (-) – *nm* article
Arzt (Ärzte) – *nm* doctor
Ärztin (-nen) – *nf* doctor
Aschenbecher (-) – *nm* ashtray

Aschermittwoch – *nm* Ash
Wednesday
asiatisch – *adj* Asian
Asien – *nnt* Asia
Ass (-e) – *nnt* ace
aß – *see essen*
Ast (Äste) – *nm* branch
Asthma – *nnt* asthma
asthmatisch – *adj* asthmatic
Atelier (-s) – *nnt* studio, workshop
Atem – *nm* breath
außer Atem – out of breath
atemlos – *adj* out of breath
Athlet (-en) – *nm wk* athlete
Athletin (-nen) – *nf* athlete
Athletik – *nf* athletics
Atlantik – *nm* Atlantic Ocean
atmen – *v reg* † breathe
Atmosphäre (-n) – *nf* atmosphere
Attest (-e) – *nnt* doctor's certificate
attraktiv – *adj* attractive
ätzend – *adj coll* a pain
auch – *adv* also, too
auch nicht – *adv* neither
auf – up (out of bed)
auf (+ acc/dat) – *prep* on, upon
(horizontal)
auf dem Lande – in the country
auf Deutsch – in German
auf einmal – *adv* all at once
auf Englisch – in English
auf links – *adv* inside out
aufbauen – *v reg sep* put up, build up
das Zelt aufbauen – *v reg sep*
pitch the tent
aufblasen – *v irreg sep* blow up,
inflate
aufbrechen* – *v irreg sep* break up,
set off
aufdrehen – *v reg sep* turn up (radio)
Aufenthalt (-e) – *nm* stay
auffordern – *v reg sep* ask, demand
aufführen – *v reg sep* put on (play)

adj - adjective	*v reg* - verb regular	*v sep* - verb separable	† - see verb info
prep - preposition	*v irreg* - verb irregular	*v refl* - verb reflexive	* - takes sein

Aufführung (-en) – *nf* show
auffüllen – *v reg sep* refill
Aufgabe (-n) – *nf* exercise, task
(school)
aufgeben – *v irreg sep* give up
aufgehen* – *v irreg sep* rise (sun)
aufgestanden sein* – *v irreg* be up
(out of bed)
aufhaben – *v irreg sep* have on
(clothes)
aufheben – *v irreg sep* pick up, lift
aufhören – *v reg sep* finish, stop
Aufkleber (-) – *nm* sticker
auflegen – *v reg sep* hang up (phone)
aufmachen – *v reg sep* open
Aufmerksamkeit (-en) – *nf*
attention
aufmuntern – *v reg sep* cheer s.o. up
aufnehmen – *v irreg sep* record
(on tape)
auf Video aufnehmen – *v irreg
sep* video
aufpassen auf (+ acc) – *v reg sep*
be careful, look after
Pass auf! – *excl* Be careful!
aufpumpen – *v reg sep* pump up
tyres
aufräumen – *v reg sep* tidy up
aufregend – *adj* exciting
Aufsatz (-sätze) – *nm* essay
Aufschlag (-schläge) – *nm* service
(tennis)
aufschlagen – *v irreg sep* open
(book)
Aufschnitt – *nm* mixed cold meats
aufschreiben – *v irreg sep* write
down
aufstehen* – *v irreg sep* get up, stand
up
aufstellen – *v reg sep* put up
Auftrag (-träge) – *nm* order
im Auftrag von (+ dat) – on
behalf of
aufwachen* – *v reg sep* wake up

aufwachsen* – *v irreg sep* grow up
sich aufwärmen – *v reg refl sep*
warm up
Auf Wiederhören! – *excl* Goodbye!
(phone)
Auf Wiedersehen! – *excl* Goodbye!
Aufzug (-züge) – *nm* lift
Auge (-n) – *nnt* eye
unter vier Augen – between you
and me, in private
Augenblick (-e) – *nm* moment,
instant
im Augenblick – at this moment
Augenbraue (-n) – *nf* eyebrow
Augenzeuge (-n) – *nm wk* eye witness
Augenzeugin (-nen) – *nf* eye witness
August – *nm* August
im August – in August
Aula (Aulen) – *nf* hall (school)
aus (+ dat) – *prep* from, out of
die Schule ist aus – school's
finished
aus – *adv* off (electrical)
aus Backstein – made of brick
aus Holz – made of wood
aus Papier – made of paper
aus Stein – built of stone
aus zweiter Hand – second-hand
Ausbildung (-en) – *nf* education,
training
Ausblick (-e) – *nm* view
Ausdruck (-e) – *nm* expression
Ausfahrt (-en) – *nf* exit, way out
ausfallen* – *v irreg sep* be cancelled
Ausflug (-flüge) – *nm* excursion
ausführen – *v reg sep* lead out
den Hund ausführen – *v reg sep*
walk the dog
Ausführung (-en) – *nf* version
ausfüllen – *v reg sep* fill in
ein Formular ausfüllen – *v reg
sep* fill in a form

Ausgang (-gänge) – *nm* exit, way out

ausgeben – *v irreg sep* spend (money)

ausgebucht – *adj* fully booked

ausgehen* – *v irreg sep* go out (light)

ausgehen* mit (+ dat) – *v irreg sep* go out with

ausgezeichnet – *adj* excellent

aushalten – *v irreg sep* put up with

aushelfen (+ dat) – *v irreg sep* help s.o. out

Aushilfe – *nf* temporary work
als Aushilfe arbeiten – *v reg* † work on a temporary basis

auskommen* mit (+ dat) – *v irreg sep* manage, get on with
gut auskommen* mit (+ dat) – *v irreg sep* get on well with (friends)

Auskunft (-en) – *nf* information
um Auskunft bitten – *v irreg* ask for information

Auskunftsbüro (-s) – *nnt* information office

Ausland – *nnt* abroad
im Ausland sein* – *v irreg* to be abroad
ins Ausland fahren* – *v irreg* to go abroad

Ausländer (-) – *nm* foreigner

Ausländerin (-nen) – *nf* foreigner

ausländisch – *adj* foreign

ausmachen – *v reg sep* put out (light)

Ausnahme (-n) – *nf* exception

auspacken – *v reg sep* unpack

Auspuff (-e) – *nm* exhaust (car)

Ausrede (-n) – *nf* excuse

ausrichten – *v reg sep* † deliver, pass on (message)

ausrufen – *v irreg sep* exclaim

Ausrufezeichen (-) – *nnt* exclamation mark (!)

sich ausruhen – *v reg refl sep* rest

Ausrüstung (-en) – *nf* equipment

ausrutschen* – *v reg sep* slip

Aussage (-n) – *nf* statement

ausschalten – *v reg sep* † switch off

ausschimpfen – *v reg sep* scold

(sich) ausschlafen – *v irreg (refl) sep* have a lie in

Aussehen (-) – *nnt* appearance

aussehen – *v irreg sep* look

aus sein* – *v irreg* be extinguished

Außen (-) – *nm* winger (sport)

Außenseite (-n) – *nf* outside

außer (+ dat) – *prep* apart from, except
außer Atem – out of breath
außer Betrieb – out of order, not working
außer Sicht – out of sight

außerdem – *adv* besides

außergewöhnlich – *adj* extraordinary

außerhalb von (+ dat) – *prep* outside

Aussicht (-en) – *nf* view

aussprechen – *v irreg sep* pronounce

ausstehen – *v irreg sep* put up with
Ich kann sie nicht ausstehen – I can't stand her

aussteigen* aus (+ dat) – *v irreg sep* get off (bus, etc)

Ausstellung (-en) – *nf* exhibition

Ausstieg (-e) – *nm* exit (bus, tram)

Austausch – *nm* school exchange
einen Austausch machen – *v reg* go on an exchange

austauschen – *v reg sep* exchange

Austauschpartner (-) – *nm* exchange partner

Austauschpartnerin (-nen) – *nf* exchange partner

austragen – *v irreg sep* deliver

Australien – *nnt* Australia

Ausverkauf – *nm* sale

Auswahl – *nf* choice

---

adj - adjective	*v reg* - verb regular	*v sep* - verb separable	† - see verb info
prep - preposition	*v irreg* - verb irregular	*v refl* - verb reflexive	* - takes sein

auswählen – v reg sep choose, pick (out)
Auswärtsspiel (-e) – nnt away game
Ausweis (-e) – nm identity card
auswendig – adj by heart
ausziehen – v irreg sep take off (clothes)
sich ausziehen – v irreg refl sep get undressed
Auto (-s) – nnt car
Autobahn (-en) – nf motorway
Autofahrer (-) – nm motorist
Autofahrerin (-nen) – nf motorist

Automat (-en) – nm wk slot machine
automatisch – adj automatic
Autor (-en) – nm author
Autorin (-nen) – nf authoress
Autoschlüssel (-) – nm car key
Autositz (-e) – nm car seat
Autotelefon (-e) – nnt car phone
Autoverleih – nm car hire
Autowaschstraße (-n) – nf car wash
Autsch! – excl Ouch! Ow!
Avocado (-s) – nf avocado pear

B

Baby (-s) – nnt baby
babysitten gehen* – v irreg go babysitting
Babysitter (-) – nm babysitter
Bach (Bäche) – nm stream
Backe (-n) – nf cheek (face, bottom)
backen – v irreg bake
Bäcker (-) – nm baker
Bäckerei (-en) – nf baker's shop
Bäckerin (-nen) – nf baker
Backofen (-öfen) – nm oven
Backstein (-e) – nm brick
Bad (Bäder) – nnt bath
Badeanzug (-züge) – nm swimsuit
Badehose (-n) – nf bathing trunks
Badekappe (-n) – nf bathing cap
Baden – nnt bathing
baden – v reg † bathe, bath
sich baden – v reg refl † have a bath
Badeort (-e) – nm seaside resort, spa
Badetuch (-tücher) – nnt bath towel
Badewanne (-n) – nf bath (tub)
Badezimmer (-) – nnt bathroom
Badminton – nnt badminton

Bahn (-en) – nf railway
Bahnhof (-höfe) – nm railway station
Bahnsteig (-e) – nm platform
Bahnübergang (-gänge) – nm level crossing
bald – adv soon
Bis bald! – See you soon!
so bald wie möglich – as soon as possible
Balkon (-s) – nm balcony
Ball (Bälle) – nm ball
Ballett (-e) – nnt ballet
Ballon (-s) – nm balloon
Banane (-n) – nf banana
Band (-s) – nf band (group)
Bangladesch – nnt Bangladesh
Bank (-en) – nf bank
Bank (Bänke) – nf bench
Bankkonto (-konten) – nnt bank account
Banknote (-n) – nf bank-note
Bankraub (-räube) – nm bank robbery
Bar (-s) – nf bar (drinks)

---

bar bezahlen – *v reg* † pay cash
Bär (-en) – *nm wk* bear
Bardame (-n) – *nf* barmaid
barfuß – *adj* barefoot
Bargeld – *nnt* cash (not a cheque)
Barmann (-männer) – *nm* barman
Bart (Bärte) – *nm* beard
  mit Bart – bearded
Basel – Basle
basiert auf (+ dat) – *adj* based on
Basis (Basen) – *nf* basis
Basketball – *nm* basketball
basteln – *v reg* do DIY
Batterie (-n) – *nf* battery
Bauarbeiter (-) – *nm* construction worker
Bauarbeiterin (-nen) – *nf* construction worker
Bauch (Bäuche) – *nm* stomach
Bauchschmerzen – *npl* stomach ache
Bauchweh – *nnt coll* stomach ache
bauen – *v reg* build
Bauer (-n) – *nm wk* farmer
Bäuerin (-nen) – *nf* female farmer
Bauernhaus (-häuser) – *nnt* farmhouse
Bauernhof (-höfe) – *nm* farm
Baum (Bäume) – *nm* tree
Baumwolle – *nf* cotton
  aus Baumwolle – made of cotton
Baustelle (-n) – *nf* roadworks; building site
Bauunternehmer (-) – *nm* builder
bayerisch – *adj* Bavarian
Bayern – *nnt* Bavaria
beachten – *v reg* † respect
Beamte – *nm* ‡ official
Beamtin (-nen) – *nf* official
beängstigend – *adj* scary
beantworten – *v reg* † reply to s.o
Becher (-) – *nm* mug (cup)

sich bedanken bei jdm – *v reg refl* † thank s.o.
bedauern – *v reg* † regret
bedeckt mit (+ dat) – *adj* covered with
bedeuten – *v reg* † mean
  Was bedeutet ...? – What does ... mean?
bedienen – *v reg* † serve
sich bedienen – *v reg refl* † serve oneself
Bedienung – *nf* service (restaurant)
Bedienung inbegriffen – service included
Bedienung (nicht) inklusive – service (not) included
Bedingung (-en) – *nf* condition (of agreement)
bedrohen – *v reg* † threaten
sich beeilen – *v reg refl* † hurry, be quick
  Beeil dich! – *excl* Hurry up!
beenden – *v reg* † finish, end
Befehl (-e) – *nm* order
befehlen – *v irreg* order
sich befinden – *v irreg refl* be situated
beflecken – *v reg* † stain
befragen – *v reg* † question s.o.
befreundet sein* mit (+ dat) – *v irreg* be good friends with
befriedigen – *v reg* † satisfy
befriedigend – *adj* satisfactory
begabt – *adj* gifted
Begabung (-en) – *nf* talent, flair
begegnen* (+ dat) – *v reg* † meet (by chance)
begehen – *v irreg* commit
  ein Verbrechen begehen – *v irreg* commit an offence
begeistert von (+ dat) – *adj* enthusiastic about
Begeisterung – *nf* enthusiasm
begießen – *v irreg* water (plants)

---

adj - adjective   *v reg* - verb regular   *v sep* - verb separable   † - see verb info
prep - preposition   *v irreg* - verb irregular   *v refl* - verb reflexive   * - takes sein

Beginn – *nm* start, beginning
beginnen – *v irreg* begin
begleiten – *v reg* † accompany
begleitet von (+ dat) – *adj* accompanied by
begonnen – *see beginnen*
im Begriff sein* – *v irreg* be about to
begrüßen – *v reg* † greet
behalten – *v irreg* keep
behandeln – *v reg* † treat (medical)
Behandlung (-en) – *nf* treatment
behilflich – *adj* helpful
behindert – *adj* handicapped
Behörde (-n) – *nf* authorities
bei (+ dat) – *prep* at the home of
   bei mir – at my house
beide – *adj* both
Beifall – *nm* applause
beilegen – *v reg sep* enclose
Bein (-e) – *nnt* leg
   sich das Bein brechen – *v irreg dat refl* break one's leg
beinahe – *adv* almost
beißen – *v irreg* bite
Beispiel (-e) – *nnt* example
   zum Beispiel – for example
beitreten* (+ dat) – *v irreg sep* join (club)
bekam – *see bekommen*
bekannt – *adj* known
Bekannte – *nmf* ‡ acquaintance
Bekanntmachung (-en) – *nf* notice, information
sich beklagen über (+ acc) – *v reg refl* † complain about
bekommen – *v irreg* receive, get
beladen – *adj* loaded (goods)
belasten – *v reg* † burden
belegt – *adj* no vacancies
beleidigen – *v reg* † offend, insult
beleidigt – *adj* offended
Belgien – *nnt* Belgium

Belgier (-) – *nm* Belgian person
Belgierin (-nen) – *nf* Belgian person
belgisch – *adj* Belgian
beliebt – *adj* popular
bellen – *v reg* bark
Belohnung (-en) – *nf* reward
bemerkbar – *adj* noticeable
bemerken – *v reg* † notice
benachbart – *adj* neighbouring
sich benehmen – *v irreg refl* behave
beneiden – *v reg* † envy
benutzen – *v reg* † use, make use of
Benutzer (-) – *nm* user
Benutzerin (-nen) – *nf* user
Benutzung – *nf* use
Benzin – *nnt* petrol
   bleifreies Benzin – *nnt* unleaded petrol
   eine Benzinpanne haben – *v irreg* run out of petrol
beobachten – *v reg* † keep an eye on
bequem – *adj* comfortable
beraten – *v irreg* advise
Berater (-) – *nm* advisor
Beraterin (-nen) – *nf* advisor
bereit – *adj* ready, willing
Berg (-e) – *nm* mountain
   in den Bergen – in the mountains
bergab fahren* – *v irreg* go downhill
Bergarbeiter (-) – *nm* miner
bergauf – *adv* uphill
Bergrad (-räder) – *nnt* mountain bike
Bergsteigen – *nnt* mountain climbing
Bergsteiger (-) – *nm* mountaineer
Bergsteigerin (-nen) – *nf* mountaineer
Bericht (-e) – *nm* report
Berliner (-) – *nm* doughnut, Berliner
die Berliner Mauer – the Berlin Wall
bersten* – *v irreg* burst
Beruf (-e) – *nm* occupation

---

nm - noun masculine   *nf* - noun feminine   *nnt* - noun neuter   *npl* - noun plural
nom- nominative   *acc* - accusative   *gen* - genitive   *dat* - dative

Was sind Sie von Beruf? – What is your occupation?

beruflich – *adj* professional

Berufs~ – *pref* occupational

Berufsberatung – *nf* careers advice

Berufsfachschulreife – *nf* GNVQ level 2

Berufspläne – *npl* career plans

Berufspraktikum (-praktika) – *nnt* work experience

Berufsschule (-n) – *nf* college (FE)

Berufswunsch (-wünsche) – *nm* preferred choice of career

sich beruhigen – *v reg refl* † calm o.s. down

berühmt – *adj* famous

berühren – *v reg* † touch

beschädigt – *adj* damaged

sich beschäftigen – *v reg refl* † busy o.s.

beschäftigt – *adj* busy

beschäftigt sein* – *v irreg* be busy

beschämend – *adj* shameful

beschämt – *adj* ashamed

Bescherung (-en) – *nf* giving out of Christmas presents

beschließen – *v irreg* decide to

Beschränkung (-en) – *nf* limit, restriction

beschreiben – *v irreg* describe

Beschreibung (-en) – *nf* description

sich beschweren über (+ acc) – *v reg refl* † complain about

Besen (-) – *nm* broom

besetzt – *adj* occupied (table, seat), engaged (toilet)

besichtigen – *v reg* † visit (tourist attraction)

besitzen – *v irreg* own

Besitzer (-) – *nm* owner

Besitzerin (-nen) – *nf* owner

besondere – *adj* particular, special

besonders – *adv* especially

besser – *adj* better

Gute Besserung! – Get well soon!

bestätigen – *v reg* † confirm

beste – *adj* best

mit besten Wünschen – best wishes

Beste – *nmf* ‡ best

sein Bestes tun – do one's best

Besteck – *nnt* cutlery

bestehen – *v irreg* pass an exam

eine Prüfung nicht bestehen – *v irreg* fail an exam

bestehen aus (+ dat) – *v irreg* consist of

bestellen – *v reg* † order (restaurant)

Bestellung (-en) – *nf* order (restaurant)

bestimmt – *adj* definite

bestrafen – *v reg* † punish

Besuch (-e) – *nm* visit

Wir haben Besuch – We have visitors

besuchen – *v reg* † visit, attend school

Ich besuche eine Gesamtschule – I go to a comprehensive school

Besucher (-) – *nm* visitor, tourist

Besucherin (-nen) – *nf* visitor, tourist

Besuchszeit (-en) – *nf* visiting time

Beton – *nm* concrete

aus Beton – made of concrete

betreffen – *v irreg* concern

betreten – *v irreg* enter on foot

Betrieb (-e) – *nm* business

außer Betrieb – out of order, not working

in Betrieb – working

betrunken – *adj* drunk

Bett (-en) – *nnt* bed

ins Bett gehen* – *v irreg* go to bed

betteln – *v reg* beg

Bettwäsche – *nf, no pl* bedding

| *adj* - adjective | *v reg* - verb regular | *v sep* - verb separable | † - see verb info |
| *prep* - preposition | *v irreg* - verb irregular | *v refl* - verb reflexive | * - takes sein |

Bettzeug – *nnt, no pl* bedclothes
sich beugen – *v reg refl* bow
Beutel (-) – *nm* purse, pouch, bag
  Teebeutel (-) – *nm* tea bag
bevor – *sub conj* before
bewegen – *v reg* † move
Bewegung (-en) – *nf* movement
  körperliche Bewegung (-en) –
  nf exercise (sport)
Beweis (-e) – *nm* evidence
beweisen – *v irreg* prove
sich bewerben um (+ acc) –
  v irreg refl apply for
Bewerber (-) – *nm* applicant
Bewerberin (-nen) – *nf* applicant
Bewerbung (-en) – *nf* job
  application
Bewohner (-) – *nm* occupant
Bewohnerin (-nen) – *nf* occupant
bewölkt – *adj* cloudy
bewundern – *v reg* † admire
bewusstlos – *adj* unconscious
bezahlen – *v reg* † pay (for)
bezahlt – *adj* paid
  gut bezahlt – *adj* well-paid
Bezahlung (-en) – *nf* payment
in Bezug auf (+ acc) – *prep*
  concerning
BH (Büstenhalter) – *nm* bra
Bibel – *nf* Bible
Bibliothek (-en) – *nf* library
Bibliothekar (-e) – *nm* librarian
Bibliothekarin (-nen) – *nf* librarian
Bidet (-s) – *nnt* bidet
biegen – *v irreg* bend
Biene (-n) – *nf* bee
Bier (-e) – *nnt* beer
Bier vom Fass – draught beer
Bierdeckel (-) – *nm* beermat
Bierkrug (-krüge) – *nm* beer mug
bieten – *v irreg* offer
Bikini (-s) – *nm* bikini

Bild (-er) – *nnt* picture
Bildschirm (-e) – *nm* screen (TV)
billig – *adj* cheap
billigen – *v reg* approve of
bin – *see sein**
binden – *v irreg* bind, fasten
Bindestrich (-e) – *nm* hyphen, dash
Biologie – *nf* biology
Birne (-n) – *nf* pear; light bulb
bis (+ acc) – *prep* till, until
  Bis bald! – See you soon!
  Bis heute Abend! – See you this
  evening!
  Bis morgen! – See you tomorrow!
  Bis Samstag! – See you on Saturday!
  Bis später! – See you later!
bis zu (+ dat) – *prep* as far as
  bis zur Ampel – as far as the
  traffic lights
Biss (-e) – *nm* bite
ein bisschen – a little
bist – *see sein**
bitte – please
  bitte sehr – it's a pleasure
  bitte wenden (b.w.) – see over
Bitte (-n) – *nf* request
bitten um (+ acc) – *v irreg* ask for
  um Auskunft bitten – *v irreg* ask
  for information
bitter – *adj* bitter
Blase (-n) – *nf* blister; bladder
blasen – *v irreg* blow
Blaskapelle (-n) – *nf* brass band
blass – *adj* pale (complexion)
Blatt (Blätter) – *nnt* leaf
Blatt Papier – *nnt* sheet of paper
blau – *adj* blue
blechen – *v reg coll* fork out, cough up
Blei – *nnt* lead (metal)
bleiben* – *v irreg* stay
  Bleiben Sie am Apparat, bitte!
  – *excl* Hold the line please!

---

nm - noun masculine   *nf* - noun feminine   *nnt* - noun neuter   *npl* - noun plural
nom- nominative   *acc* - accusative   *gen* - genitive   *dat* - dative

sitzen bleiben* – *v irreg* repeat a year (at school)
bleifrei – *adj* unleaded (petrol)
Bleistift (-e) – *nm* pencil
Bleistiftspitzer (-) – *nm* pencil sharpener
Blick (-e) – *nm* view
blicken (auf + acc) – *v reg* look (at)
blieb – *see bleiben*
blind – *adj* blind
Blinddarmentzündung (-en) – *nf* appendicitis
Blinker (-) – *nm* indicator (car)
Blitz (-e) – *nm* flash of lightning
blitzen – *v reg* flash (lightning)
es blitzt – *v reg* it's lightning
blitzsauber – *adj* spotless
Block (Blöcke) – *nm* block
Blockflöte (-n) – *nf* recorder, flute
blockieren – *v reg* † block
blöd – *adj* stupid
Blödsinn – *nm, no pl* nonsense
blond – *adj* fair-haired, blonde
bloß – *adv* merely
Blouson (-s) – *nm* blouson jacket
Blume (-n) – *nf* flower
Blumenbeet (-e) – *nnt* flower bed
Blumenkohl – *nm* cauliflower
Blumenstrauß (-sträuße) – *nm* bunch of flowers
Bluse (-n) – *nf* blouse
Blut – *nnt* blood
Blutdruck – *nm, no pl* blood pressure
Bluttat (-en) – *nf* violent deed
bluten – *v reg* † bleed
Bockwurst (-würste) – *nf* frankfurter
Boden (Böden) – *nm* ground, floor
auf dem Boden – on the ground
Bodensee – *nm* Lake Constance
Bogenschießen (-) – *nnt* archery
Bohne (-n) – *nf* bean

grüne Bohne (-n) – *nf* French bean
Bombe (-n) – *nf* bomb
Bombenalarm (-e) – *nm* bomb scare
Bon (-s) – *nm* coupon
Bonbon (-s) – *nnt* sweet
Boot (-e) – *nnt* boat
Boot fahren* – *v irreg* go boating
Bootsfahrt (-en) – *nf* boat trip
an Bord – *adv* on board
an Bord gehen* – *v irreg* board a ship
böse – *adj* angry, wicked
böse mit (+ dat) – *adj* angry, cross with
Böse – *nnt* evil
böse werden* – *v irreg* get angry
böswillig – *adj* malicious
Boxsport – *nm* boxing
brach – *see brechen*
brachte – *see bringen*
Brand (Brände) – *nm* fire (accidental or malicious)
Brandung – *nf* surf
Brandwunde (-n) – *nf* burn
braten – *v irreg* fry, roast
Braten – *nm* joint of meat
Brathähnchen (-) – *nnt* roast chicken
Bratkartoffeln – *npl* fried potatoes
Bratsche (-n) – *nf* viola
Bratwurst (-würste) – *nf* fried sausage
Brauch (Bräuche) – *nm* use, custom
brauchen – *v reg* need, use
braun – *adj* brown
Braut (Bräute) – *nf* bride
Bräutigam (-e) – *nm* bridegroom
Brautjungfer (-n) – *nf* bridesmaid
brav – *adj* good, well-behaved
BRD – *nf* Federal Republic of Germany
brechen – *v irreg* break

---

adj - adjective *v reg* - verb regular *v sep* - verb separable † - see verb info
prep - preposition *v irreg* - verb irregular *v refl* - verb reflexive * - takes sein

sich das Bein brechen – *v irreg* *dat refl* break one's leg

breit – *adj* wide, broad

Breite (-n) – *nf* width

Bremse (-n) – *nf* brake

bremsen – *v reg* brake

brennen – *v irreg* burn, go up in flames

es brennt – there is a fire

Brett (-er) – *nnt* board, plank

Brettspiel (-e) – *nnt* board game

Brezel (-n) – *nf* pretzel

Brief (-e) – *nm* letter (post)

Brieffreund (-e) – *nm* pen-friend

Brieffreundin (-nen) – *nf* pen-friend

Briefkasten (-kästen) – *nm* letter box

Briefmarke (-n) – *nf* stamp

Briefpapier (-e) – *nnt* note paper

Brieftasche (-n) – *nf* wallet

Briefträger (-) – *nm* postman

Briefträgerin (-nen) – *nf* postwoman

Briefumschlag (-schläge) – *nm* envelope

Briefwechsel (-) – *nm* correspondence

Brille (-n) – *nf* glasses

bringen – *v irreg* bring, take

Brite (-n) – *nm wk* British person

Britin (-nen) – *nf* British person

britisch – *adj* British

die Britischen Inseln – *npl* the British Isles

Brombeere (-n) – *nf* blackberry

Bronzemedaille – *nf* bronze medal

Broschüre (-n) – *nf* leaflet

Brot (-e) – *nnt* bread

belegtes Brot – *nnt* open sandwich

Brötchen (-) – *nnt* roll (bread)

Brotdose (-n) – *nf* lunch box

Brücke (-n) – *nf* bridge

Bruder (Brüder) – *nm* brother

Brunnen (-) – *nm* well (water)

Brüssel – Brussels

Brust (Brüste) – *nf* chest (body)

Bube (-n) – *nm wk* jack (cards)

Buch (Bücher) – *nnt* book

buchen – *v reg* book

Bücherei (-en) – *nf* bookshop

Bücherregal (-e) – *nnt* bookshelf

Bücherschrank (-schränke) – *nm* book case

Buchhandlung (-en) – *nf* bookshop

Buchstabe (-n) – *nm wk* letter (alphabet)

buchstabieren – *v reg* † spell

Bucht (-en) – *nf* bay (on coast)

sich bücken – *v reg refl* bend over

Bude (-n) – *nf* kiosk

büffeln – *v reg coll* swot

Büffet (-s) – *nnt* buffet

Bügeleisen (-) – *nnt* iron (clothes)

bügeln – *v reg* do ironing, iron

Bühne (-n) – *nf* stage

auf der Bühne sein* – *v irreg* be on the stage

bummeln* – *v reg* stroll

Bummelzug (-züge) – *nm coll* slow train

Bundes~ – *pref* federal, national

Bundesland (-länder) – *nnt* federal state

Bundesliga (-en) – *nf* German football league

Bundesrepublik – *nf* Federal Republic of Germany

Bundesstraße (-n) – *nf* major road

Bungalow (-s) – *nm* bungalow

bunt – *adj* multi-coloured

Burg (-en) – *nf* castle (fortified)

Bürgermeister (-) – *nm* mayor

Bürgermeisterin (-nen) – *nf* mayoress

Bürgersteig (-e) – *nm* pavement

Büro (-s) – *nnt* office

---

nm - noun masculine   *nf* - noun feminine   *nnt* - noun neuter   *npl* - noun plural
nom - nominative   *acc* - accusative   *gen* - genitive   *dat* - dative

Büroklammer (-n) – *nf* paperclip
Bürste (-n) – *nf* brush
bürsten – *v reg* † brush
  sich die Haare bürsten – *v reg*
  dat refl † brush one's hair
Bus (-se) – *nm* bus
  in den Bus einsteigen* – *v irreg*
  sep get on the bus
Busbahnhof (-höfe) – *nm* bus
station
Busfahrer (-) – *nm* bus driver

Busfahrerin (-nen) – *nf* bus driver
Bushaltestelle (-n) – *nf* bus stop
Buslinie (-n) – *nf* bus route
Butter – *nf* butter
Butterbrot (-e) – *nnt* sandwich
buttern – *v reg* spread (with butter,
etc)
b.w. – (bitte wenden) turn over
bzw. – (beziehungsweise) or, that is

C

Café (-s) – *nnt* café
campen – *v reg* camp
Camper (-) – *nm* camper
Campingbus (-se) – *nm* motor home
Camping Carnet (-s) – *nnt* camping
carnet
Campinggaz® – *nnt* camping gaz®
Campingkocher (-) – *nm* camping
stove
Campingplatz (-plätze) – *nm*
campsite
CD (-s) – *nf* CD
CD-ROM (-s) – *nm* CD ROM
CD-Spieler (-) – *nm* CD player
CD-Wechsler (-) – *nm* CD changer
Cello (-s) – *nnt* cello
Celsius – Celsius
Chance (-n) – *nf* chance, opportunity
Charakter (-e) – *nm* character
Chef (-s) – *nm* boss
Chefin (-nen) – *nf* boss
Chemie – *nf* chemistry (subject)
China – *nnt* China

Chinese – *nmf* ‡ Chinese person
chinesisch – *adj* Chinese
Chip (-s) – *nf* chip (micro)
Chipkarte (-n) – *nf* smart card
Chips – *npl* crisps
Chor (Chöre) – *nm* choir
Christ (-en) – *nm wk* Christian
Christin (-nen) – *nf* Christian
Clown (-s) – *nm* clown
Cola – *nf* Coca cola®, cola
Comic (-s) – *nm* cartoon, comic
Comicstrip (-s) – *nm* cartoon strip
Computer (-) – *nm* computer
Computerspiel (-e) – *nnt* computer
game
Couchtisch (-e) – *nm* coffee table
Cousine (-n) – *nf* cousin
Cousin (-s) – *nm* cousin
Creme (n) – *nf* cream (medical)
Cursor – *nm* cursor
Currywurst (-würste) – *nf* curried
sausage

---

adj - adjective	*v reg* - verb regular	*v sep* - verb separable	† - see verb info
prep - preposition	*v irreg* - verb irregular	*v refl* - verb reflexive	* - takes sein

D

da – *adv* there
　da drüben – *adv* over there
da – *sub conj* since
dabei – *adv* with that, etc
Dach (Dächer) – *nnt* roof
Dachboden (-böden) – *nm* attic, loft
dachte – *see denken*
Dackel (-) – *nm* dachshund
dagegen – *adv* on the other hand
dahin – *adv* there (motion)
damals – *adv* at that time
Dame – *nf* draughts
Dame (-n) – *nf* lady
Damen – Ladies' toilets
Damenbinde (-n) – *nf* sanitary towel
Damenkonfektion – *nf* ladies'
　clothes department
damit – *adv* with that
Dampf – *nm* steam
Damfper (-) – *nm* steamer (ship)
danach – *adv* then
Däne (-n) – *nm wk* Dane
Dänemark – *nnt* Denmark
Dänin (-nen) – *nf* Dane
dänisch – *adj* Danish
dank (+ gen/dat) – *prep* thanks to
dankbar (+ dat) – *adj* grateful (to)
danke – *adv* thank you
　danke sehr – thank you very much
　danke schön – thank you very much
　(nein) danke – no thank you
　Nichts zu danken! – You're
　welcome!
　Vielen Dank – Thank you very
　much
danken (+ dat) – *v reg* thank
dann – *adv* then
dann und wann – *adv* from time to
　time
darauf – *adv* then

darf – *see dürfen*
das – *pron nt* the, *rel pron nt* who, which
　Das geht – That's OK
　Das macht .... – That'll be (+ price)
　Das stimmt – That's right
dass – *sub conj* that
Datei (-en) – *nf* file (computer)
Daten – *npl* data
Datenautobahn (-en) – *nf*
　information super highway
Datenbank (-en) – *nf* database
Datum (Daten) – *nnt* date
Dauer – *nf* length (time)
Dauerkarte (-n) – *nf* season ticket
dauern – *v reg* last
Daumen (-) – *nm* thumb
dazu – *adv* with that
DB (Deutsche Bundesbahn) – *nf*
　German railways
DDR – *nf* East Germany
　in der ehemaligen DDR – in the
　former East Germany
Debatte (-n) – *nf* debate
Decke (-n) – *nf* blanket; ceiling
Deckel (-) – *nm* lid (top)
decken – *v reg* cover
　den Tisch decken – *v reg* set the
　table
Defekt (-) – *nm* fault (defect)
dein – *poss adj sing* your (informal)
Dein – *poss adj* With best wishes from
　(male, informal)
Deine – *poss adj* With best wishes
　from (female, informal)
dekorieren – *v reg* † decorate (shop
　window)
Delikatessengeschäft (-e) – *nnt*
　delicatessen
Demonstration (-en) – *nf*
　demonstration
demonstrieren – *v reg* † demonstrate

---

nm - noun masculine	nf - noun feminine	nnt - noun neuter	npl - noun plural
nom - nominative	acc - accusative	gen - genitive	dat - dative

den 12. November – 12th of
November (letter heading)
denken – *v irreg* think
denken an (+ acc) – *v irreg* think of
Ich denke nicht daran! – Not
likely!
Denkmal (-mäler) – *nnt* monument
denn – *co-ord conj* for, as
deprimierend – *adj* depressing
deprimiert – *adj* depressed
der – *pron m* the, *rel pron m* who,
which, that
derselbe – *dem pron* the same
deshalb – *adv* therefore
Designer (-) – *nm* designer
Designerin (-nen) – *nf* designer
deswegen – *adv* consequently
Detektiv (-e) – *nm* detective
Detektivfilm (-e) – *nm* detective film
deutlich – *adv* clearly
deutsch – *adj* German
auf Deutsch – in German
Wie sagt man ... auf Deutsch?
– How do you say ... in German?
Deutsch – *nnt* German (language)
Seit wann lernst du Deutsch? –
How long have you been learning
German?
Deutsch sprechen – *v irreg* speak
German
Deutsche Bundesbahn (DB) – *nf*
German railways
Deutsche – *nmf* ‡ German person
Er ist kein Deutscher – He's not
German
Deutschland – *nnt* Germany
Dezember – *nm* December
im Dezember – in December
d.h. (das heißt) – i.e. (that is)
Dia (-s) – *nnt* slide (transparency)
Diät (-en) – *nf* diet
dich – *pron acc sing* you (informal)
dick – *adj* fat, thick

die – *def art f, pl* the; *rel pron f, pl*
who, which, that
Dieb (-e) – *nm* thief
Diebin (-nen) – *nf* thief
Diebstahl – *nm* theft
Diele (-n) – *nf* hallway
dienen – *v reg* serve
Dienst (-e) – *nm* service
(maintenance)
Dienstag – *nm* Tuesday
am Dienstag – on Tuesday
diese – *dem pron* these, this
Diesel – *nm* diesel
dieser – *dem pron* this
diesig – *adj* hazy
diesmal – *adv* this time
Ding (-e) – *nnt* thing
Dingsbums – *nnt coll* whatsit
Dinosaurier (-) – *nm* dinosaur
Diplom (-e) – *nnt* diploma, university
degree
dir – *pron dat sing* you, to you,
yourself (singular, informal)
direkt – *adj* direct, straight
direkt – *adv* directly
Direktor (-en) – *nm* head teacher
Direktorin (-nen) – *nf* head teacher
Dirndl (-) – *nnt* dirndl dress
Disco (-s) – *nf* disco
Diskette (-n) – *nf* floppy disk
Diskettenlaufwerk (-e) – *nnt* disk
drive
Disko (-s) – *nf coll* disco
Diskothek (-en) – *nf* discotheque
Diskussion (-en) – *nf* discussion
diskutieren über (+ acc) – *v reg* †
discuss
DJH – *nf* German Youth Hostel
DM – *nf* Deutschmark, German
currency
doch – *adv* yes, really
Doktor (-en) – *nm* academic doctor,
PhD

---

adj - adjective	*v reg* - verb regular	*v sep* - verb separable	† - see verb info
prep - preposition	*v irreg* - verb irregular	*v refl* - verb reflexive	* - takes sein

Dokumentarfilm (-e) – *nm* documentary

Dokumentarsendung (-en) – *nf* documentary programme

dolmetschen – *v reg* interpret

Dolmetscher (-) – *nm* interpreter

Dolmetscherin (-nen) – *nf* interpreter

Dom (-e) – *nm* cathedral

Donau – *nf* River Danube

Donner – *nm* thunder

donnern – *v reg* thunder

Donnerstag – *nm* Thursday
  am Donnerstag – on Thursday

doof – *adj coll* stupid

Doppel~ – *pref* double

Doppelbett (-en) – *nnt* double bed

Doppeldecker (-) – *nm* double decker

Doppelhaus (-häuser) – *nnt* semi-detached house

Doppelpunkt (-e) – *nm* colon (:)

doppelt – *adv* doubly

Doppelzimmer (-) – *nnt* double room

Dorf (Dörfer) – *nnt* village

dort – *adv* there (position towards)

dort drüben – *adv* over there

dort oben – *adv* up there

Dose (-n) – *nf* tin, can

Dosenöffner (-) – *nm* tin opener

Dosis (Dosen) – *nf* dose

Drachen (-) – *nm* kite

Drachenfliegen – *nnt* hang gliding

Drama (Dramen) – *nnt* drama

Drama machen – *v reg* do drama

dran sein* – *v irreg* have your turn
  Wer ist dran? – Who's next?

draußen – *adv* outdoors, outside

Dreck – *nm* dirt

dreckig – *adj* dirty

drehen – *v reg* turn

drei – three

Dreieck (-e) – *nnt* triangle

dreimal – *adv* three times

dreißig – *adj* thirty

dreißigste – *adj* thirtieth

drei viertel – three quarters

Dreiviertelstunde (-n) – *nf* three quarters of an hour

dreizehn – *adj* thirteen

dressieren – *v reg* † train (animal)

dringend – *adj* urgent

Dringlichkeit – *nf* urgency

drinnen – *adv* indoors, inside

Drittel (-) – *nnt* third (fraction)

dritte – *adj* third (in order)

Droge (-n) – *nf* drug (narcotic)

drogenabhängig – *adj* drug-dependent

Drogenabhängige – *nmf* ‡ drug addict

Drogenopfer (-) – *nnt* drugs victim

drogensüchtig – *adj* addicted to drugs

Drogenszene (-n) – *nf* drugs scene

Drogerie (-n) – *nf* chemist, drug store

Drogist (-en) – *nm wk* chemist

Drogistin (-nen) – *nf* chemist

Druckbuchstabe (-n) – *nm wk* block letter

drucken – *v reg* print

drücken – *v reg* push, press

Drucker (-) – *nm* printer

Dschungel (-) – *nm* jungle

du – *pron nom sing* you (informal)

dumm – *adj* stupid

Dummheit (-en) – *nf* silly mistake
  eine Dummheit begehen – *v irreg* do something stupid

dunkel – *adj* dark

dunkelblau – *adj* navy blue

dünn – *adj* thin

durch (+ acc) – *prep* through

---

nm - noun masculine   *nf* - noun feminine   *nnt* - noun neuter   *npl* - noun plural
nom- nominative   *acc* - accusative   *gen* - genitive   *dat* - dative

Durcheinander – *nnt* mess
durcheinander – *adv* in a mess
durchfahren* – *v irreg sep* go direct (train)
Durchfahrt (-en) – *nf* through way
Durchfahrt verboten – no entry
Durchfall – *nm* diarrhoea
durchfallen* – *v irreg sep* fail
  in einer Prüfung durchfallen* – *v irreg sep* fail an exam
Durchgang (-gänge) – *nm* way through
Durchgangszug (-züge) – *nm* express train, through train
gut durchgebraten – *adj* well-cooked (steak)
durchgefallen – *adj* failed
durchnässt – *adj* soaked
  völlig durchnässt – *adj* soaked to the skin
durchnehmen – *v irreg sep* do, learn at school

sich durchschlagen – *v irreg refl sep* cope
sich gut durchschlagen – *v irreg refl sep* do well
Durchschnitt (-e) – *nm* average
durchschnittlich – *adj* average
durchstreichen – *v irreg sep* cross out
durchsuchen – *v reg insep* search
dürfen – *v irreg* be allowed, may
durfte – *see dürfen*
Durst – *nm* thirst
Durst haben – *v irreg* be thirsty
  Ich habe Durst – I am thirsty
durstig – *adj* thirsty
Dusche (-n) – *nf* shower
sich duschen – *v reg refl* have a shower
Düsenflugzeug (-e) – *nnt* jet
düster – *adj* gloomy
Dutzend (-e) – *nnt* dozen
D-Zug (D-Züge) – *nm* express train, through train

E

E111-Schein (-e) – *nm* E111 form
Ebbe (-n) – *nf* tide (low)
eben – *adv* just
ebenso – *adv* just as
ebenso ... wie – *adv* just as ... as
echt – *adj* real, genuine
Ecke (-n) – *nf* corner
  an der Ecke – at the corner of
  um die Ecke gehen* – *v irreg* go round a corner
eckig – *adj* square, angular; awkward
Edel~ – high quality
Edelstein (-e) – *nm* jewel
Edinburg – Edinburgh
EDV-Bearbeiter (-) – *nm* computer operator

EG – *nf* EC (European Community)
egal – *adj* equal
  Es ist mir egal – I don't mind
egoistisch – *adj* selfish
ehe – *sub conj* before
Ehe (-n) – *nf* marriage
Ehefrau (-en) – *nf* wife
ehemalig – *adj* ex-, former, previous
Ehemann (-männer) – *nm* husband
Ehepaar (-e) – *nnt* married couple
eher – rather, sooner *adv*
Ehre (-n) – *nf* honour
ehrlich – *adj* honest
Ei (-er) – *nnt* egg

---

adj - adjective	*v reg* - verb regular	*v sep* - verb separable	† - see verb info
prep - preposition	*v irreg* - verb irregular	*v refl* - verb reflexive	* - takes sein

ein gekochtes Ei – a boiled egg
ein hart gekochtesEi – a hard
boiled egg
Eiche (-n) – *nf* oak tree
eifersüchtig auf (+ acc) – *adj*
jealous of
eigen – *adj* own
Eigenname (-n) – *nm wk* proper
noun
Eigentum – *nnt, no pl* belongings
Eile – *nf* hurry
eilen* – *v reg* hurry
eilig – *adj* hurried
es eilig haben – *v irreg* be in a hurry
Ich habe es eilig – I am in a hurry
Eilzug (-züge) – *nm* local train
Eimer (-) – *nm* bucket
ein – *indef art m, nt* a, an
ein bisschen – *pron inv* a little
ein paar – *pron inv* some
einander – *pron* each other
Einbahnstraße (-n) – *nf* one way
street
Einbildung (-en) – *nf* imagination
einbrechen* – *v irreg sep* break in,
burgle
Einbrecher (-) – *nm* burglar
Eindruck (-e) – *nm* impression
eindrucksvoll – *adj* impressive
eine – *indef art f* a, an
einem – *pron dat sing* you (persons
unspecified)
einen – *pron acc sing* you (persons
unspecified)
einerseits – *adv* on the one hand
eines Tages – one day
einfach – *adj* easy
einmal einfach nach Hamburg
– a single to Hamburg
einfache Fahrkarte (-n) – *nf* single
ticket
Einfahrt (-en) – *nf* entrance, drive
(road in)

Einfahrt frei halten! – Keep
entrance clear!
einfallen* – *v irreg sep* occur to
es fällt mir ein, dass ... – it
occurs to me that ...
Einfamilienhaus (-häuser) – *nnt*
detached house
Einführungsbrief (-e) – *nm* letter of
introduction
Eingang (-gänge) – *nm* entrance,
way in
eingebildet – *adj* snobbish
eingeschlafen – *adj* asleep
Einheit (-en) – *nf* unit, unity
der Tag der deutschen Einheit
– *nm* Day of German Unity
(3rd October)
einige – *adj* some
Einkäufe machen – *v reg* do the
shopping
einkaufen – *v reg sep* shop
einkaufen gehen* – *v irreg* do the
shopping
Einkaufen – *nnt* shopping
einen Einkaufsbummel machen
– *v reg* go round the shops
Einkaufsliste (-n) – *nf* shopping list
Einkaufspassage (-n) – *nf* arcade
(shops)
Einkaufstasche (-n) – *nf* shopping bag
Einkaufswagen (-) – *nm* trolley
(supermarket)
Einkaufszentrum (-zentren) – *nnt*
shopping centre
einladen – *v irreg sep* invite, ask s.o.
for dinner, etc
Freunde einladen – *v irreg sep*
have friends round
Einladung (-en) – *nf* invitation
sich einleben – *v reg refl sep* settle
down
einlösen – *v reg sep* cash in

---

nm - noun masculine	*nf* - noun feminine	*nnt* - noun neuter	*npl* - noun plural
nom - nominative	*acc* - accusative	*gen* - genitive	*dat* - dative

einen Scheck einlösen – *v reg sep* cash a cheque

einmal – *adv* once

einmal nach Dresden, hin und zurück – a return ticket to Dresden

einmalig – *adj* one off, unique

einordnen – *v reg sep* † sort, file

bitte einordnen – get in lane

einpacken – *v reg sep* wrap up (present)

als Geschenk einpacken – *v reg sep* gift wrap

einreiben – *v irreg sep* rub in (cream, fat)

Einrichtung (-en) – *nf* establishment

einsam – *adj* lonely

einschalten – *v reg sep* † switch on (light, radio)

einschenken – *v reg sep* pour a drink

einschl. – including

einschlafen* – *v irreg sep* fall asleep

einschließen – *v irreg sep* shut in

einschließlich – *adv* including

einschränken – *v reg sep* restrict

Einschreibebrief (-e) – *nm* registered letter

einsehen – *v irreg sep* understand, realise

einsteigen* in (+ acc) – *v irreg sep* get into (bus, etc)

in den Zug einsteigen* – *v irreg sep* get on the train

Einstieg (-e) – *nm* entry route

Eintopf – *nm* stew

eintreten* – *v irreg sep* enter

Eintritt (-e) – *nm* entrance (price)

Eintrittsgeld (-er) – *nnt* entrance fee

Eintrittskarte (-n) – *nf* entrance ticket

Eintrittsprüfung (-en) – *nf* entrance examination

einundzwanzig – *adj* twenty-one

einundzwanzigste – *adj* twenty-first

einverstanden – *adj* agreed

einwerfen – *v irreg sep* post

einen Brief einwerfen – *v irreg sep* post a letter

Einwohner (-) – *nm* inhabitant

Einwohnerin (-nen) – *nf* resident

Einwurf – *nm* post letters here

Einzel~ – *pref* single

Einzelbett (-en) – *nnt* single bed

Einzelheit (-en) – *nf* detail

Einzelkind (-er) – *nnt* only child

einzeln – *adj* individual

Einzelzimmer (-) – *nnt* single room

einziehen* – *v irreg sep* move in

einzig – *adj* single, only

Eis~ – *pref* ice

Eis – *nnt* ice, ice-cream

Schokoladeneis – *nnt* chocolate ice-cream

Vanilleeis – *nnt* vanilla ice-cream

Eisbahn (-en) – *nf* ice-rink

Eisbecher (-) – *nm* mixed ice cream

Eisen~ – *pref* iron (metal)

Eisenbahn (-en) – *nf* railway

Eisenwarengeschäft (-e) – *nnt* hardware shop

eisig – *adj* icy

eitel – *adj* vain (conceited)

Eitelkeit (-en) – *nf* vanity

ekelhaft – *adj* disgusting

eklig – *adj* revolting

Elefant (-en) – *nm wk* elephant

elegant – *adj* elegant

Elektriker (-) – *nm* electrician

elektrisch – *adj* electric(al)

Elektrizität – *nf* electricity

Elektro~ – *pref* electric(al)

Elektroherd (-e) – *nm* electric cooker

Elektronik – *nf* electronics

elf – *adj* eleven

---

adj - adjective	*v reg* - verb regular	*v sep* - verb separable	† - see verb info
prep - preposition	*v irreg* - verb irregular	*v refl* - verb reflexive	* - takes sein

elfte – *adj* eleventh
Elbe – *nf* River Elbe
Ellenbogen (-) – *nm* elbow
Eltern – *npl* parents
Empfang (Empfänge) – *nm* reception
Empfänger (-) – *nm* receiver
Empfangsdame (-n) – *nf* receptionist
empfehlen – *v irreg* recommend
empfindlich – *adj* sensitive
empfohlen – *adj* recommended
Ende (-n) – *nnt* end
  am Ende – at the end
  am Ende des Ganges – at the end of the corridor
  zu Ende – over, out (finished)
enden – *v reg* † end
endlich – *adv* at last
endlos – *adj* endless
Endspiel (-e) – *nnt* final (sport)
Endstation (-en) – *nf* terminus, end of line
Endsumme (-n) – *nf* total
Energie – *nf* energy
eng – *adj* narrow, tight
engagiert – *adj* committed, keen on
England – *nnt* England
Engländer (-) – *nm* Englishman
Engländerin (-nen) – *nf* Englishwoman
Englisch – *nnt* English (language)
  auf Englisch – in English
englisch – *adj* English
englischsprachig – *adj* English speaking
Englischstunde (-n) – *nf* English lesson
Enkel (-) – *nm* grandson
Enkelin (-nen) – *nf* granddaughter
Enkelkind (-er) – *nnt* grandchild
enorm – *adj* immense
entdecken – *v reg* † discover

Ente (-n) – *nf* duck
entfalten – *v reg* † unfold
entfernen – *v reg* † remove
entfernt – away (distance)
  weit entfernt – *adv* far away
  zehn Kilometer von ... entfernt – 10 kilometres from ...
Entfernung (-en) – *nf* distance
entfliehen* – *v irreg* flee
entführen – *v reg* † kidnap
Entführer (-) – *nm* kidnapper
Entführerin (-nen) – *nf* kidnapper
entgegen – *adv* towards
enthalten – *v irreg* contain
entkommen* – *v irreg* escape
entlang (+ acc) – *prep* along
  hier entlang – *adv* this way
  die Straße entlang – along the street
entmutigt – *adj* discouraged
(sich) entscheiden – *v irreg (refl)* decide
sich entscheiden für (+ acc) – *v irreg refl* opt for
Entscheidung (-en) – *nf* decision
sich entschließen – *v irreg refl* to make up one's mind
sich entschuldigen bei (+ dat) – *v reg refl* † to apologise to, to make excuses
  Entschuldigen Sie, bitte! – Excuse me!
Entschuldigung (-en) – *nf* apology
Entschuldigung! – sorry!
entsetzlich – *adj* horrifying
entsetzt – *adj* horrified
sich entspannen – *v reg refl* † relax
entspannt – *adj* relaxed
Entspannung – *nf* relaxation
enttäuschend – *adj* disappointing
enttäuscht – *adj* disappointed
entweder ... oder ... – *conj* either ... or ...

---

nm - noun masculine	*nf* - noun feminine	*nnt* - noun neuter	*npl* - noun plural
nom- nominative	*acc* - accusative	*gen* - genitive	*dat* - dative

entwerten – *v reg* † cancel ticket
Entwerter (-) – *nm* ticket cancelling machine
entwickeln – *v reg* † develop
Entwicklung (-en) – *nf* development
Entwurf (Entwürfe) – *nm* rough draft
entzückend – *adj* delightful
entzückt – *adj* delighted
er – *pron nom* he, it
erbärmlich – *adj* pathetic
erbeuten – *v reg* † escape with
sich erbrechen – *v irreg refl* vomit
Erbse (-n) – *nf* pea
Erdbeben (-) – *nnt* earthquake
Erdbeere (-n) – *nf* strawberry
Erde (-n) – *nf* earth, ground
Erdgas – *nnt* natural gas
Erdgeschoss – *nnt* ground floor
  im Erdgeschoss – on the ground floor
Erdkunde – *nf* geography
Erdnuss (-nüsse) – *nf* peanut
erdrosseln – *v reg* † strangle
Ereignis (-se) – *nnt* event
erfahren – *v irreg* experience
erfahren – *adj* experienced
Erfahrung (-en) – *nf* experience
erfinden – *v irreg* invent
Erfolg (-e) – *nm* success
erfolgreich – *adj* successful
erforschen – *v reg* † explore
erfreut – *adj* pleased
Erfrischung (-en) – *nf* refreshment
ergänzen – *v reg* † complete
Ergebnis (-se) – *nnt* result
ergreifen – *v irreg* grip, seize
erhalten – *v irreg* receive
erhältlich – *adj* obtainable
sich erheben – *v irreg refl* rise (mountain)

sich erholen – *v reg refl* † get better, recover
erinnern an (+ acc) – *v reg* † remind of
sich erinnern an (+ acc) – *v reg refl* † remember
sich erkälten – *v reg refl* † catch cold
erkältet sein* – *v irreg* have a cold
Erkältung (-en) – *nf* cold (illness)
erkennen – *v irreg* recognise
erklären – *v reg* † explain
Erklärung (-en) – *nf* explanation
sich erkundigen (nach + dat) – *v reg refl* † enquire (about)
erlauben – *v reg* † allow, let
Erlaubnis (-se) – *nf* permission
erlaubt – *adj* permitted
  nicht erlaubt – not allowed
Ermäßigung (-en) – *nf* reduction (price)
  10% Ermäßigung – 10% off
  Schülerermäßigung (-en) – *nf* student reduction
ermüdend – *adj* tiring
ermutigen – *v reg* † encourage
erneuern – *v reg* † renew
ernst – *adj* serious
Ernte (-n) – *nf* harvest
ernten – *v reg* † harvest
erreichen – *v reg* † reach
Ersatz – *nm* substitute
Ersatzrad (-räder) – *nnt* spare wheel
Ersatzteil (-e) – *nnt* spare part
erscheinen* – *v irreg* appear
erschießen – *v irreg* shoot dead
erschöpft – *adj* exhausted
erschrecken – *v irreg* terrify
erschreckend – *adj* startling
erschrocken – *adj* frightened
erschüttern – *v reg* † shock
erschüttert – *adj* distressed
ersetzen – *v reg* † replace

---

adj - adjective   *v reg* - verb regular   *v sep* - verb separable   † - see verb info
prep - preposition   *v irreg* - verb irregular   *v refl* - verb reflexive   * - takes sein

Ersparnisse – *npl* savings
erstaunen – *v reg* † astonish
erstaunt – *adj* amazed
erst – *adv* not until, only (+ time)
erste – *adj* first
   einmal erster Klasse, bitte – a
   first class ticket, please
erste Hilfe – *nf* first aid
erstens – *adv* firstly
ertragen – *v irreg* stand (put up with)
ertrinken* – *v irreg* drown
erwachsen – *adj* adult, grown up
Erwachsene – *nmf* ‡ adult
erwähnen – *v reg* † bring up
   (mention)
erwarten – *v reg* † expect
erwidern – *v reg* † reply
erzählen – *v reg* † recount
Erzähler (-) – *nm* storyteller
Erzählerin (-nen) – *nf* storyteller
erzeugt – *adj* produced
es (nom/acc) – *pron nt* it
   Es grüßt dich herzlich –
   Greetings from
   Es hat geklappt – It worked
   Es kommt darauf an – It depends
   Es macht nichts – It doesn't
   matter
   Es tut mir leid – I'm sorry
Esel (-) – *nm* donkey
essbar – *adj* edible
essen – *v irreg* eat

Essen – *nnt* food
   zu Abend essen – *v irreg* have
   dinner
Essig – *nm* vinegar
Esslöffel (-) – *nm* tablespoon(ful)
Esszimmer (-) – *nnt* dining room
Etage (-n) – *nf* storey
   auf der Etage – upstairs
etwa – *adv* approximately
etwas – *adj inv* some (uncountable)
etwas – something, anything
   etwas anderes – something else
   etwas Schlechtes – something bad
   Sonst noch etwas? – Anything
   else?
EU – *nf* European Union
euch – *pron acc/dat pl* you (informal)
euer – *poss adj pl* your (informal)
Europa – *nnt* Europe
Europäer (-) – *nm* European person
Europäerin (-nen) – *nf* European
   person
europäisch – *adj* European
die Europäische Union – *nf* the
   European Union
Euroscheck (-s) – *nm* Eurocheque
evangelisch – *adj* Protestant
existieren – *v reg* † exist
Experiment – *nnt* experiment
extrem – *adj* extreme

F

fabelhaft – *adj* fabulous

Fabrik (-en) – *nf* factory

Fabrikarbeiter (-) – *nm* factory worker

Fabrikarbeiterin (-nen) – *nf* factory worker

Fach (Fächer) – *nnt* subject (school)

Facharzt (-ärzte) – *nm* specialist (doctor)

Fachärztin (-nen) – *nf* specialist (doctor)

Fachhochschulreife – *nf* GNVQ Level 3

Fachmann (-männer) – *nm* expert

Fachwerk~ – *pref* half-timbered

fähig – *adj* capable

Fahne (-n) – *nf* flag

Fahrausweis (-e) – *nm* ticket

Fähre (-n) – *nf* ferry

fahren – *v irreg* drive (a car, etc)

fahren* – *v irreg* travel, go

  mit dem Bus fahren* – *v irreg* get the bus

Fahrer (-) – *nm* driver

Fahrerin (-nen) – *nf* driver

Fahrgast (-gäste) – *nm* passenger

Fahrgeld (-er) – *nnt* fare

Fährhafen (-häfen) – *nm* ferry terminal

Fahrkarte (-n) – *nf* ticket (bus, train)

  Fahrkarte erster Klasse – *nf* first class ticket

  einfache Fahrkarte – *nf* single ticket

Fahrkartenautomat (-en) – *nm wk* ticket machine

Fahrkartenschalter (-) – *nm* ticket office

Fahrplan (-pläne) – *nm* timetable (transport)

Fahrpreis (-e) – *nm* full fare

zum vollen Fahrpreis (-e) – at full fare

fahrplanmäßig – *adj* according to timetable

Fahrprüfung (-en) – *nf* driving test

Fahrrad (-räder) – *nnt* bicycle

Fahrschein (-e) – *nm* ticket

Fahrstuhl (-stühle) – *nm* lift

Fahrt – *nf* journey

  Gute Fahrt! – *excl* Have a good journey!

Fahrzeit (-en) – *nf* journey time

Fahrzeug (-e) – *nnt* vehicle

fair – *adj* fair (just)

Fall (Fälle) – *nm* case, situation

  auf keinen Fall – on no account

  in diesem Fall – in this case

fallen* – *v irreg* fall

fallen lassen – *v irreg* drop

falls – *sub conj* in case

falsch – *adj* wrong

falsch 'rum – wrong way round

falsch verbunden – wrong number

falten – *v reg* † fold

Familie (-n) – *nf* family

Familienname (-n) – *nm wk* surname

Familienzimmer (-) – *nnt* family room (hotel)

Fan (-s) – *nm* fan (supporter)

fand – *see* finden

fangen – *v irreg* catch (fish)

fantastisch – *adj* fantastic

Farbe (-n) – *nf* colour

Fasching – *nm* Carnival

Faschingsdienstag – *nm* Shrove Tuesday

fassen – *v reg* grasp

fast – *adv* almost

faszinierend – *adj* fascinating

---

faul – *adv* lazy, rotten
faulenzen – *v reg* laze about
Faust (Fäuste) – *nf* fist
Fax (-) – *nnt* fax
faxen – *v reg* fax
Faxgerät (-e) – *nnt* fax machine
Faxnummer (-n) – *nf* fax number
Februar – *nm* February
  im Februar – in February
Feder (-n) – *nf* feather
Federball – *nm* badminton
Federmäppchen (-) – *nnt* pencil case
fehlen – *v reg* lack, be missing, miss
Fehler (-) – *nm* mistake
Feier (-n) – *nf* celebration
Feierabend (-e) – *nm* end of the
  working day
feierlich – *adj* solemn
feiern – *v reg* celebrate
Feiertag (-e) – *nm* public holiday
fein – *adj* fine (delicate)
Feld (-er) – *nnt* field, square
Feldbett (-en) – *nnt* camp bed
feminin – *adj* feminine (grammar)
Fenster (-) – *nnt* window
Ferien – *npl* holiday (school)
  die Ferien verbringen – *v irreg*
  spend one's holiday
Ferienhaus (-häuser) – *nnt* holiday
  cottage
fern – *adj* distant
Fernbedienung – *nf* remote control
  (TV)
Ferne – *nf* distance
  in der Ferne – in the distance
Ferngespräch (-e) – *nnt* phone call
Fernseh~ – *pref* TV
Fernsehapparat (-e) – *nm* TV set
Fernsehen – *nnt* television
  im Fernsehen – on television
fernsehen – *v irreg sep* watch TV
Fernseher (-) – *nm* television set

Fernsprecher (-) – *nm* telephone
Ferse (-n) – *nf* heel (foot)
fertig – *adj* ready
  sich fertig machen – *v reg refl*
  get ready
Fertiggericht (-e) – *nnt* ready-made
  meal
fesseln – *v reg* grip (interest)
fesselnd – *adj* gripping
fest – *adj* firm, steady (job)
Fest (-e) – *nnt* festival, fête
Festland – *nnt* continent (-not island)
festhalten – *v irreg sep* hold tight
festmachen – *v reg sep* fasten
Festplatte (-n) – *nf* hard disk
festsetzen – *v reg sep* arrange (time)
feststellen – *v reg sep* establish,
  determine
Festspiele – *npl* drama festival
fettig – *adj* greasy
feucht – *adj* damp
Feuer (-) – *nnt* fire
  Haben Sie Feuer? – Have you
  got a light?
Feueralarm (-e) – *nm* fire alarm
Feuerleiter (-n) – *nf* fire escape
Feuerwehr (-en) – *nf* fire brigade
Feuerwehrmann (-männer) – *nm*
  fireman
Feuerwehrwagen (-) – *nm* fire-engine
Feuerwerk – *nnt, no pl* firework
Fieber (-) – *nnt* fever, high temperature
  Fieber haben – *v irreg* have a
  temperature
Fieberthermometer (-) – *nnt*
  thermometer (medical)
fiel – *see fallen*
Figur (-en) – *nf* figure
Filiale (-n) – *nf* branch (firm)
Film (-e) – *nm* film
Filmstar (-s) – *nm* film star
Filterkaffee – *nm* filter coffee
Filzstift (-e) – *nm* felt tip pen

---

finden – *v irreg* find
Finger (-) – *nm* finger
  Ich habe mir den Finger
  verbrannt – I have burnt my finger
Finne (-n) – *nm wk* Finnish person
Finnin (-nen) – *nf* Finnish person
finnisch – *adj* Finnish
Finnland – *nnt* Finland
Firma (Firmen) – *nf* firm
Fisch (-e) – *nm* fish
Fische – Pisces (horoscope)
fischen – *v reg* fish
Fischer (-) – *nm* fisherman
Fischereihafen (-häfen) – *nm*
  fishing port
Fischerin (-nen) – *nf* fisherwoman
Fischhändler (-) – *nm* fishmonger
Fischhändlerin (-nen) – *nf*
  fishmonger
Fischstäbchen (-) – *nnt* fish finger
fit – *adj* fit
Fitness – *nf* fitness (condition)
Fitnesszentrum (-zentren) – *nnt*
  fitness centre
flach – *adj* flat, level
Flagge (-n) – *nf* flag
Flamme (-n) – *nf* flame
Flasche (-n) – *nf* bottle
  eine Flasche Wein – a bottle of
  wine
Flaschenöffner (-) – *nm* bottle opener
Fleck (-en) – *nm* stain
  ein blauer Fleck (-e) – *nm* a
  bruise
Fledermaus (-mäuse) – *nf* bat
  (mammal)
Fleisch – *nnt* meat
Fleischer (-) – *nm* butcher
Fleischsorte (-n) – *nf* type of meat
fleißig – *adj* hardworking
Fliege (-n) – *nf* fly (insect), bow tie
Fliegen – *nnt* flying (in plane)

fliegen* – *v irreg* fly
fliehen* – *v irreg* flee
fließen* – *v irreg* flow
fließend – *adj* fluent (speech)
flirten – *v reg* † flirt
flog – *see fliegen**
Floh (Flöhe) – *nm* flea
Flohmarkt (-märkte) – *nm* flea
  market
Flöte (-n) – *nf* flute
Flug (Flüge) – *nm* flight (plane)
Flügel (-) – *nm* piano (grand)
Flughafen(-häfen) – *nm* airport
Flugzeug (-e) – *nnt* aeroplane
  mit dem Flugzeug – by plane
Flur (-e) – *nm* hallway
Fluss (Flüsse) – *nm* river
Flüssigkeit (-en) – *nf* liquid
flüstern – *v reg* whisper
Flut (-en) – *nf* high tide
Föhn (-e) – *nm* hair dryer; warm
  alpine wind
Folge (-n) – *nf* consequence
folgen* (+ dat) – *v reg* follow
folgend – *adj* following
Forelle (-n) – *nf* trout
Form (-en) – *nf* shape
Formular (-e) – *nnt* form (paper)
  ein Formular ausfüllen – *v reg*
  sep fill in a form
fort – *adv* away
fortfahren* – *v irreg sep* go on
  (continue)
fortgehen* – *v irreg* go away
Fortschritt (-e) – *nm* progress
  Fortschritte machen – *v reg*
  make progress
Foto (-s) – *nnt* photo
  Fotos machen – *v reg* take photos
Fotoapparat (-e) – *nm* camera
Fotograf (-en) – *nm wk* photographer

---

adj - adjective	*v reg* - verb regular	*v sep* - verb separable	† - see verb info
prep - preposition	*v irreg* - verb irregular	*v refl* - verb reflexive	* - takes sein

Fotografie – *nf* photography
fotografieren – *v reg* † take a photo
Fotografin (-nen) – *nf* photographer
Fotokopie (-n) – *nf* photocopy
fotokopieren – *v reg* † photocopy
Fotokopiergerät(-e) – *nnt*
photocopier
Frage (-n) – *nf* question
eine mündliche Frage (-n) – *nf*
an oral question
das kommt nicht in Frage –
that's out of the question
fragen – *v reg* ask
sich fragen – *v reg refl* wonder
Fragezeichen – *nnt* question mark (?)
Franc (-s) – *nm* franc (French)
Franken (-) – *nm* franc (Swiss)
Frankreich – *nnt* France
Franzose (-n) – *nm wk* French person
Französin (-nen) – *nf* French person
französisch – *adj* French
Französisch – *nnt* French (language)
auf Französisch – in French
Frau – Mrs, Ms
Frau (-en) – *nf* woman, wife
Frauenarzt (-ärzte) – *nm*
gynaecologist
Frauenärztin (-nen) – *nf*
gynaecologist
Frauenzeitschrift (-en) – *nf*
women's magazine
Fräulein (-) – *nnt* Miss
Fräulein! – *excl* Waitress!
frech – *adj* cheeky
frei – *adj* free
im Freien – in the open air
Freibad (-bäder) – *nnt* open air
swimming pool
frei halten– *v irreg* keep free, keep
clear
Freiheit (-en) – *nf* freedom
Freitag (-e) – *nm* Friday
am Freitag – on Friday

freitags – *adv* on Fridays
freiwillig – *adj* voluntary
Freiwillige – *nmf* ‡ volunteer
Freizeit – *nf* free time
Freizeitsbeschäftigung (-en) – *nf*
hobby
Freizeitzentrum (-zentren) – *nnt*
leisure centre
fremd – *adj* foreign, not local
ich bin hier fremd – I'm a stranger
Fremde – *nmf* ‡ stranger
Fremdenzimmer (-) – *nnt* room to
let, B & B
Fremdsprache (-n) – *nf* foreign
language
fressen – *v irreg* eat (of animal)
Frettchen (-) – *nnt* ferret
Freude (-n) – *nf* joy
Freudenfeuer – *nnt* bonfire
sich freuen auf (+ acc) – *v reg refl*
look forward to
sich freuen über (+ acc) – *v reg*
refl be pleased about
Freund (-e) – *nm* friend, boyfriend
ein Freund/eine Freundin von
mir – a friend of mine
Freundin (-nen) – *nf* friend, girlfriend
freundlich – *adj* friendly
mit freundlichen Grüßen –
Kind regards, Yours sincerely
Freundlichkeit (-en) – *nf* kindness
Freundschaft (-en) – *nf* friendship
Frieden (-) – *nm* peace
friedlich – *adj* peaceful
frieren – *v irreg* freeze
Es friert – It is freezing (ice)
Mir friert's – I'm freezing
Frikadelle (-n) – *nf* rissole
frisch – *adj* fresh
frisch gestrichen – wet paint
Friseuse (-n) – *nf* hairdresser
Frisör (-e) – *nm* hairdresser
Frisur (-en) – *nf* hairstyle

---

froh – *adj* happy, merry
  Frohe Weihnachten! – Happy Christmas!

fröhlich – *adj* merry
  Fröhliche Weihnachten! – Merry Christmas!

Frosch (Frösche) – *nm* frog

Frost – *nm* frost

frostig – *adj* frosty

Frucht~ – *pref* fruit

Fruchtsaft (-säfte) – *nm* fruit juice

früh – *adj* early
  morgen früh – tomorrow morning

früher – *adv* in the past, formerly

Frühjahr – *nnt* spring

Frühling – *nm* spring
  im Frühling – in spring

frühmorgens – *adv* in the early morning

Frühstück (-e) – *nnt* breakfast

frühstücken – *v reg* have breakfast

fühlen – *v reg* feel

sich fühlen – *v reg refl* feel (person)
  Ich fühle mich wohl – I feel well, I feel at ease
  Ich fühle mich unwohl – I feel ill

fuhr – *see fahren**

führen – *v reg* lead

Führer (-) – *nm* guide, leader

Führerin (-nen) – *nf* guide, leader

Führerschein (-e) – *nm* driving licence
  den Führerschein machen – *v reg* take a driving test

Führung (-en) – *nf* guided tour
  in Führung – in the lead

füllen – *v reg* fill

Füller (-) – *nm* fountain pen

Fundbüro (-s) – *nnt* lost property office

Fundsachen – *npl* lost property

fünf – *adj* five

fünfte – *adj* fifth

fünfzehn – *adj* fifteen

fünfzig – *adj* fifty

Fünfzigmarkschein (-e) – *nm* 50 mark note

funktionieren – *v reg* † work

für (+ acc) – *prep* for

Furcht – *nf* fear

furchtbar – *adj* awful, terrible

furchtbar – *adv* tremendously

fürchterlich – *adj* horrible

Fuß (Füße) – *nm* foot
  zu Fuß gehen* – *v irreg* go on foot
  sich den Fuß verrenken – *v reg dat refl* † to sprain one's ankle

Fußball (-bälle) – *nm* football

Fußballplatz (-plätze) – *nm* football field

Fußballschuh (-e) – *nm* football boot

Fußballspiel (-e) – *nnt* football match

Fußballspieler (-) – *nm* footballer

Fußboden (-böden) – *nm* floor (ground)

Fußgänger (-) – *nm* pedestrian

Fußgängerin (-nen) – *nf* pedestrian

Fußgängerüberweg (-e) – *nm* pedestrian crossing

Fußgängerzone (-n) – *nf* pedestrian zone

Fußgelenk (-e) – *nnt* ankle
  sich das Fußgelenk verstauchen – *v reg dat refl* † sprain one's ankle
  sich das Fußgelenk verrenken – *v reg dat refl* † twist an ankle

Fußweg (-e) – *nm* footpath

füttern – *v reg* feed (animal)

G

g – gramme
gab – *see geben*
  es gab – there was, there were
  es gäbe – there would be
Gabel (-n) – *nf* fork
gähnen – *v reg* yawn
Galerie (-n) – *nf* gallery
Gang (Gänge) – *nm* corridor,
  gear (car)
  (den Gang) schalten – *v reg* †
  change gear
Gans (Gänse) – *nf* goose
ganz – *adv* quite (totally)
  ganz allein – all alone
  ganz viel – quite a lot
ganz – *adj* whole
  das ganze Jahr – all year round
  den ganzen Tag – all day
  die ganze Zeit – the whole time
  im Großen und Ganzen – on the
  whole
ganztägig – *adj* full time (job)
Ganztagsschule (-n) – *nf* all-day
  school
gar – *adj* cooked
gar – *adv* even
  gar nicht – not at all
  gar nichts – nothing at all
Garage (-n) – *nf* garage (house)
Garantie (-n) – *nf* guarantee
Garderobe (-n) – *nf* cloak-room
Gardine (-n) – *nf* curtain (net)
Garten (Gärten) – *nm* garden
  im Garten arbeiten – *v reg* †
  do (the) gardening
Gartenarbeit – *nf* gardening
Gartenhäuschen (-) – *nnt* shed
Gärtner (-) – *nm* gardener
Gas (-e) – *nnt* gas
Gasflasche (-n) – *nf* gas cylinder

Gasherd (-e) – *nm* gas cooker
Gasse (-n) – *nf* lane, alley
Gast (Gäste) – *nm* guest
Gastarbeiter (-) – *nm* guest worker
Gastfreundschaft – *nf* hospitality
Gastgeber (-) – *nm* host
Gastgeberin (-nen) – *nf* hostess
Gasthaus (-häuser) – *nnt* pub, inn
Gasthof (-höfe) – *nm* pub, inn
Gaststätte (-n) – *nf* pub
geb. – born
Gebäck – *nnt* biscuits, pastries
Gebäude (-) – *nnt* building
geben – *v irreg* give
  Geben Sie mir... – Give me...
  (formal)
  Es wird ... geben – There will be ...
Gebiet (-e) – *nnt* area
Gebirge (-) – *nnt* mountain range,
  range of hills
geblieben – *see bleiben**
geboren – *adj* born
  am 6. Januar geboren – born on
  6th January
geboren sein* – *v irreg* be born
gebracht – *see bringen*
Gebrauch (Gebräuche) – *nm*
  custom
Gebrauch – *nm, no pl* use
gebrauchen – *v reg* † use
Gebrauchsanweisung (-en) – *nf*
  user instructions
gebraucht – *adj* second-hand
gebräunt – *adj* sun-tanned
gebrochen – *adj* broken
Gebühr (-en) – *nf* fee
Geburt (-en) – *nf* birth
gebürtig – *adj* native
Geburtsdatum (-daten) – *nnt* date
  of birth

Geburtsort (-e) – *nm* place of birth
Geburtstag (-e) – *nm* birthday
Herzlichen Glückwunsch zum Geburtstag! – *excl* Happy Birthday!
Geburtstagsgeschenk (-e) – *nnt* birthday present
Geburtstagskarte (-n) – *nf* birthday card
Geburtstagskuchen (-) – *nm* birthday cake
Geburtsurkunde (-n) – *nf* birth certificate
gedacht – *see denken*
Gedächtnis (-se) – *nnt* memory
Gedanke (-n) – *nm wk* thought
Gedränge – *nnt* scrum
gedruckt – *adj* printed
Geduld – *nf* patience
geduldig – *adj* patient
geehrt – *adj* honoured
Sehr geehrter Herr! – Dear Sir
geeignet – *adj* fit (suitable)
Gefahr (-en) – *nf* danger
gefahren – *see fahren**
gefährlich – *adj* dangerous
gefallen (+ dat) – *v irreg* be pleasing
Die Hose gefällt mir – I like the trousers
Gefängnis (se) – *nnt* prison
geflogen – *see fliegen**
Geflügel – *nnt* poultry
gefolgt von (+ dat) – *adj* followed by
gefroren – *adj* frozen
tiefgefroren – *adj* deep-frozen
Gefühl (-e) – *nnt* feeling
gefunden – *see finden*
gegangen – *see gehen**
gegeben – *see geben*
gegen (+ acc) – *prep* against, towards
gegen Mittag – towards midday

Gegend – *nf* area, district
hier in der Gegend – round here
Gegenstand (-stände) – *nm* item
Gegenstück (-e) – *nnt* equivalent
Gegenteil (-e) – *nnt* opposite
gegenüber (+ dat) – *prep* opposite
gegenwärtig – *adj* present (current)
gegessen – *see essen*
gehabt – *see haben*
gehacktes Rindfleisch – minced beef
Gehalt (Gehälter) – *nnt* salary
Gehaltserhöhung (-en) – *nf* pay rise
gehässig – *adj* spiteful
geheim – *adj* secret
Geheimnis (-se) – *nnt* secret
geheimnisvoll – *adj* mysterious
gehen* – *v irreg* walk, go
Meine Uhr geht vor – My watch is fast
Mir geht es gut – I am well
mit jdm gehen* – *v irreg* go out with s.o.
nach Hause gehen* – *v irreg* go home
nach oben gehen* – *v irreg* go upstairs
Gehirn (-e) – *nnt* brain
geholfen – *see helfen*
gehorchen (+ dat) – *v reg* † obey
gehören (+ dat) – *v reg* † belong to
Das gehört ihnen – It's theirs
Es gehört mir – It's mine
gehorsam – *adj* obedient
Geige (-n) – *nf* violin
Geige spielen – *v reg* play the violin
geil – *adj coll* excellent; randy
Geisteswissenschaften – *npl* humanities
geizig – *adj* mean
gekannt – *see kennen*
gekommen – *see kommen**
gel? – *adv* isn't it?, etc

---

adj - adjective	*v reg* - verb regular	*v sep* - verb separable	† - see verb info
prep - preposition	*v irreg* - verb irregular	*v refl* - verb reflexive	* - takes sein

Gel – *nnt* hair gel
gelaufen – *see laufen**
gelaunt – *adj* mood
  schlecht gelaunt – in a bad mood
  gut gelaunt – in a good mood
gelb – *adj* yellow
Geld – *nnt* money, cash
  Geld verdienen – *v reg* † make money
  Geld wechseln – *v reg* change money
Geldautomat (-en) – *nm wk* cash machine (dispenser)
Geldbeutel (-) – *nm* purse
Geldbörse (-n) – *nf* purse
Geldrückgabe (-n) – *nf* refund, return coins
Geldschein (-e) – *nm* bank-note
Geldstrafe (-n) – *nf* fine (punishment)
Geldwechsel – *nm* currency exchange, bureau de change
Gelee – *nnt* jelly, aspic
gelegen – *adj* situated
Gelegenheit (-en) – *nf* opportunity
  die Gelegenheit haben – *v irreg* have the opportunity to
Gelegenheitsarbeiten – *npl* odd jobs
Gelegenheitsarbeiten verrichten – *v reg* † do odd jobs
gelegentlich – *adj* occasional
gelesen – *see lesen*
gelingen* – *v irreg* succeed
  Es ist mir gelungen – I've succeeded
Gemäldegalerie (-n) – *nf* art gallery
gemein – *adj* mean (nasty)
Gemeinde (-n) – *nf* parish, district
Gemeinderat – *nm* local council
der Gemeinsame Markt – *nm* the Common Market

Gemeinschaftskunde – *nf* social studies
gemischt – *adj* mixed, coeducational
Gemüse – *nnt no pl* vegetables, greens
Gemüsehändler (-) – *nm* greengrocer
Gemüsehändlerin (-nen) – *nf* greengrocer
gemütlich – *adj* snug, cosy, sociable, pleasant
genau – *adj* exact
  genau so – *adv* in the same way as
genauso – *adv* just as
Genehmigung (-en) – *nf* licence
Generalprobe (-n) – *nf* dress rehearsal
Genf – Geneva
geniert – *adj* embarrassed
genießen – *v irreg* enjoy
Genitiv – *nnt* genitive
genommen – *see nehmen*
genug – *adj* enough
geöffnet – *adj* open
Geographie – *nf* geography
Geologie – *nf* geology
Gepäck – *nnt, no pl* luggage
Gepäckaufbewahrung (-en) – *nf* left luggage office
Gepäckausgabe (-n) – *nf* luggage carousel
Gepäcknetz (-e) – *nnt* train luggage rack
Gepäckschließfach (-fächer) – *nnt* left luggage locker
Gepäckstück (-e) – *nnt* piece of luggage
Gepäckträger (-) – *nm* porter; carrier on bicycle
Gepäckzettel (-) – *nm* left luggage ticket
geparkt – *adj* parked
gepunktet – *adj* spotty (fabric)
gerade – *adj* even, just, straight

Ich bin gerade angekommen – I have just arrived

Er wollte gerade anrufen – He was on the point of phoning

geradeaus – *adv* straight on

Gehen Sie geradeaus! – Go straight on!

Gerät (-e) – *nnt* appliance

ins Schleudern geraten* – *v irreg* skid

Geräusch (-e) – *nnt* noise (quiet)

geräuschlos – *adj* silent

gerecht – *adj* fair, just

Das ist nicht gerecht – It's not fair!

gereizt – *adj* irritated

Gericht (-e) – *nnt* dish (recipe)

gern – *adv* gladly

gern haben – *v irreg* like

gern machen – *v reg* be keen on

Ich tanze gern – I like dancing

Geruch (Gerüche) – *nm* smell

gesagt – *see sagen* told

Gesamtschule (-n) – *nf* comprehensive school

Geschäft (-e) – *nnt* shop, business

Geschäftsfrau (-en) – *nf* business woman

Geschäftsführer (-) – *nm* manager

Geschäftsführerin (-nen) – *nf* manageress

Geschäftsmann (-männer) – *nm* business man

Geschäftszeiten – *npl* opening hours

geschehen* – *v irreg* happen

Gern geschehen! – *excl* It's a pleasure!

Geschenk (-e) – *nnt* gift

als Geschenk einpacken – *v reg sep* gift wrap

Geschichte – *nf* history; story

geschickt – *adv* skilfully

geschickt – *adj* skilled

geschieden – *adj* divorced

Geschirr – *nnt, no pl* crockery

Geschirrspülautomat (-en) – *nm wk* dishwasher

Geschirrspülmaschine (-n) – *nf* dishwasher

Geschirrtuch (-tücher) – *nnt* tea towel

geschlafen – *see schlafen*

geschlagen – *adj* defeated

Geschlecht (-er) – *nnt* gender

geschlossen – *adj* closed

Geschmack (Geschmäcke) – *nm* taste, flavour

mit Zitronengeschmack – lemon flavoured

geschnitten – *see schneiden*

Geschoss (-e) – *nnt* floor

im obersten Geschoss – on the top floor

geschrieben – *see schreiben*

geschützt von (+ dat) – *adj* sheltered from

Geschwindigkeit (-en) – *nf* speed

mit hoher Geschwindigkeit – at high speed

Geschwindigkeitsbegrenzung (-en) – *nf* speed limit

Geschwindigkeitsbeschränkung (-en) – *nf* speed limit

Geschwister – *npl* brothers and sisters

geschwollen – *adj* swollen

geschwommen – *see schwimmen* (*)

gesehen – *see sehen*

Gesellschaft (-en) – *nf* society; company; firm

Gesellschaftsspiel (-e) – *nnt* board game

gesessen – *see sitzen*

Gesetz (-e) – *nnt* law

Gesicht (-er) – *nnt* face

ein Gesicht ziehen – *v irreg* pull a face

---

adj - adjective	*v reg* - verb regular	*v sep* - verb separable	† - see verb info
prep - preposition	*v irreg* - verb irregular	*v refl* - verb reflexive	* - takes sein

gespannt – *adj* eager
Gespenst (-er) – *nnt* ghost
gesperrt – *adj* closed (road)
Gespräch (-e) – *nnt* conversation
gesprächig – *adj* talkative
gesprochen – *see sprechen*
gestattet – *adj* permitted
Gestell (-e) – *nnt* frame (spectacles)
gestern – *adv* yesterday
  gestern Abend – *adv* last night,
  yesterday evening
gestochen werden* – *v irreg* get
  stung
gestorben – *adj* dead
gestreift – *adj* striped
gestresst – *adj* stressed out
gesund – *adj* healthy, well
Gesundheit! – *excl* Bless you!
Gesundheit – *nf* health
getestet – *adj* checked
getragen – *see tragen*
Getränk (-e) – *nnt* drink
  ein alkoholfreies Getränk – *nnt*
  a soft drink
Getränkekarte (-n) – *nf* wine list
getrennt – *adj* separated
getrennt – *adv* separately
  Geht das getrennt oder
  zusammen? – Do you want to
  pay separately or all together?
getrunken – *see trinken*
Gewächshaus (-häuser) – *nnt*
  greenhouse
Gewalt – *nf* violence
gewaltig – *adj* violent (storm)
gewalttätig – *adj* violent (person)
gewaschen – *see waschen*
Gewehr (-e) – *nnt* gun (rifle)
gewesen – *see sein** been
Gewicht (-e) – *nnt* weight
gewinnen – *v irreg* win

einen Punkt gewinnen – *v irreg*
  score a point
gewiss – *adj* certain
Gewitter (-) – *nnt* thunderstorm
  Es wird Gewitter geben – There
  will be thunderstorms
sich gewöhnen an (+ acc) – *v reg*
  refl † get used to
Gewohnheit (-en) – *nf* habit
  Ich habe die Gewohnheit – I am
  in the habit of
gewöhnlich – *adj* ordinary, usual
  wie gewöhnlich – *adv* as usual
gewonnen – *see gewinnen*
geworden – *see werden**
gewusst – *see wissen*
Gib mir ... – give me ... (informal)
gibt – *see geben*
Es gibt (+ acc) – There are, There is
  Es gibt keinen/keine/kein ... –
  There is no ...
  Es gibt keine ... – There are no ...
gierig – *adj* greedy
Gift (-e) – *nnt* poison
giftig – *adj* poisonous
ging – *see gehen**
Gipfel (-) – *nm* summit
Gips (-e) – *nm* plaster (broken arm)
Gitarre (-n) – *nf* guitar
Gitarre spielen – *v reg* play the
  guitar
Glück – *nnt* happiness
glänzend – *adj* shiny
Glas (Gläser) – *nnt* glass, jar
  ein Glas Marmelade – *nnt* a jar
  of jam
Glasscheibe (-n) – *nf* (pane of) glass
glatt – *adj* smooth, straight (hair)
Glatteis – *nnt* black ice
Glatze (-n) – *nf* bald patch
  Er hat eine Glatze – He's bald
glauben – *v reg* think

---

glauben (an + acc) – *v reg* believe (in)
gleich – *adj* same, equal
gleich – *adv* immediately, in a moment
 Ich esse gleich – I am about to eat
gleichaltrig – *adj* of the same age
Gleichfalls! – *excl* I wish you the same!
Gleichheit (-en) – *nf* equality
gleichmäßig – *adj* evenly
gleichzeitig – *adv* at the same time
Gleis – *nnt* track, rails
 auf Gleis 8 – from platform 8
Gletscher (-) – *nm* glacier
glitschig – *adj* slippery
global – *adj* global
Glocke (-n) – *nf* bell (church)
Glotze – *nf coll* telly
Glück – *nnt* luck
 Viel Glück! – *excl* Good luck!
Glück haben – *v irreg* to be lucky
glücklich – *adj* happy, fortunate
 Ein glückliches neues Jahr! – *excl* Happy New Year!
 Herzlichen Glückwunsch zum Geburtstag! – *excl* Happy Birthday!
glücklicherweise – *adv* fortunately
Glückwunschkarte (-n) – *nf* greetings card
Glühbirne (-e) – *nf* light bulb
glühen – *v reg* glow
Gokart (-s) – *nm* go-kart
Gokart fahren* – *v irreg* to go go-karting
Gokart-Fahren – *nnt* go-karting
Gold – *nnt* gold
 aus Gold – made of gold
golden – *adj* golden
Goldfisch (-e) – *nm* goldfish
Goldmedaille – *nf* gold medal
Golf – *nm* golf
Golfplatz (-plätze) – *nm* golf course
Gott (Götter) – *nm* God

Gottesdienst (-e) – *nm* church service
Grad – *nm* degree (temperature)
Gramm – *nnt* gramme
Grammatik – *nf* grammar
Gras (Gräser) – *nnt* grass
gratis – *adj* free
gratulieren (+ dat) – *v reg* †
 congratulate
 Ich gratuliere – Congratulations!
grau – *adj* grey
Graubrot – *nnt* wholemeal bread
grausam – *adj* cruel
greifen – *v irreg* grab
Grenze (-n) – *nf* border, limit
Grieche (-n) – *nm wk* Greek person
Griechenland – *nnt* Greece
Griechin (-nen) – *nf* Greek person
griechisch – *adj* Greek
Griff (-e) – *nm* handle
grillen – *v reg* grill (food)
 vom Grill – grilled
Grillfest (-e) – *nnt* barbecue
grinsen – *v reg* grin
Grippe – *nf* flu
grölen – *v reg* yell
Groschen (-) – *nm* 10 Pfennig piece
groß – *adj* big, tall
 im Großen und Ganzen – on the whole
 nicht so groß wie – not as big as
Groß~ – *pref* big
großartig – *adj* magnificent
Großbritannien – *nnt* Great Britain
Großbuchstabe (-n) – *nm wk* capital letter
Größe (-n) – *nf* size, height
Großeltern – *npl* grandparents
größer als – bigger than
Großmutter (-mütter) – *nf* grandmother
Großstadt (-städte) – *nf* city

---

adj - adjective	*v reg* - verb regular	*v sep* - verb separable	† - see verb info
prep - preposition	*v irreg* - verb irregular	*v refl* - verb reflexive	* - takes sein

Großvater (-väter) – *nm* grandfather

großzügig – *adj* generous

grün – *adj* green

grüner Salat – *nm* green salad

Grund (Gründe) – *nm* reason

im Grunde – *adv* basically

Grund~ – *pref* basic

Grundschule (-n) – *nf* primary school

Grundschullehrer (-) – *nm* primary school teacher

Grundschullehrerin (-nen) – *nf* primary school teacher

Grundstück (-stücke) – *nnt* plot of land

Gruppe (-n) – *nf* group, band

gruselig – *adj* gory

Gruselroman (-e) – *nm* horror story

Gruß (Grüße) – *nm* greeting

Grüß dich! – *excl* Hello!

Grüß Gott! – *excl* Hello!

mit freundlichen Grüßen – Yours sincerely, Kind regards

grüßen – *v reg* greet

gucken – *v reg coll* watch

Gulasch – *nm* stew

gültig – *adj* valid

Gummiband (-bänder) – *nnt* rubber band

günstig – *adj* good value, favourable

Gurke (-n) – *nf* cucumber

Gürtel (-) – *nm* belt

Gürteltasche (-n) – *nf* bumbag

gut – *adj* good

Alles Gute – love from

Gute Besserung! – *excl* Get well soon!

Gute Fahrt! – *excl* Have a good journey!

Gute Heimreise! – *excl* Have a good journey home!

Gute Idee! – *excl* Good idea!

Gute Nacht! – *excl* Good night!

Gute Reise! – *excl* Have a good trip!

Guten Abend! – *excl* Good evening!

Guten Appetit! – *excl* Enjoy your meal!

Guten Morgen! – *excl* Good morning!

Guten Tag! – *excl* Hello, Good afternoon!

guter Laune – in a good mood

gut zu Tieren – kind to animals

gut – *adv* well

Es geht mir gut – I'm fine

gut gelaunt – *adj* good-tempered

Gut gemacht! – *excl* Well done!

gut aussehend – *adj* good looking

Güte – *nf* goodness

gut erzogen – *adj* well brought up

gut in .... sein* – *v irreg* be good at

Gymnasium (-ien) – *nnt* grammar school

Gymnastik machen – *v reg* do gymnastics

H

h – o'clock
Haar (-e) – *nnt* hair
  sich die Haare bürsten – *v reg dat refl* † brush one's hair
  sich die Haare schneiden lassen – *v irreg dat refl* have a haircut
  sich die Haare wachsen lassen – *v irreg dat refl* grow one's hair
  sich die Haare trocknen – *v reg dat refl* † dry one's hair
  sich die Haare waschen – *v irreg dat refl* wash one's hair
Haarbürste (-n) – *nf* hairbrush
Haarschnitt (-e) – *nm* haircut
haben – *v irreg* have, get
  Recht haben – *v irreg* be right
  Urlaub haben – *v irreg* have a holiday
Hackfleisch – *nnt* mince (meat)
Hafen (Häfen) – *nm* harbour, port
Hafenstadt (-städte) – *nf* port
Hagel – *nm* hail
hageln – *v reg* hail
  Es hagelt – It is hailing
Hähnchen (-) – *nnt* chicken
Haken (-) – *nm* hook, tick, snag
halb – *adj* half
  eine halbe Stunde – half an hour
  zum halben Preis – half-price
halb – half past
  um halb vier – at half past three
Halb~ – *pref* half
Halbbruder (-brüder) – *nm* half-brother
Halbfinale (-n) – *nnt* semi-final
Halbjahresferien – *npl* February half-term holiday
Halbjahreszeugnis (se) – *nnt* mid-year report

Halbpension – *nf* half board
Halbschwester (-n) – *nf* half-sister
halbtags – *adv* part-time
halbwegs – *adv* half way
half – *see helfen*
Hälfte (-n) – *nf* half
Halle (-n) – *nf* hall (public, sport)
Hallenbad (-bäder) – *nnt* pool, indoor pool
Hallo! – *excl* Hello! Hi!
Hals (Hälse) – *nm* neck, throat
Halskette (-n) – *nf* necklace
Halsschmerzen – *npl* sore throat
Halstablette (-n) – *nf* throat pastille
Halt! – *excl* Halt! Stop!
Halt machen – *v reg* halt
Halteverbot – *nnt* no stopping
halten – *v irreg* hold
Haltestelle (-n) – *nf* stop
Hamburger (-) – *nm* beefburger
Hameln – Hamelin
Hammelfleisch – *nnt* mutton
Hammer (-) – *nm* hammer
Hamster (-) – *nm* hamster
Hand (Hände) – *nf* hand
  jdm die Hand geben – *v irreg* shake hands with s.o.
Hand~ – *pref* manual
Handarbeit – *nf* needlework
Handball (-bälle) – *nm* handball
Handel – *nm* trade, drugs traffic
handeln – *v reg* trade
  Worum handelt es sich? – What is it about?
Handgelenk (-e) – *nnt* wrist
handgemacht – *adj* handmade
Handgepäck – *nnt* hand luggage
handgeschrieben – *adj* handwritten
Händler (-) – *nm* shopkeeper

---

adj - adjective   *v reg* - verb regular   *v sep* - verb separable   † - see verb info
prep - preposition   *v irreg* - verb irregular   *v refl* - verb reflexive   * - takes sein

Handlung (-en) – *nf* shop
Handschrift (-en) – *nf* handwriting
Handschuh (-e) – *nm* glove
Handtasche (-n) – *nf* handbag
Handtuch (-tücher) – *nnt* hand towel
Handwerker (-) – *nm* craftsman
Handwerkerin (-nen) – *nf* craftswoman
Hang (Hänge) – *nm* slope
hängen – *v irreg* hang
   Es hängt vom Wetter ab – It depends upon the weather
Hannover – Hanover
Hansaplast® – *nnt* elastoplast®
hart – *adj* hard
Haselnuss (-nüsse) – *nf* hazelnut
hassen – *v reg* hate
hässlich – *adj* ugly
hast – *see* haben
hat – *see* haben
Hat er welche? – Has he got any?
hatte – *see* haben
Haube (-n) – *nf* bonnet
Haufen – *nm* heap, pile
häufig – *adj* frequent
Haupt~ – *pref* main, chief
Hauptbahnhof (-höfe) – *nm* main railway station
Hauptgericht (-e) – *nnt* main course
Hauptschule (-n) – *nf* secondary modern school
Hauptstadt (-städte) – *nf* capital (city)
Hauptstraße (-n) – *nf* high street, major road
Hauptverkehrszeit (-en) – *nf* rush hour
Haus (Häuser) – *nnt* home, house
   ins Haus gehen* – *v irreg* to go inside

Kommen Sie/Komm gut gut nach Hause! – *excl* Have a safe journey home!
nach Hause gehen* – *v irreg* go home
zu Hause bleiben* – *v irreg* stay at home
zu Hause sein* – *v irreg* be at home
Hausarbeit – *nf* housework
Hausarbeit machen – *v reg* do housework
Hausaufgaben – *npl* homework
Hausaufgaben machen – *v reg* do homework
Häuschen (-) – *nnt* cottage
Hausflur (-e) – *nm* hall (domestic)
Hausfrau (-en) – *nf* housewife
Haushalt (-e) – *nm* household
Haushaltslehre – *nf* home economics
häuslich – *adj* domestic
Hausmann (-männer) – *nm* househusband
Hausmeister (-) – *nm* caretaker
Hausmeisterin (-nen) – *nf* caretaker
Hausmutter (-mütter) – *nf* matron
Hausnummer (-n) – *nf* house number
Hausschuh (-e) – *nm* slipper
Haustier (-e) – *nnt* pet
Haustür (-en) – *nf* front door
Hauswirtschaftslehre – *nf* home economics
Haut – *nf* skin
Hbf. – main railway station
heben – *v irreg* lift
   hochheben – *v irreg sep* lift up
Heck – *nnt, no pl* back (of car)
Hecke (-n) – *nf* hedge
Heft (-e) – *nnt* exercise book, jotter
Heftklammer (-n) – *nf* staple
Heftmaschine (-n) – *nf* stapler
heilig – *adj* holy
Heiligabend – *nm* Christmas Eve

| *nm* - noun masculine | *nf* - noun feminine | *nnt* - noun neuter | *npl* - noun plural |
| *nom*- nominative | *acc* - accusative | *gen* - genitive | *dat* - dative |

Heilige – *nmf* ‡ saint
Heiliger Abend – *nm* Christmas Eve
Heimat – *nf* home area
Heimatstadt – *nf* native town
  Gute Heimreise! – *excl* Have a
  good journey home!
Heimspiel (-e) – *nnt* home game
Heimweh – *nnt* homesickness
  Ich habe Heimweh – I'm
  homesick
Heimwerker (-) – *nm* handyman
heiraten – *v reg* † marry, get married
heiß – *adj* hot
heiß sein* – *v irreg* be hot (weather)
  Mir ist heiß – I am hot
heißen – *v irreg* be called
  das heißt (d.h.) – that is to say (i.e.)
  Ich heiße ... – My name is ...
  **Wie heißt du?/Wie heißen
  Sie?** – What is your name?
  Wie heißt ...? – What does ... mean?
heiter – *adj* cheerful, bright (of
  weather)
heizen – *v reg* heat
Heizgerät (-e) – *nnt* heater
Heizkörper (-) – *nm* radiator (in
  building)
Heizung (-en) – *nf* heating
Held (-en) – *nm wk* hero
Heldin (-nen) – *nf* heroine
helfen (+ dat) – *v irreg* help, aid,
  assist
hell – *adj* bright, light
hell~ – *pref* pale
hellblau – *adj* pale blue
Helm (-e) – *nm* helmet
Hemd (-en) – *nnt* shirt
Henne (-n) – *nf* hen
her – *adv* towards (speaker)
heraufkommen* – *v irreg sep* come
  up
herausfinden – *v irreg sep* find out

herauskommen* – *v irreg sep* come
  out
herausnehmen – *v irreg sep* take
  out, remove
Herberge (-n) – *nf* hostel
Herbergsmutter (-mütter) – *nf*
  youth hostel warden
Herbergsvater (-väter) – *nm* youth
  hostel warden
Herbst – *nm* autumn
  im Herbst – in autumn
Herbstferien – *npl* autumn half-term
  holiday
Herd (-e) – *nm* cooker, oven, stove
Herde (-n) – *nf* flock, herd
Herein! – *excl* Come in!
hereinkommen* – *v irreg sep* come in
hereinplatzen* – *v reg sep coll* gate-
  crash
Hering (-e) – *nm* herring
Heroin – *nnt* heroin (drug)
Herr (-en) – *nm wk* gentleman,
  master
Herr – Mr, Sir
  Herr Ober! – *excl* Waiter!
  mein Herr – Sir
Herren – Men's toilets
Herrenhaus (-häuser) – *nnt*
  mansion
Herrenkonfektion – *nf* men's
  clothes department
herrlich – *adj* gorgeous
herrschsüchtig – *adj* bossy
herstellen – *v reg sep* manufacture
herüber – *adv* over (across, towards
  speaker)
herum – *adv* about, around (place)
herumalbern – *v reg sep* mess about
herunterkommen* – *v irreg sep*
  come down
hervorragend – *adj* outstanding,
  very good
Herz (-en) – *nnt wk* heart
herzlich – *adj* sincere

---

adj - adjective	*v reg* - verb regular	*v sep* - verb separable	† - see verb info
prep - preposition	*v irreg* - verb irregular	*v refl* - verb reflexive	* - takes sein

Herzlichen Glückwunsch! – *excl* Congratulations!

heulen – *v reg* cry, weep, howl

Heuschnupfen – *nm* hay fever

heute – *adv* today

heute Abend – tonight (evening)

heute Nacht – tonight (night-time)

heutzutage – *adv* nowadays, today

hielt – *see halten*

hier – *adv* here

hier in der Nähe – nearby

hieß – *see heißen*

Hilfe – *nf* aid, assistance, help
  erste Hilfe – *nf* first aid

Hilfe! – *excl* Help!

hilflos – *adj* helpless

hilfsbereit – *adj* helpful

Hilfspolizist (-en) – *nm wk* traffic warden

Himbeere (-n) – *nf* raspberry

Himbeertorte (-n) – *nf* raspberry tart

Himmel (-) – *nm* sky

himmelblau – *adj* sky blue

hin – *adv* away (from speaker)

hin und wieder – *adv* occasionally

hin und her laufen* – *v irreg* run backwards and forwards

hin und zurück – *adv* return, there and back

hinauflaufen* – *v irreg sep* run up

hinausgehen* – *v irreg sep* go out

hinauslaufen* aus (+ dat) – *v irreg sep* run out of (building)

sich hinauslehnen – *v reg refl sep* lean out
  Nicht hinauslehnen! – *excl* Do not lean out!

Hindernis (-se) – *nnt* obstacle

hindu – *adj* Hindu

Hindu (-s) – *nm* Hindu person

hineingehen* – *v irreg sep* go in (to)

hinfallen* – *v irreg sep* trip over, fall

hinlegen – *v reg sep* deposit; lay down

sich hinlegen – *v reg refl sep* lie down

sich hinsetzen – *v reg refl sep* sit down

hinstellen – *v reg sep* put down (vertical)

hinten – *adv* back

hinter (+ acc/dat) – *prep* behind, past (beyond)

Hintern (-) – *nm* behind

hinüber – *adv* over (across, away from speaker)

sich hinüberbeugen – *v reg refl sep* lean over

hinunterkommen* – *v irreg sep* come down, go down

hinunterlaufen* – *v irreg sep* run down
  Sie ist die Straße hinuntergelaufen – She ran down the street

Hinweis (-e) – *nm* tip, clue

hinzufügen – *v reg sep* add

historisch – *adj* historic

Hit (-s) – *nm* hit song (in English)

Hitze – *nf* heat

hitzefrei – *adj* school closure due to hot weather

Hitzewelle (-n) – *nf* heatwave

Hobby (-s) – *nnt* hobby

hoch – *adj* high

Hochachtungsvoll – *adv* Yours faithfully (very formal)

Hochhaus (-häuser) – *nnt* block of flats

Hochschule (-n) – *nf* university

höchst – *adj* highest

Höchst~ – *pref* maximum

Höchstgeschwindigkeit (-en) – *nf* maximum speed
  mit Höchstgeschwindigkeit – at full speed

Höchsttemperatur (-en) – *nf* maximum temperature

---

nm - noun masculine	*nf* - noun feminine	*nnt* - noun neuter	*npl* - noun plural
nom- nominative	*acc* - accusative	*gen* - genitive	*dat* - dative

höchstwahrscheinlich – *adv* very probably

Hochwasser – *nnt* high tide
  bei Hochwasser – at high tide

Hochzeit (-en) – *nf* marriage (ceremony), wedding

Hochzeitskleid (-er) – *nnt* wedding dress

Hocker (-) – *nm* stool

Hockey – *nnt* hockey

Hof (Höfe) – *nm* yard (place)

hoffen – *v reg* hope

hoffentlich – *adv* hopefully

Hoffnung (-en) – *nf* hope

höflich – *adj* polite

Höflichkeit (-en) – *nf* politeness

Höhe – *nf* height (geographical)

höher – *adj* higher

hohl – *adj* hollow

Höhle (-n) – *nf* cave

holen – *v reg* fetch, get

Holland – *nnt* Holland

Holländer (-) – *nm* Dutchman
  Der Fliegende Holländer – The Flying Dutchman

Holländerin (-nen) – *nf* Dutchwoman

holländisch – *adj* Dutch

Holz – *nnt* wood
  aus Holz – wooden

Honig (-e) – *nm* honey

hören – *v reg* hear, listen (to)
  Kassetten hören – *v reg* listen to tapes
  von (+ dat) hören – *v reg* hear from

Hörer (-) – *nm* hand set, receiver (phone)
  den Hörer abnehmen – *v irreg sep* pick up phone

Horizont (-e) – *nm* horizon
  am Horizont – on the horizon

Horn (Hörner) – *nnt* horn (music)

Horror – *nm* horror

Horrorfilm (-e) – *nm* horror film

Horrorgeschichte (-n) – *nf* horror story

Hose (-n) – *nf* trousers
  eine kurze Hose – *nf* a pair of shorts

Hotel (-s) – *nnt* hotel

Hotelverzeichnis (-se) – *nnt* list of hotels

hübsch – *adj* pretty

Hubschrauber (-) – *nm* helicopter

Hubschrauberlandeplatz (-plätze) – *nm* heliport

Hüfte (-n) – *nf* hip

Hügel (-n) – *nf* hill

Huhn (Hühner) – *nnt* chicken, hen

Humor – *nm* humour

Hund (-e) – *nm* dog
  ein junger Hund – *nm* a puppy
  Warnung vor dem Hund – beware of the dog

hundert – *adj* hundred

hundertste – *adj* hundredth

Hündin (-nen) – *nf* dog

Hunger – *nm* hunger

Hunger haben – *v irreg* be hungry
  Ich habe Hunger – I am hungry

hungrig – *adj* hungry

hungrig sein* – *v irreg* be hungry

Hupe (-n) – *nf* horn (car)

hupen – *v reg* blow the horn (car)

Hürde (-n) – *nf* hurdle

Husten (-) – *nm* cough

husten – *v reg* † cough

Hustensaft (-säfte) – *nm* cough medicine

Hut (Hüte) – *nm* hat
  ohne Hut – bare-headed

Hüttenkäse – *nm* cottage cheese

hygienisch – *adj* hygienic

---

adj - adjective   *v reg* - verb regular   *v sep* - verb separable   † - see verb info
prep - preposition   *v irreg* - verb irregular   *v refl* - verb reflexive   * - takes sein

I

ich – *pron* I
IC-Zug (-Züge) – *nm* Inter-City train
ideal – *adj* ideal
Idee (-n) – *nf* idea
  ein paar Ideen – some ideas
identifizieren – *v reg* † identify
Identität (-en) – *nf* identity
Idiot (-en) – *nm wk* idiot
idiotisch – *adj* idiotic
ihm – *pron dat m, nt* him, it, to him, to it
ihn – *pron acc m* him, it
ihnen – *pron dat* them, to them
Ihnen – *pron dat sing or pl* you (formal)
ihr – *pron dat f* her, it, to her, to it
ihr – *pron nom pl* you (informal)
ihr – *poss adj* her, its, their
Ihr – *poss adj* your (formal)
Ihr – *poss adj* With best wishes from (male, formal)
Ihre – *poss adj* With best wishes from (female, formal)
Illustration (-en) – *nf* illustration
Illustrierte – *nf* ‡ glossy magazine
im – (= in dem) in the
  im Bus – on the bus
  im Freien – *adv* outdoors
  im Frühling – in spring
  im Moment – *adv* at present
  im Notfall – in an emergency
  im Sommer – in summer
  im Zug – on the train
Imbiss (-e) – *nm* snack
Imbissstube (-n) – *nf* snack bar
immer – *adv* always
  für immer – *adv* for ever
immer noch – *adv* still
immer schlimmer – *adv* worse and worse
immer wieder – *adv* again and again

Immobilienmakler (-) – *nm* estate agent
Imperfekt – *nnt* imperfect tense
in (+ acc/dat) – *prep* in, into, to, at (place)
  in die Stadt – into town
  in der Stadt – in town
  in Ordnung! – *excl* OK!
in – *adj inv* trendy
inbegr./inbegriffen – included
  alles inbegriffen – all included
  Bedienung inbegriffen – service included
  nicht inbegriffen – not included
indem – *sub conj* whilst
Inder (-) – *nm* Indian person (Asia)
Inderin (-nen) – *nf* Indian person (Asia)
Indianer (-) – *nm* Indian (America)
Indianerin (-nen) – *nf* Indian (America)
indianisch – *adj* Indian (America)
Indien – *nnt* India (Asia)
indisch – *adj* Indian (Asia)
individuell – *adj* individual
Individuum (Individuen) – *nnt* individual
Industrie (-n) – *nf* industry
Industriegebiet (-e) – *nnt* industrial area
industriell – *adj* industrial
Infektion (-en) – *nf* infection
Informatik – *nf* IT, information technology, computer studies
Informatiker (-) – *nm* computer scientist
Informatikerin (-nen) – *nf* computer scientist
Information (-en) – *nf* information
Informationsbüro (-s) – *nnt* tourist information office
informatisieren – *v reg* † computerise

---

nm - noun masculine   *nf* - noun feminine   *nnt* - noun neuter   *npl* - noun plural
nom- nominative   *acc* - accusative   *gen* - genitive   *dat* - dative

informieren – *v reg* † inform, let s.o. know
Ingenieur (-e) – *nm* engineer
Ingwer – *nm* ginger
Inhalt – *nm, no pl* contents
Inhaltsverzeichnis (-se) – *nnt* contents (book)
inkl. – included
inklusive – *adv* included
Inland – *nnt* home (not abroad)
Inliner – *npl* roller blades
Innenstadt (-städte) – *nf* town centre
Innere – *nnt* ‡ inside
Insekt (-en) – *nnt* insect
Insel (-n) – *nf* island
Inserat (-e) – *nnt* advert (small ad)
insgesamt – *adv* altogether
installieren – *v reg* † install
Instrument (-e) – *nnt* instrument
intelligent – *adj* intelligent, smart
Intelligenz – *nf* intelligence
Inter-City-Zug (-Züge) – *nm* Inter-City train
interessant – *adj* interesting
Interesse (-n) – *nnt* interest
sich interessieren für (+ acc) – *v reg refl* † be interested in
Internat (-e) – *nnt* boarding school
international – *adj* international
Interne – *nmf* ‡ boarder

Internet – *nnt* internet
das Internet benutzen – *v reg* † surf the net
Interview (-s) – *nnt* interview
inzwischen – *adv* meanwhile
Ire (-n) – *nm wk* Irishman
Ich bin Ire – I am Irish
irgend~ – *pref* some (unspecified)
irgendein – *adj* any
irgendwann – *adv* sometime
irgendwie – somehow
irgendwo – *adv* somewhere
irgendwo anders – somewhere else
Irin (-nen) – *nf* Irishwoman
Ich bin Irin – I am Irish
irisch – *adj* Irish
Irland – *nnt* Eire, Ireland
   Nordirland – *nnt* Northern Ireland
   Die Republik Irland – *nf* Eire
islamisch – *adj* Islamic
Island – *nnt* Iceland
isländisch – *adj* Icelandic
isst – *see essen*
ist – *see sein**
es ist (+ nom) – it is
Italien – *nnt* Italy
Italiener (-) – *nm* Italian
Italienerin (-nen) – *nf* Italian
italienisch – *adj* Italian
Italienisch – *nnt* Italian (language)

J

ja – *adv* yes
Jacht (-en) – *nf* yacht
Jachthafen (-häfen) – *nm* yacht marina
Jacke (-n) – *nf* jacket
Jagd – *nf* hunt, chase
auf die Jagd gehen * – *v irreg* hunt

jagen – *v reg* chase
Jahr (-e) – *nnt* year
das ganze Jahr – all year round
Ein glückliches neues Jahr! – *excl* Happy New Year!

---

adj - adjective	*v reg* - verb regular	*v sep* - verb separable	† - see verb info
prep - preposition	*v irreg* - verb irregular	*v refl* - verb reflexive	* - takes sein

jedes Jahr – every year
letztes Jahr – last year
nächstes Jahr – next year
X Jahre alt sein* – be X years old
Jahrestag (-e) – *nm* anniversary
Jahreszeit (-en) – *nf* season of the year
Jahrhundert (-e) – *nnt* century
  im 20. Jahrhundert – in the 20th
  century
jährlich – *adj* annual, yearly
Jahrmarkt (-märkte) – *nm* fun fair
Jahrtausend – *nnt* millennium
Januar – *nm* January
  im Januar – in January
Japan – *nnt* Japan
Japaner (-) – *nm* Japanese person
Japanerin (-nen) – *nf* Japanese
  person
japanisch – *adj* Japanese
jawohl – *adv* yes, certainly
Jazz – *nm* jazz
Jazzgruppe (-n) – *nf* jazz band
je – *adv* ever
Jeans – *nf* jeans, a pair of jeans
jede – *adj* each, every
jeden Abend – every evening
jeden Tag – every day
jeder/jede – *indef pron* anybody, each
  one
jeder Einzelne – *pron* every one
jedes Mal – every time
jedoch – *adv* however
jemand – *pron nom, acc* somebody
jemand anders – *pron* someone else
jemandem – *pron dat* somebody
jene – *dem pron* those
jener – *dem pron* that
jetzt – *adv* now
jeweils – *adv* respectively, at that time
Job (-s) – *nm* job (for student)
Joga – *nm, no pl* yoga

jodeln – *v reg* yodel
joggen – *v reg* go jogging
Jogging – *nnt* jogging
Jogginganzug (-züge) – *nm* track suit
Joghurt (-s) – *nm* yoghurt
rote Johannisbeere (-n) – *nf*
  redcurrant
schwarze Johannisbeere (-n) – *nf*
  blackcurrant
Journalist (-en) – *nm wk* journalist
Journalistin (-nen) – *nf* journalist
Joystick (-s) – *nm* joystick (IT)
Jude (-n) – *nm wk* Jew
Jüdin (-nen) – *nf* Jewess
jüdisch – *adj* Jewish
  das jüdische Neujahr – *nnt* Rosh
  Hashanah
Judo – *nnt* judo
Jugend – *nf, no pl* youth, young people
Jugendherberge (-n) – *nf* youth hostel
Jugendklub (-s) – *nm* youth club
Jugendliche – *nmf* ‡ teenager, young
  person
Juli – *nm* July
  im Juli – in July
Julei – *see* Juli
Jumbojet (-s) – *nnt* jumbo jet
jung – *adj* young
Junge (-n) – *nm wk* boy
jünger – *adj* younger
Jungfrau – (horoscope) Virgo
Junggeselle (-n) – *nm wk* bachelor
jüngste – *adj* youngest
Juni – *nm* June
  im Juni – in June
Juno – *see* Juni
Juwelier (-) – *nm* jeweller
Juweliergeschäft (-e) – *nnt*
  jeweller's shop
Juwelierin (-nen) – *nf* jeweller

---

nm - noun masculine	nf - noun feminine	nnt - noun neuter	npl - noun plural
nom- nominative	acc - accusative	gen - genitive	dat - dative

K

Kabelfernsehen (-) – *nnt* cable TV
Kabine (-n) – *nf* cabin
Käfer (-) – *nm* beetle
Kaffee – *nm* coffee
Einen schwarzen Kaffee, bitte
– A black coffee, please
Kaffee Hag ® – *nm* decaffeinated coffee
Kaffee mit Milch – coffee with milk
Kaffee mit Sahne – white coffee
Kaffeekanne (-n) – *nf* coffee pot
Kaffeelöffel (-) – *nm* teaspoon
Kaffeesatz – *nm* coffee grounds
Käfig (-e) – *nm* cage
kahl – *adj* bald
Kai (-s) – *nm* quay
Kakao – *nm* cocoa
Kalb (Kälber) – *nnt* calf
Kalbfleisch – *nnt* veal
Kalender (-) – *nm* diary, calendar
kalt sein* – *v irreg* be cold (weather)
Es ist kalt – It is cold
Es ist sehr kalt – It is freezing
kalt – *adj* cold
Mir ist kalt – I am cold
kaltes Wasser – *nnt* cold water
Kälte – *nf* cold
kam – *see* kommen*
Kamel (-e) – *nnt* camel
Kamera (-s) – *nf* (video) camera
Kamerad (-en) – *nm wk* friend, mate
Kameradin (-nen) – *nf* friend, mate
Kamin (-e) – *nm* fire-place
Kamm (Kämme) – *nm* comb
sich kämmen – *v reg refl* comb one's hair
Kampf (Kämpfe) – *nm* fight
kämpfen – *v reg* fight
Kanada – *nnt* Canada

Kanal (Kanäle) – *nm* canal
Kanal – *nm* English Channel
Kanaltunnel – *nm* Channel Tunnel
Kanarienvogel (-vögel) – *nm* canary
Kandidat (-en) – *nm wk* candidate
Kandidatin (-nen) – *nf* candidate
Kaninchen (-) – *nnt* rabbit
kann – *see* können
Kännchen (-) – *nnt* small pot
ein Kännchen Kaffee/Tee – an individual pot of coffee/tea
Kanne (-n) – *nf* pot
kannte – *see* kennen
Kantine (-n) – *nf* canteen
Kanton (-e) – *nm* canton
Kanu (-s) – *nm* canoe
Kanu fahren* – *v irreg* canoe
Kanzler (-) – *nm* Chancellor
Kapelle (-n) – *nf* chapel
Kapitän (-e) – *nm* captain (ship)
Kapitel (-) – *nnt* chapter
kaputt – *adj* damaged
kaputt machen – *v reg* spoil, ruin
Karambolage (-n) – *nf* multiple crash
Karate – *nnt* karate
Karfreitag – *nm* Good Friday
kariert – *adj* check pattern
Karneval – *nm* Carnival
Karo (-s) – *nnt* square, diamond, check pattern
Karotte (-n) – *nf* carrot
Karriere (-n) – *nf* career
Karte (-n) – *nf* card
Karten spielen – *v reg* play cards
Kartenspiel (-e) – *nnt* card game
Kartoffel (-n) – *nf* potato
Kartoffelpüree – *nnt* mashed potato
Kartoffelsalat – *nm* potato salad
Karton (-s) – *nm* cardboard box

---

adj - adjective	*v reg* - verb regular	*v sep* - verb separable	† - see verb info
prep - preposition	*v irreg* - verb irregular	*v refl* - verb reflexive	* - takes sein

aus Karton – made of cardboard
Karussell (-s) – *nnt* roundabout (fair)
Käse – *nm* cheese
Käsebrot (-e) – *nnt* cheese sandwich
Käsekuchen (-) – *nm* cheesecake
Kasse (-n) – *nf* cash desk, checkout, till
an die Kasse gehen* – *v irreg* go
to the cash desk
Kassette (-n) – *nf* cassette, tape
Kassettenrekorder (-) – *nm* tape
recorder
Kassierer (-) – *nm* cashier
Kassiererin (-nen) – *nf* cashier
Kasten (Kästen) – *nm* box
Katalysator (-en) – *nm* catalytic
converter
mit Kat – with a catalytic converter
katastrophal – *adj* disastrous
Katastrophe (-n) – *nf* disaster
Kater (-) – *nm* tomcat; hangover
Katholik (-en) – *nm wk* Catholic
Katholikin (-nen) – *nf* Catholic
katholisch – *adj* Catholic
Kätzchen (-) – *nnt* kitten
Katze (-n) – *nf* cat
Kauf (Käufe) – *nm* purchase
kaufen – *v reg* buy, purchase
Kauffrau (-en) – *nf* businesswoman
Kaufhaus (-häuser) – *nnt*
department store
Kaufmann (-männer) – *nm*
businessman
Kaugummi (-s) – *nm* chewing gum
kaum – *adv* hardly, scarcely
Kaution (-en) – *nf* deposit (against
damage)
Kegelbahn (-en) – *nf* bowling alley
kegeln – *v reg* play skittles, bowl
kehren – *v reg* sweep
Kehrseite (-n) – *nf* wrong side
kein – *adj* no, not any
keine – *adj* not any

Keks (-e) – *nm* biscuit
Keller (-) – *nm* cellar, basement
Kellner (-) – *nm* waiter
Kellnerin (-nen) – *nf* waitress
kennen – *v irreg* know (person)
kennen lernen – *v reg* get to know,
meet
Kennzeichen (-) – *nnt* number plate,
registration number (car)
Kerl (-e) – *nm* chap
Kern (-e) – *nm* kernel, nucleus
Kernenergie – *nf* nuclear power
Kernkraftwerk (-e) – *nnt* nuclear
power station
Kerze (-n) – *nf* candle
Ketchup – *nm* ketchup
Kette (-n) – *nf* chain
kichern – *v reg* giggle
Kilo – *nnt* kilo(gram)
pro Kilo – by the kilo
zwei Kilo Äpfel – two kilos of apples
Kilometer – *nm* kilometre
zehn Kilometer von ... entfernt
– 10 kilometres from ...
Kind (-er) – *nnt* child (ren)
Kindergarten (-gärten) – *nm*
nursery school
Kindergeld – *nnt* child benefit
kinderleicht – *adj* child's play
Kindermädchen (-) – *nnt* nanny
Kindheit (-en) – *nf* childhood
Kinn (-e) – *nnt* chin
Kino (-s) – *nnt* cinema
Kiosk (-e) – *nm* kiosk
Kirche (-n) – *nf* church
Kirsche (-n) – *nf* cherry
Kissen (-) – *nnt* pillow, cushion
Kissenbezug (-züge) – *nm*
pillowcase
Kiste (-n) – *nf* box; banger (car)
Kiwi (-s) – *nf* kiwi fruit
Klammer (-n) – *nf* brackets
in Klammern – in brackets

---

klappen – *v reg* work, function
klar – *adj* clear, distinct
Klarinette (-n) – *nf* clarinet
 Klarinette spielen – *v reg* play
 the clarinet
Klasse (-n) – *nf* class, form
 einmal erster Klasse, bitte –
 a first class ticket, please
Klasse! – *excl* Great!
Klassenarbeit (-en) – *nf* formal
 class test
Klassenfahrt (-en) – *nf* school trip
Klassenkamerad (-en) – *nm wk*
 school friend
Klassenkameradin (-nen) – *nf*
 school friend
Klassenschwächste – *nmf* ‡ bottom
 of class
Klassenzimmer (-) – *nnt* classroom
klassisch – *adj* classical
klauen – *v reg coll* steal
Klaviatur (-en) – *nf* keyboard (piano)
Klavier – *nnt* upright piano
Klavier spielen – *v reg* play the
 piano
kleben – *v reg* stick, paste
Klebstoff (-e) – *nm* glue
Kleid (-er) – *nnt* dress
Kleider (-) – *npl* clothes
Kleiderbügel (-) – *nm* coat hanger
Kleiderschrank (schränke) – *nm*
 wardrobe
Kleidung (-en) – *nf* clothes, outfit
Kleidungsstück (-e) – *nnt* article of
 clothing
klein – *adj* small, short (not tall)
Kleinanzeige (-n) – *nf* classified
 (small) ad
Kleinbus (-se) – *nm* minibus
Kleingeld – *nnt* change (coins)
 Haben Sie Kleingeld? – Have
 you any change?
Klempner (-) – *nm* plumber

Klempnerin (-nen) – *nf* plumber
klettern – *v reg* climb
Klima (-s) – *nnt* climate
Klimaanlage (-n) – *nf* air conditioning
 mit Klimaanlage – air conditioned
Klingel (-n) – *nf* bell (door, school)
klingeln – *v reg* ring the (door)bell
 Es klingelte – The doorbell rang
Klinik (-en) – *nf* hospital, clinic
Klippe (-n) – *nf* cliff
Klo (-s) – *nnt coll* toilet
klopfen – *v reg* knock
 Es klopft – There's a knock at the door
 an die Tür klopfen – knock on
 the door
Klub (-s) – *nm* club
klug – *adj* clever
knackig – *adj* crisp, crunchy
Knall (-e) – *nm* bang
Knallkörper (-) – *nm* firework
knapp – *adj* short of
 Ich bin knapp bei Kasse – I'm
 broke
Kneipe (-n) – *nf* pub
Knie (-n) – *nnt* knee
knien – *v reg* kneel
Knoblauch – *nm* garlic
Knochen (-) – *nm* bone
Knopf (Knöpfe) – *nm* button
Knüller (-) – *nm* blockbuster
knurren – *v reg* growl
knusprig – *adj* crunchy
Koch (Köche) – *nm* cook
kochen – *v reg* cook, boil, be boiling
Kochen – *nnt* cookery
Köchin (-nen) – *nf* cook
Koffer (-) – *nm* suitcase
 Koffer packen – *v reg* pack cases
Kofferkuli (-s) – *nm* luggage trolley
Kofferradio (-s) – *nnt* transistor radio
Kofferraum (-räume) – *nm* boot (car)

---

adj - adjective   *v reg* - verb regular   *v sep* - verb separable   † - see verb info
prep - preposition   *v irreg* - verb irregular   *v refl* - verb reflexive   * - takes sein

Kohl – *nm* cabbage
Kohle (-n) – *nf* coal
Kollege (-n) – *nm wk* colleague
Kollegin (-nen) – *nf* colleague
Köln – Cologne
kölnisch Wasser – *nnt* eau de Cologne
Komfort – *nm* comfort
komisch – *adj* funny, amusing
Komma (-s) – *nnt* comma (,)
kommen* – *v irreg* come
　ans Ziel kommen* – *v irreg* finish (sport)
　Es kommt darauf an – It depends
　ums Leben kommen* – *v irreg* lose one's life
Kommode (-n) – *nf* chest of drawers
Kommunismus – *nm* communism
Komödie (-n) – *nf* comic film
Komplize (-n) – *nm wk* accomplice
kompliziert – *adj* complicated
Komplizin (-nen) – *nf* accomplice
Kompott (-e) – *nnt* stewed fruit
Konditorei (-en) – *nf* cake shop
Kondom (-e) – *nnt* condom
Konfektion (-en) – *nf* ready-made clothes
König (-e) – *nm* king
Königin (-nen) – *nf* queen
das Vereinigte Königreich – *nnt* the United Kingdom
königsblau – *adj* royal blue
können – *v irreg* be able to, can
konnte – *see* können could, was able to
Kontaktlinse (-n) – *nf* contact lense
Kontinent (-e) – *nm* continent (geographical)
Konto (Konten) – *nnt* account (bank)
Kontoauszug (-züge) – *nm* bank statement
Kontrabass (-bässe) – *nm* double bass
Kontrolle (-en) – *nf* check, control

kontrollieren – *v reg* † check tickets
　den Ölstand kontrollieren – *v reg* † check the oil level
　den Reifendruck kontrollieren – *v reg* † check the tyre pressure
　Fahrkarten kontrollieren – *v reg* † check tickets
Konzert (-e) – *nnt* concert; concerto
Kopf (Köpfe) – *nm* head
　auf den Kopf gestellt – *adj* upside down
　Kopf oder Zahl? – Heads or tails?
Kopfhörer (-) – *nm* headphones
Kopfkissen (-) – *nnt* pillow
Kopfsalat – *nm* lettuce
Kopfschmerzen – *npl* headache
Kopfschmerzen haben – *v irreg* have a headache
kopieren – *v reg* † copy, write down
Koppel (-n) – *nf* paddock
Koran – *nm* Koran
Korb (Körbe) – *nm* basket
Korbball – *nm* netball
Korken (-) – *nm* cork
Korkenzieher (-) – *nm* corkscrew
Kornett (-e) – *nnt* cornet (music)
Körper (-) – *nm* body
körperlich – *adj* physical
körperliche Bewegung (-en) – *nf* exercise (sport)
korrigieren – *v reg* † correct, mark
Kosmetikerin (-nen) – *nf* beautician
Kosmetiktäschchen (-) – *nnt* make-up bag
Kosten – *npl* costs
kosten – *v reg* † cost, taste
　Was kostet das? – How much is it?
kostbar – *adj* precious
kostenlos – *adj* free
köstlich – *adj* delicious, yummy
Kostüm (-e) – *nnt* lady's suit
Kotelett (-s) – *nnt* chop, cutlet
kotzen – *v reg coll* vomit

Krabbe (-n) – *nf* crab, shrimp
Krach (Kräche) – *nm* din, loud noise, row
Kraft (Kräfte) – *nf* strength
Kragen (-) – *nm* collar
krank – *adj* ill, unwell
krank werden* – *v irreg* fall ill
Kranke – *nmf* ‡ sick person
Krankenhaus (-häuser) – *nnt* hospital
Krankenpfleger (-) – *nm* male nurse
Krankenschwester (-n) – *nf* nurse
Krankenwagen (-) – *nm* ambulance
Krankheit (-en) – *nf* illness
Kräutertee (-s) – *nm* herbal tea
Krawatte (-n) – *nf* tie
Krebs – *nm* cancer
Kreditkarte (-n) – *nf* credit card
Kreide – *nf* chalk
Kreis (-e) – *nm* circle; district (political)
Kreisdiagramm (-e) – *nnt* pie chart
Kreuz (-e) – *nnt* cross; small of back
  Autobahnkreuz – *nnt* motorway junction
Kreuzfahrt (-en) – *nf* cruise
Kreuzung (-en) – *nf* crossroads
Kreuzworträtsel (-) – *nnt* crossword
Kricket – *nnt* cricket
Krieg (-e) – *nm* war
kriegen – *v reg coll* get, obtain
Kriegsmarine (-n) – *nf* navy
Krimi (-s) – *nm* detective story
Kriminalfilm (-e) – *nm* detective film
Krokodil (-e) – *nnt* crocodile
Krug (Krüge) – *nm* jug
Küche (-n) – *nf* kitchen
Kuchen (-) – *nm* cake, tart
Küchenmaschine (-n) – *nf* food processor
Kuckucksuhr (-en) – *nf* cuckoo clock

Kugelschreiber (-) – *nm* ball-point pen, biro®
Kuh (Kühe) – *nf* cow
kühl – *adj* cool
Kühler (-) – *nm* radiator (in car)
Kühlschrank (-schränke) – *nm* fridge
Kuli (-s) – *nm* ball point pen
sich kümmern um (+ acc) – *v reg refl* care for, look after, be concerned with
Kunde (-n) – *nm wk* customer
Kundin (-nen) – *nf* customer
Kündigung (-en) – *nf* notice, dismissal
künftig – *adj* future
Kunst – *nf* art
Kunsterziehung – *nf* art (education)
Kunstgalerie (-n) – *nf* art gallery
Kunsthochschule (-n) – *nf* art school
Künstler (-) – *nm* artist, performer
Künstlerin (-nen) – *nf* artist, performer
Kunststoff (-e) – *nm* plastic
  aus Kunststoff – made of plastic
Kupplung (-en) – *nf* clutch (car)
Kur (-en) – *nf* cure, course of treatment
Kurort (-e) – *nm* spa
Kurs (-e) – *nm* course; rate of exchange
Kursivschrift – *nf* italic
Kurstadt (-städte) – *nf* spa town
Kurzentrum (-zentren) – *nnt* spa centre
Kurve (-n) – *nf* bend
kurvenreich – *adj* twisty
kurz – *adj* short, brief
kurzsichtig – *adj* short-sighted
Kusine (-n) – *nf* cousin
Kuss (Küsse) – *nm* kiss
küssen – *v reg* kiss
Küste (-n) – *nf* coast
  an der Küste – by the sea, at the seaside

---

adj - adjective	*v reg* - verb regular	*v sep* - verb separable	† - see verb info
prep - preposition	*v irreg* - verb irregular	*v refl* - verb reflexive	* - takes sein

L

l – litre
Labor (-s) – *nnt* laboratory
Lächeln (-) – *nnt* smile
lächeln – *v reg* smile
lächelnd – *adj* smiling
lachen – *v reg* laugh
lächerlich – *adj* ridiculous
Lachs (-e) – *nm* salmon
laden – *v irreg* load
Laden (Läden) – *nm* shop
  Tante-Emma-Laden (-Läden)
  – *nm* small shop
Ladendieb (-e) – *nm* shoplifter
Ladentisch (-e) – *nm* counter (shop)
lag – *see liegen*
Lage (-n) – *nf* position
Lagerfeuer (-) – *nnt* camp-fire
Laken (-) – *nnt* sheet (bed)
Lamm (Lämmer) – *nnt* lamb
  (animal)
Lammfleisch – *nnt* lamb (meat)
Lampe (-n) – *nf* light, lamp
Land (Länder) – *nnt* country, land
  auf dem Lande – in the country
Landarbeiter (-) – *nm* farm worker
landen* – *v reg* † land
Landkarte (-n) – *nf* map
ländlich – *adj* rural
Landschaft (-en) – *nf* countryside,
  scenery
landschaftlich – *adj* scenic
Landstraße (-n) – *nf* country road
Landtag (-e) – *nm* regional parliament
Landung (-en) – *nf* landing (plane)
landwirtschaftlich – *adj* agricultural
lang – *adj* long
  vor langer Zeit – long ago
lange – *adv* for a long time, a long while
  Es war schon lange her – It was
  a long time ago

Länge (-n) – *nf* length (measurement)
länger – *adj* longer
  nicht länger – *adv* no longer
Langeweile – *nf* boredom
langsam – *adj* slow
langsamer werden* – *v irreg* slow
  down
Langspielplatte (-n) – *nf* LP
langweilen – *v reg* bore
  sich langweilen – *v reg refl* to be bored
langweilig – *adj* boring
Laptop (-s) – *nm* laptop
Lärm – *nm* loud noise
las – *see lesen*
Laserdrucker (-) – *nm* laser printer
lassen – *v irreg* let
  den Arzt kommen lassen –
  v irreg send for the doctor
  etwas machen lassen – *v irreg*
  get sthg done
  etwas reinigen lassen – *v irreg*
  have sthg cleaned
  etwas reparieren lassen –
  v irreg have sthg repaired
  fallen lassen – *v irreg* drop
Lastwagen (-) – *nm* lorry, truck
Lastwagenfahrer (-) – *nm* lorry driver
Lastwagenfahrerin (-nen) – *nf*
  lorry driver
Latein – *nnt* Latin
lateinisch – *adj* Latin
Laterne (-n) – *nf* lantern
Lauf (Läufe) – *nm* run, course
laufen* – *v irreg* run
  Was läuft? – What's on? (cinema)
Läufer (-) – *nm* half back
Laune (-n) – *nf* mood
  schlechter Laune – in a bad
  mood

guter Laune – in a good mood
laut – *adj* loud, noisy, aloud
läuten – *v reg* † ring (bell)
Lautsprecher (-) – *nm* loudspeaker
Lazarett (-e) – *nnt* sick bay (school)
Leben – *nnt* life
  im täglichen Leben – in daily life
  ums Leben kommen* – *v irreg* lose one's life
leben – *v reg* live (be alive)
lebend – *adj* alive, living
lebendig – *adj* lively, alive
Lebenskunde – *nf* PSE
lebenslänglich – *adj* lifelong
Lebenslauf (-läufe) – *nm* CV, curriculum vitae
Lebensmittel (-) – *nnt* groceries
Lebensmittelgeschäft (-e) – *nnt* grocer's shop
Lebensmittelhändler (-) – *nm* grocer
Lebensmittelhändlerin (-nen) – *nf* grocer
Lebensstandard – *nm* standard of living
Leber (-n) – *nf* liver
Leberwurst – *nf* liver sausage
lebhaft – *adj* lively
Lebkuchen – *nm* ginger bread
lecken – *v reg* lick
lecker – *adj* delicious, appetizing
Leder (-) – *nnt* leather
  aus Leder – made of leather
Lederhose – *nf* leather shorts
Lederwaren – *npl* leather goods
ledig – *adj* unmarried
Ledige – *nf* ‡ single person
leer – *adj* empty
leeren – *v reg* empty
legen – *v reg* place, lay sthg down
Leggings – *npl* leggings
lehnen – *v reg* lean
Lehnstuhl (-stühle) – *nm* armchair

Lehre (-n) – *nf* apprenticeship
lehren – *v reg* teach
Lehrer (-) – *nm* teacher, instructor
Lehrerin (-nen) – *nf* teacher, instructor
Lehrerzimmer (-) – *nnt* staff room
Lehrling (-e) – *nm* apprentice
leicht – *adj* light (not heavy)
Leichtathletik – *nf* athletics
Leichtathletik treiben – *v irreg* do athletics
Es tut mir Leid! – I'm sorry!
leiden – *v irreg* suffer
leider – *adv* unfortunately, sadly
leihen – *v irreg* lend
Leine (-n) – *nf* lead (dog)
Leinwand (-wände) – *nf* screen (cinema)
leise – *adj* quiet (without noise)
leise – *adv* silently
leisten – *v reg* † achieve
sich leisten – *v reg dat refl* † afford
Leistung (-en) – *nf* achievement, performance
Leistungsfach (-fächer) – *nnt* A Level subject
Leistungsgruppe (-n) – *nf* set (school)
Leiter (-n) – *nf* ladder
Leitung (-en) – *nf* leadership, management
  eine elektrische Leitung – an electrical lead
Leitungswasser – *nnt* tap water
Lektüre – *nf* reading matter
Lenkrad (-räder) – *nnt* steering wheel
lernen – *v reg* learn, study
  Seit wann lernst du Deutsch? – How long have you been learning German?
Lernprogramm (-e) – *nnt* curriculum
lesen – *v irreg* read
Lesen – *nnt* reading
Leser (-) – *nm* reader

---

adj - adjective	*v reg* - verb regular	*v sep* - verb separable	† - see verb info
prep - preposition	*v irreg* - verb irregular	*v refl* - verb reflexive	* - takes sein

Leserin (-nen) – *nf* reader
letzte – *adj* last, final
  letzte Woche – last week
  letztes Jahr – last year
Leuchtturm (-türme) – *nm* lighthouse
Leute – *npl* people
Licht (-er) – *nnt* light
  das Licht anmachen – *v reg sep* put on light
Lichtstift (-e) – *nm* light pen
Lidschatten – *nm* eye shadow
lieb – *adj* likeable, loveable, sweet
  Ich habe dich lieb – I am fond of you
Liebe – Dear (in letter to female)
Liebe (-n) – *nf* love
lieben – *v reg* love, adore
liebenswürdig – *adj* agreeable (nice)
Lieber – Dear (in letter to male)
lieber – *adv* preferably
  Ich trinke lieber Tee als Kaffee – I prefer tea to coffee
lieber haben – *v irreg* prefer
Liebesroman (-e) – *nm* love story
liebevoll – *adj* affectionate
Liebling – *nm* favourite
Lieblings~ – *pref* favourite
am liebsten – *adv* most of all
Lied (-er) – *nnt* song
lief – *see laufen**
liefern – *v reg* deliver
Lieferung (-en) – *nf* delivery
Lieferwagen (-) – *nm* van
liegen – *v irreg* lie (be situated)
liegen lassen – *v irreg* leave lying around
Liegesitz (-e) – *nm* couchette
Liegestuhl (-stühle) – *nm* deckchair
liest – *see lesen*
Lift – *nm* lift
Liga (Ligen) – *nf* league
lila – *adj inv* mauve

Limo – *nf coll* lemonade
Limonade (-n) – *nf* lemonade
Lineal (-e) – *nnt* ruler
Linie (-n) – *nf* line, route (tram, bus)
  Nehmen Sie den Bus Linie 3! – Catch the number three bus!
linke – *adj* left
  auf der linken Seite – on the left hand side
links – *adv* on the left
  nach links gehen – to go left
Linksaußen (-) – *nm* left wing (sport)
linkshändig – *adj* left-handed
  Ich bin Linkshänder – (male) I am left-handed
  Ich bin Linkshänderin – (female) I am left-handed
Linse (-n) – *nf* lens; lentil
Lippe (-n) – *nf* lip
  von den Lippen ablesen – *v irreg sep* lip-read
Lippenstift (-e) – *nm* lipstick
Liste (-n) – *nf* list
Liter – *nm* litre
Literatur – *nf* literature
Litfaßsäule (-n) – *nf* advertising pillar
live – *adj* live (radio, TV)
Livesendung (-en) – *nf* live broadcast
LKW (-s) – *nm* lorry (HGV)
loben – *v reg* praise
Loch (Löcher) – *nnt* hole
lockig – *adj* curly
Löffel (-) – *nm* spoon, spoonful
Lohn (Löhne) – *nm* wages, pay
sich lohnen – *v reg refl* be worthwhile
  Es lohnt sich nicht – It's not worth it
Lokal (-e) – *nnt* pub
Los! – *excl* Go on! Go ahead!
  Was ist los? – What's wrong?
löschen – *v reg* extinguish
lösen – *v reg* solve

---

nm - noun masculine	*nf* - noun feminine	*nnt* - noun neuter	*npl* - noun plural
nom- nominative	*acc* - accusative	*gen* - genitive	*dat* - dative

losfahren* – *v irreg sep* set off
Lösung (-en) – *nf* solution
loswerden* – *v irreg sep* get rid of
Lotterie (-n) – *nf* lottery, draw
Lotto (-s) – *nnt* bingo
Löwe (-n) – *nm wk* lion; Leo
(horoscope)
Luft – *nf, no pl* air
Luftdruck – *nm* air pressure
Luftkissenboot (-e) – *nnt* hovercraft
Luftkrankheit – *nf* air sickness
Luftmatratze (-n) – *nf* air-bed
Luftpost – *nf* air mail
   per Luftpost – by air mail
Luftwaffe – *nf, no pl* air force

lügen – *v irreg* lie, tell lies (untruth)
Lügner (-) – *nm* liar
Lügnerin (-nen) – *nf* liar
Lunchpaket (-e) – *nnt* packed lunch
Lust haben zu – *v irreg* wish to
lustig – *adj* amusing
   sich lustig machen über
   (+ acc) – *v reg refl* make fun of
Lutscher (-) – *nm* lollipop
Lüttich – *nnt* Liège
Luxemburg – *nnt* Luxembourg
Luxemburger (-) – *nm* Luxembourger
Luxemburgerin (-nen) – *nf*
   Luxembourger
luxuriös – *adj* luxurious

M

m – metre
machen – *v reg* make, do
   Mach schnell! – *excl* Get a move on!
   Das macht zehn Mark – That
   comes to ten marks
   Es macht nichts – Never mind
   Das macht mir nichts aus –
   I don't mind
   eine Prüfung machen – *v reg* go
   in for an exam
   einen Einkaufsbummel machen
   – *v reg* go round the shops
   einen Schaufensterbummel
   machen – *v reg* go window
   shopping
   einen Spaziergang machen –
   v reg have a walk
   einen Stadtbummel machen –
   v reg go round town
   Notizen machen – *v reg* take notes
   Pause machen – *v reg* have a rest
mächtig – *adj* powerful
Mädchen (-) – *nnt* girl

Mädchenname (-n) – *nm wk*
   maiden name
mag – *see mögen*
Magazin (-e) – *nnt* magazine
Magen (-) – *nm* stomach
Magenschmerzen – *npl* stomach ache
den Rasen mähen – *v reg* mow the
   lawn
Mahlzeit (-en) – *nf* meal
Mahlzeit! – *excl* Enjoy your meal!
Mai – *nm* May
   im Mai – in May
Mailand – Milan
Main – *nm* River Main
majestätisch – *adj* majestic
Make-Up – *nnt* make-up
Mal (-e) – *nnt* occasion, time
   zum ersten Mal – for the first time
   zum letzten Mal – for the last time
malen – *v reg* paint (art)
Maler (-) – *nm* painter
Malerin (-nen) – *nf* painter

malerisch – *adj* picturesque

Mallorca – *nnt* Majorca

man – *pron nom sing* they, you (people in general), one

mangelhaft – *adj* poor; below pass mark

manchmal – *adv* sometimes

Manieren – *npl* manners

Mann (Männer) – *nm* man, husband

Mannequin (-s) – *nnt* model (fashion)

männlich – *adj* male, masculine

Mannschaft (-en) – *nf* team

Mantel (Mäntel) – *nm* coat, overcoat

Mappe (-n) – *nf* briefcase

Märchen (-) – *nnt* fairy tale, myth

Margarine (-n) – *nf* margarine

marineblau – *adj* navy blue

Mark (-) – *nf* mark (money)

Marke (-n) – *nf* make, brand name

Markstück (-) – *nnt* mark piece, mark coin

Markt (Märkte) – *nm* market

der Gemeinsame Markt – *nm* the Common Market

Markthalle (-n) – *nf* market hall

Marktplatz(-plätze) – *nm* market place

Marmelade (-n) – *nf* jam
  ein Glas Marmelade – *nnt* a jar of jam

März – *nm* March
  im März – in March

Maschine (-n) – *nf* machine

maschinengeschrieben – *adj* typewritten

Maschinenschreiben – *nnt* typewriting

mäßig – *adj* moderate

Maskenkostüm (-e) – *nnt* fancy dress

Materialien – *npl* materials

Mathe – *nf* maths

Mathematik – *nf* mathematics

Matratze (-n) – *nf* mattress

Matrose (-n) – *nm wk* sailor (navy)

Matura – *nf* Swiss and Austrian A Level/GNVQ Level 3 equivalent

Mauer (-n) – *nf* wall; The Berlin Wall

Maurer (-) – *nm* bricklayer

Maus (Mäuse) – *nf* mouse

Mayonnaise – *nf* mayonnaise

Mechaniker (-) – *nm* mechanic

Mechanikerin (-nen) – *nf* mechanic

Medaille (-n) – *nf* medal

Medien – *npl* media

Medikament (-e) – *nnt* medicine (remedy)

Medizin – *nf* medicine (science)

Meer (-e) – *nnt* sea

Meeresfrüchte – *npl* seafood

Meerschweinchen (-) – *nnt* guinea-pig

Mehl – *nnt* flour

mehr – *adv* more
  ein bisschen mehr – a little more
  mehr als – more than
  immer mehr – *adv* more and more
  mehr oder weniger – *adv* more or less
  Es ist nichts mehr da – There is no more

mehrere – *adj* several

Mehrwertsteuer (MwSt) – *nf* VAT

Meile (-n) – *nf* mile

mein – *poss adj* my, mine

meinen – *v reg* think, feel (have opinion)

Meinung (-en) – *nf* opinion
  meiner Meinung nach – in my opinion

Meinungsumfrage (-n) – *nf* survey, opinion poll

die meisten – most (people)

am meisten – *adv* most

meistens – *adv* for the most part

Meister (-) – *nm* champion

Meisterin (-nen) – *nf* champion

Meisterschaft (-en) – *nf* championship

Meldeschein (-e) – *nm* residence registration document

Melodie (-n) – *nf* tune (music)

Melone (-n) – *nf* melon

Menge (-n) – *nf* crowd, quantity, amount

eine Menge – lots of

Mensch (-en) – *nm wk* man (person)

Menü (-s) – *nnt* set price menu

merken – *v reg* realise

merkwürdig – *adj* remarkable

messen – *v irreg* measure

Messer (-) – *nnt* knife

Metall (-) – *nnt* metal

Meter – *nm* metre

Methode (-n) – *nf* method

Metzger (-) – *nm* butcher

Metzgerei (-en) – *nm* butcher's shop

mich – *pron acc* me, myself

mies – *adj* lousy, awful

Miete (-n) – *nf* hire, rent

mieten – *v reg* † hire, rent

Mieter (-) – *nm* tenant

Mieterin (-nen) – *nf* tenant

Mietwohnung (-en) – *nf* lodging

Mikrochip (-s) – *nm* microchip

Mikrocomputer (-) – *nm* microcomputer

Mikrofon (-e) – *nnt* microphone

Mikroskop (-e) – *nnt* microscope

Mikrowelle (-n) – *nf* microwave

Mikrowellenherd (-e) – *nm* microwave oven

Milch – *nf* milk

Milchmann (-männer) – *nm* milkman

mild – *adj* mild

Militär – *nnt* armed forces

beim Militär – in the services

Milkshake – *nm* milk shake

Million (-en) – *nf* million

minderjährig – *adj* minor

Minderjährige – *nmf* ‡ minor (under 18)

Mindest~ – *pref* minimum

Mindesttemperatur (-en) – *nf* minimum temperature

Mineralwasser – *nnt* mineral water

Minimum (Minima) – *nnt* minimum

minus – *prep* minus (maths)

Minute (-n) – *nf* minute

alle zehn Minuten – every ten minutes

mir – *pron dat* me, to me, myself

mischen – *v reg* mix

Missverständnis (-se) – *nnt* misunderstanding

mit (+ dat) – *prep* with

mit dem Auto – by car

mit dem Bus – by bus

mit der Bahn – by train

mit dem Reisebus fahren* – *v irreg* travel by coach

mit dem Wagen fahren* – *v irreg* travel by car

mit freundlichen Grüßen – *adv* Yours sincerely

mit Höchstgeschwindigkeit – at top speed

mitbringen – *v irreg sep* bring

Mitglied (-er) – *nnt* member

Mitgliedskarte (-n) – *nf* membership card

mitmachen – *v reg sep* participate, take part

mitnehmen – *v irreg sep* take away

Kannst du mich mitnehmen? – Can I have a lift?

zum Mitnehmen – take away (food); please take one

Mittag – *nm* midday

um Mittag – at midday

zu Mittag essen – *v irreg* have lunch

Mittagessen (-) – *nnt* lunch, midday meal

---

adj - adjective	*v reg* - verb regular	*v sep* - verb separable	† - see verb info
prep - preposition	*v irreg* - verb irregular	*v refl* - verb reflexive	* - takes sein

Mittagspause (-n) – *nf* lunch hour
Mitte (-n) – *nf* middle, centre
 in der Mitte von (+ dat) – in the
 middle of
Mitteilung (-en) – *nf* message
Mittel gegen (+ acc) – *nnt* remedy for
Mittel~ – *pref* medium
mittelalterlich – *adj* medieval
Mittelengland – *nnt* Midlands
mittelgroß – *adj* medium size
Mittellandkanal – *nm* canal between
 the rivers Ems and Elbe
mittellang – *adj* medium length
mittelmäßig – *adj* fair (average)
Mittelmeer – *nnt* Mediterranean
Mitternacht – *nf* midnight
 um Mitternacht – at midnight
Mittwoch – *nm* Wednesday
 am Mittwoch – on Wednesday
Möbel – *npl* furniture
Möbelstück (-e) – *nnt* piece of
 furniture
Möbelwagen (-) – *nm* removal van
möbliert – *adj* furnished
mochte – *see mögen*
ich möchte – I would like
 ich möchte gern – I'd love to
Mode (-n) – *nf* fashion
Modell (-e) – *nnt* design, model
 ein maßstabgerechtes Modell
 – *nnt* a scale model
Modem (-s) – *nnt* modem
Moderator (-en) – *nm wk* presenter
 (TV)
Moderatorin (-nen) – *nf* presenter
 (TV)
moderieren – *v reg* † present (radio,
 TV)
modern – *adj* modern
Modezeichner (-) – *nm* fashion
 designer
Modezeichnerin (-nen) – *nf* fashion
 designer

modisch – *adj* fashionable, smart
mogeln – *v reg* cheat
mögen – *v irreg* like
möglich – *adj* possible
 so bald wie möglich – as soon as
 possible
möglicherweise – *adv* possibly
Möglichkeit (-en) – *nf* possibility,
 opportunity
Mohammedaner (-) – *nm* Muslim
Mohammedanerin (-nen) – *nf* Muslim
mohammedanisch – *adj* Muslim
mollig – *adj* plump
Moment (-e) – *nm* moment
 im Moment – at the moment
momentan – *adj* current, present
Monat (-e) – *nm* month
 im Monat – per month
 pro Monat – per month
monatelang – *adj* for months on end
monatlich – *adj* monthly
Mond (-e) – *nm* moon
Montag (-e) – *nm* Monday
 am Montag – on Monday
Moped (-s) – *nnt* moped
Morgen (-) – *nm* morning
 am nächsten Morgen – next
 morning
 Guten Morgen! – *excl* Good
 morning!
morgen – *adv* tomorrow
 Bis morgen! – See you tomorrow!
 morgen Abend – tomorrow evening
 morgen früh – tomorrow morning
Morgenrock (-röcke) – *nm*
 dressing gown
morgens – *adv* in the morning
Moschee (-n) – *nf* mosque
Mosel – *nf* Moselle
Moselwein (-e) – *nm* Moselle wine
Moskau – Moscow
Moskito (-s) – *nm* mosquito
Motor (-en) – *nm* engine, motor

Motorboot (-e) – *nnt* motor boat
Motorrad (-räder) – *nnt* motorbike
Motorradfahrer (-) – *nm* motorcyclist
Motorradfahrerin (-nen) – *nf* motorcyclist
Mountainbike (-s) – *nnt* mountain bike
Möwe (-n) – *nf* seagull
müde – *adj* tired
Mühe (-n) – *nf* effort
sich die Mühe geben – *v irreg dat refl* take trouble to, bother
Müll – *nm* rubbish
Müllabfuhr – *nf* refuse collection
Mülleimer (-) – *nm* rubbish bin
Müllhalde (-n) – *nf* tip (rubbish)
Mülltonne (-n) – *nf* dustbin
München – Munich
Mund (Münder) – *nm* mouth
Mundharmonika (-harmoniken) – *nf* mouth organ
mündlich – *adj* oral
  mündliche Frage (-n) – *nf* oral question
  mündliche Prüfung (-en) – *nf* speaking test
Mundvoll (-) – *nm* mouthful
Münster – Munster
munter – *adj* cheerful

Münzautomat (-en) – *nm wk* slot machine
Münze (-n) – *nf* coin
Münzfernsprecher (-) – *nm* pay phone
Münzwäscherei (-en) – *nf* laundrette
murren – *v reg* grumble
Museum (Museen) – *nnt* museum
Musik – *nf* music
  klassische Musik – *nf* classical music
Musikabteilung (-en) – *nf* music department
Musiker (-) – *nm* musician
Musikerin (-nen) – *nf* musician
Musikraum (räume) – *nm* music room
muss – *see* müssen
müssen – *v irreg* have to, got to (must)
musste – *see* müssen
Mut – *nm* courage
mutig – *adj* bold
Mutter (Mütter) – *nf* mother
mütterlich – *adj* motherly
Muttersprache (-n) – *nf* mother tongue
Mutti (-s) – *nf* mum(my)
Mütze (-n) – *nf* cap, hat
MwSt (Mehrwertsteuer) – *nf* VAT

N

na und? – so what?
nach (+ dat) – *prep* after, to, past (time), according to
  fünf nach vier – five past four
  meiner Meinung nach – in my opinion
  nach Berlin – to Berlin
  nach unten gehen* – *v irreg* go downstairs
Nachbar (-en) – *nm wk* neighbour

Nachbarin (-nen) – *nf* neighbour
Nachbarschaft (-en) – *nf* neighbourhood
nachdem – *sub conj* after
nachdenken über (+ acc) – *v irreg sep* think about
nachgeben – *v irreg sep* give in
nachher – *adv* afterwards
nachholen – *v reg sep* catch up with

| *adj* - adjective | *v reg* - verb regular | *v sep* - verb separable | † - see verb info |
| *prep* - preposition | *v irreg* - verb irregular | *v refl* - verb reflexive | * - takes sein |

nachmachen – *v reg sep* copy (imitate)
Nachmittag (-e) – *nm* afternoon
am Nachmittag – in the afternoon
nachmittags – *adv* p.m.
Nachname (-n) – *nm wk* surname
Nachrichten – *npl* news (radio, TV)
eine gute Nachricht – good news
nachschauen – *v reg sep* check
nachsehen – *v irreg sep* check
das Wasser nachsehen – *v irreg sep* check the water level
Nachsitzen – *nnt* detention
nachsitzen müssen – *v irreg* be in detention
Nachspeise (-n) – *nf* dessert
nächst – *adj* next, nearest
am nächsten Tag – next day
nächstes Jahr – next year
nächste Woche – next week
Nacht (Nächte) – *nf* night
Gute Nacht! – *excl* Good night!
Nachteil (-e) – *nm* disadvantage
Nachthemd (-en) – *nnt* nightdress
Nachtisch (-e) – *nm* pudding, dessert
Nachtklub (-s) – *nm* night club
nachts – *adv* at night
Nachttisch (-e) – *nm* bedside table
Nachttischlampe (-n) – *nf* bedside light
Nacken (-) – *nm* back of neck
nackt – *adj* bare, naked
Nadel (-n) – *nf* needle
Nagel (Nägel) – *nm* nail
nagelneu – *adj* brand new
nah – *adj* close (-near)
Nähe – *nf* vicinity, surrounding area
hier in der Nähe – around here
in der Nähe – close by
in der Nähe (von + dat) – near (to)
nähen – *v reg* sew
Nähen – *nnt* sewing

näher – *adj* nearer
sich nähern (+ dat) – *v reg refl* go near to, approach
nahm – *see* nehmen
Nähmaschine (-n) – *nf* sewing machine
Nahverkehrszug (-züge) – *nm* local train, slow train
Name (-n) – *nm wk* name
im Namen (+ gen) – in the name (of)
im Namen Smith – in the name of Smith
Narr (-en) – *nm wk* fool
Närrin (-nen) – *nf* fool
Nase (-n) – *nf* nose
sich die Nase putzen – *v reg dat refl* blow one's nose
Ich habe die Nase voll – I've had enough, I'm fed up
Nasenbluten (-) – *nnt* nosebleed
Nashorn (-hörner) – *nnt* rhinoceros
nass – *adj* wet
national – *adj* national
nationalistisch – *adj* nationalist
Natur – *nf* nature
Naturkunde – *nf* natural history
natürlich – *adj* natural
natürlich – *adv* of course, naturally
Naturschutzgebiet (-e) – *nnt* nature reserve
Naturwissenschaft (-en) – *nf* science
Naturwissenschaften – *npl* natural sciences
Nebel – *nm* fog, mist
nebelig – *adj* foggy, misty
neben (+ acc/dat) – *prep* next to, beside
nebenan – *adv* next door
nebeneinander – *adv* side by side
neblig – *adj* foggy, misty
necken – *v reg* tease

Neffe (-n) – *nm wk* nephew

negativ – *adj* negative

nehmen – *v irreg* take, catch (bus, etc)

    den Bus nehmen – *v irreg* catch the bus

    Nehmen Sie den Bus Linie 3! – Catch the number three bus!

    Nehmen Sie die erste Straße links! – Take the first on the left!

nein – *adv* no

Nektarine (-n) – *nf* nectarine

nennen – *v irreg* call, name

nennenswert – *adj* noteworthy

Nerven – *npl* nerves

    Er geht mir auf die Nerven – He gets on my nerves

nervös – *adj* nervous, tense

nett – *adj* nice, kind, sweet

neu – *adj* new, recent

    Ein glückliches neues Jahr! – *excl* Happy New Year!

neuest – *adj* latest

neugierig – *adj* curious, nosy

Neujahr (-e) – *nnt* New Year

Neujahrstag (-e) – *nm* New Year's Day

neulich – *adv* recently, the other day

neun – *adj* nine

neunte – *adj* ninth

neunzehn – *adj* nineteen

neunzig – *adj* ninety

Neuseeland – *nnt* New Zealand

Neusprache(-n) – *nf* modern language

Neutrum – *nnt* neuter

nicht – not

    bitte nicht – please do not ...

    nicht gut in (+ dat) – no good at

    nicht länger – no longer

    nicht mehr – no more

    nicht wahr? – don't you, doesn't he?

noch nicht – *adv* not yet

Nichte (-n) – *nf* niece

Nichtraucher (-) – *nm* non-smoker

Nichtraucher~ – *pref* non smoking

nichts – nothing

    nichts anderes – nothing else

    nichts Neues – nothing new

    Nichts zu danken! – You're welcome!

nichtsdestoweniger – *adv* none the less

nie – *adv* never

    noch nie – *adv* never before

Niederlande – *npl* Netherlands

Niedersachsen – Lower Saxony

Niederschlag – *nm* precipitation, rain or snow

niederschlagsfrei – *adj* dry

niedlich – *adj* sweet (cute)

niedrig – *adj* low

niemand – *pron* no-one, nobody

    sonst niemand – no-one else

niesen – *v reg* sneeze

nimmt – *see nehmen*

nirgendwo – *adv* nowhere, anywhere (negative)

Niveau – *nnt* standard, level (school)

noch – *adv* another (more)

    noch einmal – *adv* once more

    Noch etwas Brot? – Any more bread?

noch – *adv* still, yet

    noch nicht – *adv* not yet

    noch besser – *adj* even better

    noch nie – *adv* never before

    weder ... noch – *adv* neither ... nor

nochmals – *adv* yet again, once more

Nord~ – *pref* north

Nordamerika – *nnt* North America

Norddeutschland – *nnt* North Germany

Norden – *nm* north

---

adj - adjective	*v reg* - verb regular	*v sep* - verb separable	† - see verb info
prep - preposition	*v irreg* - verb irregular	*v refl* - verb reflexive	* - takes sein

im Norden – in the north
Nordire (-n) – *nm wk* Northern Irishman
Nordirin (-nen) – *nf* Northern Irishwoman
nordirisch – *adj* North Irish
Nordirland – *nnt* Northern Ireland
nördlich von (+ dat) – *adj* north of
nördlich – *adj* northerly
Nordsee – *nf* North Sea
normal – *adj* normal, usual, ordinary
normalerweise – *adv* usually, normally
Norwegen – *nnt* Norway
norwegisch – *adj* Norwegian
Not~ – *pref* emergency
Notarzt (-ärzte) – *nm* emergency doctor
Notausgang (-gänge) – *nm* emergency exit
Notdienst (-e) – *nm* emergency service
Note (-n) – *nf* mark, grade (school)
Notfall (-fälle) – *nm* emergency
Nothilfe (-n) – *nf* emergency aid
notieren – *v reg* † note down
nötig – *adj* necessary
Notiz (-en) – *nf* note (message)
Notizblock (-blöcke) – *nm* notepad

Notizbuch (-bücher) – *nnt* notebook
Notizen machen – *v reg* take notes
Notruf (-e) – *nm* emergency phone number
notwendig – *adj* necessary
Notwendigkeit (-en) – *nf* necessity
November – *nm* November
im November – in November
Nr. – number
Nudeln – *npl* noodles, pasta
null – *adj* nil
zwei zu null – 2:0, two - nil
Null (-en) – *nf* zero, nought
null zu null Unentschieden – *nnt* goalless draw
Nummer (-n) – *nf* number (house, etc)
die Nummer wählen – *v reg* dial the number
nun – *adv* now
nur – *adv* only, just
nicht nur – not only
nicht nur ... sondern auch – not only ... but also
Nuss (Nüsse) – *nf* nut
nützlich – *adj* useful
nutzlos – *adj* useless
Nylon – *nnt* nylon
aus Nylon – made of nylon

O

ob – *sub conj* if, whether
oben – *adv* above, at the top, upstairs
oben auf (+ dat) – *adv* on top of
nach oben gehen* – *v irreg* go upstairs
ober~ – *pref* upper, senior
Herr Ober! – *excl* Waiter!
Obergeschoss (-e) – *nnt* upper floor

im zweiten Obergeschoss – on the second floor
Oberlippenbart (-bärte) – *nm* moustache
Oberstufe (-n) – *nf* sixth form
in der Oberstufe sein* – be in Year 12
Oberstufenkolleg (-kollegien) – *nnt* sixth form college

---

nm - noun masculine	*nf* - noun feminine	*nnt* - noun neuter	*npl* - noun plural
nom- nominative	*acc* - accusative	*gen* - genitive	*dat* - dative

obgleich – *sub conj* although
obligatorisch – *adj* obligatory
Oboe (-n) – *nf* oboe
Obst – *nnt* fruit
Obstbaum (-bäume) – *nm* fruit tree
Obsthändler (-) – *nm* fruit seller
Obstsorten – *npl* fruits
obwohl – *sub conj* although
oder – *coord conj* or
   entweder ... oder ... – *conj*
   either ... or ...
Oder – *nf* River Oder
Ofen (Öfen) – *nm* stove (oven)
offen – *adj* open, frank
offensichtlich – *adj* obvious
öffentlich – *adj* public
   öffentliche Verkehrsmittel –
   npl public transport
offiziell – *adj* official
öffnen – *v reg* † open
Öffnung (-en) – *nf* opening
Öffnungszeiten – *npl* opening hours
oft – *adv* often, frequently
   sehr oft – many, many times
ohne (+ acc) – *prep* without
ohnmächtig werden* – *v irreg*
   faint (swoon)
Ohr (-en) – *nnt* ear
Ohrenschmerzen – *npl* earache
Ohrring (-e) – *nm* earring
Öko~ – ecological
Ökologe (-n) – *nm wk* ecologist
Ökologie (-n) – *nf* ecology
Ökologin (-en) – *nf* ecologist
Oktober – *nm* October
   im Oktober – in October
Öl – *nnt* oil
Ölgemälde – *nnt* oil painting
Olivenöl – *nnt* olive oil
die Olympischen Spiele – *npl* the
   Olympic Games
Oma (-s) – *nf* granny

Omelett (-s) – *nnt* omelette
Omi (-s) – *nf* granny
Onkel (-) – *nm* uncle
Opa (-s) – *nm* grandpa
Oper (-n) – *nf* opera
Operation (-en) – *nf* operation
operieren – *v reg* † operate
   sich operieren lassen – *v irreg*
   refl have an operation
Opernhaus (-häuser) – *nnt* opera
   house
Opfer (-) – *nnt* victim
Opi (-s) – *nm* grandpa
Optiker (-) – *nm* optician
Optikerin (-nen) – *nf* optician
Optimist (-en) – *nm wk* optimist
optimistisch – *adj* optimistic
orange – *adj inv* orange
Orangenmarmelade (-n) – *nf*
   marmalade
Orangensaft – *nm* orange juice
Orchester (-) – *nnt* orchestra
ordentlich – *adj* neat, tidy, orderly
Ordinalzahl (-en) – *nf* ordinal
   number
ordnen – *v reg* † put in the right order
Ordner (-) – *nm* file, ring binder
Ordnung (-en) – *nf* order (tidiness)
   In Ordnung! – *excl* Alright! Fine!
organisieren – *v reg* † organise
organisiert – *adj* organised
original – *adj* original
   im Originalton – in the original
   version (soundtrack)
Ort (-e) – *nm* place (town, etc)
örtlich – *adj* local
Ortschaft (-en) – *nf* town, built up area
Ost~ – *pref* eastern
Osten – *nm* east
   im Osten – in the east
Osterei (-er) – *nnt* Easter egg
Osterferien – *npl* Easter holidays

---

adj - adjective   *v reg* - verb regular   *v sep* - verb separable   † - see verb info
prep - preposition   *v irreg* - verb irregular   *v refl* - verb reflexive   * - takes sein

Osterhase (-n) – *nm wk* Easter bunny
Ostern – *npl* Easter
  zu Ostern – at Easter
Österreich – *nnt* Austria
Österreicher (-) – *nm* Austrian
Österreicherin (-nen) – *nf* Austrian
österreichisch – *adj* Austrian

Ostersonntag – *nm* Easter Day
östlich von (+ dat) – *prep* east of
Ostsee – *nf* Baltic Sea
oval – *adj* oval
Overall (-s) – *nm* overalls
Ozean (-e) – *nm* ocean
Ozonschicht (-en) – *nf* ozone layer

P

Paar – *nnt* pair (of)
  ein Paar Schuhe – *nnt* a pair of
  shoes
ein paar – a few
  Ein paar Leute waren da – A
  few people were there
Päckchen (-) – *nnt* packet
packen – *v reg* pack (case)
Packung (-en) – *nf* packet
Paket (-e) – *nnt* parcel, package
Pakistan – *nnt* Pakistan
Pakistaner (-) – *nm* Pakistani person
Pakistanerin (-nen) – *nf* Pakistani
person
pakistanisch – *adj* Pakistani
Pampelmuse (-n) – *nf* grapefruit
Panne (-n) – *nf* breakdown
  eine Panne haben – *v irreg* break
  down
Pantoffel (-n) – *nm* slipper
Papagei (-en) – *nm* parrot
Papier (-e) – *nnt* paper
  ein Blatt Papier – *nnt* a sheet of
  paper
Papierkorb (-körbe) – *nm* waste
paper basket
Papiertaschentuch (-tücher) – *nnt*
tissue
Pappe – *nf* cardboard
Paprika (-s) – *nm* green pepper

Parfüm – *nnt* perfume
Park (-s) – *nm* park
Parkanlage (-n) – *nf* park
Parken verboten – no parking
parken – *v reg* park
Parken – *nnt* parking
Parkett – *nnt* stalls (theatre)
Parkhaus (-häuser) – *nnt* multi-
storey car park
Parkplatz (-plätze) – *nm* car park
Parkuhr (-en) – *nf* parking meter
Parkverbot (-e) – *nnt* parking
forbidden
Parlament (-e) – *nnt* parliament
(national)
Partei (-en) – *nf* party (political)
Parterre (-s) – *nnt* stalls (theatre)
Partizip (-ien) – *nnt* participle
Partner (-) – *nm* partner
Partnerin (-nen) – *nf* partner
Partnerstadt (-städte) – *nf* twin town
Party (-s) – *nf* party (celebration)
Pass (Pässe) – *nm* passport
Passagier (-e) – *nm* passenger
Passagierin (-nen) – *nf* passenger
Passahfest (-e) – *nnt* Passover
Passant (-en) – *nm wk* passer-by
Passantin (-nen) – *nf* passer-by
passen – *v reg* be convenient, suit

Es passt mir nicht – It doesn't fit me, It doesn't suit me, It's not convenient

passend – *adj* suitable, convenient

passieren* – *v reg* † happen

Pastete (-n) – *nf* pâté

Pastor (-en) – *nm* protestant vicar

Pastorin (-nen) – *nf* protestant vicar (female)

Patient (-en) – *nm wk* patient

Patientin (-nen) – *nf* patient

pauken – *v reg* swot

pauschal – *adj* all-inclusive

Pauschalreise (-n) – *nf* package tour

Pause (-n) – *nf* break, pause

Pause machen – *v reg* have a rest

PC (-s) – *nm* PC

Pech! – *excl* Too bad! Hard luck!

Pech – *nnt* bad luck

Pech haben – *v irreg* be unlucky

peinlich – *adj* embarrassing, awkward

pendeln* – *v reg* commute

Pension – *nf* guest house, board (food)

per – *prep* by

perfekt – *adj* perfect

Periode (-n) – *nf* period (menstrual)

Person (-en) – *nf* person, character (drama) (male or female)

pro Person – per person

Personalausweis (-e) – *nm* identity card

Personenzug (-züge) – *nm* slow train

persönlich – *adj* personal; *adv* in person

Pf – pfennig

Pfadfinder (-) – *nm* scout

Pfadfinderin (-nen) – *nf* guide

Pfand – *nm* deposit (on empty bottle)

Pfanne (-n) – *nf* frying pan

Pfannkuchen (-) – *nm* pancake

Pfeffer – *nm* pepper (spice)

Pfefferminz – *nm* mint

Pfefferminztee – *nm* mint tea

Pfeife (-n) – *nf* pipe

pfeifen – *v irreg* whistle

Pfeil (-e) – *nm* arrow

Pfennig – *nm* pfennig (100 Pf = 1DM)

Pferd (-e) – *nnt* horse

Pferderennen – *nnt* races

Pferdeschwanz (-schwänze) – *nm* pony tail

Pferdestall (-ställe) – *nm* stable

Pfingsten – *npl* Whitsun

Pfingstferien – *npl* summer half-term holiday (Whitsuntide)

Pfirsich (-e) – *nm* peach

Pflanze (-n) – *nf* plant

pflanzen – *v reg* plant

Pflaster – *nnt* plaster (sticking)

Pflaume (-n) – *nf* plum

pflegen – *v reg* care for

Pflicht – *nf* duty

Pflichtfach (-fächer) – *nnt* compulsory subject

pflücken – *v reg* pick, collect fruit

Pfote (-n) – *nf* paw

Pfund – *nnt* pound

ein Pfund Käse – a pound of cheese

phantastisch – *adj* fantastic

Physik – *nf* physics

Physiotherapeut (-en) – *nm wk* physiotherapist

Physiotherapeutin (-nen) – *nf* physiotherapist

Pickel (-) – *nm* spot, zit

pickelig – *adj* spotty (zits)

Picknick (-s) – *nnt* picnic

picknicken – *v reg* picnic

Pille (-n) – *nf* pill (contraceptive)

Pilot (-en) – *nm wk* pilot (air)

Pils – *nm* lager

Pilsener – *nm* lager

Pilz (-e) – *nm* mushroom

pingelig – *adj coll* fussy

---

adj - adjective	*v reg* - verb regular	*v sep* - verb separable	† - see verb info
prep - preposition	*v irreg* - verb irregular	*v refl* - verb reflexive	* - takes sein

Pinsel (-) – *nm* brush (painting)
Piste (-n) – *nf* ski-run, course (route)
Pistole (-n) – *nf* gun (handgun)
Pizza (-s) – *nf* pizza
PKW (-s) – *nm* car
Plakat (-e) – *nnt* placard
Plan (Pläne) – *nm* plan
planen – *v reg* plan
Plastik – *nnt* plastic
Plastiktüte (-n) – *nf* plastic bag
platt – *adj* flat (of tyre, etc)
Platte (-n) – *nf* dish; record
  kalte Platte – *nf* mixed cold meats
Plattenspieler (-) – *nm* record player
Platz (Plätze) – *nm* place, seat;
square (town); ground, pitch (sport);
site (camping)
  einen Platz reservieren – *v reg* †
  book a seat
  Platz nehmen – *v irreg* take one's
  place
Platzanweiserin (-nen) – *nf*
usherette
Platzregen (-) – *nm* downpour
plaudern – *v reg* chat
pleite – *adj inv* broke
  Ich bin pleite – *sl* I'm broke
Plombe (-n) – *nf* filling (teeth)
plötzlich – *adj* sudden, *adv* suddenly
Plural (-e) – *nm* plural
  im Plural – in the plural
plus – *prep* plus
Plusquamperfekt – *nnt* pluperfect
Pokal (-e) – *nm* cup (trophy)
Pokalendspiel (-e) – *nnt* cup final
Polen – Poland
polieren – *v reg* † polish
Politesse (-n) – *nf* female traffic warden
Politik – *nf* policy
Politiker (-) – *nm* politician
Politikerin (-nen) – *nf* politician
Polizei – *nf* police

Polizeiwache (-n) – *nf* police station
Polizist (-en) – *nm wk* policeman
Polizistin (-nen) – *nf* police woman
polnisch – *adj* Polish
Pommes – *npl* chips
Pommes frites – *npl* chips
Pony (-s) – *nnt* pony
Pony (-s) – *nm* fringe
Popmusik – *nf* pop music
Portemonnaie (-s) – *nnt* purse
Portion (-en) – *nf* portion
Portugal – *nnt* Portugal
Portugiese (-n) – *nm wk* Portuguese
person
Portugiesin (-nen) – *nf* Portuguese
person
portugiesisch – *adj* Portuguese
Posaune (-n) – *nf* trombone
positiv – *adj* positive
Post – *nf* post office; mail
Postamt (-ämter) – *nnt* post office
Postanweisung (-en) – *nf* postal order
Poster (-) – *nnt* poster
Postkarte (-n) – *nf* postcard
Postleitzahl (-en) – *nf* post code
Postwertzeichen – *npl* stamps
praktisch – *adj* practical, useful
Praline (-n) – *nf* chocolate (individual)
Präsens – *nnt* present (tense)
Praxis (Praxen) – *nf* clinic (surgery)
Preis (-e) – *nm* cost, price, charge;
prize
  zum halben Preis – half-price
  zum Preis von (+ dat) – *prep*
  costing
Preisliste (-n) – *nf* price list
Preistafel (-n) – *nf* price list
preiswert – *adj* good value
Presse – *nf* press (media)
Priester (-) – *nm* priest (RC)
prima! – *excl* great!
Prinzip (-ien) – *nnt* principle

---

nm - noun masculine	*nf* - noun feminine	*nnt* - noun neuter	*npl* - noun plural
nom- nominative	*acc* - accusative	*gen* - genitive	*dat* - dative

privat – *adj* private
private Grundschule (-n) – *nf* prep(aratory) school
Privatschule (-n) – *nf* private school, public school (UK)
pro (+ acc) – *prep* per
pro Kilo – by the kilo
pro Stunde – by the hour
pro Tag – per day
Probe (-n) – *nf* rehearsal
probieren – *v reg* † taste, try (food)
Problem (-e) – *nnt* problem
Probleme haben – *v irreg* be in trouble
Produkt (-e) – *nnt* product
Programm (-e) – *nnt* programme, channel (TV)
im zweiten Programm – on the second channel
programmieren – *v reg* † program
Programmierer (-) – *nm* computer programmer
Programmiererin (-nen) – *nf* computer programmer
Projekt (-e) – *nnt* project
Pronomen (-) – *nnt* pronoun
Prospekt (-e) – *nm* leaflet
Prost! – *excl* Cheers!
Protestant (-en) – *nm wk* Protestant
Protestantin (-nen) – *nf* Protestant
protestieren – *v reg* † protest
Proviant – *nm* food, provisions
Provinz (-en) – *nf* province
Prozent – *nnt* per cent
Prozess (-e) – *nm* process
prüfen – *v reg* examine
Prüfung (-en) – *nf* examination (school)

eine Prüfung bestehen – *v irreg* pass an exam
eine Prüfung machen – *v reg* take an exam
eine Prüfung wiederholen – *v reg insep* † resit an exam
in einer Prüfung durchfallen* – *v irreg* fail an exam
mündliche Prüfung (-en) – *nf* speaking test
schriftliche Prüfung – *nf* written test
Publikum – *nnt* audience
Pudding (-s) – *nm* cold milk dessert
Pudel (-) – *nm* poodle
Puder (-) – *nm* powder (cosmetic)
Pulli (-s) – *nm* pullover
Pullover (-) – *nm* pullover
Pullunder (-) – *nm* sleeveless pullover
Pulver (-) – *nnt* powder
Pulverkaffee – *nm* instant coffee
Punkt (-e) – *nm* point, full stop (.)
einen Punkt gewinnen – *v irreg* score a point
zehn Punkte haben – *v irreg* get ten out of ten
pünktlich – *adj* punctual
pünktlich – *adv* on time
Puppe (-n) – *nf* doll
purpur – *adj inv* purple
putzen – *v reg* clean
sich die Nase putzen – *v reg dat refl* blow one's nose
sich die Zähne putzen – *v reg dat refl* clean one's teeth
Putzfrau (-en) – *nf* cleaning lady

---

adj - adjective	*v reg* - verb regular	*v sep* - verb separable	† - see verb info
prep - preposition	*v irreg* - verb irregular	*v refl* - verb reflexive	* - takes sein

Q

Qualifikation (-en) – *nf* qualification
Qualität (-en) – *nf* quality
  guter Qualität – good quality
  schlechter Qualität – poor quality
Quark – *nm* curd cheese
Quatsch – *nm* nonsense

quatschen – *v reg* chatter
Quelle (-n) – *nf* source, spring
quer – *adv* across, at an angle
quetschen – *v reg* squeeze
Quittung (-en) – *nf* receipt
Quiz (-) – *nnt* quiz

R

Rabatt (-e) – *nm* discount
Rad (Räder) – *nnt* cycle, bike, wheel
Rad fahren* – *v irreg* cycle, go for a bike ride
Radfahren – *nnt* cycling
Radfahrer (-) – *nm* cyclist
Radfahrerin (-nen) – *nf* cyclist
Radiergummi (-s) – *nm* rubber (eraser)
Radio (-s) – *nnt* radio
  im Radio sein* – *v irreg* be on the radio
Radiokassettenrekorder (-) – *nm* radio cassette player
Radiowecker (-) – *nm* clock radio
Radtour (-en) – *nf* bike ride
  eine Radtour machen – *v reg* go for a bike ride
Radverleih – *nm* cycle hire
Rahmen (-) – *nm* frame (photo, etc)
Ramadan – *nm* Ramadan
Rand (Ränder) – *nm* edge, outskirts
  am Rand – on the edge
Rang (Ränge) – *nm* row (cinema)
Ranzen (-) – *nm* schoolbag
Rappen (-) – *nm* Swiss coin (SF1 = 100 Rappen)
Rasen (-) – *nm* lawn

  den Rasen mähen – *v reg* mow the lawn
Rasierapparat (-e) – *nm* razor
sich rasieren – *v reg refl* † shave
Rasse (-n) – *nf* race (nationality)
Rastplatz (-plätze) – *nm* picnic area (motorway)
Rasthof (-höfe) – *nm* motorway service area
Raststätte (-n) – *nf* motorway service area
Rat – *nm, no pl* advice
raten – *v irreg* guess
Rathaus (-häuser) – *nnt* town hall
Ratschlag (-schläge) – *nm* piece of advice
Rätsel (-) – *nnt* puzzle
Ratte (-n) – *nf* rat
Rattenfänger (-) – *nm* rat catcher, the Pied Piper
Rauch – *nm* smoke
rauchen – *v reg* smoke
Rauchen verboten – no smoking
Raucher (-) – *nm* smoker
Raucher~ – *pref* smoking (area)
Raucherin (-nen) – *nf* smoker
Rasierapparat (-e) – *nm* electric razor
Raum (Räume) – *nm* room, space

---

nm - noun masculine	*nf* - noun feminine	*nnt* - noun neuter	*npl* - noun plural
nom- nominative	*acc* - accusative	*gen* - genitive	*dat* - dative

'Raus! – *excl* Get out!

Realschule (-n) – *nf* technical secondary school

Rebstock – *nm* vine

Rechnen – *nnt* arithmetic

rechnen – *v reg* † calculate, reckon

Rechnung (-en) – *nf* bill, account, sum

Recht haben – *v irreg* be right
  Du hast Recht – You are right

rechts – *adv* right, on the right, to the right

rechts fahren* – *v irreg* keep to the right, drive on the right hand side of the road

Rechts halten! – *excl* Keep to the right!

Rechtsanwalt (-anwälte) – *nm* solicitor, lawyer

Rechtsanwältin (-nen) – *nf* solicitor, lawyer

Rechtsaußen (-) – *nm* right wing (sport)

Rechtschreibung – *nf* spelling

rechtshändig – *adj* right-handed

recyceln – *v reg* † recycle

Rede (-n) – *nf* speech (in public)

reduzieren – *v reg* † reduce

reduziert – *adj* reduced

Reflexivverbum (-verben) – *nnt* reflexive verb

Reformkost – *nf* health food

Regal (-e) – *nnt* shelf

Regel (-n) – *nf* rule
  in der Regel – as a rule

regelmäßig – *adj* regular

Regen – *nm* rain
  der saure Regen – *nm* acid rain
  im Regen – in the rain

Regenbogen (-bögen) – *nm* rainbow

Regenjacke (-n) – *nf* cagoule

Regenmantel (-mäntel) – *nm* raincoat

Regenschauer (-) – *nm* shower (rain)

Regenschirm (-e) – *nm* umbrella

Region (-en) – *nf* region

regnen – *v reg* † rain
  Es regnet – It is raining
  Es regnete – It was raining
  Es wird regnen – It will rain

regnerisch – *adj* rainy

reiben – *v irreg* rub

reich – *adj* rich

reichen – *v reg* pass (at table), be enough
  Das reicht – That's enough

reif – *adj* ripe

Reife – *nf* maturity
  Hochschulreife – *nf* A Level/GNVQ Level 3 equivalent

Reifen (-) – *nm* tyre

Reifendruck – *nm* tyre pressure
  den Reifendruck kontrollieren – *v reg* † check the tyre pressure

Reifenpanne (-n) – *nf* puncture, flat tyre

Reihe (-n) – *nf* row
  der Reihe nach – in turn
  in alphabetischer Reihenfolge – in alphabetical order

Reihenhaus (-häuser) – *nnt* terraced house

rein – *adj* clean

reinigen – *v reg* clean
  etwas reinigen lassen – *v irreg* have something cleaned

Reis – *nm* rice

Reise (-n) – *nf* journey, trip
  Gute Reise! – *excl* Have a good trip!

Reisebüro (-s) – *nnt* travel agency

Reisebus (-se) – *nm* coach

Reiseführer (-) – *nm* guide book

reisen* – *v reg* travel

Reisende – *nmf* ‡ traveller

Reisescheck (-s) – *nm* travellers' cheque

Reisetasche (-n) – *nf* holdall

Reißverschluss (-verschlüsse) – *nm* zip

reiten (*) – *v irreg* ride (horse)
reiten gehen* – *v irreg* go horse riding
Reiten – *nnt* horse riding
Reitkappe (-n) – *nf* riding hat
reizbar – *adj* irritable
reizen – *v reg* irritate
Reklame (-n) – *nf* advertisement (for products)
Rekord (-e) – *nm* record (sport, etc)
relativ – *adv* relatively
Religion (-en) – *nf* RE, RS, religion
Rennboot (-e) – *nnt* speedboat
Rennen (-) – *nnt* race (sport)
Rentner (-) – *nm* retired person, senior citizen, pensioner
Rentnerin (-nen) – *nf* retired person, senior citizen, pensioner
Reparatur (-en) – *nf* repair
Reparaturwerkstatt (-werkstätten) – *nf* repair workshop, garage
reparieren – *v reg* † repair, mend, fix
etwas reparieren lassen – *v irreg* have something repaired
Reporter (-) – *nm* reporter
Reporterin (-nen) – *nf* reporter
Republik (-en) – *nf* republic
die Republik Irland – the Irish Republic, Eire
reservieren – *v reg* † reserve
reserviert – *adj* reserved, booked
Reservierung (-en) – *nf* reservation
Respekt – *nm* respect
Rest – *nm* remainder, the rest
Restaurant (-s) – *nnt* restaurant
retten – *v reg* † save, rescue
Rettungsring (-e) – *nm* lifebelt
Rettungsschwimmer (-) – *nm* lifeguard
Revolver (-) – *nm* revolver
Rezept (-e) – *nnt* recipe; prescription
Rezeption – *nf* reception desk (hotel)

Rhein – *nm* River Rhine
Rhein-Main-Donau-Kanal – *nm* Rhine-Main-Danube Canal
Rheinwein (-e) – *nm* Rhine wine, hock
Richter (-) – *nm* judge
Richterin (-nen) – *nf* judge
richtig – *adj* right, true, correct
Richtlinien – *npl* code (guidelines)
Richtung (-en) – *nf* direction
Gehen Sie in diese Richtung! – Go that way!
in alle Richtungen – in all directions
in entgegengesetzter Richtung – in the opposite direction
in Richtung – towards, in the direction of
riechen (nach + dat) – *v irreg* smell (of)
rief – *see rufen*
rief an – *see anrufen*
Riese (-n) – *nm wk* giant
riesengroß – *adj* enormous
riesig – *adj* gigantic, huge
Rinderbraten (-) – *nm* roast beef
Rindfleisch – *nnt* beef
gehacktes Rindfleisch – minced beef
Ring (-e) – *nm* ring
Rippe (-n) – *nf* rib
Risiko (Risiken) – *nnt* risk
Rock (Röcke) – *nm* skirt
Rockmusik – *nf* rock music
roh – *adj* raw
Rollladen (Rolllläden) – *nm* blind, shutter
Rollbrett (-er) – *nnt* skateboard
Rollbrett fahren* – *v irreg* skateboard
Rolle (-n) – *nf* role, part, reel
Rollenspiel (-e) – *nnt* role play
Roller (-) – *nm* scooter

---

nm - noun masculine   *nf* - noun feminine   *nnt* - noun neuter   *npl* - noun plural
nom- nominative   *acc* - accusative   *gen* - genitive   *dat* - dative

Rollschuh fahren* – *v irreg* roller skate

Rollschuhe – *npl* roller skates

Rollstuhl (-stühle) – *nm* wheelchair

Rolltreppe (-n) – *nf* escalator

Rom – Rome

Roman (-e) – *nm* novel

romantisch – *adj* romantic

röntgen – *v reg* X-ray
  sich röntgen lassen – *v irreg refl* to be X-rayed

Röntgenbild – *nnt* X-ray

rosa – *adj inv* pink

Rose (-n) – *nf* rose

Rosenkohl – *nm, no pl* Brussels sprout

Roséwein (-e) – *nm* rosé wine

rot – *adj* red
  rot werden* – *v irreg* go red

rotbraun – *adj* auburn

Rotkäppchen – Little Red Riding Hood

rothaarig – *adj* red haired, ginger

Rotwein (-e) – *nm* red wine

Routine (-n) – *nf* routine

Rowdy (-s) – *nm* hooligan

Rücken (-) – *nm* back

Rückfahrkarte (-n) – *nf* return ticket

Rückfahrt (-en) – *nf* return journey

Rucksack (-säcke) – *nm* rucksack

rücksichtslos – *adj* careless

Rückspiegel (-) – *nm* driving mirror

rückwärts – *adv* backwards
  rückwärts fahren* – *v irreg* reverse, back (car)

rudern – *v reg* row (boat)

Ruf (-e) – *nm* reputation

rufen – *v irreg* shout, call, cry

Rugby – *nnt* rugby

Ruhe – *nf* peace, tranquillity
  Lass mich in Ruhe! – *excl* Leave me in peace!

Ruhestand – *nm* retirement
  in den Ruhestand treten* – *v irreg* retire
  im Ruhestand – retired

Ruhetag (-e) – *nm* rest day (hotel, etc)

ruhig – *adj* calm, quiet
  Sei ruhig! – *excl* Be quiet! (informal)

Rührei (-er) – *nnt* scrambled egg

rülpsen – *v reg* belch

Rumänien – *nnt* Romania

Rumpelkammer (-n) – *nf* junk room

rund – *adj* round

rund – *adv* approximately

Runde (n) – *nf* round of drinks
  eine Runde drehen – *v reg* go for a short walk

Rundfahrt (-en) – *nf* guided tour (by coach, etc)

runzeln – *v reg* wrinkle
  die Stirn runzeln – *v reg* frown

Russe (-n) – *nm wk* Russian person

Rüssel (-) – *nm* elephant's trunk

Russin (-nen) – *nf* Russian person

russisch – *adj* Russian

Russland – *nnt* Russia

Rutschbahn (-en) – *nf* slide (playground)

S

Saal (Säle) – *nm* hall (public, smart)
Sache (-n) – *nf* thing
Sachen – *npl* belongings
Sachsen – Saxony
Sack (Säcke) – *nm* sack
Sackgasse (-n) – *nf* cul de sac
Saft (Säfte) – *nm* juice, syrup
  Fruchtsaft – *nm* fruit juice
  Orangensaft – *nm* orange juice
sagen – *v reg* say
  Wie sagt man ... auf Deutsch?
  – How do you say ... in German?
  jdm sagen – *v reg* tell
sah – *see sehen*
Sahne – *nf* cream (milk)
Saison (-s) – *nf* season (football, etc)
  außerhalb der Saison – out of
  season
Saite (-n) – *nf* string (violin, racket)
Salami – *nf* salami
Salat (-e) – *nm* lettuce
  gemischter Salat – *nm* mixed
  salad
  grüner Salat – *nm* green salad
Salbe (-n) – *nf* cream (medicine)
Salz – *nnt* salt
salzig – *adj* salty
Salzkartoffeln – *npl* boiled potatoes
sammeln – *v reg* collect (stamps, etc)
  Briefmarken sammeln – *v reg*
  collect stamps
Sammelstelle (-n) – *nf* collection
point
Sammlung (-en) – *nf* collection
Samstag (-e) – *nm* Saturday
  am Samstag – on Saturday
  Bis Samstag! – See you on
  Saturday!
Samt – *nm* velvet
Sand – *nm* sand

Sandale (-n) – *nf* sandal
Sandburg (-en) – *nf* sand castle
sanft – *adj* gentle
Sänger (-) – *nm* singer
Sängerin (-nen) – *nf* singer
Sanitäranlage (-n) – *nf* toilet block
Sankt – *adj inv* saint
Sardine (-n) – *nf* sardine
saß – *see sitzen*
Satellit (-en) – *nm wk* satellite
Satellitenschüssel (-n) – *nf* satellite
dish
satt – *adj* fed up
Sattel (Sättel) – *nm* saddle
Satz (Sätze) – *nm* sentence
sauber – *adj* clean
sauber machen – *v reg* clean
Saubermachen – *nnt* cleaning
sauer – *adj* sour
Sauerkraut – *nnt* sauerkraut, hot
  pickled cabbage
Sauerstoff – *nm* oxygen
saufen – *v irreg coll* booze
der saure Regen – *nm* acid rain
Saxophon (-e) – *nnt* saxophone
SB (Selbstbedienung) – *nf* self-
service
S-Bahn (-en) – *nf* city and suburban
railway
Schach – *nnt* chess
Schachtel (-n) – *nf* box (cardboard)
schade – *adj* pity
schade! – it is a pity!
  Wie schade! – *excl* What a pity!
Schaden (Schäden) – *nm* damage
Schadstoffe – *npl* harmful substances
Schaf (-e) – *nnt* sheep
etwas schaffen – *v reg* manage to do
sthg
Schaffner (-) – *nm* ticket inspector

---

nm - noun masculine	*nf* - noun feminine	*nnt* - noun neuter	*npl* - noun plural
nom- nominative	*acc* - accusative	*gen* - genitive	*dat* - dative

Schaffnerin (-nen) – *nf* ticket inspector

Schal (-s) – *nm* scarf (long)

schälen – *v reg* peel

Schallplatte (-n) – *nf* record (pop, etc)

(den Gang) schalten – *v reg* † change gear

Schalter (-) – *nm* ticket office; counter; switch
am Schalter – at the ticket office

sich schämen vor (+ dat) – *v reg refl* be ashamed of

schändlich – *adj* disgraceful

scharf – *adj* sharp; spicy

Schatten (-) – *nm* shade
im Schatten – in the shade

Schatz (Schätze) – *nm* treasure

schätzen – *v reg* appreciate

schauen – *v reg* look

Schauer (-) – *nm* shower (rain)
es wird Schauer geben – there will be showers

Schaufenster (-) – *nnt* shop window
einen Schaufensterbummel machen – *v reg* go window shopping

Schaukel (-n) – *nf* swing (child's)

schaukeln – *v reg* swing

Schaukelstuhl (-stühle) – *nm* rocking chair

Schaumwein (-e) – *nm* sparkling wine

Schauspieler (-) – *nm* actor

Schauspielerin (-nen) – *nf* actress

Scheck (-s) – *nm* cheque
einen Scheck einlösen – *v reg sep* cash a cheque

Scheckheft (-e) – *nnt* cheque book

Scheckkarte (-n) – *nf* cheque card

Scheibe (-n) – *nf* slice

Scheibenwischer (-) – *nm* windscreen wiper

sich scheiden lassen – *v irreg refl* get a divorce

Schein (-e) – *nm* banknote; certificate

E-111-Schein (-e) – *nm* E111 certificate

scheinen – *v irreg* seem, shine

Scheinwerfer (-) – *nm* headlight

Schenkel (-) – *nm* thigh

schenken – *v reg* give as a present

Schere (-n) – *nf* scissors (pair of)

scheu – *adj* shy, timid

Scheune (-n) – *nf* barn

scheußlich – *adj* vile

schick – *adj* smart, chic

schicken – *v reg* send

schieben – *v irreg* push (a car)

Schiedsrichter (-) – *nm* referee

Schiedsrichterin (-nen) – *nf* referee

schief gehen* – *v irreg* go wrong

schießen – *v irreg* shoot

Schießen – *nnt* shooting

Schiff (-e) – *nnt* ship

schikanieren – *v reg* † hassle

Schild (-er) – *nnt* sign

Schildkröte (-n) – *nf* tortoise

Schilling – *nm* schilling (Austrian currency)

Schinken (-) – *nm* ham

Schinkenbrot (-e) – *nnt* ham sandwich

Schirm (-e) – *nm* umbrella

Schlacht (-en) – *nf* battle

Schlaf – *nm* sleep

Schlafanzug (-züge) – *nm* pyjamas

schlafen – *v irreg* sleep

Schlafenszeit (-en) – *nf* bedtime

Schlafraum (-räume) – *nm* dormitory

schläfrig – *adj* sleepy

Schlafsack (-säcke) – *nm* sleeping bag

Schlafwagen (-) – *nm* sleeper car

Schlafzimmer (-) – *nnt* bedroom

---

adj - adjective	*v reg* - verb regular	*v sep* - verb separable	† - see verb info
prep - preposition	*v irreg* - verb irregular	*v refl* - verb reflexive	* - takes sein

Schlag (Schläge) – *nm* blow (hit)
schlagen – *v irreg* hit, strike
Schlager (-) – *nm* hit song (in German)
Schläger (-) – *nm* racket, bat
Schlagsahne – *nf* whipped cream
Schlagzeile (-n) – *nf* headline
Schlagzeug – *nnt* drum kit
Schlamm – *nm* mud
schlammig – *adj* muddy
Schlange (-n) – *nf* queue; snake
Schlange stehen – *v irreg* queue
schlank – *adj* slim
eine Schlankheitskur machen – *v reg* be on a diet
schlau – *adj* crafty
Schlauchboot (-e) – *nnt* dinghy (inflatable)
schlecht – *adj* bad
schlecht gelaunt – bad-tempered
Schleier (-) – *nm* veil
schlendern* – *v reg* stroll
schleppen – *v reg* tow
ins Schleudern geraten* – *v irreg* skid
schlief – *see schlafen*
schließen – *v irreg* shut
Schließfach (-fächer) – *nnt* locker
schließlich – *adv* finally
schlimm – *adj* bad
schlimmer – *adj* worse
Schlips (-e) – *nm* tie
Schlitten (-) – *nm* sledge
Schlittschuh (-e) – *nm* skate
Schlittschuh laufen* – *v irreg* skate
Schlittschuhlaufen – *nnt* ice-skating
Schloss (Schlösser) – *nnt* castle; lock (door)
Schlüssel (-) – *nm* key
Schlüsselbund (-e) – *nm* bunch of keys
Schlüsselloch (-löcher) – *nnt* keyhole

Schlüsselring (-e) – *nm* key ring
Schluss (Schlüsse) – *nm* end, conclusion
Schluss machen mit jdm – *v reg* to finish with s.o.
Schlussverkauf (-verkäufe) – *nm* sale
im Schlussverkauf – in the sales
schmal – *adj* narrow
schmecken – *v reg* taste
Es schmeckt – It tastes good
Schmerz (-en) – *nm* pain
Schmerzen haben – *v irreg* be in pain
schmerzhaft – *adj* painful
Schmetterling (-e) – *nm* butterfly
schmieren – *v reg* spread (with butter, etc)
Schmierheft (-e) – *nnt* rough book
sich schminken – *v reg refl* put on make-up
schmollen – *v reg* sulk
Schmuck – *nm* jewellery
Schnaps (Schnäpse) – *nm* spirits, schnaps
Schnapsidee (-n) – *nf coll* daft idea
Schmutz – *nm* dirt
schmutzig – *adj* dirty
schnarchen – *v reg* snore
Schnecke (-n) – *nf* snail
Schnee – *nm* snow
Schneeball (-bälle) – *nm* snowball
Schneefall (-fälle) – *nm* snowfall
Schneemann (-männer) – *nm* snowman
Schneesturm (-stürme) – *nm* snowstorm
schneiden – *v irreg* cut, slice
Ich habe mich in den Finger geschnitten – I have cut my finger
sich die Haare schneiden lassen – *v irreg dat refl* have a haircut

---

nm - noun masculine   *nf* - noun feminine   *nnt* - noun neuter   *npl* - noun plural
nom - nominative   *acc* - accusative   *gen* - genitive   *dat* - dative

Schneider (-) – *nm* tailor
Schneiderin (-nen) – *nf* tailor
schneien – *v reg* snow
schnell – *adj* quick
Schnellimbiss (-e) – *nm* snack
Schnellhefter (-) – *nm* folder (file)
Schnellzug (-züge) – *nm* express train
schnitt – *see schneiden*
Schnitzel (-) – *nnt* escalope
schnuggeln – *v reg* snuggle
Schnupfen (-) – *nm* cold
Schnur (Schnüre) – *nf* string
Schnurrbart (-bärte) – *nm* moustache
schnurren – *v reg* purr
Schokolade – *nf* chocolate (bar)
Schokoladen~ – *pref* chocolate
schon – *adv* already
schön – *adj* beautiful, fine
  Einen schönen Tag! – *excl* Have a nice day!
  Einen schönen Abend! – *excl* Have a nice evening!
  Schönes Wochenende! – *excl* Have a good weekend!
Schönheit (-en) – *nf* beauty
Schornstein (-e) – *nm* chimney
Schotte (-n) – *nm wk* Scotsman
Schottenmuster – *nnt* tartan
Schottin (-nen) – *nf* Scotswoman
schottisch – *adj* Scottish
Schottland – *nnt* Scotland
schräg – *adj* sloping
Schrank (Schränke) – *nm* cupboard
Schraubenzieher (-) – *nm* screwdriver
Schrebergarten (-gärten) – *nm* allotment
Schreck (-e) – *nm* fright
schrecklich – *adj* terrible
Schrei (-e) – *nm* shout

Schreibblock (-blöcke) – *nm* pad (writing)
schreiben – *v irreg* write
  eine Prüfung schreiben – *v irreg* take an exam
  Wie schreibt man das? – How do you spell that?
schreiben an (+ acc) – *v irreg* write to
Schreibmaterial – *nnt* writing materials
Schreibmaschine (-n) – *nf* typewriter
Schreibpapier – *nnt* writing paper
Schreibtisch (-e) – *nm* desk
Schreibwarengeschäft (-e) – *nnt* stationer's shop
Schreibwarenhandlung (-en) – *nf* stationer's shop
schreien – *v irreg* shout (scream)
schrieb – *see schreiben*
Schrift (-en) – *nf* writing, handwriting
schriftlich – *adj* in writing
schriftliche Prüfung (-en) – *nf* written test
Schriftsteller (-) – *nm* writer
Schriftstellerin (-nen) – *nf* writer
Schritt (-e) – *nm* footstep
Schubkarre (-n) – *nf* wheelbarrow
Schublade (-n) – *nf* drawer
schüchtern – *adj* shy
Schuh (-e) – *nm* shoe
  ein Paar Schuhe – *nnt* a pair of shoes
  schmutzige Schuhe – *npl* muddy shoes
Schuhgeschäft (-e) – *nnt* shoe shop
Schuhgröße (-n) – *nf* shoe size
Schul~ – *pref* educational
Schulbuch (-bücher) – *nnt* text book
Schulbus (-busse) – *nm* school bus
Schuld – *nf* blame, fault
  jdm die Schuld geben – *v irreg* blame s.o.

---

adj - adjective	*v reg* - verb regular	*v sep* - verb separable	† - see verb info
prep - preposition	*v irreg* - verb irregular	*v refl* - verb reflexive	* - takes sein

Es ist meine Schuld – It's my
fault
schulden – *v reg* † owe (money)
schuldig – *adj* guilty
Schuldirektor (-en) – *nm*
headmaster
Schuldirektorin (-nen) – *nf*
headmistress
Schule (-n) – *nf* school, academy
Die Schule ist aus – School is
finished
in der Schule – in school
Ich gehe zu Fuß zur Schule –
I walk to school
Schüler (-) – *nm* schoolboy
Schülerin (-nen) – *nf* schoolgirl
Schulferien – *npl* school holidays
schulfrei – *adj* off school
Schulhof (-höfe) – *nm* school
playground
Schuljahr (-e) – *nnt* school year
im sechsten Schuljahr – in Year 7
im siebten Schuljahr – in Year 8
im achten Schuljahr – in Year 9
im neunten Schuljahr –
in Year 10
im zehnten Schuljahr –
in Year 11
Schuljahresanfang (-anfänge) –
nm start of school year
Schulleiter (-) – *nm* headmaster
Schulleiterin (-nen) – *nf*
headmistress
Schulregel (-n) – *nf* school rule
Schultasche (-n) – *nf* school bag
Schulter (-n) – *nf* shoulder
Schuluniform (-en) – *nf* school
uniform
Schulweg (-e) – *nm* way to school
auf dem Schulweg – on the way
to school
Schürze (-n) – *nf* apron
Schüssel (-n) – *nf* bowl (dish)

Schutz (-e) – *nm* protection
Schutzbrille (-n) – *nf* goggles
Schütze – (horoscope) Sagittarius
schützen vor (+ dat) – *v reg* protect
from
schwach – *adj* weak
Schwager (Schwäger) – *nm*
brother-in-law
Schwägerin (-nen) – *nf* sister-in-law
Schwalbe (-n) – *nf* swallow (bird)
Schwamm (Schwämme) – *nm*
sponge
schwanger – *adj* pregnant
Schwanz (Schwänze) – *nm* tail
schwänzen – *v reg* truant
schwärmen für (+ acc) – *v reg* be
keen on
schwarz – *adj* black
Schwarzbrot (-e) – *nnt* black bread
Schwarzfahrer (-) – *nm* fare dodger
Schwarzfahrerin (-nen) – *nf* fare
dodger
Schwarzwälderkirschtorte (-n) –
nf Black Forest Gateau
Schwede (-n) – *nm wk* Swedish
person
Schweden – *nnt* Sweden
Schwedin (-nen) – *nf* Swedish
person
schwedisch – *adj* Swedish
schweigen – *v irreg* be silent
Schwein (-e) – *nnt* pig
Schwein haben – *v irreg coll*
be lucky
Schweinebraten – *nm* roast pork
Schweinefleisch – *nnt* pork
Schweinekotelett (-s) – *nnt* pork
chop
die Schweiz – *nf* Switzerland
in der Schweiz – in Switzerland
Schweizer (-) – *nm* Swiss person
Schweizerin (-nen) – *nf* Swiss
person
schweizerisch – *adj* Swiss

---

nm - noun masculine   *nf* - noun feminine   *nnt* - noun neuter   *npl* - noun plural
nom - nominative   *acc* - accusative   *gen* - genitive   *dat* - dative

schwer – *adj* difficult, heavy, severe
schwerhörig – *adj* hard of hearing
Schwester (-n) – *nf* sister
Schwiegermutter (-mütter) – *nf* mother-in-law
Schwiegersohn (-söhne) – *nm* son-in-law
Schwiegertochter (-töchter) – *nf* daughter-in-law
Schwiegervater (-väter) – *nm* father-in-law
schwierig – *adj* difficult
Schwierigkeit (-en) – *nf* difficulty
Schwierigkeiten haben – *v irreg* have difficulty
Schwimmbad (-bäder) – *nnt* swimming pool
schwimmen (*) – *v irreg* swim, float
Schwimmen – *nnt* swimming
Schwimmweste (-n) – *nf* lifejacket
schwindlig – *adj* dizzy
Mir ist schwindlig – I'm dizzy
schwül – *adj* sultry
Sciencefiction – *nf* science fiction
Sciencefiction Film (-e) – *nm* science fiction film
Sciencefiction Roman (-e) – *nm* science fiction story, book
sechs – *adj* six
sechste – *adj* sixth
sechzehn – *adj* sixteen
sechzehnte – *adj* sixteenth
sechzig – *adj* sixty
See (-n) – *nm* lake
See (-n) – *nf* sea
Seebad (-bäder) – *nnt* seaside resort
seekrank – *adj* seasick
Seemann (-männer) – *nm* sailor (civilian)
Segel (-) – *nnt* sail
Segelboot (-e) – *nnt* dinghy (sailing)
segeln – *v reg* sail
segeln gehen* – *v irreg* go sailing

Segelschiff (-e) – *nnt* sailing ship
sehen – *v irreg* see
sehenswert – *adj* worth seeing
Sehenswürdigkeit (-en) – *nf* sight (tourist)
sehr – *adv* very
Sehr geehrte Herren – Dear Sirs
seid – *see sein***
Seide (-n) – *nf* silk
aus Seide – made of silk
Seife (-n) – *nf* soap
Seifenoper (-n) – *nf* soap opera
Seilbahn (-en) – *nf* cable car
sein – *poss adj* his, its
sein* – *v irreg* be
seit (+ dat) – *prep* since, for (since)
Seit wann lernst du Deutsch? – How long have you been learning German?
seit wann? – how long?
seitdem – *sub conj* since
Seite (-n) – *nf* page, side
auf der anderen Seite – on the other side
auf der linken Seite – on the left hand side
auf Seite 51 – on page 51
unten auf der Seite – at the bottom of the page
oben auf der Seite – at the top of the page
Sekretär (-e) – *nm* secretary
Sekretärin (-nen) – *nf* secretary
Sekt – *nm* German champagne
Sekunde (-n) – *nf* second (time)
selbst – *pron* itself, oneself, yourself
selbst gemacht – *adj* home-made
Selbstbedienung – *nf* self-service
Selbstbedienungsrestaurant (-s) – *nnt* self-service restaurant
selbstbewusst – *adj* self-confident
selbstständig – *adj* independent
selbstverständlich – *adv* of course

adj - adjective	*v reg* - verb regular	*v sep* - verb separable	† - see verb info
prep - preposition	*v irreg* - verb irregular	*v refl* - verb reflexive	* - takes sein

selten – *adj* rare
selten – *adv* seldom
seltsam – *adj* strange, odd
Semester (-) – *nnt* term (university)
Semikolon (-s) – *nnt* semi-colon (;)
Semmel (-n) – *nf* bread roll
senden – *v reg* † broadcast
Sendung (-en) – *nf* programme (TV)
Senf – *nm* mustard
sensationell – *adj* sensational
sensibel – *adj* sensitive
September – *nm* September
  im September – in September
Serie (-n) – *nf* serial
Serviette (-n) – *nf* serviette
Servus! – *excl* Hi!; Goodbye!
Sessel (-) – *nm* armchair
Sesselbahn (-en) – *nf* chair lift
setzen – *v reg* set (put)
setzen auf (+ acc) – *v reg* place on
sich setzen – *v reg refl* sit down
  Setz dich! – Sit down! (informal)
  Setzen Sie sich! – Sit down!
  (formal)
sexistisch – *adj* sexist
Shampoo (-s) – *nm* shampoo
Sherry (-s) – *nm* sherry
Shorts – *npl* shorts
Show (-s) – *nf* show (variety)
sich – *pron refl* herself, himself,
  oneself,
sicher – *adj* certain, safe
Sicherheit – *nf* safety
Sicherheitsgurt (-e) – *nm* seat belt
sicherlich – *adv* surely
Sicht – *nf, no pl* visibility, sight
  in Sicht – in sight
sichtbar – *adj* visible
sie – *pron nom/acc* she, her, it, they,
  them
Sie – *pron nom/acc sing or pl* you
  (singular or plural polite)

sieben – *adj* seven
siebte – *adj* seventh
siebzehn – *adj* seventeen
siebzig – *adj* seventy
Siedlung (-en) – *nf* housing estate
Sieg (-e) – *nm* victory
siegen – *v reg* win
Sieger (-) – *nm* winner
Siegerin (-nen) – *nf* winner
siegreich – *adj* victorious
sieht – *see sehen*
Signal (-e) – *nnt* signal, tone (on
  phone)
Silber – *nnt* silver
Silbermedaille – *nf* silver medal
silbern – *adj* silver
Silvester – *nnt* New Year's Eve
sind – *see sein**
singen – *v irreg* sing
Singular – *nm* singular (grammar)
  im Singular – in the singular
sinken* – *v irreg* sink
Sinn (-e) – *nm* sense
  Es hat keinen Sinn – There's no
  point
sinnvoll – *adj* sensible
Situation (-en) – *nf* situation
sitzen – *v irreg* sit
sitzen bleiben* – *v irreg* repeat a
  year (at school)
Ski (-er) – *nm* ski
Ski fahren* – *v irreg* go skiing
Skifahren – *nnt* skiing
Skilaufen – *nnt* skiing
Skilift (-s) – *nm* ski lift
Skischuh (-e) – *nm* ski boot
Skistiefel (-) – *nm* ski boot
Skorpion – Scorpio (horoscope)
Slip (-s) – *nm* knickers
die Slowakei – *nf* Slovakia
Snooker – *nnt* snooker
so – so

---

nm - noun masculine   *nf* - noun feminine   *nnt* - noun neuter   *npl* - noun plural
nom- nominative   *acc* - accusative   *gen* - genitive   *dat* - dative

sobald – *sub conj* as soon as
sobald wie möglich – *adv* as soon as possible
so viel – *adv* so much
so viele – so many
so ... wie – *adv* as ... as
  Sie ist so groß wie ich – She is as big as me
Socke (-n) – *nf* sock
Sofa (-s) – *nnt* settee
sofort – *adv* immediately, at once
sofortig – *adj* immediate (instant)
Software – *nf* software
sogar – *adv* even
sogleich – *adv* at once
Sohn (Söhne) – *nm* son
Soja~ – *pref* soya
solche – such
  ein solcher – such a
Soldat (-en) – *nm wk* soldier
solide – *adj* solid
sollen – *v irreg* ought
  Ich sollte es tun – I ought to do it
sollte – *see sollen*
Sommer – *nm* summer
  im Sommer – in summer
Sommerferien – *npl* summer holidays
sommerlich – *adj* summery
Sommerschlussverkauf (-verkäufe) – *nm* summer sales
Sonderangebot (-e) – *nnt* special offer
Sonderpreis (-e) – *nm* special price
Sonnabend (-e) – *nm* Saturday
  am Sonnabend – on Saturday
Sonne (-n) – *nf* sun
sich sonnen – *v reg refl* sunbathe
Sonnenaufgang (-gänge) – *nm* sunrise
Sonnenbrand – *nm* sunburn
Sonnenbrille (-n) – *nf* sun-glasses
Sonnencreme – *nf* sun cream

Sonnenmilch – *nf* sun milk
Sonnenöl – *nnt* sun-tan oil
Sonnenschein – *nm* sunshine
Sonnenschirm (-e) – *nm* sunshade
Sonnenstich – *nm* sun-stroke
Sonnenstrahl (-en) – *nm* sunbeam
Sonnenuntergang (-gänge) – *nm* sunset
sonnig – *adj* sunny
Sonntag – *nm* Sunday
  am Sonntag – on Sunday
  Bis Sonntag! – See you on Sunday!
sonst – *adv* otherwise
Sonst noch etwas? – Anything else?
Sorge (-n) – *nf* worry
sich Sorgen machen über (+ acc) – *v reg dat refl* worry
sorgen für (+ acc) – *v reg* look after
sorgfältig – *adv* carefully
Sorte (-n) – *nf* sort, kind
Soße (-n) – *nf* sauce, gravy
Souvenir (-s) – *nnt* souvenir
so viel – so much
so viel wie möglich – *adv* as much as possible
sowieso – *adv* anyway
sozial – *adj* social
Sozialkunde – *nf* social studies
Sozialwohnung (-en) – *nf* council flat
Spaghetti – *nf* spaghetti
Spanien – *nnt* Spain
Spanier (-) – *nm* Spaniard
Spanierin (-nen) – *nf* Spaniard
spanisch – *adj* Spanish
Spanisch – *nnt* Spanish (language)
spannend – *adj* exciting
Sparbuch (-bücher) – *nnt* savings pass book
sparen für (+ acc) – *v reg* save up for
  Geld sparen – *v reg* save money
Spargel – *nm* asparagus

---

adj - adjective	*v reg* - verb regular	*v sep* - verb separable	† - see verb info
prep - preposition	*v irreg* - verb irregular	*v refl* - verb reflexive	* - takes sein

Sparkasse (-n) – *nf* bank
sparsam – *adj* economical
Sparschwein (-e) – *nnt* piggy bank
Spaß (Späße) – *nm* fun
   Es macht (mir) Spaß – It's fun
Spaß haben – *v irreg* to have fun
   Viel Spaß! – *excl* Have a good time!
spät – *adj* late
   Wie spät ist es? – What time is it?
Spaten (-) – *nm* spade
später – *adj* later
   Bis später! – See you later!
spazieren gehen* – *v irreg* go for a walk
   mit dem Hund spazieren gehen* – *v irreg* take the dog for a walk
Spaziergang (-gänge) – *nm* walk (stroll)
   einen Spaziergang machen – *v reg* go for a walk
Speck – *nm* bacon
Speicher (-) – *nm* memory (computer); attic
speichern – *v reg* save (computer)
Speisekarte (-n) – *nf* menu
Speisesaal (-säle) – *nm* dining hall
Speisewagen (-) – *nm* dining car
Sperre (-n) – *nf* barrier
Spezialität (-en) – *nf* speciality
Spiegel (-) – *nm* mirror
Spiegelei (-er) – *nnt* fried egg
Spiel (-e) – *nnt* game, match; pack of cards
   ein Spiel verlieren – *v irreg* lose a match
Spielautomat (-en) – *nm wk* fruit machine
spielen – *v reg* play, act (drama)
   Fußball spielen – *v reg* play football

Gitarre spielen – *v reg* play the guitar
Spieler (-) – *nm* player
Spielerin (-nen) – *nf* player
Spielfilm (-e) – *nm* feature film
Spielhalle (-n) – *nf* amusement arcade
Spielkarte (-n) – *nf* playing card
Spielplatz (-plätze) – *nm* playground
Spielraum (-räume) – *nm* games room
Spielwaren – *npl* toys
Spielwarengeschäft (-e) – *nnt* toy shop
Spielzeug (-e) – *nnt* toy
Spinat – *nm* spinach
Spinne (-n) – *nf* spider
Spion (-e) – *nm* spy
Spionage – *nf* spying
Spionagefilm (-e) – *nm* spy film
Spionagegeschichte (-n) – *nf* spy story
Spionin (-nen) – *nf* spy
Spirituosen – *npl* spirits (alcohol)
spitz – *adj* pointed
spitze – *adj inv coll* excellent
Spitzenpolitiker (-) – *nm* top politician
Spitzname (-n) – *nm wk* nickname
Sport (Sportarten) – *nm* PE, games, sport
Sport treiben – *v irreg* do games
   gern Sport treiben – *v irreg* be keen on sport
Sportart (-en) – *nf* type of sport
sportlich – *adj* athletic
Sportmöglichkeit (-en) – *nf* sporting facility
Sportplatz (-plätze) – *nm* sports ground
Sportverein (-e) – *nm* sports club
Sportwagen (-) – *nm* sports car; push chair

Sportzentrum (-zentren) – *nnt* sports centre

sprach – *see sprechen*

Sprache (-n) – *nf* language

Sprachlabor (-s) – *nnt* language laboratory

sprachlos – *adj* speechless

sprechen (mit + dat) – *v irreg* speak (to)

   Deutsch sprechen – *v irreg* speak German

   jdm sprechen – *v irreg* speak to s.o.

   laut sprechen – *v irreg* speak loudly

Sprechstunde (-n) – *nf* surgery (time)

spricht – *see sprechen*

springen* – *v irreg* jump

   Trampolin springen* – *v irreg* trampoline

Spritze (-n) – *nf* injection

spritzen – *v reg* spray; inject

Sprudel (-) – *nm* sparkling water

sprudelnd – *adj* fizzy

Sprühdose (-n) – *nf* aerosol

Sprungbrett (-er) – *nnt* springboard

Spülbecken (-) – *nnt* sink

spülen – *v reg* do washing up

Spülmaschine (-n) – *nf* dishwasher

Spülmittel (-) – *nnt* washing up liquid

Squash – *nnt* squash (sport)

Stöpsel (-) – *nm* plug (bath)

Staat (-en) – *nm* state (nation)

Staatsangehörigkeit (-en) – *nf* nationality

Staatsexamen (-) – *nnt* degree (university exam)

Stachelbeere (-n) – *nf* gooseberry

Stadion (Stadien) – *nnt* stadium

Stadt (Städte) – *nf* town

   in der Stadt – in town

Sam fährt in die Stadt – Sam goes into town

Stadtbummel – *nm* stroll around town

   einen Stadtbummel machen – *v reg* go round town

Stadtführung (-en) – *nf* guided tour of town

städtisch – *adj* urban, municipal

Stadtmitte (-n) – *nf* town centre

   in der Stadtmitte – in the town centre

Stadtplan (-pläne) – *nm* town plan

Stadtrand (-ränder) – *nm* edge of town, outskirts

   am Stadtrand – on the edge of town

Stadtrundfahrt (-en) – *nf* tour of town (coach, boat, etc)

Stadtteil (-e) – *nm* part of town

Stadtviertel (-) – *nnt* district of city

Stadtzentrum (-zentren) – *nnt* town centre

stahl – *see stehlen*

stammeln – *v reg* stutter

Stammtisch (-e) – *nm* table reserved for regular customers

stand – *see stehen*

Stand (Stände) – *nm* stall

Star (-s) – *nm* celebrity

starb – *see sterben**

stark – *adj* strong

   Es regnet stark – It's raining heavily

   stark gebaut – *adj* well-built (person)

Startbahn (-en) – *nf* runway

starten* – *v reg* † take off (aircraft)

Station (-en) – *nf* station (underground)

statt – *conj* instead of

statt (+ gen) – *prep* instead of

stattfinden – *v irreg sep* take place

---

adj - adjective	*v reg* - verb regular	*v sep* - verb separable	† - see verb info
prep - preposition	*v irreg* - verb irregular	*v refl* - verb reflexive	* - takes sein

Stau (-s) – *nm* traffic jam

Staub – *nm* dust

staubsaugen – *v reg* vacuum

Staubsauger (-) – *nm* vacuum
cleaner

Steak (-s) – *nnt* steak

stechen – *v irreg* sting

Stechpalme (-n) – *nf* holly

Steckdose (-n) – *nf* socket, power
point

stecken – *v reg* put, place (insert)

Stecker (-) – *nm* plug (electric)

stehen (*) – *v irreg* stand (on feet)

stehen – *v irreg* suit
    Es steht mir – It suits me

Stehlampe (-n) – *nf* standard lamp

stehlen – *v irreg* steal

steif – *adj* stiff

steigen* – *v irreg* climb

steil – *adj* steep (hill)

Stein (-e) – *nm* stone

Steinbock – Capricorn (horoscope)

Steinbruch (-brüche) – *nm* quarry

Stelle (-n) – *nf* place, job; passage
(in book)

stellen – *v reg* place (vertical)
    den Wecker stellen – *v reg* set
    the alarm
    eine Frage stellen – *v reg* ask a
    question

Stellenangebot (-e) – *nnt* job offer

Stenographie – *nf* shorthand

Stenotypist (-en) – *nm wk* typist

Stenotypistin (-nen) – *nf* typist

Steppdecke (-n) – *nf* duvet, quilt

Steppdeckenbezug (-bezüge) –
nm duvet cover

sterben* – *v irreg* die

Stereoanlage (-n) – *nf* stereo, Hi-Fi
system

Stern (-e) – *nm* star (sky)

Steuer (-n) – *nf* tax

Steuerberater (-) – *nm* accountant

Steuerberaterin (-nen) – *nf*
accountant

Steward (-s) – *nm* steward

Stewardess (-en) – *nf* air hostess,
stewardess

Stich (-e) – *nm* bite, sting (insect)

Stiefbruder (-brüder) – *nm*
stepbrother

Stiefel (-) – *nm* boot (shoe)

Stiefmutter (-mütter) – *nf*
stepmother

Stiefschwester (-n) – *nf* stepsister

Stiefsohn (-söhne) – *nm* stepson

Stieftochter (-töchter) – *nf*
stepdaughter

Stiefvater (-väter) – *nm* stepfather

Stier (-e) – *nm* bull; Taurus
(horoscope)

Stift (-e) – *nm* pen

Stil (-e) – *nm* style

still – *adj* still, quiet, peaceful

Stille (-n) – *nf* silence

stillstehen – *v irreg sep* stand still

Stimme (-n) – *nf* voice

stimmen – *v reg* tune (instrument)
    Das stimmt – That's right
    Das stimmt so – Keep the change

stinken – *v irreg* smell (stink)

stinkig – *adj* smelly

Stock (Stöcke) – *nm* stick

Stock (Stockwerke) – *nm* floor
    im ersten Stock – on the first
    floor
    im nächsten Stock – on the next
    floor
    im obersten Stock – on the top
    floor

Stockung (-en) – *nf* blockage

Stockwerk (-e) – *nnt* storey

Stoff (-e) – *nm* cloth

stöhnen – *v reg* moan

stolz (auf + acc) – *adj* proud (of)

stören – *v reg* bother, disturb
Stoßstange (-n) – *nf* bumper
Str. (Straße) – St. (Street), Rd.
Strafe (-n) – *nf* punishment
Straftat (-en) – *nf* offence
Strafzettel (-) – *nm* parking ticket
Strand (Strände) – *nm* beach
    am Strand – on the beach
Strandbad (-bäder) – *nnt* bathing beach
Strandburg (-en) – *nf* windbreak
Strandkorb (-körbe) – *nm* wicker beach seat
Straßburg – Strasbourg
Straße (-n) – *nf* street, road
    auf der Straße – in the street
Straßenbahn (-en) – *nf* tram
Straßenkarte (-n) – *nf* road map
Straßenschild (-er) – *nnt* road sign
Straßenverkehrsordnung (StVO) – *nf* highway code
Strauch (Sträuche) – *nm* bush
Streber (-) – *nm coll* swot
Streberin (-nen) – *nf coll* swot
streichen – *v irreg* cancel; cross out
streichen – *v irreg* decorate (paint)
Streichholz (-hölzer) – *nnt* match
Streichholzschachtel (-n) – *nf* matchbox
Streichinstrument (-e) – *nnt* stringed instrument (with bow)
Streichorchester (-) – *nnt* string orchestra
Streifenkarte (-n) – *nf* book of tickets
Streik (-s) – *nm* strike (walk-out)
streiken – *v reg* go on strike
Streikende – *nmf* ‡ striker (on strike)
Streit (-e) – *nm* row (argument)
sich streiten – *v irreg refl* argue, quarrel
Streitkräfte – *npl* armed forces

streng – *adj* strict, harsh
Stress – *nm* stress
stressig – *adj coll* stressful
stricken – *v reg* knit
Strickjacke (-n) – *nf* cardigan
Strohdach (-dächer) – *nnt* thatched roof
Strohhalm (-e) – *nm* drinking straw
Strom – *nm* current (electricity)
Strumpf (Strümpfe) – *nm* stocking
Strumpfhose (-n) – *nf* pair of tights
Stube (-n) – *nf* room
Stück (-) – *nnt* piece (of), coin
    ein Stück Schokolade – a piece of chocolate
    ein Zweimarkstück – a 2 DM coin
Student (-en) – *nm wk* student
Studentin (-nen) – *nf* student
studieren – *v reg* † study (at university)
Studio (-s) – *nnt* studio (TV)
Studium (Studien) – *nnt* studies
Stufe (-n) – *nf* step (on stairs)
    Vorsicht Stufe! – *excl* Mind the step!
Stuhl (Stühle) – *nm* chair
stumm – *adj* dumb
stumpf – *adj* dull, blunt
stumpfsinnig – *adj* apathetic, tedious
Stunde (-n) – *nf* hour, lesson
    eine halbe Stunde – half an hour
    pro Stunde – per hour
stundenlang – *adv* for hours on end
Stundenplan (-pläne) – *nm* timetable (school)
stündlich – *adj* hourly
stur – *adj* stubborn, obstinate
Sturm (Stürme) – *nm* storm, gale
Stürmer (-) – *nm* striker, forward (football)
stürmisch – *adj* stormy

---

adj - adjective	*v reg* - verb regular	*v sep* - verb separable	† - see verb info
prep - preposition	*v irreg* - verb irregular	*v refl* - verb reflexive	* - takes sein

Sturzhelm (-e) – *nm* crash helmet
StVO – *nf* highway code
Substantiv (-e) – *nnt* noun
suchen – *v reg* hunt for, look for
Südafrika – *nnt* South Africa
Südamerika – *nnt* South America
Süden – *nm* south
  im Süden – in the south
  in Süddeutschland – in South
  Germany
südlich – *adj* southern
südlich von (+ dat) – *prep* south of
super – *adj inv* super
Super bleifrei – *nm* super unleaded
  petrol
Super verbleit – *nnt* 4-star leaded
  petrol

Supermarkt (-märkte) – *nm*
  supermarket
Suppe (-n) – *nf* soup
Surfbrett (-er) – *nnt* surfboard,
  sailboard
Surfen (-) – *nnt* surfing
  das Internet surfen – *v reg* surf
  the net
süß – *adj* sweet (tasting)
Süßigkeit (-en) – *nf* sweet
Sweatshirt (-s) – *nnt* sweatshirt
sympathisch – *adj* likeable
Synagoge (-n) – *nf* synagogue
Synchronisierung – *nf* dubbing
System (-e) – *nnt* system
Szene (-n) – *nf* scene (play)

T

T-Shirt (-s) – *nnt* T-shirt
Tabak – *nm* tobacco
Tabakhändler (-) – *nm* tobacconist
Tabakhändlerin (-nen) – *nf*
  tobacconist
Tabakhandlung (-en) – *nf*
  tobacconist's shop
Tablett (-s) – *nnt* tray
Tablette (-n) – *nf* tablet
Tafel (-n) – *nf* blackboard, bar of
  chocolate
Tafelwein (-e) – *nm* table wine
Tag (-e) – *nm* day
  am nächsten Tag – next day
  am Tag – by day
  den ganzen Tag – all day long
  Einen schönen Tag! – *excl* Have
  a nice day!
  eines Tages – some day
  Guten Tag! – *excl* Hello! Good
  afternoon!

  jeden Tag – every day
  pro Tag – per day
  der Tag der Deutschen
  Einheit – *nm* German Unity Day
  (3rd October)
  vierzehn Tage – fortnight
  vor ein paar Tagen – the other
  day, a few days ago
Tage – *npl* period (menstrual)
  Ich habe meine Tage – I've got
  my period
Tagebuch (-bücher) – *nnt* diary
  (reminiscences)
Tagesablauf – *nm* daily routine
Tagesgericht (-e) – *nnt* dish of the
  day
Tageskarte (-n) – *nf* menu of the day
Tageslichtprojektor (-en) – *nm*
  overhead projector
Tagesmutter (-mütter) – *nf* child-
  minder

---

nm - noun masculine	*nf* - noun feminine	*nnt* - noun neuter	*npl* - noun plural
nom- nominative	*acc* - accusative	*gen* - genitive	*dat* - dative

Tagesrückfahrkarte (-n) – *nf* day return
Tagesschüler (-) – *nm* day boy
Tagesschülerin (-nen) – *nf* day girl
Tageszeitung (-en) – *nf* daily paper
täglich – *adj* daily
  im täglichen Leben – in daily life
tagsüber – by day
Taille (-n) – *nf* waist(line)
taktlos – *adj* tactless
taktvoll – *adj* tactful
Tal (Täler) – *nnt* valley
talentiert – *adj* talented
Tampon (-s) – *nm* tampon
tanken – *v reg* fill up with petrol
Tankstelle (-n) – *nf* petrol station
Tankstellenbesitzer (-) – *nm* garage owner
Tankwart (-e) – *nm* petrol-pump attendant
Tannenbaum (-bäume) – *nm* fir tree
Tante (-n) – *nf* aunt
Tanz~ – *pref* dance
Tanz (Tänze) – *nm* dance
tanzen – *v reg* dance
Tänzer (-) – *nm* dancer
Tänzerin (-nen) – *nf* dancer
Tapete (-n) – *nf* wallpaper
tapezieren – *v reg* † wallpaper
tapfer – *adj* brave
Tarif (-e) – *nm* charge, rate, fare
Tasche (-n) – *nf* bag, pocket
Taschenbuch (-bücher) – *nnt* paperback
Taschendieb (-e) – *nm* pickpocket
Taschengeld – *nnt* pocket money
Taschenlampe (-n) – *nf* torch
Taschenmesser (-) – *nnt* penknife
Taschenrechner (-) – *nm* calculator
Taschentuch (-tücher) – *nnt* handkerchief

Tasse (-n) – *nf* cup
  eine Tasse Tee – cup of tea
Tastatur (-en) – *nf* keyboard (IT)
Taste (-n) – *nf* key (keyboard)
Tat (-en) – *nf* action (deed)
  in der Tat – *adv* in fact
tat – *see tun*
Tätigkeit (-en) – *nf* activity
Tatort (-e) – *nm* scene (crime)
Tatsache (-n) – *nf* fact
tatsächlich – *adv* in fact
taub – *adj* deaf
taubstumm – *adj* deaf and dumb
tauchen* – *v reg* dive
Taufe (-n) – *nf* christening
tauschen – *v reg* swap
täuschen – *v reg* deceive
tausend – *adj* thousand
Tausende von (+ dat) – thousands of
Taxi (-s) – *nnt* taxi
Taxifahrer (-) – *nm* taxi driver
Taxifahrerin (-nen) – *nf* taxi driver
Taxistand (-stände) – *nm* taxi rank
Technik – *nf* technology
Techniker (-) – *nm* technician
Technikerin (-nen) – *nf* technician
technisch – *adj* technical
technisches Zeichnen – *nnt* engineering drawing
Technologie (-n) – *nf* technology
Teddybär (-en) – *nm wk* teddy bear
Tee – *nm* tea
Teebeutel (-) – *nm* teabag
Teekanne (-n) – *nf* teapot
Teetasse (-n) – *nf* tea cup
TEE-Zug (-Züge) – *nm* Trans-European express train
Teich (-e) – *nm* pond
Teig (-e) – *nm* pastry
Teil (-e) – *nm* part

---

adj - adjective   *v reg* - verb regular   *v sep* - verb separable   † - see verb info
prep - preposition   *v irreg* - verb irregular   *v refl* - verb reflexive   * - takes sein

teilen – *v reg* share, separate
teilnehmen an (+ dat) – *v irreg sep* take part in
am Austausch teilnehmen – *v irreg sep* go on an exchange
Teilnehmer (-) – *nm* competitor
Teilnehmerin (-nen) – *nf* competitor
Teilzeit~ – *pref* part-time
Teilzeitarbeit (-en) – *nf* part-time work
Telefon (-e) – *nnt* phone
am Telefon – on the phone
Telefonbuch (-bücher) – *nnt* telephone directory
telefonieren mit (+ dat) – *v reg* † telephone s.o.
telefonisch – *adv* by phone
Telefonkabine (-n) – *nf* phone box
Telefonkarte (-n) – *nf* phone card
Telefonnummer (-n) – *nf* phone number
Telefonzelle (-n) – *nf* phone box
Telegramm (-e) – *nnt* telegram
Teller (-) – *nm* plate
Temperatur (-en) – *nf* temperature
Tendenz (-en) – *nf* trend
Tennis – *nnt* tennis
Tennisball (-bälle) – *nm* tennis ball
Tennisplatz (-plätze) – *nm* tennis court
Tennisschläger (-) – *nm* tennis racket
Tennisschuh (-e) – *nm* tennis shoe
Tennisspiel (-e) – *nnt* game of tennis
Teppich (-e) – *nm* carpet, rug
Teppichboden (-böden) – *nm* fitted carpet
Termin (-e) – *nm* appointment
einen Termin ausmachen – *v reg sep* make an appointment
Terrasse (-n) – *nf* terrace, patio
Tesafilm® – *nm* sellotape®

Test (-s) – *nm* test
Testbogen (-bögen) – *nm* paper (exam)
teuer – *adj* expensive
Textverarbeitung – *nf* word processing
Textverarbeitungsprogramm (-e) – *nnt* word processing program
Theater – *nnt* theatre; *coll* fuss
Theater machen über (+ acc) – *v reg coll* make a fuss about sthg
Theaterkunde – *nf* performing arts (school)
Theaterstück (-e) – *nnt* play
Thema (Themen) – *nnt* topic
Themse – *nf* River Thames
Thermometer (-) – *nnt* thermometer
Thunfisch (-e) – *nm* tuna
Ticket (-s) – *nnt* ticket (plane)
tief – *adj* deep, low
tiefgefroren – *adj* deep frozen
Tiefkühltruhe (-n) – *nf* deep freeze
Tiefseetauchen – *nnt* scuba diving
Tiefsttemperatur (-en) – *nf* minimum temperature
bei Tiefwasser – at low tide
Tier (-e) – *nnt* animal
Tierarzt (-ärzte) – *nm* vet
Tierärztin (-nen) – *nf* vet
Tiergarten (-gärten) – *nm* zoo
Tiger (-) – *nm* tiger
Tinte (-n) – *nf* ink
Tintenfisch (-e) – *nm* squid; octopus; cuttlefish
Tintenlöscher (-) – *nm* ink eraser pen
Tintenstrahldrucker (-) – *nm* ink jet printer
Tipp (-s) – *nm* tip (hint)
tippen – *v reg* type
Tisch (-e) – *nm* table
den Tisch decken – *v reg* set the table

---

den Tisch verlassen – *v irreg*
leave the table
zu Tisch kommen* – *v irreg* sit
down at table
Tischdecke (-n) – *nf* table-cloth
Tischtennis – *nnt* table tennis
Titel (-) – *nm* title, heading
Toast – *nm* toast (bread)
Tochter (Töchter) – *nf* daughter
Tod (-e) – *nm* death
Toilette (-n) – *nf* toilet
Toilettenpapier – *nnt* toilet paper
Toilettentisch (-e) – *nm* dressing
table
tolerieren – *v reg* † tolerate
toll – *adj* great; mad
Tollwut – *nf* rabies
Tomate (-n) – *nf* tomato
Tomatensalat – *nm* salad (tomato)
Ton (Töne) – *nm* tone
Tonband (-bänder) – *nnt* tape
Tonbandgerät (-e) – *nnt* tape
recorder
Tonne (-n) – *nf* ton
Topf (Töpfe) – *nm* saucepan
Töpferei (-en) – *nf* pottery (workshop)
Topfpflanze (-n) – *nf* pot plant
Tor (-e) – *nnt* gate, goal (sport)
ein Tor schießen – *v irreg* score a
goal
Torpfosten (-) – *nm* goalpost
Torte (-n) – *nf* flan
Torwart (-e) – *nm* goalkeeper
tot – *adj* dead
total – *adv* totally
töten – *v reg* † kill
Toto – *nnt* National Lottery
Tour (-en) – *nf* tour
Tourismus – *nm* tourism
Tourist (-en) – *nm wk* tourist
Touristenstadt (-städte) – *nf*
tourist centre

Touristin (-nen) – *nf* tourist
Tournier (-e) – *nnt* tournament
Tradition (-en) – *nf* tradition
Tracht (-en) – *nf* national costume
traditionell – *adj* traditional
tragen – *v irreg* carry, wear
Tragflügelboot (-e) – *nnt* hydrofoil
Trainer (-) – *nm* trainer (person)
trainieren – *v reg* † train (sport)
Trainingsanzug (-anzüge) – *nm*
tracksuit
Trainingsschuhe – *npl* trainers
Traktor (-en) – *nm* tractor
Trampolin (-e) – *nnt* trampoline
trank – *see trinken*
Transportmittel (-) – *nnt* transport
Traube (-n) – *nf* grapes
Traubensaft (-säfte) – *nm* grape juice
trauen – *v reg* trust
Traum (Träume) – *nm* dream
träumen – *v reg* dream
traurig – *adj* sad
Traurigkeit – *nf* sadness
Treffen (-) – *nnt* meeting
treffen – *v irreg* meet; hit target
sich treffen – *v irreg refl* meet (by
arrangement)
treiben – *v irreg* do (sport)
gern Sport treiben – *v irreg* be
keen on sport
Treibhauseffekt – *nm* greenhouse
effect
Trend (-s) – *nm* trend
trennbares Verb – *nnt* separable
verb
trennen – *v reg* separate
sich trennen – *v reg refl* separate (by
agreement)
Trennung (-en) – *nf* separation
Treppe (-n) – *nf* flight of stairs
**Er ist die Treppe
hinaufgelaufen** – He ran up the
stairs

adj - adjective	*v reg* - verb regular	*v sep* - verb separable	† - see verb info
prep - preposition	*v irreg* - verb irregular	*v refl* - verb reflexive	* - takes sein

Treppenflur (-e) – *nm* landing (house)

Tresor (-e) – *nnt* safe

treten – *v irreg* kick (ball, etc)

treten* – step, tread

in den Ruhestand treten* – *v irreg* retire

Trickfilm (-e) – *nm* cartoon film

Trimester (-) – *nnt* term (school)

trimmen – *v reg* keep fit

trinkbar – *adj* drinkable

trinken – *v irreg* drink

Trinkgeld (-er) – *nnt* tip (money)

Trinkwasser – *nnt* drinking water

kein Trinkwasser – non-drinking water

trocken – *adj* dry

Trockenreinigung (-en) – *nf* dry cleaner's

trocknen – *v reg* † dry

sich die Haare trocknen – *v reg dat refl* † dry one's hair

Trompete (-n) – *nf* trumpet

trotz (+ gen) – *prep* in spite of

trotzdem – *adv* nevertheless

trug – *see tragen*

Truthahn (-hähne) – *nm* turkey

die Tschechische Republik – *nf* the Czech Republic

Tschüs! – *excl coll* Goodbye!

T-Shirt (-s) – *nnt* T-shirt

Tube (-n) – *nf* tube (toothpaste, etc)

Tuch (Tücher) – *nnt* scarf (square)

Tulpe (-n) – *nf* tulip

tun – *v irreg* do

tun so, als ob – *v irreg* pretend

Tunnel (-) – *nm* tunnel

Tür (-en) – *nf* door

an die Tür klopfen – knock on the door

Türke (-n) – *nm wk* Turk

die Türkei – *nf* Turkey

Türkin (-nen) – *nf* Turk

türkis – *adj inv* turquoise

türkisch – *adj* Turkish

Turm (Türme) – *nm* tower

Turnen – *nnt* gym(nastics)

turnen – *v reg* do gymnastics

Turnhalle (-n) – *nf* gym(nasium)

Turnschuh (-e) – *nm* trainer (shoe)

tut – *see tun*

Tütchen (-) – *nnt* cornet (ice cream)

Tüte (-n) – *nf* bag (paper, plastic)

TÜV – *nm* MOT; technical approval agency

Typ (-en) – *nm* type, bloke

typisch – *adj* typical

U

U-Bahn (-en) – *nf* underground

U-Bahnfahrkarte (-n) – *nf* underground ticket

U-Bahnstation (-en) – *nf* underground station

übel – *adj* bad

Mir ist übel – I feel sick

sich übel fühlen – *v reg refl* feel sick

üben – *v reg* practise

über (+ acc/dat) – *prep* above, over, across, about

Überdosis – *nf* overdose

Überfahrt (-en) – *nf* crossing (channel)

überall – *adv* everywhere

übereinstimmen mit (+ dat) – *v reg sep* agree with

überfahren – *v irreg insep* run over (accident)

Überfall (-fälle) – *nm* holdup (robbery)

überfallen – *v irreg insep* attack, mug

Übergang (-gänge) – *nm* crossing

sich übergeben – *v irreg refl insep* vomit

überhaupt – *adv* at all

überhaupt nicht – *adv* not at all

überholen – *v reg insep* overtake

überlegen – *adj* superior

sich etwas anders überlegen – *v reg dat refl insep* change one's mind

Ich habe mir das anders überlegt – I've changed my mind

übermorgen – *adv* day after tomorrow

übernachten – *v reg insep* † stay the night

in einem Hotel übernachten – *v reg insep* † stay at a hotel

Übernachtung (-en) – *nf* overnight stay

überqueren – *v reg insep* go across

überraschen – *v reg insep* surprise

überraschend – *adj* surprising

überrascht – *adj* surprised

Überraschung (-en) – *nf* surprise

überreden – *v reg insep* † persuade

sich überschlagen – *v irreg refl insep* overturn (car)

Überschrift (-en) – *nf* title (homework)

Überschwemmung (-en) – *nf* flood

Übersee~ – *pref* overseas

übersetzen – *v reg insep* translate (in writing)

Übersetzung (-en) – *nf* translation

überwachen – *v reg insep* supervise

überzeugt – *adj* convinced

übrig – *adv* over (left)

übrig bleiben* – *v irreg* remain (left over)

übrigens – by the way

Übung (-en) – *nf* practice

Übung macht den Meister – practice makes perfect

Ufer (-) – *nnt* bank (river)

Uhr (-en) – *nf* clock, time

Meine Uhr geht vor/nach – My watch is fast/slow

um sechs Uhr – at six o'clock

um wie viel Uhr? – at what time?

Uhrzeit (-en) – *nf* time

um (+ acc) – *prep* around, about, at (time)

um ... zu – *conj* in order to

um ... herum (+ acc) – *prep* round about

sich umdrehen – *v reg refl sep* turn round

Umfrage (-n) – *nf* survey

umgangssprachlich – *adj* colloquial

umgeben von (+ dat) – *adj* surrounded by

Umgebung (-en) – *nf* area (surrounding)

Umgehungstraße (-n) – *nf* bypass

umkippen* – *v reg sep* overturn (boat)

Umkleidekabine (-n) – *nf* fitting room

Umkleideraum (-räume) – *nm* changing-room (sport)

Umleitung (-en) – *nf* diversion

Umschlag (Umschläge) – *nm* envelope

sich umsehen – *v irreg refl sep* look round

umsonst – *adv* free; in vain

umsteigen* – *v irreg sep* change (trains)

Umtausch (-e) – *nm* exchange

umtauschen – *v reg sep* change (exchange)

Umwelt – *nf* environment

---

adj - adjective	*v reg* - verb regular	*v sep* - verb separable	† - see verb info
prep - preposition	*v irreg* - verb irregular	*v refl* - verb reflexive	* - takes sein

umweltbelastend – *adj* environmentally undesirable

umweltbewusst – *adj* environmentally aware

umweltfeindlich – *adj* environmentally damaging

umweltfreundlich – *adj* environmentally friendly

umweltschonend – *adj* environmentally friendly

Umweltschmutz – *nm* pollution

Umweltschutz – *nm* protection of the environment

umziehen* – *v irreg sep* move house

sich umziehen – *v irreg refl sep* get changed

un~ – *pref* un~

unangenehm – *adj* unpleasant

unartig – *adj* naughty

unbedingt – *adv* absolutely

unbedingt notwendig – *adj* vital

unbekannt – *adj* unknown

unbequem – *adj* uncomfortable

und – *co-ord conj* and

undankbar – *adj* ungrateful

unehrlich – *adj* untruthful

unentbehrlich – *adj* essential

unentschieden – *adj* drawn (score)

unentschieden spielen – *v reg* draw (match)

unerträglich – *adj* unbearable

unerwartet – *adj* unexpected

unfair – *adj* unfair

Unfall (Unfälle) – *nm* accident

Unfallstation (-en) – *nf* emergency department (hospital)

unfit – *adj inv* unfit

unfreundlich – *adj* unfriendly, nasty

Ungarn – *nnt* Hungary

ungarisch – *adj* Hungarian

Ungeduld – *nf* impatience

ungeduldig – *adj* impatient

ungefähr – *adv* approximately

Ungeheuer (-) – *nnt* monster

ungenau – *adj* vague

ungerade – odd (number)

ungerecht – *adj* unjust

ungern – *adv* reluctantly

ungeschickt – *adj* awkward (clumsy)

ungewiss – *adj* uncertain

ungewöhnlich – *adj* unusual

ungewohnt – *adj* unaccustomed

ungezogen – *adj* rude (very)

unglaublich – *adj* incredible

ungleich – *adj* uneven

Unglück – *nnt* accident, misfortune

unglücklich – *adj* unhappy, unlucky

unglücklicherweise – *adv* unfortunately

ungünstig – *adj* unfavourable

unhöflich – *adj* rude (impolite)

uni – *adj inv* plain (no pattern)

Uni (-s) – *nf coll* university

Uniform (-en) – *nf* uniform

Union – *nf* union

die Europäische Union – *nf* the European Union

Universal~ – *pref* universal

Universität (-en) – *nf* university

Universum (Universen) – *nnt* universe

Unkraut – *nnt, no pl* weeds

unmöglich – *adj* impossible

Unmöglichkeit (-en) – *nf* impossibility

unnötig – *adj* unnecessary

unordentlich – *adj* untidy

unpraktisch – *adj* impractical

Unrecht haben – *v irreg* be wrong

Ich habe Unrecht – I am wrong

uns – *pron refl* ourselves

uns – *pers pron acc/dat* us

unser – *poss adj* our

Unsinn – *nm* nonsense, rubbish

unten – *adv* downstairs, down

nach unten gehen* – *v irreg* go
downstairs
weiter unten – *adv* lower down
unter (+ acc/dat) – *prep* under,
below; among
unter Freunden – among friends
unter~ – *pref* sub~
unterbringen – *v irreg sep* put up
(guest)
Unterführung (-en) – *nf* subway
(under road)
Untergeschoss (-e) – *nnt* basement
unterhalb von (+ dat) – *prep*
beneath
sich unterhalten mit (+ dat) –
v irreg refl insep talk to s.o.
Unterhaltung (-en) – *nf*
entertainment
Unterhemd (-er) – *nnt* vest
Unterhose (-n) – *nf* underpants (pair
of)
Unterkunft – *nf* accommodation
Untermieter (-) – *nm* lodger
Untermieterin (-nen) – *nf* lodger
Unternehmen (-) – *nnt* firm,
company
unternehmen – *v irreg insep*
undertake
Unternehmer (-) – *nm* entrepreneur
Unternehmerin (-nen) – *nf*
entrepreneur
Unterricht – *nm* teaching (lesson)
unterrichten – *v reg insep* † teach
Unterschied (-e) – *nm* difference
unterschiedlich – *adj* different
(varied)
unterschreiben – *v irreg insep* sign
Unterschrift (-en) – *nf* signature

untersetzt – *adj* stocky
unterstreichen – *v irreg insep*
underline
unterstützen – *v reg insep* support
untersuchen – *v reg insep*
investigate, examine (medical)
Untersuchung (-en) – *nf*
examination (medical)
Untertasse (-n) – *nf* saucer
mit Untertiteln – subtitled
Unterwäsche – *nf, no pl* underwear
unterwegs – *adv* on the way
ununterbrochen – *adj* uninterrupted
unvergesslich – *adj* unforgettable
unverheiratet – *adj* unmarried
unverletzt – *adj* unhurt
unvermeidlich – *adj* unavoidable
unwichtig – *adj* unimportant
unwohl – *adj* unwell
Mir ist unwohl – I am unwell
unzufrieden – *adj* dissatisfied
Urgroßmutter (-mütter) – *nf*
great-grandmother
Urgroßvater (-väter) – *nm* great-
grandfather
Urlaub – *nm* holiday
auf Urlaub – on holiday
in Urlaub fahren* – *v irreg* go
on holiday
Ich habe Urlaub–I'm on holiday
Urlauber (-) – *nm* holiday maker
Urlauberin (-nen) – *nf* holiday
maker
Urlaubspläne – *npl* holiday plans
Ursache (-n) – *nf* cause
USA – *npl* USA
usw. (und so weiter) – etc

---

adj - adjective   *v reg* - verb regular   *v sep* - verb separable   † - see verb info
prep - preposition   *v irreg* - verb irregular   *v refl* - verb reflexive   * - takes sein

V

Vanille – *nf* vanilla
Vanilleeis – *nnt, no pl* vanilla ice cream
Vanillesoße – *nf* custard
Vase (-n) – *nf* flower vase
Vater (Väter) – *nm* father, dad(dy)
Vati – *nm* daddy
vegan – *adj* vegan
Veganer (-) – *nm* vegan
Veganerin (-nen) – *nf* vegan
Vegetarier (-) – *nm* vegetarian
Vegetarierin (-nen) – *nf* vegetarian
vegetarisch – *adj* vegetarian
sich verabschieden – *v reg refl* † say goodbye to s.o.
veränderlich – *adj* changeable
veranstalten – *v reg* † organise (event)
verantwortlich – *adj* responsible
Verantwortung – *nf* responsibility
veräppeln – *v reg* † *coll* make fun of, play a trick on
Verb (-en) – *nnt* verb
ein trennbares Verb – *nnt* separable verb
Verband (-bände) – *nm* bandage, dressing
Verbandkasten (-kästen) – *nm* first aid kit
verbessern – *v reg* † correct, improve
Verbesserungen – *npl* corrections
verbieten – *v irreg* forbid
verbinden – *v irreg* join (together)
Verbindung (-en) – *nf* connection
verbleit – *adj* leaded
verblüfft – *adj* dumbfounded
verboten – *adj* forbidden
  Parken verboten – no parking
  Rauchen verboten – no smoking
verbracht – *see verbringen*
verbrachte – *see verbringen*

Verbrechen(-) – *nnt* crime, offence
ein Verbrechen begehen – *v irreg* commit an offence
Verbrecher (-) – *nm* criminal
Verbrecherin (-nen) – *nf* criminal
sich verbrennen – *v irreg refl* burn o.s.
verbringen – *v irreg* spend (time)
Verbum (Verben) – *nnt* verb
verbunden – *adj* connected
falsch verbunden – wrong number (phone)
Verdacht – *nm* suspicion
verdächtigen – *v reg* † suspect
Verdammt! – *excl* Blast!
jdm etwas verdanken – *v reg* † owe s.o. sthg (eg thanks)
verdienen – *v reg* † earn, deserve
(sich) seinen Lebensunterhalt verdienen – *v reg (dat refl)* † earn one's living
verdrießlich – *adj* grumpy
Verein (-e) – *nm* club
wie vereinbart – *adj* as agreed
vereinigen – *v reg* † unify
das Vereinigte Königreich – *nnt* UK
die Vereinigten Staaten – *npl* USA
Vereinigung – *nf* unification
vereist – *adj* icy (road)
verekelt – *adj* disgusted
verfügbar – *adj* available
zur Verfügung haben – *v irreg* to have at one's disposal
sich verfahren – *v irreg refl* lose one's way (by car, etc)
verfaulen* – *v reg* † go bad (food)
Verflucht! – *excl* Blow!
vergangen – *adj* previous
Vergangenheit (-en) – *nf* past tense
vergaß – *see vergessen*

---

nm - noun masculine   *nf* - noun feminine   *nnt* - noun neuter   *npl* - noun plural
nom - nominative   *acc* - accusative   *gen* - genitive   *dat* - dative

vergeben – *v irreg* forgive
vergebens – *adv* in vain
vergessen – *v irreg* forget
vergisst – *see vergessen*
Vergleich (-e) – *nm* comparison
vergleichen – *v irreg* compare
Vergnügen (-) – *nnt* pleasure
mit Vergnügen – with pleasure
Vergnügungspark (-s) – *nm* amusement park
verhaften – *v reg* † arrest
sich verhalten – *v irreg refl* act (behave)
Verhältnis (se) – *nnt* relationship
verheiratet – *adj* married
verhindern – *v reg* † prevent
verhüten – *v reg* † stop (prevent)
Verkauf (Verkäufe) – *nm* sale
verkaufen – *v reg* † sell
zu verkaufen – for sale
Verkäufer (-) – *nm* shop assistant
Verkäuferin (-nen) – *nf* shop assistant
verkauft – *adj* sold
Verkehr – *nm* traffic (vehicles)
Verkehrsamt (-ämter) – *nnt* tourist office
Verkehrskreisel (-) – *nm* roundabout (traffic)
öffentliche Verkehrsmittel – *npl* public transport
Verkehrsteilnehmer (-) – *nm* road user
Verkehrsteilnehmerin (-nen) – *nf* road-user
verlangen – *v reg* † demand
verlassen – *v irreg* leave (house, etc)
sich verlaufen – *v irreg refl* get lost (on foot)
verlegen – *adj* embarrassed
Verlegenheit – *nf* embarrassment
verletzen – *v reg* † injure

sich verletzen – *v reg refl* † hurt oneself
verletzt – *adj* injured
verletzt werden* – *v irreg* get hurt
Verletzung (-en) – *nf* injury
verleugnen – *v reg* † deny
in jdn verliebt sein* – *v irreg* be in love with s.o.
Ich bin in dich verliebt – I'm in love with you
verlieren – *v irreg* lose
ein Spiel verlieren – *v irreg* lose a match
verließ – *see verlassen*
verlobt – *adj* engaged (to marry)
Verlobte – *nm* ‡ fiancé
Verlobte – *nf* ‡ fiancée
verlor – *see verlieren*
verloren – *adj* lost
vermeiden – *v irreg* avoid
vermeintlich – *adj* imaginary
vermieten – *v reg* † let (rent out)
zu vermieten – to let, for hire
Vermietung (-en) – *nf* renting out
vermissen – *v reg* † miss (person)
vermutlich – *adj* probable
vernachlässigen – *v reg* † neglect
vernachlässigt – *adj* neglected
vernünftig – *adj* sensible (wise)
verpassen – *v reg* † miss (train, etc)
Verpflegung – *nf* provisions, picnic
verpflichtet – *adj* obliged
verreisen* – *v reg* † go away on holiday
sich das Fußgelenk verrenken – *v reg dat refl* † twist an ankle
verrückt – *adj* crazy, mad
Versammlung (-en) – *nf* assembly
versäumen – *v reg* † miss (lesson)
verschieben – *v irreg* postpone
verschieden – *adj* different
verschieden sein* – *v irreg* vary

---

verschleißen – *v irreg* wear out

verschlissen – *adj* worn out

verschlucken – *v reg* † swallow

Verschmutzung – *nf* pollution

verschmutzt – *adj* polluted

verschnupft sein* – *v irreg* have a cold

verschreiben – *v irreg* prescribe

verschwand – *see verschwinden*

verschwenden – *v reg* † waste

verschwenderisch – *adj* wasteful

verschwinden* – *v irreg* disappear

verschwunden – *see verschwinden*

versichern – *v reg* † assure; insure

Versicherung (-en) – *nf* insurance

verspäten – *v reg* † delay

Verspätung (-en) – *nf* delay

Versprechen (-) – *nnt* promise

jdm versprechen – *v irreg* promise s.o.

verstanden – *adj* understood

Verständnis – *nnt* understanding

sich das Fußgelenk verstauchen – *v reg dat refl* † sprain one's ankle

verstecken – *v reg* † hide

sich verstecken – *v reg refl* † hide o.s.

versteckt – *adj* hidden

verstehen – *v irreg* understand

sich verstehen mit (+ dat) – *v irreg refl* get on with (person)

verstopft – *adj* constipated; blocked

Versuch (-e) – *nm* experiment

versuchen – *v reg* † try

Verteidiger (-) – *nm* back (sport)

vertreten – *v irreg* represent

Vertreter (-) – *nm* representative, agent

Vertreterin (-nen) – *nf* representative, agent

sich vertun – *v irreg refl* be mistaken

verursachen – *v reg* † cause

einen Unfall verursachen – *v reg* † cause an accident

verwandeln – *v reg* † transform

Verwandte – *nmf* ‡ relative, relation

verweigern – *v reg* † refuse (permission)

von der Schule verweisen – *v irreg* expel

verwitwet – *adj* widowed

verwöhnen – *v reg* † spoil (child)

verwöhnt – *adj* spoilt (child)

Verzeihung! – *excl* Sorry!

Verzeihung – *nf* forgiveness

verzollen – *v reg* † declare to customs

verzweifelt – *adj* desperate

Vetter (-) – *nm* male cousin

Video~ – *pref* video

Videokamera (-s) – *nf* video camera

Videokassette (-n) – *nf* video cassette

Videokassettenrekorder (-) – *nm* video recorder

Videorekorder (-) – *nm* camcorder

Videospiel (-e) – *nnt* video game

viel – *adv* much, lot

  nicht viel – not much, nothing much

vielen Dank – thank you very much

Viel Glück! – *excl* Good luck!

Viel Spaß! – *excl* Have a good time!

viele – *adj* many

vielleicht – *adv* perhaps, maybe

vier – *adj* four

viereckig – *adj* rectangular, square

vierte – *adj* fourth

Viertel (-) – *nnt* quarter, district

Viertel nach eins – quarter past one

Viertel vor zwei – quarter to two

  um Viertel vor vier – at quarter to four

Viertelstunde – *nf* quarter of an hour

vierzehn – *adj* fourteen

---

nm - noun masculine	*nf* - noun feminine	*nnt* - noun neuter	*npl* - noun plural
nom- nominative	*acc* - accusative	*gen* - genitive	*dat* - dative

vierzig – *adj* forty
  einundvierzig – *adj* forty-one
Violine (-n) – *nf* violin
Visum (Visen) – *nnt* visa
Vogel (Vögel) – *nm* bird
Vokabel (-n) – *nf* vocabulary
  (individual items)
Volk (Völker) – *nnt* nation
Volkslied (-er) – *nnt* folk song
Volksmusik – *nf* folk music
Volkswirtschaft – *nf* economics
voll – *adj* full, full of
  Ich habe die Nase voll – I'm fed
  up (annoyed)
vollenden – *v reg* † complete
Volleyball – *nm* volleyball
völlig – *adj* complete
völlig – *adv* entirely
vollkommen – *adj* absolute
Vollkornbrot (-e) – *nnt* wholemeal
  bread
Vollpension – *nf* full board
voll tanken – *v reg* fill up (petrol,
  diesel)
von (+ dat) – *prep* from, of
  sechs von zehn – six out of ten
vor (+ acc/dat) – *prep* before, in
  front of; ago; to (clock time)
  Es ist Viertel vor vier – It's
  quarter to four
  vor 8 Tagen – a week ago
  vor 14 Tagen – a fortnight ago
  vor vielen Jahren – a long time
  ago
vor allem – above all
vor kurzem – recently
Vor~ – *pref* preparatory
vorangehen* – *v irreg sep* go
  forward
vorankommen* – *v irreg sep* get on
  (succeed)
im Voraus – *adv* beforehand
vorbei – *adv* over (finished)

an (+ dat) vorbei – *prep* past
  (travelling)
vorbeifahren* an (+ dat) – *v irreg*
  sep pass (in car)
vorbeigehen* an (+ dat) – *v irreg*
  sep pass (on foot)
  Ich gehe an der Schule vorbei
  – I'm walking past the school
vorbeikommen* – *v irreg sep* call
  on s.o.
vorbereiten – *v reg sep* † prepare
Vorbereitung (-en) – *nf* preparation
Vorderrad (-räder) – *nnt* front
  wheel
Vorderseite (-n) – *nf* front
Vorfahrt – *nf* priority (traffic)
Vorführung (-en) – *nf* showing
  (film)
vorgehen* – *v irreg sep* happen
vorgestern – *adv* the day before
  yesterday
etwas vorhaben – *v irreg sep* plan
  sthg, intend to do sthg
vorhanden – *adj* available
Vorhang (-hänge) – *nm* curtain
  (opaque)
vorig – *adj* previous
  am vorigen Tag – the day before
vorkommen* – *v irreg sep* happen
vorlesen – *v irreg sep* read aloud
Vormittag (-e) – *nm* morning
  am Vormittag – in the morning
vormittags – *adv* a.m., in the mornings
vorn – *adv* at the front
Vorname (-n) – *nm wk* first name
vornehm – *adj* posh
Vorort (-e) – *nm* suburb
  in einem Vorort – in a suburb
  in den Vororten – in the suburbs
vorschlagen – *v irreg sep* suggest,
  propose
Vorsicht! – *excl* Beware! Be careful!
vorsichtig – *adj* careful

---

adj - adjective	*v reg* - verb regular	*v sep* - verb separable	† - see verb info
prep - preposition	*v irreg* - verb irregular	*v refl* - verb reflexive	* - takes sein

Vorsichtsmaßnahme (-n) – *nf* precaution

Vorspeise (-n) – *nf* starter (food)

vorstellen – *v reg sep* introduce, present

sich vorstellen – *v reg refl sep* introduce o.s.

sich vorstellen – *v reg dat refl sep* imagine

Vorstellung (-en) – *nf* performance (drama)

Vorteil (-e) – *nm* advantage

vorteilhaft – *adj* advantageous

Vorwahl (-en) – *nf* dialling code

Vorwahlnummer (-n) – *nf* dialling code

vorwärts – *adv* forwards, onwards

vorziehen – *v irreg sep* prefer

W

Waage – Libra (horoscope)

wach – *adj* awake

Warschau – Warsaw

Wache (-n) – *nf* police station

wachsen* – *v irreg* grow (get bigger)

sich die Haare wachsen lassen – *v irreg dat refl* grow one's hair

Wackelpudding – *nm* jelly (dessert)

Waffel (-n) – *nf* waffle (edible)

Wahl (-en) – *nf* choice; election

Wagen (-) – *nm* car

wagen – *v reg* dare

Wagenheber (-) – *nm* jack (car)

Wagon (-s) – *nm* railway carriage

wählen – *v reg* choose, dial

Wahlfach (-fächer) – *nnt* optional subject

wahr – *adj* true

nicht wahr? – isn't it, don't you, doesn't he?

während – *sub conj* as, while

während (+ gen) – *prep* during

Wahrheit (-en) – *nf* truth

wahrscheinlich – *adj* probable

wahrscheinlich – *adv* probably

Währung (-en) – *nf* currency

Waise (-n) – *nf* orphan

Wald (Wälder) – *nm* forest

Waldlauf (-läufe) – *nm* cross country (run)

Wales – *nnt* Wales

Waliser (-) – *nm* Welshman

Waliserin (-nen) – *nf* Welsh woman

walisisch – *adj* Welsh

Walisisch – *nnt* Welsh (language)

Walkman® (Walkmen) – *nm* walkman®

Wand (Wände) – *nf* wall (interior)

Wanderer (-) – *nm* hiker

Wanderin (-nen) – *nf* hiker

Wanderkarte (-n) – *nf* hiker's map

wandern* – *v reg* go for a hike

Wanderschuh (-e) – *nm* walking boot

Wanderung (-en) – *nf* hike, long walk

Wange (-n) – *nf* cheek (face)

wann – *adv* when? (question)

seit wann? – how long?

war – *see sein**

es war – it was

Das wär's – That's all

Ware (-n) – *nf* merchandise

Warenhaus (-häuser) – *nnt* department store

warf – *see werfen*

---

nm - noun masculine   *nf* - noun feminine   *nnt* - noun neuter   *npl* - noun plural
nom- nominative   *acc* - accusative   *gen* - genitive   *dat* - dative

warm – *adj* warm
  Es ist warm – It is warm/hot (weather)
  Mir ist warm – I am warm/hot
  warmes Wasser – hot water
Warnblinkanlage – *nf* hazard warning lights
warnen vor (+ dat) – *v reg* warn about
Warnung (-en) – *nf* warning
  Warnung vor dem Hund! – Beware of the dog!
warten – *v reg* † wait
warten auf (+ acc) – *v reg* † wait (for)
Warteraum (-räume) – *nm* waiting room
Wartesaal (-säle) – *nm* waiting room
Wartezimmer (-) – *nnt* waiting room
warum? – *adv* why?
was – *sub conj* what
  Was ist das? – What is that?
  Was für (+ acc) – What sort of ...?
  Was für einen Wagen? – What kind of car?
  Was gibt's neues? – What's new?
  Was hast du gesagt? – What did you say?
  Was ist los? – What's going on?
  Was macht das? – How much is that altogether?
  Was sonst? – What else?
was? – *excl* eh?
Waschbecken (-) – *nnt* wash basin, basin
Wäsche – *nf, no pl* washing, linen
  die Wäsche machen – *v reg* do (the) washing
  schmutzige Wäsche – *nf* dirty linen
waschen – *v irreg* wash (clothes, etc)

sich waschen – *v irreg refl* have a wash.
sich die Haare waschen – *v irreg dat refl* shampoo one's hair
Ich habe mich gewaschen – I have washed
Wäscherei (-en) – *nf* laundry (building)
Wäschetrockner (-) – *nm* dryer, tumble drier (clothes)
Waschlappen (-) – *nm* flannel
Waschmaschine (-n) – *nf* washing machine
Waschpulver – *nnt* washing powder
Wasser – *nnt, no pl* water
  kaltes Wasser – *nnt* cold water
  warmes Wasser – hot water
Wasser kochen – *v reg* boil water
wasserdicht – *adj* waterproof
Wasserhahn (-hähne) – *nm* tap
Wassermann – Aquarius (horoscope)
Wasserskifahren – *nnt* water skiing
Wasserski laufen* – *v irreg* water-ski
Wassersport – *nm* water sports
  Wassersport treiben – *v irreg* do water sports
Watte – *nf* cotton wool
WC (-s) – *nnt* WC, toilet
Wechsel (-) – *nm* exchange (money)
wechselhaft – *adj* changeable
Wechselkurs (-e) – *nm* rate of exchange
wechseln – *v reg* change
  Geld wechseln – *v reg* change money
Wechselstube (-n) – *nf* currency exchange office
wecken – *v reg* wake s.o.
Wecker (-) – *nm* alarm clock
  den Wecker stellen – *v reg* set the alarm clock
weder ... noch – *adv* neither ... nor

---

adj - adjective	*v reg* - verb regular	*v sep* - verb separable	† - see verb info
prep - preposition	*v irreg* - verb irregular	*v refl* - verb reflexive	* - takes sein

Ich habe weder Pass noch Personalausweis – I have neither a passport nor an identity card

weg – *adv* away, off

Weg (-e) – *nm* path, way (route)

sich auf den Weg machen – *v reg refl* set out

wegen (+ gen) – *prep* because of, on account of

weggehen* – *v irreg sep* go away, depart

weglaufen* – *v irreg sep* run away

weglegen – *v reg sep* put away

Wegweiser (-) – *nm* signpost

Weh (-e) – *nm* pain

wehtun – *v irreg sep* hurt

sich wehtun – *v irreg dat refl sep* hurt o.s.

wehen – *v reg* blow (wind)

Wehrdienst – *nm* military service

Wehrpflicht – *nf* compulsory military service

wehrpflichtig – *adj* liable for military service

Weibchen (-) – *nnt* female (animals)

weiblich – *adj* female

weich – *adj* soft

sich weigern – *v reg refl* refuse (to do sthg)

Weihnachten – *npl* Christmas

zu Weihnachten – at Christmas

Frohe/Fröhliche Weihnachten! – *excl* Happy Christmas!

Weihnachtsbaum (-bäume) – *nm* Christmas tree

Weihnachtsferien – *npl* Christmas holidays

Weihnachtsgeschenk (-e) – *nnt* Christmas present

Weihnachtslied (-er) – *nnt* carol

Weihnachtsmann (-männer) – *nm* Father Christmas

der 1. Weihnachtstag – *nm* Christmas Day

der 2. Weihnachtstag – *nm* Boxing Day

weil – *sub conj* as, because, for

Weile (-n) – *nf* while

Wein (-e) – *nm* wine

Weinbauer (-n) – *nm wk* vine grower

Weinbäuerin (-nen) – *nf* vine grower

Weinberg (-e) – *nm* vineyard

weinen – *v reg* cry, weep

Weinkarte (-n) – *nf* wine list

Weinstube (-n) – *nf* wine bar

Weintraube (-n) – *nf* grape

Weise (-n) – *nf* manner

auf diese Weise – in this way

weise – *adj* wise

weiß – *adj* white

weiß – *see* wissen

Ich weiß es nicht – I don't know

Weißwein (-e) – *nm* white wine

weit – *adj* far away

Ist es weit? – Is it far?

nicht weit von hier – not far from here

weit entfernt – *adv* far away

weit verbreitet – *adj* widely known

weit weg – a long way off

weiter – *adv* further

und so weiter (usw.) – and so on (etc)

Weiterbildung – *nf* further education

weiterfahren* – *v irreg sep* travel on

weitermachen – *v reg sep* continue, carry on

weiterstudieren – *v reg sep* † continue to study

weitsichtig – *adj* long-sighted

welche – *pron* any

welche – *adj* which? what?

Welche Farbe? – What colour?

Welle (-n) – *nf* wave (sea)

Wellensittich (-e) – *nm* budgerigar

Welt (-en) – *nf* world

---

nm - noun masculine   *nf* - noun feminine   *nnt* - noun neuter   *npl* - noun plural
nom - nominative   *acc* - accusative   *gen* - genitive   *dat* - dative

auf der Welt – in the world
Weltmeisterschaft (-en) – *nf* world championship
weltweit – *adj* worldwide
wem? – to whom?
  Wem hast du das Buch gegeben? – Who did you give the book to?
wen? – who(m)?
  Wen hast du gesehen? – Who(m) did you see?
Wende (-n) – *nf* reunification; change
sich wenden an (+ acc) – *v reg refl* † contact
bitte wenden (b.w.) – PTO
wenige – *adj* a few (not many)
weniger – *adv* less
weniger als – fewer than
weniger ... als – less ... than
  weniger als zwei Kilo – less than two kilos
wenigste – *adj* least
wenn – *sub conj* if, when (whenever)
wer? – who?
  Wer kommt mit? – Who is coming with us?
Werbung (-en) – *nf* advertising, publicity
werden* – *v irreg* become, get, go, grow
werfen – *v irreg* fling, throw, bowl
Werken – *nnt* CDT, woodwork
Werkstatt (-stätten) – *nf* garage, workshop (repair)
Werktag (-e) – *nm* working day
werktags – *adv* on working days
Werkzeug (-e) – *nnt* tool
Wert (-e) – *nm* value ,worth
  Es ist DM 2 000 wert – It's worth DM 2,000
wertlos – *adj* worthless
Wertsachen – *npl* valuables
wertvoll – *adj* precious, valuable

Weser – *nf* River Weser
Wespe (-n) – *nf* wasp
Wessen? – whose?
Weste (-n) – *nf* waistcoat
Westen – *nm* west
  im Westen – in the west
Western (-) – *nm* western (film)
Westinder (-) – *nm* West Indian (male)
Westinderin (-nen) – *nf* West Indian (female)
westindisch – *adj* West Indian
Die Westindischen Inseln – *npl* The West Indies
westlich – *adj* western
westlich von (+ dat) – *prep* to the west of
Wettbewerb (-e) – *nm* competition, contest
wetten – *v reg* † bet
Wetter – *nnt, no pl* weather
  bei schlechtem Wetter – in bad weather
  bei gutem Wetter – in good weather
Wetteraussichten – *npl* weather prospects
Wetterbericht (-e) – *nm* weather report
Wettervorhersage (-n) – *nf* weather forecast
Whisky – *nm, no pl* whisky
wichtig – *adj* important
Widder – Aries (horoscope)
widerstandsfähig – *adj* tough (resilient)
widerwärtig – *adj* vile
wie – *adv* how, what; like
  Wie bitte? – What (did you say)?
  Wie geht's? – How are you?
  Wie geht es dir? – How are you? (informal)

---

adj - adjective	*v reg* - verb regular	*v sep* - verb separable	† - see verb info
prep - preposition	*v irreg* - verb irregular	*v refl* - verb reflexive	* - takes sein

Wie geht es Ihnen? – How are you? (formal)

wie geplant – as planned

Wie heißt das auf Deutsch? – What is it in German?

Wie heißt du? – What is your name?

Wie ist ...? – What is ...like?

Wie kommt man am besten zum/zur? – What is the best way to ...? (+ building)

Wie kommt man nach ...? – What is the way to ...? (+ town name)

wie oft? – how often?

Wie schreibt man das? – How do you spell that?

Wie sieht er aus? – What does he look like?

Wie spät ist es? – What is the time?

wieder – *adv* again

immer wieder – *adv* over and over (again)

wiederholen – *v reg insep* † repeat

wieder sehen – *v irreg* see again

Auf Wiedersehen! – *excl* Goodbye!

Wiedervereinigung – *nf* reunification

wieder verwerten – *v reg* † recycle

Wiederverwertung – *nf* recycling

wiegen – *v irreg* weigh

Wien – Vienna

Wiener Schnitzel – Wiener schnitzel, veal escalope

Wiese (-n) – *nf* meadow

wieso? – *adv* why?

wie viel? – how much?

Wie viel Uhr ist es? – What time is it?

Den wie vielten haben wir heute? – What is the date today?

wie viele? – how many?

wild – *adj* fierce, wild

Wildleder – *nnt* suede

will – *see wollen*

willkommen – *adj* welcome

willkommen heißen – *v irreg* welcome

Herzlich willkommen! – Welcome!

Wind (-e) – *nm* wind

windig – *adj* windy

Windschutzscheibe (-n) – *nf* windscreen

windsurfen – *v reg* windsurf

windsurfen gehen* – *v irreg* go windsurfing

winken – *v reg* wave (hand)

Winter – *nm* winter

im Winter – in winter

Wintergarten (-gärten) – *nm* conservatory

Wintersport – *nm, no pl* winter sports

winzig – *adj* tiny

wir – *pers pron* we

wird – *see werden**

wirft – *see werfen*

wirklich – *adj* real (true)

wirklich – *adv* really

Wirklichkeit (-en) – *nf* reality

wirksam – *adj* effective

Wirtshaus (-häuser) – *nnt* pub, inn

wischen – *v reg* wipe

wissen – *v irreg* know (fact)

wissen, dass – *v irreg* be aware that

Wissenschaftler (-) – *nm* scientist

Wissenschaftlerin (-nen) – *nf* scientist

wissenschaftlich – *adj* scientific

Witwe (-n) – *nf* widow

Witwer (-) – *nm* widower

Witz (-e) – *nm* joke
wo – *sub conj* where
wo? – *adv* where?
Woche (-n) – *nf* week
  in der Woche – during the week
  jede Woche – every week
  letzte Woche – last week
  nächste Woche – next week
  pro Woche – per week
Wochenende (-n) – *nnt* weekend
  Schönes Wochenende! – *excl*
  Have a good weekend!
Wochenkarte (-n) – *nf* weekly ticket
Wochentag (-e) – *nm* weekday
wochentags – *adv* on weekdays
wöchentlich – *adj* weekly
woher? – *adv* where (from)?
  Woher kommst du? – Where do
  you come from?
Wohin? – *adv* (to) where?
  Wohin gehst du? – Where are
  you going (to)?
wohl – *adj* all right
  Zum Wohl! – *excl* Cheers!
wohlriechend – *adj* sweet-smelling
Wohnblock (-s) – *nm* block of flats,
  tower block
wohnen – *v reg* live (inhabit)
  Wo wohnst du? – Where do you
  live?
wohnen bei (+ dat) – *v reg* lodge
  with, stay with
Wohnort (-e) – *nm* town of residence
Wohnschlafzimmer (-) – *nnt* bed-
  sit
Wohnsitz (-e) – *nm* place of
  residence
Wohnung (-en) – *nf* apartment, flat
Wohnwagen (-) – *nm* caravan
Wohnzimmer (-) – *nnt* living room,
  lounge, sitting room

Wolke (-n) – *nf* cloud
Wolkenkratzer (-) – *nm* skyscraper
wolkenlos – *adj* cloudless
wolkig – *adj* cloudy
Wolle (-n) – *nf* wool
  aus Wolle – woollen
wollen – *v irreg* want (to), wish (to)
wollte – *see wollen*
Wort (Worte) – *nnt* word
Wörterbuch (-bücher) – *nnt*
  dictionary
Wortschatz – *nm* vocabulary
  (complete list)
Wortspiel (-e) – *nnt* pun
Wunde (-n) – *nf* wound
wunderbar! – *excl* great!
wunderbar – *adj* marvellous, terrific,
  wonderful
wunderschön – *adj* wonderful
Wunsch (Wünsche) – *nm* desire,
  wish
  auf Wunsch – optional
  mit besten Wünschen – Best
  wishes
wünschen – *v reg* desire, wish
wurde – *see werden**
würde – *see werden**
Würfel (-) – *nm* dice
würfeln – *v reg* throw dice
Wurm (Würmer) – *nm* worm
Wurst (Würste) – *nf* sausage
  Leberwurst – *nf* liver sausage
  Bockwurst – *nf* frankfurter
  Bratwurst – *nf* fried sausage
Würstchen – *nnt* small sausage
wusste – *see wissen*
Wüste (-n) – *nf* desert
Wüstenspringmaus (-mäuse) – *nf*
  gerbil
wütend – *adj* furious

---

adj - adjective	*v reg* - verb regular	*v sep* - verb separable	† - see verb info
prep - preposition	*v irreg* - verb irregular	*v refl* - verb reflexive	* - takes sein

Z

zäh – *adj* tough (meat)
Zahl (-en) – *nf* number (numeral)
  Kopf oder Zahl? – Heads or tails?
zahlen – *v reg* pay (bill)
zählen – *v reg* count
Zahlkarte (-n) – *nf* postal order
zahlreich – *adj* numerous
zahm – *adj* tame
Zahn (Zähne) – *nm* tooth
  sich die Zähne putzen – *v reg dat refl* clean one's teeth
Zahnarzt (-ärzte) – *nm* dentist
Zahnärztin (-nen) – *nf* dentist
Zahnbürste (-n) – *nf* toothbrush
Zahnpasta – *nf* toothpaste
Zahnschmerzen – *npl* toothache
Zapfsäule (-n) – *nf* petrol pump
zart – *adj* gentle, tender
Zauber – *nm* magic
  Die Zauberflöte – *nf* The Magic Flute
Zauberer (-) – *nm* magician
Zaun (Zäune) – *nm* fence
z.B. (zum Beispiel) – e.g. (for example)
Zebra (-s) – *nnt* zebra
Zebrastreifen – *nm* zebra crossing
Zeh (-en) – *nm* toe
zehn – *adj* ten
  zehn Kilometer entfernt – 10 kilometres away
zehnte – *adj* tenth
Zeichensetzung (-en) – *nf* punctuation
Zeichentrickfilm (-e) – *nm* cartoon film
zeichnen – *v reg* draw (picture)
  technisches Zeichnen – *nnt* engineering drawing

Zeichnung (-en) – *nf* drawing
zeigen – *v reg* show
Zeile (-n) – *nf* line (writing)
Zeit (-en) – *nf* time, period
  die ganze Zeit – all the time
  für eine lange Zeit – for a long time
  Ich habe keine Zeit mehr – I have run out of time
  vor langer Zeit – long ago
  zu derselben Zeit – at the same time as
Zeitpunkt (-e) – *nm* period (in time)
Zeitschrift (-en) – *nf* magazine
Zeitung (-en) – *nf* newspaper
  die Zeitungen austragen – *v irreg sep* deliver the papers
Zeitungshändler (-) – *nm* newsagent
Zeitungshändlerin (-nen) – *nf* newsagent
Zeitungsstand (-stände) – *nm* newspaper stand
Zeitverschwendung – *nf, no pl* a waste of time
Zeitvertreib (-e) – *nm* pastime, amusement
Zelt (-e) – *nnt* tent
  ein Zelt aufbauen – *v reg sep* pitch a tent
  ein Zelt abbauen – *v reg sep* take down a tent
zelten – *v reg* † go camping
zelten gehen* – *v irreg* go camping
Zentimeter (-) – *nm* centimetre
Zentralheizung – *nf* central heating
Zentrum (Zentren) – *nnt* centre
zerbrechlich – *adj* fragile
zerquetschen – *v reg* † crush, squash

---

zerreißen – *v irreg* tear, rip
zerrissen – *adj* torn
zerstören – *v reg* † destroy
zerstreut – *adj* absent-minded
Zettel (-) – *nm* note, slip of paper
Zeuge (-n) – *nm wk* witness
Zeugin (-nen) – *nf* witness
Zeugnis(-se) – *nnt* certificate, school report
Ziege (-n) – *nf* goat
ziehen – *v irreg* draw, pull
Ziel (-e) – *nnt* destination, goal
ans Ziel kommen* – *v irreg* finish (sport)
ziemlich – *adv* fairly, quite, rather
zierlich – *adj* delicate
Zigarette (-n) – *nf* cigarette
Zimmer (-) – *nnt* room
Zimmer frei – vacancies, B & B
Zirkus (-se) – *nm* circus
Zitat (-e) – *nnt* quotation
Zither (-n) – *nf* zither
zitieren – *v reg* † quote
Zitrone (-n) – *nf* lemon
Zitronentee – *nm* lemon tea
zittern – *v reg* shake, shiver, tremble
zitternd – *adj* trembling
Zivildienst – *nm* community service (instead of military service)
zog – *see ziehen*
zögern – *v reg* hesitate
Zoll – *nm* customs, toll
Zollbeamte – *nm* ‡ customs officer
Zollbeamtin (-nen) – *nf* customs officer
zollfrei – *adj* duty-free
Zone (-n) – *nf* zone
Zoo (-s) – *nm* zoo
Zopf (Zöpfe) – *nm* plait
Zorn – *nm* anger
zu – *adj inv* off (tap)
zu – *adv* too

zu haben – available
zu viel – too much
zu viele – too many
zu viele Leute – too many people
um ... zu – *conj* in order to
zu (+ dat) – *prep* to
zu den Gleisen – to the trains
zu Ostern – at Easter
zu Weihnachten – at Christmas
züchten – *v reg* † breed
Zucker – *nm* sugar
zuckerkrank – *adj* diabetic
Zuckerkrankheit – *nf* diabetes
Zuckerwatte – *nf* candy floss
zudecken – *v reg sep* cover
zudrehen – *v reg sep* turn off (tap)
zuerst – *adv* at first, first of all
Zufahrt (-en) – *nf* approach (road)
Zufahrtsstraße (-n) – *nf* access road
Zufall (Zufälle) – *nm* chance (fate)
zufällig – *adj* by accident
zufälligerweise – *adv* by chance
zufrieden – *adj* pleased, satisfied, glad
zufrieden mit (+ dat) – *adj* happy with
Zug (Züge) – *nm* train, procession
Zugang (Zugänge) – *nm* access
zugänglich – *adj* accessible
zugreifen – *v irreg sep* help o.s.
zugestiegen – *adj* got on train
Noch jemand zugestiegen? – Any more tickets?
zuhören – *v reg sep* listen to
Zukunft – *nf* future
in Zukunft – *adv* in future
Zukunftspläne – *npl* future plans
zuletzt – *adv* most recently
zum Mitnehmen – take away (food)
zumachen – *v reg sep* close (shut)
zunächst – *adv* first of all
Zunge (-n) – *nf* tongue

---

zur Post – to the post office
zur Schule – to the school
zurechtkommen* – v irreg sep get along, manage
zurück – adv back
zurückbekommen – v irreg sep recover (get back)
zurückbringen – v irreg sep bring back
zurückgeben – v irreg sep give back
zurückgehen* – v irreg sep go back
zurückhalten – v irreg sep hold back
zurückkehren* – v reg sep return
zurückkommen* – v irreg sep return, come back, get back
zurücklassen – v irreg sep leave behind
zurücklegen – v reg sep put back
zurücknehmen – v irreg sep take back
zurückstellen – v reg sep put back
zurzeit – at the present moment
zusammen – adv together
Geht das getrennt oder zusammen? – Do you want to pay separately or all together?
Zusammenstoß (-stöße) – nm collision, crash, bump
zusammenstoßen* mit (+ dat) – v irreg sep collide with, bump into
zusätzlich – adj extra
zuschauen – v reg sep watch
Zuschauer – npl audience
Zuschauer (-) – nm spectator, viewer
Zuschauerin (-nen) – nf spectator, viewer
Zuschlag (-schläge) – nm extra charge
zusehen – v irreg sep watch
Zustand (Zustände) – nm condition (state)
in gutem Zustand – in good condition

in schlechtem Zustand – in poor condition
Zutaten – npl ingredients
kein Zutritt – no entry (on foot)
zuverlässig – adj reliable
zwanzig – adj twenty
zwanzigste – adj twentieth
zwar – adv admittedly; to be more precise
Zweck (-e) – nm purpose
Es hat keinen Zweck – There's no point
zwecklos – adj pointless
zwei – adj two
Zweibettzimmer (-) – nnt room with twin beds
Zweifamilienhaus (-häuser) – nnt semi-detached house
zweifelhaft – adj doubtful
zweifellos – adv without doubt
zweimal – adv twice
zweisprachig – adj bilingual
zweit~ – pref second
Zweite – nmf ‡ runner up (sport)
zweite – adj second
zweiter Klasse – second class (ticket)
Zwiebel (-n) – nf onion
Zwillinge – npl twins; Gemini (horoscope)
Zwillingsbruder (-brüder) – nm twin brother
Zwillingsschwester (-n) – nf twin sister
zwingen – v irreg force
zwischen (+ acc/dat) – prep between
Zwischenzeugnis (-se) – nnt mid-year report
zwo – see zwei
zwölf – adj twelve
zwölfte – adj twelfth

A

a – ein *indef art m, n*
a – eine *indef art f*
abandon – (desert) verlassen *v irreg*
abbey – Abtei (-en) *nf*
abbreviation – Abkürzung (-en) *nf*
able – fähig *adj*
  be able to – können *v irreg*
aboard – an Bord *adv*
about – (approx) etwa, ungefähr *adv*
about – (place) herum *adv*
about – (relating to) über (+ acc/dat) *prep*
about – (place) um (+ acc) *prep*
  I am about to eat – Ich esse gleich
above – oben *adv*
above – über (+ acc/dat) *prep*
above all – vor allem *adv*
abroad – Ausland *nnt*
  be abroad – im Ausland sein* *v irreg*
  go abroad – ins Ausland fahren* *v irreg*
absence – Abwesenheit (-en) *nf*
absent – abwesend *adj*
absent-minded – zerstreut *adj*
absolute – vollkommen *adj*
absurd – absurd *adj*
academy – Schule (-n) *nf*
accent – Akzent (-e) *nm*
accept – (take) annehmen *v irreg sep*
accept – (agree) akzeptieren *v reg* †
acceptable – annehmbar *adj*
access – Zugang (Zugänge) *nm*
accessible – zugänglich *adj*
access road – Zufahrtsstraße (-n) *nf*
access only – Anlieger frei
accident – Unfall (Unfälle) *nm*
  by accident – zufällig *adj*

acclaim – Beifall *nm*
accommodation – Unterkunft *nf*
accompany – begleiten *v reg* †
accompanied by – begleitet von (+ dat) *adj*
accomplice – (male) Komplize (-n) *nm wk*
accomplice – (female) Komplizin (-nen) *nf*
according to – nach (+ dat) *prep*
account – (bank) Konto (-s) *nnt*
account – (bill) Rechnung (-en) *nf*
account – (report) Bericht (-e) *nm*
  on account of – wegen (+ gen) *prep*
  on no account – auf keinen Fall
accountant – (male) Steuerberater (-) *nm*
accountant – (female) Steuerberaterin (-nen) *nf*
accurate – genau *adj*
accuse – anklagen *v reg sep*
ace – Ass (-e) *nnt*
ache – Schmerz (-en) *nm*
  I have a headache – Ich habe Kopfschmerzen
achieve – leisten *v reg* †
achievement – Leistung (-en) *nf*
acid rain – der saure Regen *nm*
acquaintance – Bekannte *nmf* ‡
across – über (+ acc/dat) *prep*
go across – überqueren *v reg insep*
act – (behave) sich verhalten *v irreg refl*
act – (drama) spielen *v reg*
action – (deed) Tat (-en) *nf*
active – aktiv *adj*
activity – Tätigkeit (-en) *nf*
actor – Schauspieler (-) *nm*
actress – Schauspielerin (-nen) *nf*
add – hinzufügen *v reg sep*

adj - adjective	*v reg* - verb regular	*v sep* - verb separable	† - see verb info
prep - preposition	*v irreg* - verb irregular	*v refl* - verb reflexive	* - takes sein

add up – addieren *v reg* †
address – Adresse (-n) *nf*
address – ansprechen *v irreg sep*
adjective – Adjektiv (-e) *nnt*
admire – bewundern *v reg* †
adolescent – Jugendliche *nmf* ‡
adopt – adoptieren *v reg* †
adopted – Adoptiv- *pref*
adore – lieben *v reg*
adult – Erwachsene *nmf* ‡
adult – erwachsen *adj*
advance – Fortschritt (-e) *nm*
advantage – Vorteil (-e) *nm*
advantageous – vorteilhaft *adj*
adventure – Abenteuer (-) *nnt*
adventure film – Abenteuerfilm (-e) *nm*
adventure story – Abenteuerroman (-e) *nm*
advert – (small ad) Inserat (-e) *nnt*
advertisement – (for products) Reklame (-n) *nf*, Anzeige (-n) *nf*
advertising – Werbung *nf*
advice – Rat *nm, no pl*
  piece of advice – Ratschlag (-schläge) *nm*
advise – beraten *v irreg*
advisor – (male) Berater (-) *nm*
advisor – (female) Beraterin (-nen) *nf*
aerial – Antenne (-n) *nf*
aerobics – Aerobic *nnt, no pl*
aeroplane – Flugzeug (-e) *nnt*
aerosol – Sprühdose (-n) *nf*
affectionate – liebevoll *adj*
afford – sich leisten *v reg dat refl* †
(be) afraid (of) – Angst haben vor (+ dat) *v irreg*
Africa – Afrika *nnt*
African – afrikanisch *adj*
after – nach (+ dat) *prep*
after all – (finally) schließlich *adv*
afternoon – Nachmittag (-e) *nm*

afterwards – nachher *adv*
again – wieder *adv*
again and again – immer wieder *adv*
against – gegen (+ acc) *prep*
age – Alter (-) *nnt*
  I am 15 years of age – Ich bin 15 Jahre alt
  of the same age – gleichaltrig *adj*
agency – Agentur (-en) *nf*
agent – (male) Vertreter (-) *nm*
agent – (female) Vertreterin (-nen) *nf*
aggressive – aggressiv *adj*
ago – vor (+ dat) *prep*
  It was a long time ago – Es war schon lange her
  a fortnight ago – vor 14 Tagen
  a week ago – vor 8 Tagen
agree with – übereinstimmen mit (+ dat) *v reg sep*
agreeable – (nice) liebenswürdig *adj*
agreed – einverstanden *adj*
Agreed! – Abgemacht! *excl*
agricultural – landwirtschaftlich *adj*
aid – Hilfe *nf*
  first aid – erste Hilfe *nf*
aid – helfen (+ dat) *v irreg*
air – Luft *nf, no pl*
  by air mail – per Luftpost
  in the open air – im Freien
airbed – Luftmatratze (-n) *nf*
air conditioned – mit Klimaanlage
air conditioning – Klimaanlage (-n) *nf*
aircraft – Flugzeug (-e) *nnt*
air force – Luftwaffe *nf, no pl*
air hostess – Stewardess (-en) *nf*
airport – Flughafen(-häfen) *nm*
air sickness – Luftkrankheit *nf*
alarm clock – Wecker (-) *nm*
  set the alarm – den Wecker stellen *v reg*
Alas! – Ach! *excl*
alcohol – Alkohol (-e) *nm*

---

nm - noun masculine *nf* - noun feminine *nnt* - noun neuter *npl* - noun plural
nom- nominative *acc* - accusative *gen* - genitive *dat* - dative

alcohol free – alkoholfrei *adj*
A level – Abitur *nnt*
algebra – Algebra *nf*
alive – lebend *adj*
all – alle
  all alone – ganz allein
  all included – alles inbegriffen
  all in all – alles in allem
  all of us – wir alle
  all over – (everywhere) überall *adv*
  all over – (finished) zu Ende
  all sorts of – allerlei
  all the same – (however) trotzdem *adv*
  all the time – die ganze Zeit
  all year round – das ganze Jahr
  not at all – überhaupt nicht
allergic to – allergisch gegen (+ acc) *adj*
allow – erlauben *v reg* †
  be allowed – dürfen *v irreg*
allowance – (money) Geld *nnt*
almost – fast *adv*
alone – allein *adv*
along – entlang (+ acc) *prep*
aloud – laut *adj*
  read aloud – vorlesen *v irreg sep*
alphabet – Alphabet (-e) *nnt*
Alps – Alpen *npl*
already – schon *adv*
alright! – in Ordnung! *excl*
also – auch *adv*
alter – ändern *v reg*
although – obwohl, obgleich *sub conj*
altogether – zusammen *adv*, insgesamt *adv*
always – immer *adv*
am – bin *see sein**
a.m. – vormittags *adv*
amazed – erstaunt *adj*
  be amazed – erstaunt sein* *v irreg*
ambulance – Krankenwagen (-) *nm*

America – Amerika *nnt*
American – amerikanisch *adj*
American – (male) Amerikaner (-) *nm*
American – (female) Amerikanerin (-nen) *nf*
among – unter (+ acc/dat) *prep*
  among friends – unter Freunden
amount – Menge (-n) *nf*
amusement – (pastime) Zeitvertreib (-e) *nm*
amusement arcade – Spielhalle (-n) *nf*
amusement park – Vergnügungspark (-s) *nm*
amusing – lustig *adj*
an – ein *indef art m, nt*
an – eine *indef art f*
ancient – alt *adj*
and – und *co-ord conj*
anger – Zorn *nm*
angling – Angeln *nnt*
  go angling – angeln gehen* *v irreg*
angry – böse *adj*
get angry – böse werden* *v irreg*
animal – Tier (-e) *nnt*
ankle – Fußgelenk (-e) *nnt*
  sprain one's ankle – sich den Fuß verrenken *v reg dat refl* †
anniversary – Jahrestag (-e) *nm*
announce – ankündigen *v reg sep*
announcer – (male) Ansager (-) *nm*
announcer – (female) Ansagerin (-nen) *nf*
annoy – ärgern *v reg*
get annoyed – sich ärgern *v reg*
annoying – ärgerlich *adj*
annual – jährlich *adj*
anorak – Anorak (-s) *nm*
another – (more) noch *adv*
another – (different) andere *pron*
answer – Antwort (-en) *nf*
answer – antworten *v reg* †

---

answering machine –
Anrufbeantworter (-) *nm*
anti~ – Anti~ *pref*
antibiotic – Antibiotikum (-ka) *nnt*
antibiotic – antibiotisch *adj*
antiseptic – Antiseptikum (-ka) *nnt*
antiseptic – antiseptisch *adj*
anxious – ängstlich *adj*
any – irgendein *adj*
  not any – keine *adj*
any – welche *pron*
  Has he got any? – Hat er welche?
  Any more bread? – Noch etwas
  Brot?
anybody – jeder/jede, jemand *pron*
anybody – (negative) niemand *pron*
  I can't hear anyone – Ich kann
  niemand hören
anything – etwas *pron*
Anything else? – Sonst noch etwas?
anyway – sowieso *adv*
anywhere – irgendwo *adv*
  not anywhere –nirgendwo *adv*
apartment – Wohnung (-en) *nf*
apart from – außer (+ dat) *prep*
aperitif – Aperitif (-s) *nm*
apologise – sich entschuldigen *v reg
refl* †
apology – Entschuldigung (-en) *nf*
appalling – schrecklich *adj*
appear – (seem) scheinen *v irreg*
appear – erscheinen* *v irreg*
appearance – Aussehen (-) *nnt*
appendicitis – Blinddarmentzündung
(-en) *nf*
appetite – Appetit (-e) *nm*
appetizing – lecker *adj*
applause – Beifall *nm*
apple – Apfel (Äpfel) *nm*
apple cake – Apfelkuchen (-) *nm*
apple strudel – Apfelstrudel (-) *nm*
apple tree – Apfelbaum (-bäume) *nm*

appliance – Gerät (-e) *nnt*
applicant – (male) Bewerber (-) *nm*
applicant – (female) Bewerberin
(-nen) *nf*
application – (for job) Bewerbung
(-en) *nf*
apply for – sich bewerben um
(+ acc) *v irreg refl*
appointment – Termin (-e) *nm*
  make an appointment – einen
  Termin ausmachen *v reg sep*
appreciate – schätzen *v reg*
apprentice – Lehrling (-e) *nm*
apprenticeship – Lehre (-n) *nf*
approach – (road) Zufahrt (-en) *nf*
approach – sich nähern (+ dat) *v reg
refl*
approve of – billigen *v reg*
approximately – ungefähr, etwa *adv*
apricot – Aprikose (-n) *nf*
April – April *nm*
  in April – im April
apron – Schürze (-n) *nf*
Aquarius – Wassermann
arcade – (shops) Einkaufspassage (-n)
nf
archery – Bogenschießen (-) *nnt*
architect – (male) Architekt (-en)
nm wk
architect – (female) Architektin
(-nen) *nf*
are – *see sein**
area – Gebiet (-e) *nnt*
area – (surrounding) Umgebung (-en)
nf
  parking area – Parkplatz (-plätze)
  nm
  picnic area – (motorway)
  Rastplatz (-plätze) *nm*
  rest area – Raststätte (-n) *nf*
aren't – *see sein**
argue – sich streiten *v irreg refl*
argument – (discussion) Argument
nnt

---

nm - noun masculine   *nf* - noun feminine   *nnt* - noun neuter   *npl* - noun plural
nom- nominative   *acc* - accusative   *gen* - genitive   *dat* - dative

argument – (quarrel) Streit (-e) *nm*
Aries – Widder
arithmetic – Rechnen *nnt*
arm – Arm (-e) *nm*
armchair – Sessel (-) *nm*
army – Armee (-n) *nf*
around – herum *adv*
around – um (+ acc) *prep*
around here – hier in der Nähe
arrange – arrangieren *v reg* †
arrange – (time) festsetzen *v reg sep*
arrest – verhaften *v reg* †
arrival – Ankunft (-en) *nf*
arrive – ankommen* *v irreg sep*
arrow – Pfeil (-e) *nm*
art – Kunst *nf*
art gallery – Kunstgalerie (-n) *nf*
art school – Kunsthochschule (-n) *nf*
article – Artikel (-) *nm*
article of clothing – Kleidungsstück (-e) *nnt*
artist – (male) Künstler (-) *nm*
artist – (female) Künstlerin (-nen) *nf*
as – (while) während *sub conj*
as – (because) weil *sub conj*
as agreed – wie vereinbart *adj*
as ... as – so ... wie *adv*
  She is as big as me – Sie ist so groß wie ich
as far as – bis zu (+ dat) *prep*
as far as the traffic lights – bis zur Ampel
as for me – was mich angeht
as if – als ob *sub conj*
as much as possible – so viel wie möglich *adv*
as soon as – sobald *sub conj*
  as soon as possible – sobald wie möglich *adv*
as well – auch *adv*
ashamed – beschämt *adj*

be ashamed of – sich schämen vor (+ dat) *v reg refl*
ashtray – Aschenbecher (-) *nm*
Ash Wednesday – Aschermittwoch *nm*
Asia – Asien *nnt*
Asian – asiatisch *adj*
ask a question – eine Frage stellen *v reg*
ask – fragen *v reg*
ask for – (information) bitten um (+ acc) *v irreg*
ask – (s.o. for dinner, etc) einladen *v irreg sep*
asleep – eingeschlafen *adj*
  fall asleep – einschlafen* *v irreg sep*
asparagus – Spargel *nm*
assembly – Versammlung (-en) *nf*
assignment – Aufgabe (-n) *nf*
assist – helfen (+ dat) *v irreg*
assistance – Hilfe *nf*
assistant – (male) Verkäufer (-) *nm*
assistant – (female) Verkäuferin (-nen) *nf*
assure – versichern *v reg* †
asthma – Asthma *nnt*
asthmatic – asthmatisch *adj*
astonish – erstaunen *v reg* †
at – (position) an (+ dat) *prep*
at – (time) um (+ acc) *prep*
  at all – überhaupt *adv*
  at last – endlich *adv*
  at my house – bei mir
  at once – sofort *adv*
  at times – ab und zu *adv*
  at the (house of) – bei (+ dat) *prep*
  at the bottom of the page – unten auf der Seite
  at the end of – am Ende von (+ dat)

---

adj - adjective	*v reg* - verb regular	*v sep* - verb separable	† - see verb info
prep - preposition	*v irreg* - verb irregular	*v refl* - verb reflexive	* - takes sein

at the same time as – zu
derselben Zeit
at top speed – mit
Höchstgeschwindigkeit
ate – *see essen*
athlete – (male) Athlet (-en) *nm wk*
athlete – (female) Athletin (-nen) *nf*
athletic – sportlich *adj*
athletics – Leichtathletik *nf*
Atlantic Ocean – Atlantik *nm*
atmosphere – Atmosphäre (-n) *nf*
attach – festmachen *v reg sep*
attack – Angriff (-e) *nm*
attack – angreifen *v irreg sep*
attempt – versuchen *v reg* †
attend – (school) besuchen *v reg* †
attend – (be present) anwesend sein*
v irreg
attention – Aufmerksamkeit (-en) *nf*
Attention! – Achtung!
attic – Dachboden (-böden) *nm*
attract – anziehen *v irreg sep*
attractive – attraktiv *adj*
auburn – rotbraun *adj*
audience – Zuschauer *npl*,
(theatre) Puklikum *nnt*
August – August *nm*
in August – im August
aunt – Tante (-n) *nf*
Australia – Australien *nnt*
Austria – Österreich *nnt*

Austrian – österreichisch *adj*
Austrian – (male) Österreicher (-) *nm*
Austrian – (female) Österreicherin
(-nen) *nf*
author – (male) Schriftsteller (-) *nm*
author – (female) Schriftstellerin
(-nen) *nf*
authorities – Behörde (-n) *nf*
automatic – automatisch *adj*
autumn – Herbst *nm*
in autumn – im Herbst
available – verfügbar *adj*
avenue – Allee (-n) *nf*
average – durchschnittlich *adj*
average – Durchschnitt (-e) *nm*
avocado pear – Avocado (-s) *nf*
avoid – vermeiden *v irreg*
awake – wach *adj*
away – weg, fort *adv*
away – (distance) entfernt
10 kilometres away – zehn
Kilometer entfernt
go away – weggehen* *v irreg sep*
away game – Auswärtsspiel (-e) *nnt*
awful – furchtbar *adj*
awkward – (clumsy) ungeschickt *adj*
awkward – (difficult) schwierig *adj*
awkward – (embarrassing) peinlich
adj

B

B & B – Zimmer frei
baby – Baby (-s) *nnt*
babysitter – Babysitter (-) *nm*
go babysitting – babysitten gehen*
  v irreg
back – zurück *adv*
back – (reverse car, etc) rückwärts
  fahren* *v irreg*
come back – (come)
  zurückkommen* *v irreg sep*
back – hinten *adv*
at the back of – hinter (+ dat) *prep*
back – (of car) Heck *nnt, no pl*
back – (sport) Verteidiger (-) *nm*
left back – (sport) linker
  Verteidiger (-) *nm*
right back – (sport) rechter
  Verteidiger (-) *nm*
back – (body) Rücken (-) *nm*
back pack – Rucksack (-säcke) *nm*
backwards – rückwärts *adv*
run backwards and forwards
  – hin und her laufen* *v irreg*
bacon – Speck *nm*
bad – schlecht, schlimm *adj*
bad – (ill) krank *adj*
bad – (serious) ernst *adj*
bad – (wicked) böse *adj*
bad-tempered – schlecht gelaunt
Too bad! – Pech! *excl*
badge – Abzeichen (-) *nnt*
badly – schlecht *adv*
badminton – Badminton *nnt*,
  Federball *nm*
bag – Tasche (-n) *nf*
school bag – Schultasche (-n) *nf*
bag – (paper, plastic) Tüte (-n) *nf*
baggage – Gepäck *nnt, no pl*
bake – backen *v irreg*
baker – (male) Bäcker (-) *nm*

baker – (female) Bäckerin (-nen) *nf*
baker's shop – Bäckerei (-en) *nf*
balcony – Balkon (-s) *nm*
bald – kahl *adj*
bald patch – Glatze (-n) *nf*
ball – Ball (Bälle) *nm*
ballet – Ballett *nnt*
ball-point pen – Kugelschreiber (-)
  nm
balloon – Ballon (-s) *nm*
Baltic Sea – Ostsee *nf*
banana – Banane (-n) *nf*
band – (group) Band (-s) *nf*,
  Gruppe (-n) *nf*
bandage – Verband (Verbände) *nm*
bang – Knall (-e) *nm*
banger – (car) Kiste (-n) *nf coll*
banger – (firework) Knallkörper (-)
  nm
banger – (sausage) Bratwurst
  (-würste) *nf*
Bangladesh – Bangladesch *nnt*
Bangladeshi – bangladeschisch *adj*
Bangladeshi person – (male)
  Bangladescher (-) *nm*
Bangladeshi person – (female)
  Bangladeschin (-nen) *nf*
bank – (river) Ufer (-) *nnt*
bank – Bank (-en) *nf*, Sparkasse (-n) *nf*
bank account – Bankkonto (-konten)
  nnt
banker's card – Scheckkarte (-n) *nf*
Bank holiday – Feiertag (-e) *nm*
banknote – Geldschein (-e) *nm*
bank robbery – Bankraub (-räube) *nm*
bar – (drinks) Bar (s) *nf*
bar – (chocolate) Tafel (-n) *nf*
barbecue – Grillfest (-e) *nnt*
barber – Frisör (-e) *nm*
bare – (room) leer *adj*

---

adj - adjective	*v reg* - verb regular	*v sep* - verb separable	† - see verb info
prep - preposition	*v irreg* - verb irregular	*v refl* - verb reflexive	* - takes sein

bare – (naked) nackt *adj*
barefoot – barfuß *adj*
bare-headed – ohne Hut
bargain – Sonderangebot (-e) *nnt*
bark – bellen *v reg*
barmaid – Bardame (-n) *nf*
barman – Barmann (-männer) *nm*
barn – Scheune (-n) *nf*
based on – basiert auf (+ dat) *adj*
basement – Keller (-) *nm*
basic – Grund- *pref*
basically – im Grunde *adv*
basin – Waschbecken (-) *nnt*
basis – Basis (Basen) *nf*
basket – Korb (Körbe) *nm*
basketball – Basketball *nm*
Basle – Basel
bat – (table tennis, etc) Schläger (-) *nm*
bat – (mammal) Fledermaus (-mäuse) *nf*
bath – (tub) Badewanne (-n) *nf*
bath – (wash) Bad (Bäder) *nnt*
   have a bath – sich baden *v reg refl* †
bathe – baden *v reg* †
bathing – Baden *nnt*
bathing cap – Badekappe (-n) *nf*
bathing trunks – Badehose (-n) *nf*
bathroom – Badezimmer (-) *nnt*
bath towel – Badetuch (-tücher) *nnt*
battery – Batterie (-n) *nf*
battle – Schlacht (-en) *nf*
Bavaria – Bayern *nnt*
Bavarian – bayerisch *adj*
bay – (on coast) Bucht (-en) *nf*
be – sein* *v irreg*
be able to – können *v irreg*
be afraid – Angst haben *v irreg*
be amazed – erstaunt sein* *v irreg*
be ashamed of – sich schämen vor (+ dat) *v reg refl*
be at – anwesend sein* *v irreg*
be aware that – wissen, dass *v irreg*

be bored – sich langweilen *v reg refl*
be born – geboren sein* *v irreg*
be busy – beschäftigt sein* *v irreg*
be careful – vorsichtig sein* *v irreg*
Be careful! – Vorsicht! Pass auf! *excl*
be cold – (weather) kalt sein* *v irreg*
   I am cold – Mir ist kalt
be fine – (weather) schön sein* *v irreg*
be fit – fit sein* *v irreg*
be good at – gut in .... sein* *v irreg*
be hot – (weather) heiß sein* *v irreg*
   I am hot – Mir ist heiß
be hungry – Hunger haben *v irreg*, hungrig sein* *v irreg*
be ill – krank sein* *v irreg*
be in a hurry – es eilig haben *v irreg*
be in detention – nachsitzen müssen *v irreg*
be interested in – sich interessieren für (+ acc) *v reg refl* †
be keen on – schwärmen für (+ acc) *v reg*
be lucky – Glück haben *v irreg*, Schwein haben *v irreg coll*
be mistaken – sich vertun *v irreg refl*
be obliged to – müssen *v irreg*
be on stage – auf der Bühne sein* *v irreg*
be on television – im Fernsehen sein* *v irreg*
be on the radio – im Radio sein* *v irreg*
be on the staff – angestellt sein* *v irreg*
be out of breath – außer Atem sein* *v irreg*
Be quiet! – (informal) Sei ruhig! *excl*
be right – Recht haben *v irreg*
be situated – sich befinden *v irreg refl*
be sleepy – schläfrig sein* *v irreg*
be sorry – bedauern *v reg* †
be thirsty – durstig sein* *v irreg*, Durst haben *v irreg*

---

be up – (out of bed) auf sein* *v irreg*
be well – gesund sein* *v irreg*
be warm – (weather) warm sein*
  v irreg
I am warm – Mir ist warm
be worried – sich Sorgen machen
  v reg dat refl
be wrong – Unrecht haben *v irreg*
beach – Strand (Strände) *nm*
  on the beach – am Strand
bean – Bohne (-n) *nf*
bear – Bär (-en) *nm wk*
beard – Bart (Bärte) *nm*
bearded – mit Bart
beastly – scheußlich *adj*
beat – schlagen *v irreg*
beaten – geschlagen *adj*
beautician – Kosmetikerin (-nen) *nf*
beautiful – schön *adj*
beauty – Schönheit (-en) *nf*
because – weil *sub conj*
because of – wegen (+ gen) *prep*
become – werden* *v irreg*
bed – Bett (-en) *nnt*
  air bed – Luftmatratze (-n) *nf*
  camp bed – Feldbett (-en) *nnt*
  double bed – Doppelbett (-en) *nnt*
  flower bed – Blumenbeet (-e) *nnt*
  go to bed – ins Bett gehen* *v irreg*
  make the bed – das Bett machen
    v reg
  single bed – Einzelbett (-en) *nnt*
bedding – Bettwäsche *nf, no pl*
bedroom – Schlafzimmer (-) *nnt*
bedside table – Nachttisch (-e) *nm*
bedside light – Nachttischlampe (-n)
  nf
bed-sit – Wohnschlafzimmer (-) *nnt*
bedtime – Schlafenszeit (-en) *nf*
bee – Biene (-n) *nf*
beef – Rindfleisch *nnt*
beefburger – Hamburger (-) *nm*

beefsteak – Steak (-s) *nnt*
minced beef – gehacktes
  Rindfleisch
beer – Bier (-e) *nnt*
beer mug – Bierkrug (-krüge) *nm*
beermat – Bierdeckel (-) *nm*
beetle – Käfer (-) *nm*
before – bevor *sub conj*
before – ehe *sub conj*
before – vor (+ acc/dat) *prep*
before long – bald *adv*
  never before – noch nie *adv*
beforehand – im Voraus *adv*
before leaving – vor der Abfahrt
  the day before – am vorigen Tag
  the day before yesterday –
    vorgestern *adv*
beg – betteln *v reg*
begin – anfangen *v irreg sep*, beginnen
  v irreg
beginner – (male) Anfänger (-) *nm*
beginner – (female) Anfängerin
  (-nen) *nf*
begin again – wieder von vorne
  anfangen *v irreg sep*
beginning – Anfang (Anfänge) *nm*
  at the beginning – am Anfang
behave – sich benehmen *v irreg refl*
behind – Hintern (-) *nm*
behind – hinter (+ acc/dat) *prep*
  leave behind – zurücklassen
    v irreg sep
belch – rülpsen *v reg*
Belgian – belgisch *adj*
Belgian person – (male) Belgier (-)
  nm
Belgian person – (female) Belgierin
  (-nen) *nf*
Belgium – Belgien *nnt*
believe (in) – glauben (an + acc) *v reg*
bell – (church) Glocke (-n) *nf*
bell – (door, school) Klingel (-n) *nf*
belong to – gehören (+ dat) *v reg* †

---

belongings – Sachen *npl*, Eigentum *nnt, no pl*
below – unter (+ acc/dat) *prep*
belt – Gürtel (-) *nm*
 seat belt – Sicherheitsgurt (-e) *nm*
bench – Bank (Bänke) *nf*
bend – Kurve (-n) *nf*
bend – biegen *v irreg*
 bend over – sich bücken *v reg refl*
beneath – unterhalb von (+ dat) *prep*
benefit – Geld (-er) *nnt*
 child benefit – Kindergeld *nnt*
beside – neben (+ acc/dat) *prep*
besides – außerdem *adv*
best – Beste *nmf* ‡
best – am besten *adv*
 do one's best – sein Bestes tun
Best Wishes – mit besten Wünschen
bet – Wette (-n) *nf*
bet – wetten *v reg* †
better – besser *adj*
 get better – sich erholen *v reg refl* †
between – zwischen (+ acc/dat) *prep*
 between you and me – unter vier Augen
Beware! – Vorsicht! *excl*
Bible – Bibel *nf*
bicycle – Fahrrad (-räder) *nnt*
bidet – Bidet (s) *nnt*
big – groß *adj*
bigger than – größer als
bike – Rad (Räder) *nnt*
 go for a bike ride – Rad fahren* *v irreg*
biker – (motorbike, male) Motorradfahrer (-) *nm*
biker – (motorbike, female) Motorradfahrerin (-nen) *nf*
bikini – Bikini (s) *nm*
bilingual – zweisprachig *adj*
bill – Rechnung (-en) *nf*
bin – (rubbish) Abfalleimer (-) *nm*

bind – (fasten) binden *v irreg*
bingo – Lotto (-s) *nnt*
biology – Biologie *nf*
bird – Vogel (Vögel) *nm*
biro® – Kugelschreiber (-) *nm*
birth – Geburt (-en) *nf*
 date of birth – Geburtsdatum (-daten) *nnt*
 birth certificate – Geburtsurkunde (-n) *nf*
birthday – Geburtstag (-e) *nm*
birthday cake – Geburtstagskuchen (-) *nm*
birthday card – Geburtstagskarte (-n) *nf*
birthday present – Geburtstagsgeschenk (-e) *nnt*
birth place – Geburtsort (-e) *nm*
biscuit – Keks (-e) *nm*
bite – Biss (-e) *nm*
bite – (insect) Stich (-e) *nm*
bite – beißen *v irreg*
bitter – bitter *adj*
black – schwarz *adj*
 A black coffee, please – Einen schwarzen Kaffee, bitte
black ice – Glatteis *nnt*
blackberry – Brombeere (-n) *nf*
blackboard – Tafel (-n) *nf*
black bread – Schwarzbrot *nnt*
blackcurrant – schwarze Johannisbeere (-n) *nf*
Black Forest – der Schwarzwald *nm*
Black Forest gateau – Schwarzwälderkirschtorte (-n) *nf*
blame – Schuld *nf*
blame s.o. – jdm die Schuld geben *v irreg*
blanket – Decke (-n) *nf*
Blast! – Verdammt! *excl*
bleed – bluten *v reg* †
Bless you! – Gesundheit! *excl*
blind – blind *adj*

| *nm* - noun masculine | *nf* - noun feminine | *nnt* - noun neuter | *npl* - noun plural |
| *nom*- nominative | *acc* - accusative | *gen* - genitive | *dat* - dative |

blind – Rollladen (Rollläden) *nm*
blister – Blase (-n) *nf*
block – Block (Blöcke) *nm*
block of flats – Wohnblock (-s) *nm*
block – blockieren *v reg* †
blockbuster – Knüller (-) *nm*
bloke – Typ (-en) *nm*
blonde – blond *adj*
blood – Blut *nnt*
blouse – Bluse (-n) *nf*
blouson jacket – Blouson (-s) *nm*
blow – (hit) Schlag (Schläge) *nm*
blow – blasen *v irreg*
blow – (wind) wehen *v reg*
blow one's nose – sich die Nase
  putzen *v reg dat refl*
blow the horn – (car) hupen *v reg*
blow up – (inflate) aufblasen *v irreg*
  sep
Blow! – Verflucht! *excl*
blue – blau *adj*
  light blue – hellblau *adj*
  navy blue – dunkelblau *adj*
blunt – stumpf *adj*
board – (plank) Brett (-er) *nnt*
board – (food) Pension *nf*
  full board – Vollpension *nf*
  half board – Halbpension *nf*
board – (at school) Interne sein*
  v irreg
boarder – Interne *nmf* ‡
board a ship – an Bord gehen*
  v irreg
  on board – an Bord
board game – Gesellschaftsspiel (-e)
  nnt
boarding school – Internat (-e) *nnt*
boast – angeben *v irreg sep*
boat – Boot (-e) *nnt*
boat trip – Bootsfahrt (-en) *nf*
body – Körper (-) *nm*
boil, be boiling – kochen *v reg*

boiled egg – ein gekochtes Ei *nnt*
boiled potatoes – Salzkartoffeln *npl*
boil water – Wasser kochen *v reg*
bold – mutig *adj*
bomb – Bombe (-n) *nf*
bomb scare – Bombenalarm (-e) *nm*
bone – Knochen (-) *nm*
bonfire – Freudenfeuer *nnt*
bonnet – Haube (-n) *nf*
book – Buch (Bücher) *nnt*
  sci-fi book – Sciencefiction Buch
  (Bücher) *nnt*
book – Heft (-e) *nnt*
book – buchen *v reg*
book of tickets – Streifenkarte (-n) *nf*
book a seat – einen Platz reservieren
  v reg †
book case – Bücherschrank
  (-schränke) *nm*
booked – reserviert *adj*
  fully booked – ausgebucht *adj*
booking office – Schalter (-) *nm*
booklet – Broschüre (-n) *nf*
bookshelf – Bücherregal (-e) *nnt*
bookshop – Buchhandlung (-en) *nf*
boot (of car) – Kofferraum (-räume)
  nm
boot – Stiefel (-) *nm*
  football boot – Fußballschuh (-e)
  nm
  ski boot – Skischuh (-e) *nm*
  walking boot – Wanderschuh (-e)
  nm
booze – Alkohol *nm*
booze – saufen *v irreg coll*
border – Grenze (-n) *nf*
border – (flower) Blumenbeet (-e) *nnt*
bore – langweilen *v reg*
  to be bored – sich langweilen
  v reg refl
boredom – Langeweile *nf*
boring – langweilig *adj*
born – geboren *adj*

---

adj - adjective	*v reg* - verb regular	*v sep* - verb separable	† - see verb info
prep - preposition	*v irreg* - verb irregular	*v refl* - verb reflexive	* - takes sein

born on 6th January – am 6. Januar geboren	**branch** – (firm) Filiale (-n) *nf*
be born – geboren sein* *v irreg*	**brand name** – Marke (-n) *nf*
borrow (from) – leihen *v irreg*	**brand new** – nagelneu *adj*
boss – (male) Chef (-s) *nm*	**brass band** – Blaskapelle (-n) *nf*
boss – (female) Chefin (-nen) *nf*	**brave** – tapfer *adj*
bossy – herrschsüchtig *adj*	**bread** – Brot (-e) *nnt*
both – beide *adj*	**break** – Pause (-n) *nf*
bother – sich die Mühe geben *v irreg dat refl*	**break** – brechen *v irreg*

born on 6th January – am
6. Januar geboren
be born – geboren sein* *v irreg*
borrow (from) – leihen *v irreg*
boss – (male) Chef (-s) *nm*
boss – (female) Chefin (-nen) *nf*
bossy – herrschsüchtig *adj*
both – beide *adj*
bother – sich die Mühe geben *v irreg dat refl*
bother – stören *v reg*
bottle – Flasche (-n) *nf*
bottle opener – Flaschenöffner (-) *nm*
bottom of class – Klassenschwächste *nmf* ‡
bottom – unten *adv*
at the bottom of the page – unten auf der Seite
bow – sich beugen *v reg refl*
bow tie – Fliege (-n) *nf*
bowl – (dish) Schüssel (-n) *nf*
bowl – (skittles) kegeln *v reg*
bowl – (throw) werfen *v irreg*
bowling alley – Kegelbahn (-en) *nf*
box – Kasten (Kästen) *nm*
boxing – Boxsport *nm*
box – (wooden) Kiste (-n) *nf*
box – (cardboard) Karton (-s) *nm*
box – Schachtel (-n) *nf*
Boxing Day – der zweite Weihnachtsfeiertag *nm*
boy – Junge (-n) *nm wk*
boyfriend – Freund (-e) *nm*
bra – BH (Büstenhalter) *nm*
bracelet – Armband (-bänder) *nnt*
bracket – Klammer (-n) *nf*
in brackets – in Klammern
brain – Gehirn (-e) *nnt*
brake – Bremse (-n) *nf*
brake – bremsen *v reg*
branch – (tree) Ast (Äste) *nm*

branch – (firm) Filiale (-n) *nf*
brand name – Marke (-n) *nf*
brand new – nagelneu *adj*
brass band – Blaskapelle (-n) *nf*
brave – tapfer *adj*
bread – Brot (-e) *nnt*
break – Pause (-n) *nf*
break – brechen *v irreg*
break one's leg – sich das Bein brechen *v irreg dat refl*
breakdown – Panne (-n) *nf*
breakdown lorry – Abschleppwagen (-) *nm*
break down – eine Panne haben *v irreg*
breakfast – Frühstück (-e) *nnt*
have breakfast – frühstücken *v reg*
break in – einbrechen* *v irreg sep*
break up – aufbrechen(*) *v irreg sep*
breath – Atem *nm*
out of breath – außer Atem
breathe – atmen *v reg* †
breed – züchten *v reg* †
brick – Backstein (-e) *nm*
made of brick – aus Backstein
bricklayer – Maurer (-) *nm*
bride – Braut (Bräute) *nf*
bridegroom – Bräutigam (-e) *nm*
bridesmaid – Brautjungfer (-n) *nf*
bridge – Brücke (-n) *nf*
brief – kurz *adj*
briefcase – Mappe (-n) *nf,* Aktentasche (-n) *nf*
briefs – (pants) Unterhose (-n) *nf*
bright – (clever) intelligent *adj*
bright – (not dark) hell *adj*
bright – (weather) heiter *adj*
bring – bringen *v irreg*
bring – mitbringen *v irreg sep*
bring back – zurückbringen *v irreg sep*

---

nm - noun masculine *nf* - noun feminine *nnt* - noun neuter *npl* - noun plural
nom- nominative *acc* - accusative *gen* - genitive *dat* - dative

bring up – (be sick) sich übergeben
v irreg refl insep
bring up – (mention) erwähnen *v reg* †
British – britisch *adj*
the British Isles – die Britischen
Inseln *npl*
British person – (male) Brite (-n) *nm wk*
British person – (female) Britin
(-nen) *nf*
broad – breit *adj*
broadcast – senden *v reg* †
broadcast – Sendung (-en) *nf*
brochure – Broschüre (-n) *nf*
broke – pleite *adj inv*
I'm broke – Ich bin pleite *coll*
broken – gebrochen *adj*
broom – Besen (-) *nm*
brother – Bruder (Brüder) *nm*
brother-in-law – Schwager
(Schwäger) *nm*
brother and sisters – Geschwister
nnt, no pl
brown – braun *adj*
bruise – blauer Fleck (-e) *nm*
brush – Bürste (-n) *nf*
brush – (broom) Besen (-) *nm*
brush – (painting) Pinsel (-) *nm*
brush – bürsten *v reg* †
brush one's hair – sich die Haare
bürsten *v reg dat refl* †
Brussels – Brüssel
Brussels sprout – Rosenkohl *nm,
no pl*
bucket – Eimer (-) *nm*
budgerigar – Wellensittich (-e) *nm*
buffet – Büffet (-s) *nnt*
build – bauen *v reg*
builder – Bauunternehmer (-) *nm*
building – Gebäude (-) *nnt*
bull – Stier (-e) *nm*
bumbag – Gürteltasche (-n) *nf*
bump – Zusammenstoß (-stöße) *nm*

bumper – Stoßstange (-n) *nf*
bump into – zusammenstoßen* mit
(+ dat) *v irreg sep*
bump into – (meet) begegnen* (+ dat)
v reg †
bunch of flowers – Blumenstrauß
(-sträuße) *nm*
bunch of grapes – Trauben *npl*
bungalow – Bungalow (-s) *nm*
bureau de change – Geldwechsel *nm*
burglar – Einbrecher (-) *nm*
burgle – einbrechen* *v irreg sep*
burn – Brandwunde (-n) *nf*
burn – brennen *v irreg*
burn o.s. – sich verbrennen *v irreg
refl*
I have burnt my finger –
Ich habe mir den Finger verbrannt
burst – bersten* *v irreg*
bus – Bus (-se) *nm*
bus driver – (male) Busfahrer (-) *nm*
bus driver – (female) Busfahrerin
(-nen) *nf*
bus route – Buslinie (-n) *nf*
bus stop – Bushaltestelle (-n) *nf*
catch the bus – den Bus nehmen
v irreg
bush – Strauch (Sträuche) *nm*
business – Geschäft (-e) *nnt*
business man – Geschäftsmann
(-männer) *nm*
business woman – Geschäftsfrau
(-en) *nf*
busy – beschäftigt *adj*
busy o.s. – sich beschäftigen *v reg* †
but – aber *co-ord conj*
butcher – Metzger (-) *nm*
butcher's shop – Metzgerei (-en) *nm*
butter – Butter *nf*
butterfly – Schmetterling (-e) *nm*
button – Knopf (Knöpfe) *nm*
buy – kaufen *v reg*
by – per *prep*

| *adj* - adjective | *v reg* - verb regular | *v sep* - verb separable | † - see verb info |
| *prep* - preposition | *v irreg* - verb irregular | *v refl* - verb reflexive | * - takes sein |

by bus – mit dem Bus
by car – mit dem Auto
by coach – mit dem Reisebus
by day – am Tag, tagsüber
by the day – pro Tag

by the hour – pro Stunde
by the kilo – pro Kilo
Bye! – Tschüs *excl*
bypass – Umgehungsstraße (-n) *nf*

C

cabbage – Kohl *nm*
cable car – Seilbahn (-en) *nf*
cable TV – Kabelfernsehen (-) *nnt*
café – Café (-s) *nnt*
café terrace – Terrasse (-n) *nf*
cage – Käfig (-e) *nm*
cagoule – Regenjacke (-n) *nf*
cake – Kuchen (-) *nm*
  birthday cake –
  Geburtstagskuchen (-) *nm*
cake shop – Konditorei (-en) *nf*
calculate – rechnen *v reg* †
calculator – Taschenrechner (-) *nm*
calendar – Kalender (-) *nm*
calf – Kalb (Kälber) *nnt*
call – (phone) Anruf (-e) *nm*
call – (phone) anrufen *v irreg sep*
call – (shout) rufen *v irreg*
  be called – heißen *v irreg*
call box – Telefonzelle (-n) *nf*
call for – (friend) abholen *v reg sep*
call in on – vorbeikommen* *v irreg sep*
call the register – die Anwesenheit feststellen *v reg sep*
calm – ruhig *adj*
calm o.s. down – sich beruhigen *v reg refl* †
camcorder – Videorekorder (-) *nm*
came – *see kommen**
camel – Kamel (-e) *nnt*
camera – Fotoapparat (-e) *nm*

camp – campen *v reg*
camper – Camper (-) *nm*
camp-fire – Lagerfeuer (-) *nnt*
camping carnet – Camping Carnet (-s) *nnt*
camping cooker – Campingkocher (-) *nm*
camping gas – Campinggaz® *nnt*
campsite – Campingplatz (-plätze) *nm*
  go camping – zelten gehen* *v irreg*
can – (tin) Dose (-n) *nf*
can-opener – Dosenöffner (-) *nm*
can – (be able to) können *v irreg*
  Can I? – Kann ich?
  I can't – Ich kann nicht
Canada – Kanada *nnt*
canal – Kanal (Kanäle) *nm*
canary – Kanarienvogel (-vögel) *nm*
cancel – streichen *v irreg*
cancer – Krebs *nm*
candidate – (male) Kandidat (-en) *nm wk*
candidate – (female) Kandidatin (-nen) *nf*
candle – Kerze (-n) *nf*
candy floss – Zuckerwatte *nf*
canoe – Kanu (-s) *nm*
canoe – Kanu fahren* *v irreg*
canteen – Kantine (-n) *nf*
cap – (hat) Mütze (-n) *nf*
capable – fähig *adj*
capital – (city) Hauptstadt (-städte) *nf*

---

nm - noun masculine	*nf* - noun feminine	*nnt* - noun neuter	*npl* - noun plural
nom- nominative	*acc* - accusative	*gen* - genitive	*dat* - dative

capital letter – Großbuchstabe (-n) *nm wk*
Capricorn – (horoscope) Steinbock
captain – (ship) Kapitän (-e) *nm*
car – Auto (-s) *nnt*, Wagen (-) *nm*
  by car – mit dem Auto
  car ferry – Fähre (-n) *nf*
  car hire – Autoverleih *nm*
  car key – Autoschlüssel (-) *nm*
  car park – Parkplatz (-plätze) *nm*
  car phone – Autotelefon (-e) *nnt*
  car seat – Autositz (-e) *nm*
  car wash – Autowaschstraße (-n) *nf*
caravan – Wohnwagen (-) *nm*
card – Karte (-n) *nf*
  credit card – Kreditkarte (-n) *nf*
  identity card – Ausweis (-e) *nm*
  post card – Postkarte (-n) *nf*
  play cards – Karten spielen *v reg*
  card game – Kartenspiel (-e) *nnt*
cardboard – Pappe *nf*
cardigan – Strickjacke (-n) *nf*
care – sich kümmern um (+ acc) *v reg refl*
care for – pflegen *v reg*
career – Karriere (-n) *nf*
careers advice – Berufsberatung *nf*
careful – vorsichtig *adj*
careful with money – geizig *adj*
  be careful – aufpassen *v reg sep*
  Be careful! – Pass auf! *excl*
carefully – sorgfältig *adv*
careless – rücksichtslos *adj*
caretaker – (male) Hausmeister (-) *nm*
caretaker – (female) Hausmeisterin (-nen) *nf*
Carnival – Karneval *nm*, Fasching *nm*
carol – Weihnachtslied (-er) *nnt*
carpet – Teppich (-e) *nm*
carpet – (fitted) Teppichboden (-böden) *nm*
carrot – Karotte (-n) *nf*

carry – tragen *v irreg*
carry on – weitermachen *v reg sep*
cartoon – (cinema) Zeichentrickfilm (-e) *nm*
cartoon – Comic (-s) *nm*
cartoon strip – Comic-Strip (-s) *nm*
case – (suitcase) Koffer (-) *nm*
  pack cases – Koffer packen *v reg*
case – (example) Fall (Fälle) *nm*
cash – (money) Geld *nnt*
cash – (not a cheque) Bargeld *nnt*
  pay cash – bar bezahlen *v reg* †
cash a cheque – einen Scheck einlösen *v reg sep*
cash desk – Kasse (-n) *nf*
  go to the cash desk – an die Kasse gehen* *v irreg*
cashier – (male) Kassierer (-) *nm*
cashier – (female) Kassiererin (-nen) *nf*
cash machine – (dispenser) Geldautomat (-en) *nm wk*
cassette – Kassette (-n) *nf*
  video cassette – Videokassette (-n) *nf*
cassette recorder – Kassettenrekorder (-) *nm*
castle – (fortified) Burg (-en) *nf*
castle – (palace) Schloss (Schlösser) *nnt*
cat – Katze (-n) *nf*
  tomcat – Kater (-) *nm*
catalytic converter – Katalysator (-en) *nm*
catch – (bus, etc) nehmen *v irreg*
  Catch the number three bus! – Nehmen Sie den Bus Linie 3!
catch – (fish) fangen *v irreg*
catch cold – sich erkälten *v reg refl* †
catch up with – nachholen *v reg sep*
cathedral – Dom (-e) *nm*
Catholic – katholisch *adj*
Catholic – Katholiker (-) *nm*

---

adj - adjective
prep - preposition
v reg - verb regular
v irreg - verb irregular
v sep - verb separable
v refl - verb reflexive
† - see verb info
* - takes sein

Catholic – Katholikerin (-nen) *nf*
cauliflower – Blumenkohl *nm*
cause – Ursache (-n) *nf*
cause an accident – einen Unfall verursachen *v reg* †
cause stress – Stress verursachen *v reg* †
cave – Höhle (-n) *nf*
CD – CD (-s) *nf*
CD player – CD-Spieler (-) *nm*
CD ROM – CD-ROM (-s) *nm*
CDT – Werken *nnt*
ceiling – Decke (-n) *nf*
celebrate – feiern *v reg*
celebration – Feier (-) *nf*
celebrity – Star (-s) *nm*
cellar – Keller (-) *nm*
cello – Cello (-s) *nnt*
centimetre – Zentimeter (-) *nm*
central heating – Zentralheizung *nf*
centre – Mitte (-n) *nf*
  in the centre of – in der Mitte von (+ dat)
  in the town centre – in der Stadtmitte
century – Jahrhundert (-e) *nnt*
certain – gewiss *adj*, sicher *adj*
certificate – Zeugnis(-se) *nnt*
chain – Kette (-n) *nf*
chair – Stuhl (Stühle) *nm*
chair lift – Sesselbahn (-en) *nf*
chalk – Kreide *nf*
champagne – (German) Sekt *nm*
champion – (male) Meister (-) *nm*
champion – (female) Meisterin (-nen) *nf*
championship – Meisterschaft (-en) *nf*
chance – (opportunity) Gelegenheit (-en) *nf*
chance – (fate) Zufall (Zufälle) *nm*
  by chance – zufälligerweise *adv*

Chancellor – Kanzler (-) *nm*
change – Änderung (-en) *nf*
change – (coins) Kleingeld *nnt*
  Have you any change? – Haben Sie Kleingeld?
  Keep the change! – Das stimmt so!
change – (reunification) Wende (-n) *nf*
change – (alter) ändern *v reg*
change – (exchange) umtauschen *v reg sep*
change – (trains) umsteigen* *v irreg sep*
change clothes – sich umziehen *v irreg refl sep*
change gear – (den Gang) schalten *v reg* †
change money – Geld wechseln *v reg*
change one's mind – sich etwas anders überlegen *v reg dat refl insep*
  I've changed my mind – Ich habe mir das anders überlegt
changeable – veränderlich *adj*
changing-room – (shop) Umkleidekabine (-n) *nf*
changing-room – (sport) Umkleideraum (-räume) *nm*
channel – (TV) Programm (-e) *nnt*
  on Channel Two – im zweiten Programm
Channel Tunnel – Kanaltunnel *nm*
English Channel – Kanal *nm*
chap – Kerl (-e) *nm*
chapel – Kapelle (-n) *nf*
chapter – Kapitel (-) *nnt*
character – Charakter (-e) *nm*
character – (drama) Person (-en) *nf*
charge – Preis (-e) *nm*
charge card – Kreditkarte (-n) *nf*
charming – entzückend *adj*
chase – jagen *v reg*
chat – plaudern *v reg*

cheap – billig *adj*
cheat – mogeln *v reg*
check – Kontrolle (-n) *nf*
check – kontrollieren *v reg* †
  check the oil level – den Ölstand
  kontrollieren *v reg* †
  check the tyres –
  die Reifen kontrollieren *v reg* †
  check the water level – das
  Wasser nachsehen *v irreg sep*
checked – getestet *adj*
checked – (pattern) kariert *adj*
checkout – Kasse (-n) *nf*
check tickets – Fahrkarten
  kontrollieren *v reg* †
cheek – (face) Wange (-n) *nf*
cheek – (face, bottom) Backe (-n) *nf*
cheeky – frech *adj*
cheerful – munter *adj*, heiter *adj*
Cheers! – Prost! Zum Wohl! *excl*
cheese – Käse *nm*
cheese sandwich – Käsebrot (-e) *nnt*
chemist – (male) Apotheker (-) *nm*
chemist – (female) Apothekerin (-nen)
  nf
chemist's shop – Apotheke (-n) *nf*
  at the chemist's –
  an der Apotheke
chemistry – (subject) Chemie *nf*
cheque – Scheck (-s) *nm*
cheque book – Scheckheft (-e) *nnt*
cheque card – Scheckkarte (-n) *nf*
  cash a cheque – einen Scheck
  einlösen *v reg sep*
cherry – Kirsche (-n) *nf*
chess – Schach *nnt*
  play chess – Schach spielen *v reg*
chest – (body) Brust (Brüste) *nf*
chest – (box) Kiste (-n) *nf*
chest of drawers – Kommode (-n) *nf*
chew – kauen *v reg*
chewing gum – Kaugummi (-s) *nm*

chic – schick *adj*
chicken – Hähnchen (-) *nnt*
chief – Haupt~ *pref*
child (ren) – Kind (-er) *nnt*
  only child – Einzelkind (-er) *nnt*
childhood – Kindheit (-en) *nf*
child-minder – Tagesmutter
  (-mütter) *nf*
chimney – Schornstein (-e) *nm*
chin – Kinn (-e) *nnt*
China – China *nnt*
Chinese – chinesisch *adj*
Chinese person – Chinese *nmf* ‡
chip – (micro) Chip (-s) *nf*
chips – Pommes frites *npl*
chocolate – (bar) Schokolade *nf*
chocolate – (individual) Praline (-n)
  nf
chocolate – Schokoladen~ *pref*
choice – Auswahl *nf*
choir – Chor (Chöre) *nm*
choose – wählen *v reg*
chop – Kotelett (-s) *nnt*
Christian – (male) Christ (-en) *nm wk*
Christian – (female) Christin (-nen)
  nf
Christian name – Vorname (-n)
  nm wk
Christmas – Weihnachten *npl*
  at Christmas – zu Weihnachten
  Father Christmas –
  Weihnachtsmann (-männer) *nm*
  Happy Christmas! – Frohe
  Weihnachten!
Christmas Eve – Heiliger Abend *nm*
Christmas holidays –
  Weihnachtsferien *npl*
Christmas present –
  Weihnachtsgeschenk (-e) *nnt*
Christmas tree – Weihnachtsbaum
  (-bäume) *nm*
church – Kirche (-n) *nf*
church service – Gottesdienst (-e) *nm*

cider – Apfelwein (-e) *nm*
cigarette – Zigarette (-n) *nf*
cinema – Kino (-s) *nnt*
circle – Kreis (-e) *nm*
circus – Zirkus (-se) *nm*
city – Großstadt (-städte) *nf*
civil servant – Beamte *nm* ‡
civil servant – Beamtin (-nen) *nf*
clarinet – Klarinette (-n) *nf*
   play the clarinet – Klarinette
   spielen *v reg*
class – Klasse (-n) *nf*
classical – klassisch *adj*
classical music – klassische Musik *nf*
classified (small) ad – Kleinanzeige
   (-n) *nf*
classroom – Klassenzimmer (-) *nnt*
clean – sauber *adj*
clean – sauber machen *v reg*
clean one's teeth – sich die Zähne
   putzen *v reg dat refl*
   I cleaned my teeth – ich habe mir
   die Zähne geputzt
cleaning – Saubermachen *nnt*
cleaning lady – Putzfrau (-en) *nf*
clear – klar *adj*
clear away – abräumen *v reg sep*
clearly – deutlich *adv*
clear up – (tidy) aufräumen *v reg sep*
clever – klug *adj*
cliff – Klippe (-n) *nf*
climate – Klima (-s) *nnt*
climb – klettern *v reg*
clinic – (surgery) Praxis (Praxen) *nf*
cloak-room – Garderobe (-n) *nf*
clock – Uhr (-en) *nf*
clock radio – Radiowecker (-) *nm*
close – (near) nah *adj*
   close by – in der Nähe
close – (shut) zumachen *v reg sep*
closed – geschlossen *adj*
cloth – Stoff (-e) *nm*

clothes – Kleider (-) *npl*
clothes department – (men's)
   Herrenkonfektion *nf*
clothes department – (ladies')
   Damenkonfektion *nf*
cloud – Wolke (-n) *nf*
cloudless – wolkenlos *adj*
cloudy – wolkig *adj*
club – Verein (-e) *nm*, Klub (-s) *nm*
clutch – (car) Kupplung (-en) *nf*
clutch – (seize) greifen *v irreg*
coach – trainieren *v reg* †
coach – Reisebus (-se) *nm*
coach station – Busbahnhof (-höfe)
   nm
coal – Kohle (-n) *nf*
coast – Küste (-n) *nf*
coat – Mantel (Mäntel) *nm*
coat hanger – Kleiderbügel (-) *nm*
Coca cola® – Cola *nf*
cocoa – Kakao *nm*
code – (guidelines) Richtlinien *npl*
co-educational – gemischt *adj*
coffee – Kaffee *nm*
   a cup of coffee – eine Tasse
   Kaffee
   an individual pot of coffee –
   ein Kännchen Kaffee
   decaffeinated coffee – Kaffee
   Hag® *nm*
   filter coffee – Filterkaffee *nm*
coffee with cream – Kaffee mit Sahne
coffee pot – Kaffeekanne (-n) *nf*
coffee table – Couchtisch (-e) *nm*
coin – Münze (-n) *nf*
   2 DM coin – Zweimarkstück *nnt*
coke – Cola (-s) *nf*
cold – kalt *adj*
   I am cold – Mir ist kalt
cold water – kaltes Wasser *nnt*
cold – (illness) Erkältung (-en) *nf*
   catch cold – sich erkälten *v reg refl* †
   I have a cold – Ich bin verschnupft

| *nm* - noun masculine | *nf* - noun feminine | *nnt* - noun neuter | *npl* - noun plural |
| *nom* - nominative | *acc* - accusative | *gen* - genitive | *dat* - dative |

cold – (temperature) Kälte *nf*
collar – Kragen (-) *nm*
colleague – (male) Kollege (-n) *nm wk*
colleague – (female) Kollegin (-nen) *nf*
collect – (stamps, etc) sammeln *v reg*
collect – (pick up) abholen *v reg sep*
collection – Sammlung (-en) *nf*
college – (sixth form) Oberstufenkolleg (-ien) *nnt*
college – (FE) Berufsschule (-n) *nf*
collide with – zusammenstoßen* mit (+ dat) *v irreg sep*
collision – Zusammenstoß (-stösse) *nm*
colloquial – umgangssprachlich *adj*
Cologne – Köln
 eau de Cologne – kölnisch Wasser
colon (:) – Doppelpunkt (-e) *nm*
colour – Farbe (-n) *nf*
comb – Kamm (Kämme) *nm*
comb one's hair – sich kämmen *v reg refl*
come – kommen* *v irreg*
come back – zurückkommen* *v irreg sep*
come down – herunterkommen* *v irreg sep*
come in – hereinkommen* *v irreg sep*
Come on! – Mach schnell! *excl*
come out – herauskommen* *v irreg sep*
come up – heraufkommen* *v irreg sep*
comfort – Komfort *nm*
comfortable – bequem *adj*
comic – komisch *adj*
comic – Comic (-s) *nm*
comic film – Komödie (-n) *nf*
comic strip – Comic (-s) *nm*

coming from – (train) aus (+ dat) *prep*
comma (,) – Komma (-s) *nnt*
command – Befehl (-e) *nm*
command – befehlen *v irreg*
common – gewöhnlich *adj*
the Common Market – der Gemeinsame Markt *nm*
communism – Kommunismus *nm*
commute – pendeln* *v reg*
compact disc – CD (-s) *nf*
company – Gesellschaft (-en) *nf*
compare – vergleichen *v irreg*
comparison – Vergleich (-e) *nm*
competition – Wettbewerb (-e) *nm*
competitor – (male) Teilnehmer (-) *nm*
competitor – (female) Teilnehmerin (-nen) *nf*
complain – sich beklagen *v reg* †
complete – völlig *adj*
complete – ergänzen *v reg,* vollenden *v reg* †, beenden *v reg* †
complicated – kompliziert *adj*
compulsory – pflicht *adj inv*
compulsory subject – Pflichtfach (-fächer) *nnt*
computer – Computer (-) *nm*
computer game – Computerspiel (-e) *nnt*
computerise – informatisieren *v reg* †
computer operator – EDV-Bearbeiter (-) *nm*
computer programmer – (male) Programmierer (-) *nm*
computer programmer – (female) Programmiererin (-nen) *nf*
computer scientist – (male) Informatiker (-) *nm*
computer scientist – (female) Informatikerin (-nen) *nf*
computer studies – Informatik *nf*
concern – betreffen *v irreg*

---

adj - adjective
prep - preposition
v reg - verb regular
v irreg - verb irregular
v sep - verb separable
v refl - verb reflexive
† - see verb info
* - takes sein

be concerned with – (care for) sich kümmern um (+ acc) *v reg refl*

concerning – in Bezug auf (+ acc) *prep*

concert – Konzert (-e) *nnt*

conclusion – Schluss (Schlüsse) *nm*

concrete – Beton *nm*
made of concrete – aus Beton

condition – (of agreement) Bedingung (-en) *nf*

condition – (state) Zustand (Zustände) *nm*
in good condition – in gutem Zustand
in poor condition – in schlechtem Zustand

condom – Kondom (-e) *nnt*

confirm – bestätigen *v reg* †

congratulate – gratulieren (+ dat) *v reg* †

Congratulations! – Ich gratuliere

connection – (train) Verbindung (-en) *nf*

consequently – deswegen *adv*

conservatory – Wintergarten (-gärten) *nm*

consist (of) – bestehen (aus + dat) *v irreg*

constipated – verstopft *adj*

construct – bauen *v reg*

construction worker – (male) Bauarbeiter (-) *nm*

construction worker – (female) Bauarbeiterin (-nen) *nf*

consult – fragen *v reg*

contact – sich wenden an (+ acc) *v reg refl* †

contact lens – Kontaktlinse (-n) *nf*

contain – enthalten *v irreg*

contents – Inhalt *nm, no pl*

contents – (book) Inhaltsverzeichnis (-se) *nnt*

contest – Wettbewerb (-e) *nm*

continent – (not island) Festland *nnt*

continent – (geographical) Kontinent (-e) *nm*

continue – (doing sthg) weitermachen *v reg sep*

continue – (speaking) fortfahren* *v irreg sep*

continue – (travelling) weiterfahren* *v irreg sep*

continue – (studying) weiterstudieren *v reg sep* †

continuous – ununterbrochen *adj*

convenient – passend *adj*
It's not convenient – Das passt mir nicht

conversation – Gespräch (-e) *nnt*

convinced – überzeugt *adj*

cook – (male) Koch (Köche) *nm*

cook – (female) Köchin (-nen) *nf*

cook – kochen *v reg*

cooker – Herd (-e) *nm*

cookery – Kochen *nnt*

cool – kühl *adj*

cope – sich durchschlagen *v irreg refl sep*

copy – (imitate) nachmachen *v reg sep*

copy – (write down) kopieren *v reg* †

cork – Korken (-) *nm*

corkscrew – Korkenzieher (-) *nm*

corner – Ecke (-n) *nf*
at the corner of – an der Ecke

cornet – (music) Kornett (-e) *nnt*

cornet – (ice cream) Tütchen (-) *nnt*

correct – richtig *adj*

correct – korrigieren *v reg* †

corrections – Verbesserungen *npl*

correspondence – Briefwechsel *nm*

corridor – Gang (Gänge) *nm*

cost – (price) Preis (-e) *nm*

cost – kosten *v reg* †

costing – zum Preis von (+ dat) *prep*

cottage – Häuschen (-) *nnt*

cottage cheese – Hüttenkäse *nm*

cotton – Baumwolle *nf*

---

nm - noun masculine	*nf* - noun feminine	*nnt* - noun neuter	*npl* - noun plural
nom- nominative	*acc* - accusative	*gen* - genitive	*dat* - dative

made of cotton – aus Baumwolle
cotton wool – Watte *nf*
couchette – Liegesitz (-e) *nm*
cough – Husten (-) *nm*
cough – husten *v reg* †
cough medicine – Hustensaft (-säfte) *nm*
could – (possibly) könnte *see können*
could – (was able to) konnte *see können*
council flat – Sozialwohnung (-en) *nf*
count – zählen *v reg*
counter – (PO, bank) Schalter (-) *nm*
counter – (shop) Ladentisch (-e) *nm*
country – Land (Länder) *nnt*
   in the country – auf dem Land
countryside – Landschaft (-en) *nf*
coupon – Bon (-s) *nm*
courage – Mut *nm*
course – (school) Kurs (-e) *nm*
course – (route) Piste (-n) *nf*
   of course – natürlich *adv*
court – (outdoor sport) Platz (Plätze) *nm*
court – (indoor sport) Halle (-n) *nf*
cousin – (male) Cousin (-s) *nm*
cousin – (female) Kusine (-n) *nf*
cover – zudecken *v reg sep*
covered with – bedeckt mit (+ dat) *adj*
cow – Kuh (Kühe) *nf*
crab – Krabbe (-n) *nf*
craftsman – Handwerker (-) *nm*
craftswoman – Handwerkerin (-nen) *nf*
crafty – schlau *adj*
crash – Zusammenstoß (-stöße) *nm*
crash into – zusammenstoßen* mit (+ dat) *v irreg sep*
crazy – verrückt *adj*
cream – (milk) Sahne *nf*
cream – (medicine) Salbe (-n) *nf*
   sun cream – Sonnencreme *nf*
credit card – Kreditkarte (-n) *nf*

cricket – Kricket *nnt*
criminal – (male) Verbrecher (-) *nm*
criminal – (female) Verbrecherin (-nen) *nf*
crisps – Chips *npl*
crockery – Geschirr *nnt, no pl*
crocodile – Krokodil (-e) *nnt*
cross with – (angry) böse mit (+ dat) *adj*
cross – überqueren *v reg insep*
cross country run – Waldlauf (-läufe) *nm*
cross out – durchstreichen *v irreg sep*
crossing – (channel) Überfahrt (-en) *nf*
crossing – (level) Bahnübergang (-gänge) *nm*
crossing – (pedestrian) Fußgängerüberweg (-e) *nm*
crossroads – Kreuzung (-en) *nf*
crossword – Kreuzworträtsel (-) *nnt*
crowd – Menge (-n) *nf*
cruel – grausam *adj*
cruise – Kreuzfahrt (-en) *nf*
crunchy – knusprig *adj*
crush – zerquetschen *v reg* †
cry – (shout) rufen *v irreg*
cry – (weep) weinen *v reg*
cucumber – Gurke (-n) *nf*
cul de sac – Sackgasse (-n) *nf*
cup – Tasse (-n) *nf*
   a cup of tea – eine Tasse Tee
cup – (trophy) Pokal (-e) *nm*
cup final – Pokalendspiel (-e) *nnt*
cup tie – Pokalspiel (-e) *nnt*
cupboard – Schrank (Schränke) *nm*
curious – neugierig *adj*
curly – lockig *adj*
currency – Währung (-en) *nf*
currency exchange office – Wechselstube (-n) *nf*
current – aktuell *adj*
current – (electricity) Strom *nm*

---

adj - adjective   *v reg* - verb regular   *v sep* - verb separable   † - see verb info
prep - preposition   *v irreg* - verb irregular   *v refl* - verb reflexive   * - takes sein

curriculum – Lernprogramm (-e) *nnt*
curried sausage – Currywurst *nf*
cursor – Cursor *nm*
curtain – (opaque) Vorhang (-hänge) *nm*
curtain – (net) Gardine (-n) *nf*
cushion – Kissen (-) *nnt*
custard – Vanillesoße *nf*
custom – Gebrauch (Gebräuche) *nm*
customer – (male) Kunde (-n) *nm wk*
customer – (female) Kundin (-nen) *nf*
customs – Zoll *nm*
customs officer – (male) Zollbeamte *nm* ‡
customs officer – (female) Zollbeamtin (-nen) *nf*

cut – schneiden *v irreg*
I have cut my finger – Ich habe mich in den Finger geschnitten
cut lawn – den Rasen mähen *v reg*
cutlery – Besteck *nnt*
cutlet – Kotelett (-s) *nnt*
CV – Lebenslauf (-läufe) *nm*
cycle – Rad (Räder) *nnt*
cycle – Rad fahren* *v irreg*
cycle hire – Radverleih *nm*
cycling – Radfahren *nnt*
cyclist – (male) Radfahrer (-) *nm*
cyclist – (female) Radfahrerin (-nen) *nf*
the Czech Republic – die Tschechische Republik *nf*

D

dad(dy) – Vater (Väter) *nm*
daddy – Vati *nm*
daily – täglich *adj*
daily life – der Alltag *nm*, das tägliche Leben
in daily life – im täglichen Leben
daily paper – Tageszeitung (-en) *nf*
daily routine – Tagesablauf (-läufe) *nm*
damage – Schaden (Schäden) *nm*
damaged – beschädigt *adj*
damp – feucht *adj*
dance – Tanz (Tänze) *nm*
dance – tanzen *v reg*
dancer – (male) Tänzer (-) *nm*
dancer – (female) Tänzerin (-nen) *nf*
Dane – (male) Däne (-n) *nm wk*
Dane – (female) Dänin (-nen) *nf*
danger – Gefahr (-en) *nf*
dangerous – gefährlich *adj*
Danish – dänisch *adj*

dare – wagen *v reg*
dark – dunkel *adj*
dark – (colour) dunkel~ *pref*
dash (-) – (punctuation) Bindestrich (-e) *nm*
data – Daten *npl*
database – Datenbank (-en) *nf*
date – Datum (Daten) *nnt*
up to date – aktuell *adj*
date – (meeting) Termin (-e) *nm*
date of birth – Geburtsdatum (-daten) *nnt*
daughter – Tochter (Töchter) *nf*
daughter-in-law – Schwiegertochter (-töchter) *nf*
day – Tag (-e) *nm*
all day – den ganzen Tag
closing day – Ruhetag (-e) *nm*
next day – am nächsten Tag
one day – eines Tages
on working days – werktags
per day – pro Tag

---

nm - noun masculine   *nf* - noun feminine   *nnt* - noun neuter   *npl* - noun plural
nom - nominative   *acc* - accusative   *gen* - genitive   *dat* - dative

the **day after tomorrow** –
übermorgen *adv*
the **day before yesterday** –
vorgestern *adv*
the **other day** – vor ein paar Tagen
day boy – Tagesschüler (-) *nm*
day girl – Tagesschülerin (-nen) *nf*
day off – (public holiday) Feiertag (-e)
nm
a **day off** – (work) ein freier Tag
day return – Tagesrückfahrkarte (-n)
nf
dead – tot *adj*
dead end – Sackgasse (-n) *nf*
deaf – taub *adj*
deaf and dumb – taubstumm *adj*
dear – (expensive) teuer *adj*
Dear ... – (a letter to male) Lieber ...
Dear ... – (a letter to female) Liebe ...
Dear Sirs – Sehr geehrte Herren
death – Tod (-e) *nm*
debate – Debatte (-n) *nf*
deceive – täuschen *v reg*
December – Dezember *nm*
in **December** – im Dezember
decide – (sich) entscheiden *v irreg*
(refl)
decide to – beschließen *v irreg*
decision – Entscheidung (-en) *nf*
deckchair – Liegestuhl (-stühle) *nm*
declare – erklären *v reg* †
declare – (to customs) verzollen *v reg* †
decorate – (paint) streichen *v irreg*
decorate – (wallpaper) tapezieren
v reg †
decorate – (shop window) dekorieren
v reg †
deep – tief *adj*
deep freeze – Tiefkühltruhe (-n) *nf*
deep frozen – tiefgefroren *adj*
defeated – geschlagen *adj*
definite – bestimmt *adj*
definitely – unbedingt *adv*

degree – (temperature) Grad *nm*
degree – (university exam)
Staatsexamen (-) *nnt*
delay – Verspätung (-en) *nf*
delay – verspäten *v reg* †
delicate – zierlich *adj*
delicatessen – Delikatessengeschäft
(-e) *nnt*
delicious – lecker *adj*
delighted – entzückt *adj*
delightful – entzückend *adj*
deliver – liefern *v reg*
deliver the papers – die Zeitungen
austragen *v irreg sep*
delivery – Lieferung (-en) *nf*
demand – verlangen *v reg* †
demonstrate – demonstrieren *v reg* †
demonstration – Demonstration
(-en) *nf*
Denmark – Dänemark *nnt*
dentist – (male) Zahnarzt (-ärzte) *nm*
dentist – (female) Zahnärztin (-nen) *nf*
deny – verleugnen *v reg* †
depart – abfahren* *v irreg sep*
depart – (plane) abfliegen* *v irreg sep*
department – Abteilung (-en) *nf*
department store – Kaufhaus
(-häuser) *nnt*
departure – Abfahrt (-en) *nf*
departure – Abflug (Abflüge) *nm*
departure board – Abfahrtsplan
(-pläne) *nm*
depend – abhängen von (+ dat) *v irreg*
sep
It **depends** – Es kommt darauf an
deposit – (down payment) Anzahlung
(-en) *nf*
deposit – (on empty bottle) Pfand *nm*
deposit – (against damage) Kaution
(-en) *nf*
deposit – hinlegen *v reg sep*
depressed – deprimiert *adj*
depressing – deprimierend *adj*

describe – beschreiben *v irreg*
description – Beschreibung (-en) *nf*
desert – Wüste (-n) *nf*
deserve – verdienen *v reg* †
design – Modell (-e) *nnt*
designer – (male) Designer (-) *nm*
designer – (female) Designerin (-nen) *nf*
desire – Wunsch (Wünsche) *nm*
desire – wünschen *v reg*
desk – Schreibtisch (-e) *nm*
desperate – verzweifelt *adj*
dessert – (pudding) Nachtisch (-e) *nm*
dessert spoon – Esslöffel (-) *nm*
destination – Ziel (-e) *nnt*
destroy – zerstören *v reg* †
detached house – Einfamilienhaus (-häuser) *nnt*
detail – Einzelheit (-en) *nf*
detective – Detektiv (-e) *nm*
detective film – Kriminalfilm (-e) *nm*
detective story – Krimi (-s) *nm*
detention – Nachsitzen *nnt*
  be in detention – nachsitzen müssen *v irreg*
develop – entwickeln *v reg* †
development – Entwicklung (-en) *nf*
diabetes – Zuckerkrankheit *nf*
diabetic – zuckerkrank *adj*
dial – wählen *v reg*
dialling code – Vorwahl (-en) *nf*
dial the number – die Nummer wählen *v reg*
diarrhoea – Durchfall *nm*
diary – (appointment) Kalender (-) *nm*
diary – (reminiscences) Tagebuch (-bücher) *nnt*
dice – Würfel (-) *nm*
  throw dice – würfeln *v reg*
dictionary – Wörterbuch (-bücher) *nnt*
did – *see machen*

die – sterben* *v irreg*
diesel – Diesel *nm*
diet – Diät (-en) *nf*
  be on a diet – eine Schlankheitskur machen *v reg*
difference – Unterschied (-e) *nm*
different – (not the same) verschieden *adj*
different – (varied) unterschiedlich *adj*
differently – anders *adv*
difficult – schwierig *adj*
difficult – schwer *adj*
difficulty – Schwierigkeit (-en) *nf*
  have difficulty – Schwierigkeiten haben *v irreg*
dim – (stupid) dumm *adj*
din – Krach (Kräche) *nm*
dinghy – (inflatable) Schlauchboot (-e) *nnt*
dinghy – (sailing) Segelboot (-e) *nnt*
dining car – Speisewagen (-) *nm*
dining hall – Speisesaal (-säle) *nm*
dining room – Esszimmer (-) *nnt*
dinner – (evening meal) Abendessen (-) *nnt*
dinner hour – (lunch time) Mittagspause (-n) *nf*
dinosaur – Dinosaurier (-) *nm*
direct – direkt *adj*
direction – Richtung (-en) *nf*
  in the direction of – in Richtung
  in the opposite direction – in entgegengesetzter Richtung
  in all directions – in alle Richtungen
directly – direkt *adv*
dirty – schmutzig, dreckig *adj*
disadvantage – Nachteil (-e) *nm*
disagreeable – unangenehm *adj*
disappear – verschwinden* *v irreg*
disappointed – enttäuscht *adj*
disappointing – enttäuschend *adj*

---

nm - noun masculine   *nf* - noun feminine   *nnt* - noun neuter   *npl* - noun plural
nom - nominative   *acc* - accusative   *gen* - genitive   *dat* - dative

disaster – Katastrophe (-n) *nf*
disastrous – katastrophal *adj*
disc – (record) Schallplatte (-n) *nf*
disco – Disko (-s) *nf coll*
discount – Rabatt (-e) *nm*
discouraged – entmutigt *adj*
discover – entdecken *v reg* †
discuss – diskutieren über (+ acc) *v reg* †
discussion – Diskussion (-en) *nf*
disgraceful – schändlich *adj*
disgusted – verekelt *adj*
disgusting – ekelhaft *adj*
dish – (plate) Schüssel (-n) *nf*
dish – (recipe) Gericht (-e) *nnt*
  dish of the day – Tagesgericht (-e) *nnt*
dishwasher – Spülmaschine (-n) *nf*
disk – (computer) Diskette (-n) *nf*
disk drive – Diskettenlaufwerk (-e) *nnt*
display – Ausstellung (-en) *nf*
dissatisfied – unzufrieden *adj*
distance – Entfernung (-en) *nf*
  in the distance – in der Ferne
distant – fern *adj*
distinct – klar *adj*
distressed – erschüttert *adj*
district – Viertel (-) *nnt*
district of city – Stadtviertel (-) *nnt*
disturb – stören *v reg*
dive – tauchen* *v reg*
diversion – Umleitung (-en) *nf*
divide – teilen *v reg*
divorced – geschieden *adj*
DIY – basteln *v reg*
dizzy – schwindlig *adj*
  I'm dizzy – Mir ist schwindlig
do – machen *v reg*
do athletics – Leichtathletik treiben *v irreg*
do drama – Drama machen *v reg*

do (an) experiment – ein Experiment machen *v reg*
do gardening – im Garten arbeiten *v reg* †
do gymnastics – Gymnastik machen *v reg*
do homework – Hausaufgaben machen *v reg*
do housework – Hausarbeit machen *v reg*
do ironing – bügeln *v reg*
do odd jobs – kleinere Reparaturarbeiten machen *v reg*
do one's hair – sich kämmen *v reg refl*
do shopping – einkaufen *v reg sep*
do sport – Sport treiben *v irreg*
do (the) washing – die Wäsche machen *v reg*
do washing up – spülen *v reg*
do water sports – Wassersport treiben *v irreg*
do well – sich gut durchschlagen *v irreg refl sep*
Do you see? – Siehst du?
dock – (ship) anlegen *v reg sep*
doctor – (male) Arzt (Ärzte) *nm*
doctor – (female) Ärztin (-nen) *nf*
doctor's certificate – Attest (-e) *nnt*
documentary – Dokumentarfilm (-e) *nm*
dog – (male) Hund (-e) *nm*
dog – (female) Hündin (-nen) *nf*
  Beware of the dog! – Warnung vor dem Hund! Bissiger Hund!
dole – (on the) arbeitslos *adj*
doll – Puppe (-n) *nf*
domestic – häuslich *adj*
done – *see machen*
  Well done! – Gut gemacht!
don't you, doesn't he? – nicht wahr?
donkey – Esel (-) *nm*
door – Tür (-en) *nf*

---

knock on the door – an die Tür klopfen

dormitory – Schlafraum (-räume) *nm*

dose – Dosis (Dosen) *nf*

double – doppelt *adj*

double – Doppel~ *pref*

double bass – Kontrabass (-bässe) *nm*

double decker – Doppeldecker (-) *nm*

double room – Doppelzimmer (-) *nnt*

doubtful – zweifelhaft *adj*

doughnut – Berliner (-) *nm*

down – unten *adv*

   lower down – weiter unten *adv*

   come down, go down – hinunterkommen* *v irreg sep*

   go downhill – bergab fahren* *v irreg*

downpour – Platzregen (-) *nm*

downstairs – unten *adv*

   go downstairs – nach unten gehen* *v irreg*

dozen – Dutzend (-e) *nnt*

drama – Drama (Dramen) *nnt*

   do drama – Drama machen *v reg*

Drat! – Verflucht! *excl*

draughts – Dame *nf*

draw – (score) unentschieden *adj*

draw – (lottery) Lotterie (-n) *nf*

draw – (picture) zeichnen *v reg*

draw – (pull) ziehen *v irreg*

drawback – Nachteil (-e) *nm*

drawer – Schublade (-n) *nf*

drawing – Zeichnung (-en) *nf*

drawn – (match) unentschieden spielen *v reg*

dreadful – furchtbar *adj*

dream – Traum (Träume) *nm*

dream – träumen *v reg*

dress – Kleid (-er) *nnt*

dress o.s. – sich anziehen *v irreg refl sep*

dresser – (sideboard) Anrichte (-n) *nf*

dressing – (medical) Verband (-bände) *nm*

dressing – (sauce) Soße (-n) *nf*

dressing gown – Morgenrock (-röcke) *nm*

dressing table – Toilettentisch (-e) *nm*

dress rehearsal – Generalprobe (-n) *nf*

drink – Getränk (-e) *nnt*

drink – trinken *v irreg*

drinkable – trinkbar *adj*

drinking water – Trinkwasser *nnt*

drive – Einfahrt (-en) *nf*

drive – (travel) fahren* *v irreg*

   drive on – weiterfahren* *v irreg sep*

drive – (a car, etc) fahren *v irreg*

driver – (male) Fahrer (-) *nm*

driver – (female) Fahrerin (-nen) *nf*

driving licence – Führerschein (-e) *nm*

   take a driving test – den Führerschein machen *v reg*

driving mirror – Rückspiegel (-) *nm*

drop – fallen lassen *v irreg*

drown – ertrinken* *v irreg*

drug – (medical) Medikament (-e) *nnt*

drug – (narcotic) Droge (-n) *nf*

   addicted to drugs – drogensüchtig *adj*

drug dependent – drogenabhängig *adj*

drugs scene – Drogenszene (-n) *nf*

drum kit – Schlagzeug *nnt*

drunk – betrunken *adj*

dry – trocken *adj*

dry – trocknen *v reg* †

dry cleaner's – Trockenreinigung (-en) *nf*

dry one's hair – sich die Haare trocknen *v reg dat refl* †

---

dryer – (clothes) Wäschetrockner (-) *nm*
  hair dryer – Föhn (-e) *nm*
duck – Ente (-n) *nf*
dumb – stumm *adj*
dumbfounded – verblüfft *adj*
duration – Dauer *nf*
during – während (+ gen) *prep*
dust – Staub *nm*
dust – abstauben *v reg sep*

dustbin – Mülltonne (-n) *nf*
Dutch – holländisch *adj*
Dutchman – Holländer (-) *nm*
  The Flying Dutchman – Der Fliegende Holländer
Dutchwoman – Holländerin (-nen) *nf*
duty-free – zollfrei *adj*
duvet – Steppdecke (-n) *nf*
duvet cover – Steppdeckenbezug (-bezüge) *nm*

E

E111 certificate – E-111 Schein (-e) *nm*
each – jede *adj*
each one – jede *indef pron*
each other – einander *adv*
each time – jedes Mal *adv*
ear – Ohr (-en) *nnt*
earache – Ohrenschmerzen *npl*
earring – Ohrring (-e) *nm*
earlier – früher *adv*
early – früh *adj*
earn – verdienen *v reg* †
earth – Erde (-n) *nf*
earthquake – Erdbeben (-) *nnt*
easily – einfach *adv*
east – Osten *nm*
  in the east – im Osten
east of – östlich von (+ dat)
Easter – Ostern *npl*
  at Easter – zu Ostern
Easter Bunny – Osterhase (-n) *nm wk*
Easter egg – Osterei (-er) *nnt*
Easter holidays – Osterferien *npl*
Easter Sunday – Ostersonntag *nm*
easy – einfach *adj*
eat – essen *v irreg*

ecologist – (male) Ökologe (-n) *nm wk*
ecologist – (female) Ökologin (-en) *nf*
ecology – Ökologie (-n) *nf*
economical – sparsam *adj*
economics – Volkswirtschaft *nf*
economise – sparen *v reg*
edge – Rand (Ränder) *nm*
  on the edge – am Rand
  on the edge of town – am Stadtrand
edible – essbar *adj*
Edinburgh – Edinburg
education – Ausbildung (-en) *nf*
educational – Schul~ *pref*
effective – wirksam *adj*
effort – Mühe (-n) *nf*
egg – Ei (-er) *nnt*
  a boiled egg – ein gekochtes Ei
  a hard boiled egg – ein hart gekochtes Ei
  fried egg – Spiegelei (-er) *nnt*
  scrambled egg – Rührei (-er) *nnt*
eh? – was? *excl*
eight – acht *adj*
eighteen – achtzehn *adj*
eighth – achte *adj*
eighty – achtzig *adj*

adj - adjective	*v reg* - verb regular	*v sep* - verb separable	† - see verb info
prep - preposition	*v irreg* - verb irregular	*v refl* - verb reflexive	* - takes sein

eighty-one – einundachtzig *adj*

Eire – Irland *nnt*

either ... or... – entweder ... oder ... *conj*

elastoplast® – Hansaplast® *nnt*

elbow – Ellenbogen (-) *nm*

elder – älter *adj*

elderly – alt *adj*

eldest – ältest *adj*

election – Wahl (-en) *nf*

electric(al) – Elektro~ *pref*

electric(al) – elektrisch *adj*

electric cooker – Elektroherd (-e) *nm*

electrician – Elektriker (-) *nm*

electricity – Elektrizität *nf*

electric razor – Rasierapparat (-e) *nm*

electronics – Elektronik *nf*

elegant – elegant *adj*

elephant – Elefant (-en) *nm wk*

elephant's trunk – Rüssel (-) *nm*

eleven – elf *adj*

eleventh – elfte *adj*

embarrassed – geniert, verlegen *adj*

embarrassing – peinlich *adj*

embarrassment – Verlegenheit *nf*

emergency – Notfall (-fälle) *nm*

  in an emergency – im Notfall

emergency aid – Nothilfe (-n) *nf*

emergency dept – (hospital) Unfallstation (-en) *nf*

emergency doctor – Notarzt (-ärzte) *nm*

emergency exit – Notausgang (-gänge) *nm*

emergency service – Notdienst (-e) *nm*

employ – anstellen *v reg sep*

employee – (male) Arbeitnehmer (-) *nm*

employee – (female) Arbeitnehmerin (-nen) *nf*

employer – (male) Arbeitgeber (-) *nm*

employer – (female) Arbeitgeberin (-nen) *nf*

empty – leer *adj*

empty – leeren *v reg*

enclose – beilegen *v reg sep*

encourage – ermutigen *v reg* †

end – Ende (-n) *nnt*

  at the end – am Ende

  at the end of the corridor – am Ende des Ganges

  in the end – endlich *adv*

end – beenden *v reg* †, enden *v reg* †

endless – endlos *adj*

energy – Energie *nf*

engaged – (toilet) besetzt *adj*

engaged – (to marry) verlobt *adj*

engine – Motor (-en) *nm*

engineer – Ingenieur (-e) *nm*

engineering drawing – technisches Zeichnen *nnt*

England – England *nnt*

English – englisch *adj*

English – (language) Englisch *nnt*

  in English – auf Englisch

  English speaking – englischsprachig *adj*

English Channel – Kanal *nm*

English lesson – Englischstunde (-n) *nf*

Englishman – Engländer (-) *nm*

Englishwoman – Engländerin (-nen) *nf*

enjoy – genießen *v irreg*

Enjoy your meal! – Guten Appetit!, Mahlzeit! *excl*

enjoyable – angenehm *adj*

enormous – riesig, riesengroß *adj*

enough – genug *adj*

  I've had enough – (food) Ich bin satt

  I've had enough – (annoyance) Ich habe die Nase voll *coll*

---

enquire about – sich erkundigen nach (+ dat) *v reg refl* †
enter – eintreten* *v irreg sep*
entertainment – Unterhaltung (-en) *nf*
enthusiasm – Begeisterung *nf*
enthusiastic about – begeistert von (+ dat) *adj*
entirely – völlig *adv*
entrance – (way in) Eingang (-gänge) *nm*
entrance – (road in) Einfahrt (-en) *nf*
entrance – (price) Eintritt (-e) *nm*
entrance examination – Eintrittsprüfung (-en) *nf*
entrance fee – Eintrittsgeld (-er) *nnt*
entrance ticket – Eintrittskarte (-n) *nf*
envelope – Umschlag (Umschläge) *nm*
environment – Umwelt *nf*
environmentally aware – umweltbewusst *adj*
environmentally friendly – umweltfreundlich *adj*
environmental protection – Umweltschutz *nm*
envy – beneiden *v reg* †
equal – gleich *adj*
equality – Gleichheit (-en) *nf*
equally – genau so *adv*
equipment – Ausrüstung (-en) *nf*
equivalent – entsprechend *adj*, gleichwertig *adj*
equivalent – Gegenstück (-e) *nnt*
error – Fehler (-) *nm*
escalator – Rolltreppe (-n) *nf*
escape – entkommen* *v irreg*
especially – besonders *adv*
essay – Aufsatz (-sätze) *nm*
essential – unentbehrlich *adj*
establish – feststellen *v reg sep*
establishment – Einrichtung (-en) *nf*

estate agent – Immobilienmakler (-) *nm*
EU – Die Europäische Union *nf*
Eurocheque – Euroscheck (-s) *nm*
Europe – Europa *nnt*
European – europäisch *adj*
European person – (male) Europäer (-) *nm*
European person – (female) Europäerin (-nen) *nf*
the European Union – die Europäische Union *nf*
even – (not odd) gerade *adj*
even – sogar *adv*
even better – noch besser *adj*
even though – obwohl *sub conj*
evening – Abend (-e) *nm*
Good evening! – Guten Abend!
See you this evening! – Bis heute Abend!
evening meal – (cold) Abendbrot (-e) *nnt*
evening meal – (hot) Abendessen (-) *nnt*
evenly – gleichmäßig *adj*
event – Ereignis (-se) *nnt*
eventually – endlich *adv*
ever – je *adv*
ever since – seitdem *sub conj*
every – (all) alle *adj*
every – (each) jede *adj*
everybody – alle *pron*
everyday – alltäglich *adj*
every day – jeden Tag
every evening – jeden Abend
everyone – alle *pron*
every one – jeder Einzelne *pron*
every ten minutes – alle zehn Minuten
everything – alles
every time – jedes Mal *adv*
every week – jede Woche
everywhere – überall *adv*

---

every year – jedes Jahr
evidence – Beweis (-e) *nm*
evil – Böse *nnt*
ex- – ehemalig *adj*
exact – genau *adj*
examination – (degree)
Staatsexamen (-) *nnt*
examination – (medical)
Untersuchung (-en) *nf*
examination – (school) Prüfung (-en)
nf
  fail an exam – in einer Prüfung
  durchfallen* *v irreg sep*
  pass an exam – eine Prüfung
  bestehen *v irreg*
  take an exam – eine Prüfung
  schreiben *v irreg*
examine – prüfen *v reg*
examine – (medical) untersuchen
v reg insep
example – Beispiel (-e) *nnt*
  for example – zum Beispiel
excellent – ausgezeichnet *adj*
except – außer (+ dat) *prep*
exception – Ausnahme (-n) *nf*
exchange – (money) Wechsel (-) *nm*
exchange – (school) Austausch *nm*
  go on an exchange – einen
  Austausch machen *v reg*
exchange rate – Wechselkurs (-e)
nm
exciting – aufregend, spannend *adj*
exclaim – ausrufen *v irreg sep*
exclamation mark (!) –
Ausrufezeichen (-) *nnt*
excursion – Ausflug (-flüge) *nm*
excuse – Ausrede (-n) *nf*
  excuse o.s. – sich entschuldigen bei
  (+ dat) *v reg refl* †
Excuse me! – Entschuldigen Sie, bitte!

exercise – (sport) körperliche
Bewegung (-en) *nf*
exercise – (school) Aufgabe (-n) *nf*
exercise book – Heft (-e) *nnt*
exhaust – (car) Auspuff (-e) *nm*
exhausted – erschöpft *adj*
exhaust fumes – Abgase *npl*
exhibition – Ausstellung (-en) *nf*
exist – existieren *v reg* †
exit – (motorway) Ausfahrt (-en) *nf*
exit – (on foot) Ausgang (-gänge) *nm*
  emergency exit – Notausgang
  (-gänge) *nm*
expect – erwarten *v reg* †
expel – von der Schule verweisen
v irreg
expensive – teuer *adj*
experience – Erfahrung (-en) *nf*
experience – erfahren *v irreg*
experiment – Versuch (-e) *nm*
explain – erklären *v reg* †
explanation – Erklärung (-en) *nf*
explore – erforschen *v reg* †
express train – D-Zug,
Durchgangszug (D-Züge) *nm*
expression – Ausdruck (-e) *nm*
extinguish – löschen *v reg*
extra – zusätzlich *adj*
extra charge – Zuschlag (-schläge)
nm
extraordinary – außergewöhnlich
adj
extreme – extrem *adj*
eye – Auge (-n) *nnt*
eyebrow – Augenbraue (-n) *nf*
eye shadow – Lidschatten *nm*
eye witness – Augenzeuge (-n) *nm wk*
eye witness – Augenzeugin (-nen) *nf*

F

fabulous – phantastisch *adj*
face – Gesicht (-er) *nnt*
fact – Tatsache (-n) *nf*
  in fact – tatsächlich *adv*
factory – Fabrik (-en) *nf*
factory worker – (male)
  Fabrikarbeiter (-) *nm*
factory worker – (female)
  Fabrikarbeiterin (-nen) *nf*
fail – durchfallen* *v irreg sep*
  fail an exam – eine Prüfung nicht
  bestehen *v irreg*
failed – durchgefallen *adj*
faint – schwach *adj*
faint – (swoon) ohnmächtig werden*
  v irreg
fair – (colour) blond *adj*
fair – (average) mittelmäßig *adj*
fair – (just) fair *adj*, gerecht *adj*
  It's not fair! – Das ist nicht
  gerecht!
fair – (weather) schön *adj*
fair – (amusement) Jahrmarkt
  (-märkte) *nm*
fairly – ziemlich *adv*
fairy tale – Märchen (-) *nnt*
faithfully, Yours – mit freundlichen
  Grüßen
fall – fallen* *v irreg*
  fall asleep – einschlafen* *v irreg*
  sep
  fall ill – krank werden* *v irreg*
false – falsch *adj*
familiar – bekannt *adj*
family – Familie (-n) *nf*
family room – (hotel)
  Familienzimmer (-) *nnt*
famous – berühmt *adj*
fan – (supporter) Fan (-s) *nm*
fancy dress – Maskenkostüm (-e) *nnt*

fantastic – phantastisch *adj*
far away – weit *adj*
  Is it far? – Ist es weit?
far away – weit entfernt *adv*
fare – Fahrgeld (-er) *nnt*
fare dodger – (male) Schwarzfahrer (-)
  nm
fare dodger – (female)
  Schwarzfahrerin (-nen) *nf*
farm – Bauernhof (-höfe) *nm*
farmer – (male) Bauer (-n) *nm wk*
farmer – (female) Bäuerin (-nen) *nf*
farmhouse – Bauernhaus (-häuser)
  nnt
farm worker – Landarbeiter (-) *nm*
fascinating – faszinierend *adj*
fashion – Mode (-n) *nf*
fashion designer – (male)
  Modezeichner (-) *nm*
fashion designer – (female)
  Modezeichnerin (-nen) *nf*
fashionable – modisch *adj*
fast – schnell *adj*
  My watch is fast – Meine Uhr
  geht vor
fasten – festmachen *v reg sep*
fasten seat belt – sich anschnallen
  v reg refl sep
fast train – D-Zug (-Züge) *nm*
fat – dick *adj*
father – Vater (Väter) *nm*
Father Christmas –
  Weihnachtsmann (-männer) *nm*
father-in-law – Schwiegervater
  (-väter) *nm*
fault – (defect) Defekt (-) *nm*
fault – (blame) Schuld *nf*
  It's my fault – Es ist meine Schuld
favourable – günstig
favourite – Liebling *nm*
favourite – Lieblings~ *pref*

---

adj - adjective   *v reg* - verb regular   *v sep* - verb separable   † - see verb info
prep - preposition   *v irreg* - verb irregular   *v refl* - verb reflexive   * - takes sein

fax – Fax (-) *nnt*
fax – faxen *v reg*
fax machine – Faxgerät (-e) *nnt*
fax number – Faxnummer (-n) *nf*
fear – Furcht *nf*
feather – Feder (-n) *nf*
February – Februar *nm*
  in February – im Februar
I'm fed up – (annoyed) Ich habe die Nase voll
fee – Gebühr (-en) *nf*
feed the cat – die Katze füttern *v reg*
feel – (think) meinen *v reg*
feel – (person) sich fühlen *v reg refl*
  I feel awful – Ich fühle mich unwohl
  I feel at ease – Ich fühle mich wohl
  I feel cold – Mir ist kalt
  I feel happy – Ich bin glücklich
  I feel hot – Mir ist warm
  I feel hungry – Ich habe Hunger
  I feel ill – Ich fühle mich unwohl
  I feel like – (want) Ich möchte
  I feel sick – Mir ist übel
  I feel sleepy – Ich bin schläfrig
  I feel thirsty – Ich habe Durst
  I feel tired – Ich bin müde
  I feel well – Ich fühle mich wohl
feeling – Gefühl (-e) *nnt*
feet – *see foot*
fell – *see fall*
felt – *see feel*
felt tip pen – Filzstift (-e) *nm*
female – weiblich *adj*
female – (animals) Weibchen (-) *nnt*
feminine – (grammar) feminin *adj*
fence – Zaun (Zäune) *nm*
ferret – Frettchen (-) *nnt*
ferry – Fähre (-n) *nf*
ferry terminal – Fährhafen (-häfen) *nm*
festival – Fest (-e) *nnt*
fetch – holen *v reg*

fête – Fest (-e) *nnt*
fever – Fieber (-) *nnt*
few – (not many) wenige *adj*
  a few – (some) ein paar, einige *adj*
  A few people were there – Ein paar Leute waren da
fewer than – weniger als
fiancé – Verlobte *nm* ‡
fiancée – Verlobte *nf* ‡
fiddle – (violin) Geige (-n) *nf*
field – Feld (-er) *nnt*
fierce – wild *adj*
fifteen – fünfzehn *adj*
fifth – fünfte *adj*
fifty – fünfzig *adj*
fight – kämpfen *v reg*
fight – Kampf (Kämpfe) *nm*
figure – Figur (-en) *nf*
file – (computer) Datei (-en) *nf*
file – (ring binder) Ordner (-) *nm*
fill – füllen *v reg*
fill in a form – ein Formular ausfüllen *v reg sep*
filling station – Tankstelle (-n) *nf*
filling – (teeth) Plombe (-n) *nf*
fill up – (petrol, diesel) voll tanken *v reg*
film – Film (-e) *nm*
  detective film – Detektivfilm (-e) *nm*
  a dubbed film – ein synchronisierter Film (-e) *nm*
  sci-fi film – Sciencefiction Film (-e) *nm*
film star – Filmstar (-s) *nm*
filter coffee – Filterkaffee *nm*
filthy – schmutzig *adj*
final – letzte *adj*
final – (sport) Endspiel (-e) *nnt*
finally – schließlich *adv*
find – finden *v irreg*
find out – herausfinden *v irreg sep*

---

nm - noun masculine	*nf* - noun feminine	*nnt* - noun neuter	*npl* - noun plural
nom- nominative	*acc* - accusative	*gen* - genitive	*dat* - dative

fine – (delicate) fein *adj*
fine – (beautiful) schön *adj*
I'm fine – es geht mir gut
fine – (punishment) Geldstrafe (-n) *nf*
fine! – in Ordnung!
finger – Finger (-) *nm*
finish – beenden *v reg* †
  School is finished – Die Schule ist aus
finish – (stop doing) aufhören *v reg sep*
finish – (sport) ans Ziel kommen* *v irreg*
Finland – Finnland *nnt*
Finnish – finnisch *adj*
Finnish person – (male) Finne (-n) *nm wk*
Finnish person – (female) Finnin (-nen) *nf*
fir (tree) – Tannenbaum (-bäume) *nm*
fire – Feuer (-) *nnt*
fire – (accidental/malicious) Brand (Brände) *nm*
  Fire! – Es brennt!
fire alarm – Feueralarm (-e) *nm*
fire brigade – Feuerwehr (-en) *nf*
fire engine – Feuerwehrwagen (-) *nm*
fire escape – Feuerleiter (-n) *nf*
fireman – Feuerwehrmann (-männer) *nm*
fire-place – Kamin (e) *nm*
firework – Feuerwerk *nnt, no pl*
firm – fest *adj*
firm – Firma (Firmen) *nf*
first – erste *adj*
  at first – zuerst *adv*
  on the first floor – im ersten Stock
first aid – erste Hilfe *nf*
first aid kit – Verbandkasten (-kästen) *nm*
first class ticket – Fahrkarte erster Klasse *nf*

a first class ticket, please – einmal erster Klasse, bitte
firstly – erstens *adv*
first name – Vorname (-n) *nm wk*
first of all – zuerst *adv*
fish – Fisch (-e) *nm*
fish – angeln *v reg*
fish finger – Fischstäbchen (-) *nnt*
fisherman – Fischer (-) *nm*
fisherwoman – Fischerin (-nen) *nf*
fishing – Angeln *nnt*
  go fishing – angeln *v reg*
fishing port – Fischereihafen (-häfen) *nm*
fishing rod – Angelrute (-n) *nf*
fishmonger – (male) Fischhändler (-) *nm*
fishmonger – (female) Fischhändlerin (-nen) *nf*
  I'm going to the fish shop – Ich gehe ins Fischgeschäft
fist – Faust (Fäuste) *nf*
fit – (healthy) gesund *adj*
fit – (suitable) geeignet *adj*
  It does not fit me – Es passt mir nicht
fitness – (health) Gesundheit *nf*
fitness – (condition) Fitness *nf*
fitted carpet – Teppichboden (-böden) *nm*
fitting room – Umkleidekabine (-n) *nf*
five – fünf *adj*
fix – (repair) reparieren *v reg* †
fixed – fest *adj*
fixture – Spiel (-e) *nnt*
fizzy – sprudelnd *adj*
flag – Fahne (-n) *nf*
flame – Flamme (-n) *nf*
  go up in flames – brennen *v irreg*
flan – Torte (-n) *nf*
flannel – Waschlappen (-) *nm*
flash of lightning – Blitz (-e) *nm*

---

adj - adjective   *v reg* - verb regular   *v sep* - verb separable   † - see verb info
prep - preposition   *v irreg* - verb irregular   *v refl* - verb reflexive   * - takes sein

flat – Wohnung (-en) *nf*
  block of flats – Wohnblock (-s) *nm*
flat – (level) flach *adj*
flat – (of tyre, etc) platt *adj*
flat tyre – Reifenpanne (-n) *nf*
flavour – Geschmack (Geschmäcke) *nm*
  lemon flavoured – mit Zitronengeschmack
flea – Floh (Flöhe) *nm*
flea market – Flohmarkt (-märkte) *nm*
flee – fliehen* *v irreg*
flight – (plane) Flug (Flüge) *nm*
flight – (departure) Abflug (Abflüge) *nm*
flight of stairs – Treppe (-n) *nf*
fling – werfen *v irreg*
flip-flops – Sandale (-n) *nf*
flirt – flirten *v reg* †
float – schwimmen* *v irreg*
flock – Herde (-n) *nf*
flood – Überschwemmung (-en) *nf*
floor – (ground) Fußboden (-böden) *nm*
floor – Stock (Stockwerke) *nm*
  on the first floor – im ersten Stock
  on the ground floor – im Erdgeschoss
  on the next floor – im nächsten Stock
  on the top floor – im obersten Stock
floppy disk – Diskette (-n) *nf*
flour – Mehl *nnt*
flow – fließen* *v irreg*
flower – Blume (-n) *nf*
flower bed – Blumenbeet (-n) *nnt*
flower vase – Vase (-n) *nf*
flu – Grippe *nf*
fluent – (speech) fließend *adj*
flute – Flöte (-n) *nf*

fly – (insect) Fliege (-n) *nf*
fly – fliegen* *v irreg*
flying – (in plane) Fliegen *nnt*
fog – Nebel *nm*
foggy – neblig *adj*
fold – falten *v reg* †
folder – (file) Schnellhefter (-) *nm*
folk – Leute *npl*
folk music – Volksmusik *nf*
folk song – Volkslied (-er) *nnt*
follow – folgen* (+ dat) *v reg*
followed by – gefolgt von (+ dat) *adj*
following – folgend *adj*
food – Essen *nnt*
food processor – Küchenmaschine (-n) *nf*
fool – (male) Narr (-en) *nm wk*
fool – (female) Närrin (-nen) *nf*
foolish – albern *adj*
foot – Fuß (Füße) *nm*
  on foot – zu Fuß
football – Fußball (-bälle) *nm*
football boots – Fußballschuhe *npl*
footballer – Fußballspieler (-) *nm*
football field – Fußballplatz (-plätze) *nm*
football match – Fußballspiel (-e) *nnt*
footpath – Fußweg (-e) *nm*
footstep – Schritt (-e) *nm*
for – denn *co-ord conj*
for – weil *sub conj*
for – für (+ acc) *prep*
for – (since) seit (+ dat) *prep*
  for ever – für immer *adv*
  for example – zum Beispiel
  for hire – zu vermieten
  for sale – zu verkaufen
forbid – verbieten *v irreg*
forbidden – verboten *adj*
force – zwingen *v irreg*

---

nm - noun masculine	*nf* - noun feminine	*nnt* - noun neuter	*npl* - noun plural
nom- nominative	*acc* - accusative	*gen* - genitive	*dat* - dative

forecast – (weather) Wettervorhersage (-n) *nf*
foreign – ausländisch *adj*
foreigner – (male) Ausländer (-) *nm*
foreigner – (female) Ausländerin (-nen) *nf*
forest – Wald (Wälder) *nm*
forget – vergessen *v irreg*
forgive – vergeben *v irreg*
fork – Gabel (-n) *nf*
fork out – blechen *v reg coll*
form – (class) Klasse (-n) *nf*
form – (paper) Formular (-e) *nnt*
former – (previous) früher *adj*, ehemalig *adj*
fortnight – vierzehn Tage
fortunate – glücklich *adj*
fortunately – glücklicherweise *adv*
forty – vierzig *adj*
forty-one – einundvierzig *adj*
forwards – vorwärts *adv*
go forward – vorangehen* *v irreg sep*
forward – (sport) Stürmer (-) *nm*
found – *see find*
fountain pen – Füller (-) *nm*
four – vier *adj*
fourteen – vierzehn *adj*
fourth – vierte *adj*
fragile – zerbrechlich *adj*
frame – (photo, etc) Rahmen (-) *nm*
frame – (spectacles) Gestell (-e) *nnt*
franc – (French) Franc (-s) *nm*
franc – (Swiss) Franken (-) *nm*
France – Frankreich *nnt*
frank – offen *adj*
frankfurter – Bockwurst (-würste) *nf*
free – frei *adj*, kostenlos *adj*
freedom – Freiheit (-en) *nf*
free time – Freizeit *nf*
freeze – frieren *v irreg*
It is freezing – (ice) Es friert

It is freezing – Es ist sehr kalt
I'm freezing – Mir friert's
freezer – Tiefkühltruhe (-n) *nf*
French – französisch *adj*
in French – auf Französisch
French – (language) Französisch *nnt*
French bean – grüne Bohne (-n) *nf*
French fries – Pommes frites *npl*
French person – (male) Franzose (n) *nm wk*
French person – (female) Französin (-nen) *nf*
frequent – häufig *adj*
frequently – oft *adv*
fresh – frisch *adj*
Friday – Freitag (-e) *nm*
on Friday – am Freitag
Good Friday – Karfreitag *nm*
fridge – Kühlschrank (-schränke) *nm*
friend – (male) Freund (-e) *nm*
friend – (female) Freundin (-nen) *nf*
friendly – freundlich *adj*
friendly with – befreundet mit (+ dat) *adj*
friendship – Freundschaft (-en) *nf*
fright – Schreck (-e) *nm*
frightened – erschrocken *adj*
be frightened of – Angst haben vor (+ dat) *v irreg*
frightening – schrecklich *adj*
fringe – Pony (-s) *nm*
frog – Frosch (Frösche) *nm*
from – von (+ dat) *prep*
from – (out of) aus (+ dat) *prep*
from – (according to) nach (+ dat) *prep*
from – (date, prices) ab (+ dat) *prep*
front – Vorderseite (-n) *nf*
in front of – vor (+ acc/dat) *prep*
front door – Haustür (-en) *nf*
front wheel – Vorderrad (-räder) *nnt*
frost – Frost *nm*

---

adj - adjective   *v reg* - verb regular   *v sep* - verb separable   † - see verb info
prep - preposition   *v irreg* - verb irregular   *v refl* - verb reflexive   * - takes sein

frosty – frostig *adj*
frown – die Stirn runzeln *v reg*
frozen – gefroren *adj*
frozen – (food) tiefgefroren *adj*
fruit – Obst *nnt*
  stewed fruit – Kompott (-e) *nnt*
fruit juice – Fruchtsaft (-säfte) *nm*
fruit machine – Spielautomat (-en)
  nm wk
fruits – Obstsorten *npl*
fruit seller – Obsthändler (-) *nm*
fruit tree – Obstbaum (-bäume) *nm*
fry – braten *v irreg*
frying pan – Pfanne (-n) *nf*
full – voll *adj*
  at full fare – zum vollen Fahrpreis
full – (well fed) satt *adj*
full board – Vollpension *nf*
full of – voll *adj*
full stop (.) – Punkt (-e) *nm*
at full speed – mit
  Höchstgeschwindigkeit
full time – (job) ganztägig *adj*
fun – Spaß (Späße) *nm*

be fun – Spaß machen *v reg*
It's fun – Es macht (mir) Spaß
have fun – Spaß haben *v irreg*
make fun of – veräppeln *v reg* †
  coll
fun fair – Jahrmarkt (-märkte) *nm*
funny – (amusing) komisch *adj*
funny – (strange) seltsam *adj*
furious – wütend *adj*
furnished – möbliert *adj*
furniture – Möbel *npl*
  piece of furniture – Möbelstück
  (-e) *nnt*
further – weiter *adv*
further education – Weiterbildung
  nf
fuss – Theater *nnt coll*
  make a fuss about sthg –
    Theater machen über (+ acc)
    v reg coll
fussy – pingelig *adj coll*
future – Zukunft *nf*
future – künftig *adj*
  in future – in Zukunft *adv*

G

gale – Sturm (Stürme) *nm*
gallery – Galerie (-n) *nf*
  art gallery – Gemäldegalerie (-n)
  nf
game – Spiel (-e) *nnt*
  arcade game – Spielautomat (-en)
  nm wk
  board game – Brettspiel (-e) *nnt*
  computer game – Computerspiel
  (-e) *nnt*
  video game – Videospiel (-e) *nnt*
game of tennis – Tennisspiel (-e) *nnt*

games room – Spielraum (-räume)
  nm
games – Sport *nm*
  do games – Sport treiben *v irreg*
garage – (petrol) Tankstelle (-n) *nf*
garage – (repair) Werkstatt (-stätten)
  nf
garage – (house) Garage (-n) *nf*
garage owner – Tankstellenbesitzer
  (-) *nm*
garden – Garten (Gärten) *nm*
gardener – Gärtner (-) *nm*
gardening – Gartenarbeit *nf*

---

do the gardening – im Garten arbeiten *v reg* †

garlic – Knoblauch *nm*

garment – Kleidungsstück (-e) *nnt*

gas – Gas (-e) *nnt*

gas cooker – Gasherd (-e) *nm*

gas cylinder – Gasflasche (-n) *nf*

gate – Tor (-e) *nnt*

gate-crash – hereinplatzen* *v reg sep coll*

gather – (collect) sammeln *v reg*

GB – Großbritannien *nnt*

gear – (car) Gang (Gänge) *nm*

gel – (hair) Gel *nnt*

Gemini – Zwillinge

gender – Geschlecht (-er) *nnt*

general – allgemein *adj*
in general – im Allgemeinen *adv*

generous – großzügig *adj*

Geneva – Genf

genitive – Genitiv *nnt*

gentle – zart, sanft *adj*

gentleman – Herr (-en) *nm wk*

Gentlemen – Herren *npl*

genuine – echt *adj*

geography – Erdkunde *nf*, Geographie *nf*

geology – Geologie *nf*

gerbil – Wüstenspringmaus (-mäuse) *nf*

German – deutsch *adj*

German – (language) Deutsch *nnt*
in German – auf Deutsch

German person – Deutsche *nmf* ‡

Germany – Deutschland *nnt*

get – (become) werden* *v irreg*

get – (buy) kaufen *v reg*

get – (fetch) holen *v reg*

get – (receive) bekommen *v irreg*, kriegen *v reg coll*

get – (understand) verstehen *v irreg*

get a divorce – sich scheiden lassen *v irreg refl*

get about – (travel) fahren* *v irreg*

get across – (to the other side) überqueren *v reg insep*

get along – (manage) zurechtkommen* *v irreg sep*

get angry – böse werden* *v irreg*

get annoyed – sich ärgern *v reg refl*

get away – entkommen* *v irreg*

get back – zurückkommen* *v irreg sep*

get better – sich erholen *v reg refl* †

get changed – sich umziehen *v irreg refl sep*

get done – etwas machen lassen *v irreg*

get dressed – sich anziehen *v irreg refl sep*

get hurt – verletzt werden* *v irreg*

get in – (arrive) ankommen* *v irreg sep*

get injured – sich verletzen *v reg refl* †

get into – (bus, etc) einsteigen* in (+ acc) *v irreg sep*

get lost – (on foot) sich verlaufen *v irreg refl*

get lost – (in car) sich verfahren *v irreg refl*

get married – heiraten *v reg*

get off – (bus, etc) aussteigen* aus (+ dat) *v irreg sep*

get on – (succeed) vorankommen* *v irreg sep*

get on the train – in den Zug einsteigen* *v irreg sep*

get on with – (person) sich verstehen mit (+ dat) *v irreg refl*

get over – (illness) sich erholen *v reg refl* †

get ready – sich fertig machen *v reg refl*

get rid of – loswerden* *v irreg sep*

get round – (avoid) vermeiden *v irreg*

---

adj - adjective	*v reg* - verb regular	*v sep* - verb separable	† - see verb info
prep - preposition	*v irreg* - verb irregular	*v refl* - verb reflexive	* - takes sein

get stung – gestochen werden* *v irreg*
get the bus – mit dem Bus fahren*
  v irreg
get to – (arrive) ankommen* in (+ dat)
  v irreg sep
get to – (reach) erreichen *v reg* †
get to know – kennen lernen *v reg*
get used to – sich gewöhnen an
  (+ acc) *v reg refl* †
get undressed – sich ausziehen
  v irreg refl sep
get up – aufstehen* *v irreg sep*
ghost – Gespenst (-er) *nnt*
giant – Riese (-n) *nm wk*
gift – Geschenk (-e) *nnt*
gift wrap – als Geschenk einpacken
  v reg sep
gifted – begabt *adj*
gig – Konzert (-e) *nnt*
gigantic – riesig *adj*
giggle – kichern *v reg*
ginger – (hair) rothaarig *adj*
ginger – Ingwer *nm*
ginger bread – Lebkuchen *nm*
girl – Mädchen (-) *nnt*
girlfriend – Freundin (-nen) *nf*
give – geben *v irreg*
  Give me... – (formal) Geben Sie mir
  Give me... – (informal) Gib mir
give – (gift) schenken *v reg*
give back – zurückgeben *v irreg sep*
give in – nachgeben *v irreg sep*
give up – aufgeben *v irreg sep*
glacier – Gletscher (-) *nm*
glad – zufrieden *adj*
gladly – gern *adv*
glance – Blick (-e) *nm*
glass – (drinking) Glas (Gläser) *nnt*
glass – (mirror) Spiegel (-) *nm*
glass – (pane of) Glasscheibe (-n) *nf*
glasses – (pair of) Brille (-n) *nf sing*
glen – Tal (Täler) *nnt*

global – global *adj*
gloomy – düster *adj*
glove – Handschuh (-e) *nm*
glow – glühen *v reg*
glue – Klebstoff (-e) *nm*
GNVQ Level 2 –
  Berufsfachschulreife *nf*
GNVQ Level 3 – Fachhochschulreife
  nf
go – (on foot) gehen* *v irreg*
go – (travel) fahren* *v irreg*
go – (become) werden* *v irreg*
go – (depart) abfahren* *v irreg sep*
go – (function) funktionieren *v reg* †
go – (leave house, etc) das Haus
  verlassen *v irreg*
go – (vanish) verschwinden* *v irreg*
go and fetch someone – holen *v reg*
go and see – besuchen *v reg* †
go away – weggehen* *v irreg sep*
Go away! – Hau ab! *excl*
go babysitting – babysitten gehen*
  v irreg
go back – zurückgehen* *v irreg sep*
go by car – mit dem Auto fahren*
  v irreg
go boating – Boot fahren* *v irreg*
go camping – zelten *v reg* †
go down the street – die Straße
  entlang gehen* *v irreg sep*
go downstairs – nach unten gehen*
  v irreg
go fishing – angeln gehen* *v irreg*
go for – (fetch) holen *v reg*
go for a bike ride – eine Radtour
  machen *v reg*
go for a walk – einen Spaziergang
  machen *v reg*
go home – nach Hause gehen* *v irreg*
go horse riding – reiten gehen*
  v irreg
go in (to) – hineingehen* *v irreg sep*

---

nm - noun masculine   *nf* - noun feminine   *nnt* - noun neuter   *npl* - noun plural
nom- nominative   *acc* - accusative   *gen* - genitive   *dat* - dative

go in for an exam – eine Prüfung machen *v reg*
go jogging – joggen *v reg*
go near to – sich nähern (+ dat) *v reg refl*
go off – (depart) weggehen* *v irreg sep*
go off – (food) verfaulen* *v reg* †
go on – (continue) fortfahren* *v irreg sep*
go on an exchange – am Austausch teilnehmen *v irreg sep*
go on foot – zu Fuß gehen* *v irreg*
go on holiday – in Urlaub fahren* *v irreg*
go out – hinausgehen* *v irreg sep*
go out – (light) ausgehen* *v irreg sep*
go out with – ausgehen* mit (+ dat) *v irreg sep*
go red – rot werden* *v irreg*
go round the shops – einen Einkaufsbummel machen *v reg*
go round town – einen Stadtbummel machen *v reg*
go sailing – segeln gehen* *v irreg*
go shopping – einkaufen gehen* *v irreg*
go skiing – Ski fahren* *v irreg*
Go straight on! – Gehen Sie geradeaus!
Go that way! – Gehen Sie in diese Richtung!
go to bed – ins Bett gehen* *v irreg*
go upstairs – nach oben gehen* *v irreg*
go walking – spazieren gehen* *v irreg*
go window shopping – einen Schaufensterbummel machen *v reg*
go windsurfing – windsurfen gehen* *v irreg*
go-kart – Gokart (-s) *nm*
go-karting – Gokart Fahren *nnt*

to go go-karting – Gokart fahren* *v irreg*
goal – (aim) Ziel (-e) *nnt*
goal – (sport) Tor (-e) *nnt*
goalkeeper – Torwart (-e) *nm*
goalless draw – Null zu Null Unentschieden *nnt*
goalpost – Torpfosten (-) *nm*
goat – Ziege (-n) *nf*
God – Gott (Götter) *nm*
goggles – (pair of) Schutzbrille (-n) *nf*
going to – in Richtung
gold – Gold *nnt*
  made of gold – aus Gold
golden – golden *adj*
goldfish – Goldfisch (-e) *nm*
golf – Golf *nm*
golf course – Golfplatz (-plätze) *nm*
gone – *see fahren*, gehen**
  It's all gone – Es ist alle
good – gut *adj*
  good at – gut in (+ dat)
good – (well-behaved) brav *adj*
good – (well) gut *adv*
Good afternoon! – Guten Tag! *excl*
Goodbye! – Auf Wiedersehen! *excl*
  say goodbye – sich verabschieden *v reg refl* †
Good evening! – Guten Abend! *excl*
Good Friday – Karfreitag *nm*
Good idea! – Gute Idee! *excl*
good looking – gut aussehend *adj*
Good luck! – Viel Glück! *excl*
Good morning! – Guten Morgen! *excl*
goodness – Güte *nf*
good news – eine gute Nachricht
Good night! – Gute Nacht! *excl*
good-tempered – gut gelaunt *adj*
good value – günstig *adj*, preiswert *adj*
goose – Gans (Gänse) *nf*

---

adj - adjective | *v reg* - verb regular | *v sep* - verb separable | † - see verb info
prep - preposition | *v irreg* - verb irregular | *v refl* - verb reflexive | * - takes sein

gooseberry – Stachelbeere (-n) *nf*
gorgeous – herrlich *adj*
got to – (must) müssen *v irreg*
got – (have) haben *v irreg*
grab – greifen *v irreg*
grade – (mark) Note (-n) *nf*
gram – Gramm *nnt*
grammar – Grammatik *nf*
grammar school – Gymnasium (-ien) *nnt*
grandchild – Enkelkind (-er) *nnt*
grandad – Opa (-s) *nm*
granddaughter – Enkelin (-nen) *nf*
grandfather – Großvater (-väter) *nm*
grandmother – Großmutter (-mütter) *nf*
grandparents – Großeltern *npl*
grandson – Enkel (-) *nm*
granny – Oma (-s) *nf*
grapefruit – Pampelmuse (-n) *nf*
grape – Weintraube (-n) *nf*
grape juice – Traubensaft *nm*
grass – Gras (Gräser) *nnt*
grateful – dankbar *adj*
gravy – Soße (-n) *nf*
greasy – fettig *adj*
Great! – Klasse! Wunderbar! Prima! *excl*
great – (big) groß *adj*
great-grandfather – Urgroßvater (-väter) *nm*
great-grandmother – Urgroßmutter (-mütter) *nf*
Great Britain – Großbritannien *nnt*
Greece – Griechenland *nnt*
Greek – griechisch *adj*
Greek person – (male) Grieche (-n) *nm wk*
Greek person – (female) Griechin (-nen) *nf*
greedy – gierig *adj*
green – grün *adj*
green bean – Bohne (-n) *nf*

green pepper – Paprika (-s) *nm*
green salad – grüner Salat *nm*
greengrocer – (male) Gemüsehändler (-) *nm*
greengrocer – (female) Gemüsehändlerin (-nen) *nf*
greenhouse – Gewächshaus (-häuser) *nnt*
greenhouse effect – Treibhauseffekt *nm*
greens – Gemüse *nnt*
greet – begrüßen *v reg* †
greetings card – Glückwunschkarte (-n) *nf*
grey – grau *adj*
grill – (food) grillen *v reg*
grin – grinsen *v reg*
grip – (grasp) ergreifen *v irreg*
grip – (interest) fesseln *v reg*
gripping – fesselnd *adj*
grocer – (male) Lebensmittelhändler (-) *nm*
grocer – (female) Lebensmittelhändlerin (-nen) *nf*
groceries – Lebensmittel (-) *nnt*
grocer's shop – Lebensmittelgeschäft (-e) *nnt*
ground – (earth) Erde *nf*
   on the ground – auf dem Boden
ground – (sport) Platz (Plätze) *nm*
ground floor – Erdgeschoss *nnt*
   on the ground floor – im Erdgeschoss
group – Gruppe (-n) *nf*
grow – (become) werden* *v irreg*
grow – (plants) anbauen *v reg sep*
grow – (get bigger) wachsen* *v irreg*
grow one's hair – sich die Haare wachsen lassen *v irreg dat refl*
grow up – aufwachsen* *v irreg sep*
grown up – erwachsen *adj*
growl – knurren *v reg*
grumble – murren *v reg*

---

grumpy – verdrießlich *adj*
guarantee – Garantie (-n) *nf*
guess – raten *v irreg*
guest – Gast (Gäste) *nm*
guest house – Pension *nf*
guide – (male) Führer (-) *nm*
guide – (female) Führerin (-nen) *nf*
  girl guide – Pfadfinderin (-nen) *nf*
guide book – Reiseführer (-) *nm*
guided tour – Führung (-en) *nf*

guided tour – (by coach, etc)
  Rundfahrt (-en) *nf*
guilty – schuldig *adj*
guinea-pig – Meerschweinchen (-)
  nnt
guitar – Gitarre (-n) *nf*
gun – (handgun) Pistole (-n) *nf*
gun – (rifle) Gewehr (-e) *nnt*
guy – Typ (-en) *nm coll*
gym(nasium) – Turnhalle (-n) *nf*
gym(nastics) – Turnen *nnt*
  do gymnastics – turnen *v reg*

H

habit – Gewohnheit (-en) *nf*
  I am in the habit of – Ich habe
  die Gewohnheit
  get into the habit of – sich
  gewöhnen an (+ acc) *v reg refl* †
had – *see haben*
had to – *see müssen*
hail – Hagel *nm*
  It is hailing – Es hagelt
hair – Haar (-e) *nnt*
hairbrush – Haarbürste (-n) *nf*
haircut – Haarschnitt (-e) *nm*
  have a haircut – sich die Haare
  schneiden lassen *v irreg dat refl*
hairdresser – (male) Frisör (-) *nm*
hairdresser – (female) Friseuse (-n)
  nf
hair dryer – Föhn (-e) *nm*
hairstyle – Frisur (-en) *nf*
half – halb *adj*
  half an hour – eine halbe Stunde
  half-price – zum halben Preis
half – Halb~ *pref*
  half board – Halbpension *nf*
  half-brother – Halbbruder
  (-brüder) *nm*

half-sister – Halbschwester (-n) *nf*
half – Hälfte (-n) *nf*
half back – Läufer (-) *nm*
half past – halb
  half past two – halb drei
  half past six – halb sieben
  at half past three – um halb vier
half term holiday – (Autumn)
  Herbstferien *npl*
half term holiday – (February)
  Halbjahresferien *npl*
half term holiday – (Whitsuntide)
  Pfingstferien *npl*
half way – halbwegs *adv*
hall – (domestic) Hausflur (-e) *nm*,
  Diele (-n) *nf*
hall – (public) Halle (-n) *nf*
hall – (public, smart) Saal (Säle) *nm*
hall – (school) Aula (Aulen) *nf*
Halt! – Halt! *excl*
halt – Halt machen *v reg*
ham – Schinken (-) *nm*
  ham sandwich – Schinkenbrot (-e)
  nnt
hamburger – Hamburger (-) *nm*
hammer – Hammer (-) *nm*

---

hamster – Hamster (-) *nm*
hand – Hand (Hände) *nf*
on the one hand – einerseits *adv*
on the other hand – andererseits *adv*
give s.o. a hand – helfen (+ dat) *v irreg*
handbag – Handtasche (-n) *nf*
handball – Handball (-bälle) *nm*
handicapped – behindert *adj*
hand in – abgeben *v irreg sep*
handkerchief – Taschentuch (-tücher) *nnt*
handle – Griff (-e) *nm*
hand luggage – Handgepäck *nnt*
handmade – handgemacht *adj*
handsome – gut aussehend *adj*
handwriting – Handschrift (-en) *nf*
handwritten – handgeschrieben *adj*
handy – (useful) praktisch *adj*
handyman – Heimwerker (-) *nm*
hang – hängen *v irreg*
hang gliding – Drachenfliegen *nnt*
hang up – (phone) auflegen *v reg sep*
happen – geschehen* *v irreg*, passieren* *v reg* †
happiness – Glück *nnt*
happy – glücklich *adj*
Happy Birthday! – Herzlichen Glückwunsch zum Geburtstag! *excl*
Happy Christmas! – Frohe/Fröhliche Weihnachten! *excl*
Happy New Year! – Ein glückliches neues Jahr! *excl*
happy with – zufrieden mit (+ dat) *adj*
harbour – Hafen (Häfen) *nm*
hard – (difficult) schwer *adj*
hard – hart *adj*
hard disk – Festplatte (-n) *nf*
hardly – kaum *adv*
hard of hearing – schwerhörig *adj*

hardware shop – Eisenwarengeschäft (-e) *nnt*
hardworking – fleißig *adj*
harsh – streng *adj*
harvest – Ernte (-n) *nf*
harvest – ernten *v reg* †
has – *see haben*
has to – *see müssen*
hassle – Ärger *nm*
hassle – schikanieren *v reg* †
haste – Eile *nf*
hasten – sich beeilen *v reg refl* †
hasty – eilig *adj*
hat – Hut (Hüte) *nm*
hate – hassen *v reg*
have – haben *v irreg*
have a bath – sich baden *v reg refl* †
have a cold – erkältet sein* *v irreg*
have a flair for – eine Begabung haben *v irreg*
Have a good journey! – Gute Fahrt! *excl*
Have a good journey home! – Gute Heimreise! *excl*
Have a good time! – Viel Spaß! *excl*
Have a good trip! – Gute Reise! *excl*
Have a good weekend! – Schönes Wochenende! *excl*
have a headache – Kopfschmerzen haben *v irreg*
have a holiday – Urlaub haben *v irreg*
have a meal – essen *v irreg*
Have a nice day! – Einen schönen Tag! *excl*
Have a nice evening! – Einen schönen Abend! *excl*
have a temperature – Fieber haben *v irreg*
Have a safe journey home! – Kommen Sie gut nach Hause! *excl*

---

nm - noun masculine   *nf* - noun feminine   *nnt* - noun neuter   *npl* - noun plural
nom- nominative   *acc* - accusative   *gen* - genitive   *dat* - dative

have a sore throat – Halsschmerzen haben *v irreg*

have a walk – spazieren gehen* *v irreg*, einen Spaziergang machen *v reg*

have breakfast – frühstücken *v reg*

have difficulty – Schwierigkeiten haben *v irreg*

have dinner – zu Abend essen *v irreg*

have friends round – Freunde einladen *v irreg sep*

have lunch – zu Mittag essen *v irreg*

have on – (clothes) anhaben *v irreg sep*

have something cleaned – etwas reinigen lassen *v irreg*

have something repaired – etwas reparieren lassen *v irreg*

have stomach ache – Magenschmerzen haben *v irreg*

have the opportunity to – die Gelegenheit haben *v irreg*

have to – (must) müssen *v irreg*

have toothache – Zahnschmerzen haben *v irreg*

hay fever – Heuschnupfen *nm*

hazard – Gefahr (-en) *nf*

hazard warning lights – Warnblinkanlage *nf*

hazelnut – Haselnuss (-nüsse) *nf*

he – er *pron nom*

head – Kopf (Köpfe) *nm*

headache – Kopfschmerzen *npl*

heading – Titel (-) *nm*

headlight – Scheinwerfer (-) *nm*

headline – Schlagzeile (-n) *nf*

headmaster – Direktor (-en) *nm*

headmistress – Direktorin (-nen) *nf*

headphones – Kopfhörer (-) *nm*

Heads or tails? – Kopf oder Zahl?

headteacher – (male) Direktor (-en) *nm*

headteacher – (female) Direktorin (-nen) *nf*

health – Gesundheit *nf*

health food – Reformkost *nf*

healthy – gesund *adj*

heap – Haufen *nm*

hear – hören *v reg*

hear from – von (+ dat) hören *v reg*

heart – Herz (en) *nnt wk*

by heart – auswendig *adj*

heat – Hitze *nf*

heat – heizen *v reg*

heater – Heizgerät (-e) *nnt*

heating – Heizung (-en) *nf*

heatwave – Hitzewelle (-n) *nf*

heavy – schwer *adj*

hedge – Hecke (-n) *nf*

heel – (foot) Ferse (-n) *nf*

heel – (shoe) Absatz (-sätze) *nm*

height – (geographical) Höhe *nf*

height – (person) Größe *nf*

helicopter – Hubschrauber (-) *nm*

heliport – Hubschrauberlandeplatz (-plätze) *nm*

Hello! – Hallo! *excl*

helmet – Helm (-e) *nm*

Help! – Hilfe! *excl*

help – Hilfe *nf*

help – helfen (+ dat) *v irreg*

helpful – hilfsbereit *adj*

helpless – hilflos *adj*

help oneself – sich bedienen *v reg refl* †

hen – Henne (-n) *nf*

her – sie *pron acc*

her – ihr *pron dat*

her – ihr *poss adj*

herbal tea – Kräutertee (-s) *nm*

herd – Herde (-n) *nf*

here – hier *adv*

hero – Held (-en) *nm wk*

heroin – (drug) Heroin *nnt*

---

heroine – (heroic) Heldin (-nen) *nf*
herring – Hering (-e) *nm*
herself – sich *pron refl*
hesitate – zögern *v reg*
HGV – LKW (-s)(Lastkraftwagen) *nm*
Hi! – Hallo! *excl*
hidden – versteckt *adj*
hide – verstecken *v reg* †
hide o.s. – sich verstecken *v reg refl* †
hi-fi system – Stereoanlage (-n) *nf*
high – hoch *adj*
higher – höher *adj*
highest – höchst *adj*
high speed train – Schnellzug (-züge) *nm*
high street – Hauptstraße (-n) *nf*
high temperature – (body) Fieber *nnt*
high tide – Flut (-en) *nf*
highway – (road) Straße (-n) *nf*
highway code – Straßenverkehrsordnung (StVO) *nf*
high wind – Sturm (Stürme) *nm*
hike – Wanderung (-en) *nf*
  go for a hike – wandern* *v reg*
hiker – (male) Wanderer (-) *nm*
hiker – (female) Wanderin (-nen) *nf*
hiking boots – Wanderschuhe *npl*
hill – Hügel (-n) *nf*
him – ihn *pron acc*
him – ihm *pron dat*
himself – sich *pron refl*
Hindu – hindu *adj*
Hindu person – Hindu (-s) *nm*
hip – Hüfte (-n) *nf*
hire – (rent) Miete (-n) *nf*
hire – mieten *v reg* †
  for hire – (taxi, etc) frei
his – sein *poss adj*
historic – historisch *adj*
history – Geschichte *nf*
hit – schlagen *v irreg*

hit song – (in English) Hit (-s) *nm*
hit song – (in German) Schlager (-) *nm*
hobby – Hobby (-s) *nnt*
hockey – Hockey *nnt*
hold – halten *v irreg*
hold back – zurückhalten *v irreg sep*
Hold the line please! – Bleiben Sie am Apparat, bitte! *excl*
holdall – Reisetasche (-n) *nf*
holdup – (traffic) Stau (-s) *nm*
holdup – (robbery) Überfall (-fälle) *nm*
hold tight – festhalten *v irreg sep*
hole – Loch (Löcher) *nnt*
holiday – (school) Ferien *npl*
holiday – Urlaub *nm*
  be on holiday – auf Urlaub sein* *v irreg*
  go on holiday – in Urlaub fahren* *v irreg*
holiday – (day) Feiertag (-e) *nm*
  Easter holidays – Osterferien *npl*
  summer holidays – Sommerferien *npl*
holiday cottage – Ferienhaus (-häuser) *nnt*
holiday maker – (male) Urlauber (-) *nm*
holiday maker – (female) Urlauberin (-nen) *nf*
holiday plans – Urlaubspläne *npl*
Holland – Holland *nnt*
hollow – hohl *adj*
holly – Stechpalme (-n) *nf*
holy – heilig *adj*
home – Haus (Häuser) *nnt*
  at the home of – bei (+ dat) *prep*
  be at home – zu Hause sein* *v irreg*
  go home – nach Hause gehen* *v irreg*
home area – Heimat *nf*

---

home economics – Hauswirtschaftslehre *nf*
home game – Heimspiel (-e) *nnt*
home-made – selbst gemacht *adj*
homesickness – Heimweh *nnt*
  I'm homesick – Ich habe Heimweh
homework – Hausaufgaben *npl*
honest – ehrlich *adj*
honey – Honig (-e) *nm*
hook –Haken (-) *nm*
hooligan – Rowdy (-s) *nm*
hope – Hoffnung (-en) *nf*
hope – hoffen *v reg*
hopefully – hoffentlich *adv*
Hoping to see you soon! – Bis bald! *excl*
horizon – Horizont (-e) *nm*
  on the horizon – am Horizont
horn – (car) Hupe (-n) *nf*
horn – (music) Horn (Hörner) *nnt*
horrible – fürchterlich *adj*, furchtbar *adj*
horrified – entsetzt *adj*
horrifying – entsetzlich *adj*
horror – Horror *nm*
horror film – Horrorfilm (-e) *nm*
horror story – Horrorgeschichte (-n) *nf*
horse – Pferd (-e) *nnt*
horse riding – Reiten *nnt*
  go horse riding – reiten gehen* *v irreg*
hospital – Krankenhaus (-häuser) *nnt*
hospitality – Gastfreundschaft *nf*
host – Gastgeber (-) *nm*
hostel – Herberge (-n) *nf*
  youth hostel – Jugendherberge (-n) *nf*
hostess – Gastgeberin (-nen) *nf*
hot – heiß *adj*
  I am hot – Mir ist warm
  It is hot – Es ist warm

hot water – warmes Wasser
hotel – Hotel (-s) *nnt*
hour – Stunde (-n) *nf*
hourly – stündlich *adj*
house – Haus (Häuser) *nnt*
  at my house – bei mir
  detached house – Einfamilienhaus (-häuser) *nnt*
  semi-detached house – Doppelhaus (-häuser) *nnt*
household – Haushalt (-e) *nm*
househusband – Hausmann (-männer) *nm*
house number – Hausnummer (-n) *nf*
housewife – Hausfrau (-en) *nf*
housework – Hausarbeit *nf*
housing estate – Siedlung (-en) *nf*
hovercraft – Luftkissenboot (-e) *nnt*
how – wie *adv*
How are things? – Wie geht's?
How are you? – (formal) Wie geht es Ihnen?
How are you? – (informal) Wie geht es dir?
How do you say ... in German? – Wie sagt man ... auf Deutsch?
How do you spell that? – Wie schreibt man das?
how long? – seit wann?
How long have you been learning German? – Seit wann lernst du Deutsch?
how many? – wie viele?
how much? – wie viel?
How much is it? – Was kostet das?
How much is that altogether? – Was macht das?
however – jedoch *adv*
huge – riesig *adj*
humanities – Geisteswissenschaften *npl*
humour – Humor *nm*
hundred – hundert *adj*

---

adj - adjective	*v reg* - verb regular	*v sep* - verb separable	† - see verb info
prep - preposition	*v irreg* - verb irregular	*v refl* - verb reflexive	* - takes sein

hundredth – hundertste *adj*
hunger – Hunger *nm*
hungry – hungrig *adj*
  be hungry – Hunger haben *v irreg*
  I am hungry – Ich habe Hunger
hunt – auf die Jagd gehen* *v irreg*
hunt for – suchen *v reg*
hurdle – Hürde (-n) *nf*
hurried – eilig *adj*
hurry – Eile *nf*

I am in a hurry – Ich habe es
  eilig
hurry – sich beeilen *v reg refl* †
Hurry up! – Beeil dich! *excl*
hurt oneself – sich verletzen *v reg*
  refl †
husband – Mann (Männer) *nm*
hydrofoil – Tragflügelboot (-e) *nnt*
hygienic – hygienisch *adj*
hyphen (-) – Bindestrich (-e) *nm*

I

I – ich *pron*
  I would like – Ich möchte
ice – Eis *nnt*
ice – Eis~ *pref*
ice-cream – Eis *nnt*
  chocolate ice-cream –
  Schokoladeneis *nnt*
  strawberry ice-cream –
  Erdbeereis *nnt*
  vanilla ice-cream – Vanilleeis *nnt*
Iceland – Island *nnt*
Icelandic – isländisch *adj*
ice-rink – Eisbahn (-en) *nf*
ice-skating – Schlittschuhlaufen *nnt*
icy – eisig *adj*
icy – (road) vereist *adj*
ID – Ausweis (-e) *nm*
idea – Idee (-n) *nf*
  Good idea! – Gute Idee! *excl*
No idea! – Keine Ahnung!
ideal – ideal *adj*
identify – identifizieren *v reg* †
identity – Identität (-en) *nf*
identity card – Personalausweis (-e)
  nm
idiot – Idiot (-en) *nm wk*
idiotic – idiotisch *adj*

i.e. – d.h. (das heißt)
if – (whenever) wenn *sub conj*
if – (whether) ob *sub conj*
ill – krank *adj*
illness – Krankheit (-en) *nf*
illustration – Illustration (-en) *nf*
imaginary – vermeintlich *adj*
imagination – Einbildung (-en) *nf*
imagine – sich vorstellen *v reg dat*
  refl sep
immediate – (instant) sofortig *adj*
immediately – sofort *adv*
immense – enorm *adj*
impatience – Ungeduld *nf*
impatient – ungeduldig *adj*
imperfect tense – Imperfekt *nnt*
important – wichtig *adj*
impossibility – Unmöglichkeit (-en)
  nf
impossible – unmöglich *adj*
impractical – unpraktisch *adj*
impression – Eindruck (-e) *nm*
impressive – eindrucksvoll *adj*
in – in (+ acc/dat) *prep*
  in autumn – im Herbst
  in capital letters – in
  Druckbuchstaben

---

nm - noun masculine	*nf* - noun feminine	*nnt* - noun neuter	*npl* - noun plural
nom- nominative	*acc* - accusative	*gen* - genitive	*dat* - dative

in case – falls *sub conj*	**in turn** – der Reihe nach
in English – auf Englisch	**in winter** – im Winter
in fact – in der Tat *adv*	**included** – inklusive *adv*
in fashion – modisch *adj*	**service included** – Bedienung
in front of – vor (+ acc/dat) *prep*	inbegriffen
in future – in Zukunft	**including** – einschließlich *adv*
in general – im Allgemeinen	**incorrect** – falsch *adj*
in German – auf Deutsch	**incredible** – unglaublich *adj*
in good condition – in gutem	**indeed** – tatsächlich *adv*
Zustand	**independent** – selbstständig *adj*
in Malvern – in Malvern	**India** – (Asia) Indien *nnt*
in my opinion – meiner Meinung	**Indian** – indisch *adj*
nach	**Indian person** – (male) Inder (-) *nm*
in order to – um ... zu	**Indian person** – (female) Inderin
in poor condition – in schlechtem	(-nen) *nf*
Zustand	**Indian** – (American) indianisch *adj*
in spite of – trotz (+ gen) *prep*	**Indian** – (male) Indianer (-) *nm*
in spring – im Frühling	**Indian** – (female) Indianerin (-nen) *nf*
in summer – im Sommer	**indicator** – (car) Blinker (-) *nm*
in the 20th century – im 20.	**individual** – individuell *adj*
Jahrhundert	**individual** – Individuum (Individuen)
in the afternoon – am Nachmittag	*nnt*
in the country – auf dem Lande	**indoors** – drinnen *adv*
in the east – im Osten	**to go indoors** – ins Haus gehen
in the end – schließlich *adv*	**industrial** – industriell *adj*
in the evening – abends *adv*	**industrial area** – Industriegebiet (-e)
in the middle of – in der Mitte	*nnt*
von (+ dat)	**industry** – Industrie (-n) *nf*
in the morning – morgens *adv*	**infection** – Infektion (-en) *nf*
in the mountains – in den Bergen	**inform** – informieren *v reg* †
in the name of Fidler – im	**information** – Auskunft (-en) *nf*
Namen Fidler	**ask for information** – um
in the north – im Norden	Auskunft bitten *v irreg*
in the open air – im Freien	**information office** –
in the past – früher *adv*	Informationsbüro (-s) *nnt*
in the process of – dabei sein*	**information super highway** –
v irreg	Datenautobahn (-en) *nf*
in the rain – im Regen	**information technology** –
in the south – im Süden	Informatik *nf*
in the suburbs – in den Vororten	**ingredients** – Zutaten *npl*
in the west – im Westen	**inhabitant** – Einwohner (-) *nm*
in the world – auf der Welt	**injection** – Spritze (-n) *nf*
in this case – in diesem Fall	**injure** – verletzen *v reg* †
in town – in der Stadt	

adj - adjective	*v reg* - verb regular	*v sep* - verb separable	† - see verb info
prep - preposition	*v irreg* - verb irregular	*v refl* - verb reflexive	* - takes sein

injured – verletzt *adj*
injury – Verletzung (-en) *nf*
ink – Tinte (-n) *nf*
ink jet printer – Tintenstrahldrucker (-) *nm*
in line skates – Inliner *npl*
insect – Insekt (-en) *nnt*
inside – Innere *nnt* ‡
inside – drinnen *adv*
  to go inside – ins Haus gehen* *v irreg*
inside out – auf links *adv*
inspect tickets – kontrollieren *v reg* †
inspector – (male) Schaffner (-) *nm*
inspector – (female) Schaffnerin (-nen) *nf*
install – installieren *v reg* †
instant – Augenblick (-e) *nm*
instant coffee – Pulverkaffee *nm*
instantly – sofort *adv*
instead of – statt (+ gen) *prep*
instead of – (an)statt *conj*
instructor – (male) Lehrer (-) *nm*
instructor – (female) Lehrerin (-nen) *nf*
instrument – Instrument (-e) *nnt*
insurance – Versicherung (-en) *nf*
insure – versichern *v reg* †
intelligence – Intelligenz *nf*
intelligent – intelligent *adj*
intention – Absicht (-en) *nf*
intentionally – absichtlich *adv*
interest – Interesse (-n) *nnt*
  be interested in – sich interessieren für (+ acc) *v reg refl* †
interesting – interessant *adj*
international – international *adj*
internet – Internet *nnt*
  surf the internet – das Internet surfen *v reg*
interview – Interview (-s) *nnt*
into – in (+ acc) *prep*

introduce – vorstellen *v reg sep*
introduce o.s. – sich vorstellen *v reg refl sep*
in vain – umsonst
invent – erfinden *v irreg*
investigate – untersuchen *v reg insep*
invitation – Einladung (-en) *nf*
invite – einladen *v irreg sep*
Ireland – Irland *nnt*
Irish – irisch *adj*
Irishman – Ire (-n) *nm wk*
  I am Irish – Ich bin Ire
Irish Republic – die Republik Irland *nf*
Irishwoman – Irin (-nen) *nf*
  I am Irish – Ich bin Irin
iron – (clothes) Bügeleisen (-) *nnt*
iron – (metal) Eisen~ *pref*
iron – (clothes) bügeln *v reg*
irritable – reizbar *adj*
irritate – reizen *v reg*
irritated – gereizt *adj*
is – ist
  isn't it? – nicht wahr?
  It is – Es ist (+ nom)
  It is about... – Es geht um (+ acc)
  There is – Es gibt (+ acc)
Islamic – islamisch *adj*
island – Insel (-n) *nf*
isolated – einsam *adj*
IT – Informatik *nf*
it – er (nom) *pron m*
it – sie (nom/acc) *pron f*
it – es (nom/acc) *pron nt*
it – ihn (acc) *pron m*
it – ihm (dat) *pron m, nt*
it – ihr (dat) *pron f*
It depends – Es kommt drauf an
  It depends upon the weather – Es hängt vom Wetter ab
It is – Es ist
It is a pity! – Schade! *excl*

It is cold – Es ist kalt
It was – Es war
Italian – italienisch *adj*
Italian – (language) Italienisch *nnt*
Italian – (male) Italiener (-) *nm*
Italian – (female) Italienerin (-nen) *nf*

italic – Kursivschrift *nf*
Italy – Italien *nnt*
item – Gegenstand (-stände) *nm*
its – sein *poss adj m, nt,* ihr *poss adj f*
itself – selbst *pron*

J

jack – (car) Wagenheber (-) *nm*
jack – (cards) Bube (-n) *nm wk*
jacket – Jacke (-n) *nf*
jam – Marmelade (-n) *nf*
 a jar of jam – ein Glas Marmelade *nnt*
jam – (traffic) Stau (-s) *nm*
January – Januar *nm*
 in January – im Januar
Japan – Japan *nnt*
Japanese – japanisch *adj*
Japanese person – (male) Japaner (-) *nm*
Japanese person – (female) Japanerin (-nen) *nf*
jar – (jam, etc) Glas (Gläser) *nnt*
jazz – Jazz *nm*
jazz band – Jazzgruppe (-n) *nf*
jealous of – eifersüchtig auf (+ acc) *adj*
jeans – Jeans (-) *nf*
 a pair of jeans – eine Jeans
jelly – (dessert) Wackelpudding *nm*
jelly – Gelee *nnt*
jet – Düsenflugzeug (-e) *nnt*
jewel – Edelstein (-e) *nm*
jeweller – (male) Juwelier (-) *nm*
jeweller – (female) Juwelierin (-nen) *nf*
jeweller's shop – Juweliergeschäft (-e) *nnt*
jewellery – Schmuck *nm*

Jew – Jude (-n) *nm wk*
Jewess – Jüdin (-nen) *nf*
Jewish – jüdisch *adj*
job – Stelle (-n) *nf,* Job (-s) *nm*
 What's your job? – Was sind Sie von Beruf?
 do odd jobs – aushelfen (+ dat) *v irreg sep*
job offer – Stellenangebot (-e) *nnt*
jog – joggen *v reg*
jogging – Joggen *nnt*
join – (together) verbinden *v irreg*
join – (club) beitreten* (+ dat) *v irreg sep*
joint – (meat) Braten *nm*
joke – Witz (-e) *nm*
jotter – Heft (-e) *nnt*
journalist – (male) Journalist (-en) *nm wk*
journalist – (female) Journalistin (-nen) *nf*
journey – Reise (-n) *nf*
joy – Freude (-n) *nf*
joystick – (IT) Joystick (-s) *nm*
judge – (male) Richter (-) *nm*
judge – (female) Richterin (-nen) *nf*
judo – Judo *nnt*
jug – Krug (Krüge) *nm*
juice – Saft (Säfte) *nm*
 apple juice – Apfelsaft *nm*
 fruit juice – Fruchtsaft *nm*

adj - adjective	*v reg* - verb regular	*v sep* - verb separable	† - see verb info
prep - preposition	*v irreg* - verb irregular	*v refl* - verb reflexive	* - takes sein

orange juice – Orangensaft *nm*
July – Juli *nm*
in July – im Juli
jumbo jet – Jumbojet (-s) *nnt*
jump – springen* *v irreg*
jumper – Pullover (-) *nm*
June – Juni *nm*
in June – im Juni

jungle – Dschungel (-) *nm*
junior school – Grundschule (-n) *nf*
junk room – Rumpelkammer (-n) *nf*
just – (fair) gerecht *adj*
just – (only) nur *adv*
just – (recently) gerade, eben *adv*
I have just arrived – Ich bin
gerade angekommen

K

karate – Karate *nnt*
kebab – Schaschlik (-s) *nnt*
keen – begeistert *adj*
be keen on – gern machen *v reg*
be keen on sport – gern Sport
treiben *v irreg*
keep – behalten *v irreg*
keep an eye on – beobachten *v reg* †
keep fit – trimmen *v reg*
Keep the change! – Das stimmt so!
Keep to the right! – Rechts halten!
excl
ketchup – Ketchup *nm*
key – Schlüssel (-) *nm*
bunch of keys – Schlüsselbund
(-e) *nm*
key ring – Schlüsselring (-e) *nm*
keyhole – Schlüsselloch (-löcher) *nnt*
key – (keyboard) Taste (-n) *nf*
keyboard – (IT) Tastatur (-en) *nf*
keyboard – (piano) Klaviatur (-en) *nf*
kick – treten *v irreg*
kid – (child) Kind (-er) *nnt*
kidnap – entführen *v reg* †
kidnapper – (male) Entführer (-) *nm*
kidnapper – (female) Entführerin
(-nen) *nf*
kill – töten *v reg* †
kilo(gram) – Kilo *nnt*

kilometre – Kilometer *nm*
10 kilometres from – zehn
Kilometer von ... entfernt
kind – nett *adj*
Kind regards – mit freundlichen
Grüßen
kind to animals – gut zu Tieren
kind – Art (-en) *nf*
kind – (brand) Sorte (-n) *nf*
What kind of car? – Was für
einen Wagen?
kindergarten – Kindergarten
(-gärten) *nm*
kindly – freundlich *adj*
kindness – Freundlichkeit (-en) *nf*
king – König (-e) *nm*
kiosk – Kiosk (-e) *nm*
kiss – Kuss (Küsse) *nm*
kiss – küssen *v reg*
kitchen – Küche (-n) *nf*
kite – Drachen (-) *nm*
kitten – Kätzchen (-) *nnt*
kiwi fruit – Kiwi (-s) *nf*
knee – Knie (-) *nnt*
kneel – knien *v reg*
knickers – Slip (-s) *nm*
knife – Messer (-) *nnt*
knit – stricken *v reg*
knock – klopfen *v reg*

There's a knock at the door –
Es klopft
knock on the door – an die Tür
klopfen *v reg*
knock s.o. over – (car) anfahren
v irreg sep

know – (fact) wissen *v irreg*
I don't know – Ich weiß es nicht
know – (person) kennen *v irreg*
get to know – kennen lernen *v reg*
known – bekannt *adj*
Koran – Koran *nm*

L

laboratory – Labor (-s) *nnt*
lad – Junge (-n) *nm wk*
ladder – Leiter (-n) *nf*
Ladies' toilets – Damen
lady – Dame (-n) *nf*
  cleaning lady – Putzfrau (-en) *nf*
lady's suit – Kostüm (-e) *nnt*
lake – See (-n) *nm*
lamb – (animal) Lamm (Lämmer) *nnt*
lamb – (meat) Lammfleisch *nnt*
lamp – Lampe (-n) *nf*
land – (country) Land (Länder) *nnt*
land – (earth) Erde (-n) *nf*
  plot of land – Grundstück
  (-stücke) *nnt*
land – landen* *v reg* †
landing – (plane) Landung (-en) *nf*
landing – (house) Treppenflur (-e) *nm*
language – Sprache (-n) *nf*
  foreign language – Fremdsprache
  (-n) *nf*
  modern language – Neusprache
  (-n) *nf*
language laboratory – Sprachlabor
(-s) *nnt*
lantern – Laterne (-n) *nf*
laptop – Laptop (-s) *nm*
large – groß *adj*
laser printer – Laserdrucker (-) *nm*
last – letzt *adj*
  at last – endlich *adv*

last night – gestern Abend
last week – letzte Woche
last year – letztes Jahr
last – dauern *v reg*
late – spät *adj*
later – später *adj*
  See you later! – Bis später!
latest – neuest *adj*
Latin – lateinisch *adj*
Latin – Latein *nnt*
laugh – lachen *v reg*
laundrette – Münzwäscherei (-en) *nf*
law – Gesetz (-e) *nnt*
lawn – Rasen (-) *nm*
  mow lawn – den Rasen mähen
  v reg
lawyer – (male) Rechtsanwalt
(-anwälte) *nm*
lawyer – (female) Rechtsanwältin
(-nen) *nf*
lay down – sich hinlegen *v wk refl sep*
laze about – faulenzen *v reg*
lazy – faul *adv*
lead – (dog) Leine (-n) *nf*
lead – (metal) Blei *nnt*
  leaded – verbleit *adj*
  lead free – bleifrei *adj*
lead – führen *v reg*
  in the lead – in Führung
leader – (male) Führer (-) *nm*

---

adj - adjective	*v reg* - verb regular	*v sep* - verb separable	† - see verb info
prep - preposition	*v irreg* - verb irregular	*v refl* - verb reflexive	* - takes sein

leader – (female) Führerin (-nen) *nf*

leaf – Blatt (Blätter) *nnt*

leaflet – Broschüre (-n) *nf,* Prospekt (-e) *nm*

league – Liga (Ligen) *nf*

lean – lehnen *v reg*

lean over – sich hinüberbeugen *v reg refl sep*

Do not lean out! – Nicht hinauslehnen! *excl*

learn – lernen *v reg*

least – wenigste *adj*

leather – Leder (-) *nnt*

made of leather – aus Leder

leather goods – Lederwaren *npl*

leave – (depart) abfahren* *v irreg sep*

leave – (house, etc) verlassen *v irreg*

leave ... lying around – liegen lassen *v irreg*

leave the table – den Tisch verlassen *v irreg*

left – linke *adj*

on the left – links *adv*

on the left hand side – auf der linken Seite

left-handed – linkshändig *adj*

I am left-handed – (male) Ich bin Linkshänder

I am left-handed – (female) Ich bin Linkshänderin

left luggage locker – Gepäckschließfach (-fächer) *nnt*

left luggage office – Gepäckaufbewahrung (-en) *nf*

left luggage ticket – Gepäckzettel (-) *nm*

left winger – Linksaußen (-) *nm*

leg – Bein (e) *nnt*

leggings – Leggings *npl*

leisure – Freizeit (-en) *nf*

leisure centre – Freizeitzentrum (-zentren) *nnt*

lemon – Zitrone (-n) *nf*

lemon tea – Zitronentee *nm*

lemonade – Limonade (-n) *nf*

lend – leihen *v irreg*

lend a hand – helfen (+ dat) *v irreg*

length – (measurement) Länge (-n) *nf*

length – (time) Dauer *nf*

at length – (finally) endlich *adv*

lens – Linse (-n) *nf*

contact lens – Kontaktlinse (-n) *nf*

Leo – (horoscope) Löwe

less – weniger *adv*

less than – weniger als

less than two kilos – weniger als zwei Kilo

lesson – Stunde (-n) *nf*

let – lassen *v irreg*

let – (allow) erlauben (+ dat) *v reg* †

let s.o. know – informieren *v reg* †

let – (rent out) vermieten *v reg* †

to let – zu vermieten

letter – (alphabet) Buchstabe (-n) *nm wk*

letter – (post) Brief (-e) *nm*

registered letter – Einschreibebrief (-e) *nm*

letter box – Briefkasten (-kästen) *nm*

lettuce – Salat (-e) *nm*

level – flach *adj*

level – (school) Niveau (-s) *nnt*

level crossing – Bahnübergang (-gänge) *nm*

liar – (male) Lügner (-) *nm*

liar – (female) Lügnerin (-nen) *nf*

Libra – (horoscope) Waage

librarian – (male) Bibliothekar (-e) *nm*

librarian – (female) Bibliothekarin (-nen) *nf*

library – Bibliothek (-en) *nf*

licence – Genehmigung (-en) *nf*

driving licence – Führerschein (-e) *nm*

lick – lecken *v reg*

---

nm - noun masculine   *nf* - noun feminine   *nnt* - noun neuter   *npl* - noun plural

nom- nominative   *acc* - accusative   *gen* - genitive   *dat* - dative

lid – (top) Deckel (-) *nm*
lie – (be situated) liegen *v irreg*
lie – (untruth) lügen *v irreg*
lie down – sich hinlegen *v reg refl sep*
  have a lie in – (sich) ausschlafen
  v irreg (refl) sep
Liège – Lüttich *nnt*
life – Leben *nnt*
  daily life – das tägliche Leben *nnt*
  lose one's life – ums Leben
  kommen* *v irreg*
lifebelt – Rettungsring (-e) *nm*
lifeguard – Rettungsschwimmer (-)
nm
lifejacket – Schwimmweste (-n) *nf*
lifelong – lebenslänglich *adj*
lift – Lift *nm,* Aufzug (-züge) *nm,*
Fahrstuhl (-stühle) *nm*
lift – heben *v irreg*
  Can I have a lift? – Kannst du
  mich mitnehmen?
lift up – hochheben *v irreg sep*
light – (not heavy) leicht *adj*
light – (not dark) hell *adj*
light blue – hellblau *adj*
light – Licht (-er) *nnt*
light – (lamp) Lampe (-n) *nf*
  put the light on – das Licht
  anmachen *v reg sep*
light bulb – Glühbirne (-e) *nf*
light pen – Lichtstift (-e) *nm*
lighthouse – Leuchtturm (-türme) *nm*
lightning – (flash) Blitz (-e) *nm*
like – (similar) ähnlich *adj*
like – wie *prep*
  What does he look like? – Wie
  sieht er aus?
like that – auf diese Weise
like – mögen *v irreg*
  I like dancing – Ich tanze gern
  I like fish – Ich esse gern Fisch
  I like the trousers – Die Hose
  gefällt mir

I would like … – Ich möchte …
I would very much like … –
Ich möchte gern …
likeable – sympathisch *adj*
likely – wahrscheinlich *adv*
  Not likely! – Ich denke nicht
  daran!
limit – (border) Grenze (-n) *nf*
limit – (restriction) Beschränkung
(-en) *nf*
  speed limit –
  Geschwindigkeitsbeschränkung
  (-en) *nf*
line – (queue) Schlange (-n) *nf*
line – (tram, bus) Linie (-n) *nf*
line – (writing) Zeile (-n) *nf*
linen – (household) Wäsche *nf, no pl*
  dirty linen – schmutzige Wäsche
  nf
lion – Löwe (-n) *nm wk*
lip – Lippe (-n) *nf*
lip-read – von den Lippen ablesen
v irreg sep
lipstick – Lippenstift (-e) *nm*
liquid – Flüssigkeit (-en) *nf*
list – Liste (-n) *nf*
listen (to) – (zu)hören *v reg (sep)*
listen to tapes – Kassetten hören
v reg
literature – Literatur *nf*
litre – Liter *nm*
litter – Abfall *nm*
little – klein *adj*
  a little – ein bisschen
  a little more – ein bisschen mehr
live – (alive) lebendig *adj*
live – (radio, TV) live *adj*
live broadcast – Livesendung (-en)
nf
live – (be alive) leben *v reg*
live – (inhabit) wohnen *v reg*
  Where do you live? – Wo
  wohnst du?

---

adj - adjective	*v reg* - verb regular	*v sep* - verb separable	† - see verb info
prep - preposition	*v irreg* - verb irregular	*v refl* - verb reflexive	* - takes sein

lively – lebhaft *adj*
lively – lebendig *adj*
liver – Leber (-n) *nf*
liver sausage – Leberwurst *nf*
living – lebend *adj*
  earn one's living – (sich) seinen
  Lebensunterhalt verdienen *v reg*
  (dat refl) †
living room – Wohnzimmer (-) *nnt*
load – laden *v irreg*
loaded – beladen *adj*
loads of – eine Menge
loaf – Brot (-e) *nnt*
local – örtlich *adj*
lock – (door) Schloss (Schlösser) *nnt*
lock – abschließen *v irreg sep*
locker – Schließfach (-fächer) *nnt*
lodge with – bei (+ dat) wohnen *v reg*
lodger – (male) Untermieter (-) *nm*
lodger – (female) Untermieterin (-nen) *nf*
lodging – Mietwohnung (-en) *nf*
loft – Dachboden (-böden) *nm*
lollipop – Lutscher (-) *nm*
lonely – einsam *adj*
long – lang *adj*
  all day long – den ganzen Tag
  a long way – weit *adj*
  Don't be long! – Beeil dich! *excl*
  for a long time – lange *adv*
long ago – vor langer Zeit
longer – länger *adj*
  no longer – nicht länger *adv*
long-sighted – weitsichtig *adj*
long walk – Wanderung (-en) *nf*
look – schauen *v reg*
look – sehen *v irreg*
look – (appearance) aussehen *v irreg sep*
look after – (watch) aufpassen
  auf (+ acc) *v reg sep*
look after – (take care of) sich
  kümmern um (+ acc) *v reg refl*

look at – ansehen *v irreg sep*
look for – suchen *v reg*
look forward to – sich freuen auf
  (+ acc) *v reg refl*
look like – aussehen wie *v irreg sep*
Look out! – Achtung! *excl*
look round – sich umsehen *v irreg sep*
lorry – Lastwagen (-) *nm*
lorry – (HGV) LKW (-s) *nm*
lorry driver – (male)
  Lastwagenfahrer (-) *nm*
lorry driver – (female)
  Lastwagenfahrerin (-nen) *nf*
lose – verlieren *v irreg*
  lose a match – ein Spiel verlieren
  v irreg
lose one's way – (on foot) sich
  verlaufen *v irreg refl*
lose one's way – (by car, etc) sich
  verfahren *v irreg refl*
lose weight – abnehmen *v irreg sep*
lost – verloren *adj*
lost property – Fundsachen *npl*
lost property office – Fundbüro (-s) *nnt*
lot (of) – viel *adv*
  quite a lot – ganz viel
  the lot – alles
lottery – Lotterie (-n) *nf*
loud – laut *adj*
loudspeaker – Lautsprecher (-) *nm*
lounge – Wohnzimmer (-) *nnt*
lousy – mies *adj coll*
love – Liebe (-n) *nf*
love – lieben *v reg*
  I'd love to – Ich möchte gern
  be in love with s.o. – verliebt in
  jdn sein* *v irreg*
  I'm in love with you – Ich bin in
  dich verliebt
love from – Alles Gute
love story – Liebesroman (-e) *nm*

| *nm* - noun masculine | *nf* - noun feminine | *nnt* - noun neuter | *npl* - noun plural |
| *nom*- nominative | *acc* - accusative | *gen* - genitive | *dat* - dative |

lovely – schön *adj*
low – niedrig *adj*
LP – Langspielplatte (-n) *nf*
luck – Glück *nnt*
  Bad luck! – Pech! *excl*
  bad luck – Pech *nnt*
  be lucky – Glück haben *v irreg*
  Good luck! – Viel Glück! *excl*
luggage – Gepäck *nnt, no pl*
  piece of luggage – Gepäckstück
  (-e) *nnt*
luggage rack – Gepäcknetz (-e) *nnt*
luggage trolley – Kofferkuli (-s) *nm*

luggage carousel –
  Gepäckausgabe (-n) *nf*
lunch – Mittagessen (-) *nnt*
lunch box – Brotdose (-n) *nf*
lunch hour – Mittagspause (-n) *nf*
  have lunch – zu Mittag essen
  v irreg
Luxembourg – Luxemburg *nnt*
Luxembourger – (male)
  Luxemburger (-) *nm*
Luxembourger – (female)
  Luxemburgerin (-nen) *nf*
luxurious – luxuriös *adj*
lyrics – Worte *npl*

M

machine – Maschine (-n) *nf*
mad – verrückt *adj*
magazine – Zeitschrift (-en) *nf*
  glossy magazine – Illustrierte *nf* ‡
  women's magazine –
  Frauenzeitschrift (-en) *nf*
magic – Zauber *nm*
  The Magic Flute – Die Zauberflöte
magician – Zauberer (-) *nm*
magnificent – wunderbar, großartig
adj
maiden name – Mädchenname (-n)
nm wk
mail – Post *nf*
main – Haupt~ *pref*
  main course – Hauptgericht (-e)
  nnt
  main street – Hauptstraße (-n) *nf*
  main station – Hauptbahnhof
  (-höfe) *nm*
majestic – majestätisch *adj*
Majorca – Mallorca *nnt*
major road – Hauptstraße (-n) *nf*
make – Marke (-n) *nf*

make – machen *v reg*
make fun of – sich lustig machen
  über (+ acc) *v reg refl*
make money – Geld verdienen *v reg* †
make up one's mind – sich
  entscheiden *v irreg refl*
make-up – Make-Up *nnt*
make-up bag – Kosmetiktäschchen
  (-) *nnt*
put on make-up – sich schminken
  v reg refl
male – (person) Mann (Männer) *nm*
male – männlich *adj*
male nurse – Krankenpfleger (-) *nm*
malicious – böswillig *adj*
man – (male) Mann (Männer) *nm*
man – (person) Mensch (-en) *nm wk*
manage – zurechtkommen* *v irreg*
sep
manage – (as boss) leiten *v reg* †
manage to do sthg – etwas schaffen
v reg
manager – Geschäftsführer (-) *nm*

---

adj - adjective   *v reg* - verb regular   *v sep* - verb separable   † - see verb info
prep - preposition   *v irreg* - verb irregular   *v refl* - verb reflexive   * - takes sein

manageress – Geschäftsführerin (-nen) *nf*

manner – Weise (-n) *nf,* Art (-en) *nf*
  in this manner – auf diese Art und Weise

manners – Manieren *npl*

mansion – Herrenhaus (-häuser) *nnt*

manual – Hand~ *pref*

manufacture – herstellen *v reg sep*

many – viele *adj*

map – (area) Landkarte (-n) *nf*

map – (town) Stadtplan (-pläne) *nm*

March – März *nm*
  in March – im März

margarine – Margarine (-n) *nf*

mark – (school) Note (-n) *nf*

mark – (money) Mark (-) *nf*

mark – (stain) Fleck (-e) *nm*

mark – (books) korrigieren *v reg* †

mark with a cross – ankreuzen *v reg sep*

market – Markt (Märkte) *nm*

market hall – Markthalle (-n) *nf*

market place – Marktplatz(-plätze) *nm*

marmalade – Orangenmarmelade (-n) *nf*

marriage – Ehe (-n) *nf*

marriage – (ceremony) Hochzeit (-en) *nf*

married – verheiratet *adj*

married couple – Ehepaar (-e) *nnt*

marry – heiraten *v reg* †
  get married – heiraten *v reg* †

marvellous – wunderbar *adj*

masculine – männlich *adj*

mashed potato – Kartoffelpüree *nnt*

massive – riesig *adj*

master – Herr (-en) *nm wk*

master – (teacher) Lehrer (-) *nm*

match – (sport) Spiel (-e) *nnt*

match – Streichholz (-hölzer) *nnt*

matchbox – Streichholzschachtel (-n) *nf*

materials – Materialien *npl*

mathematics – Mathematik *nf*

maths – Mathe *nf*

matron – Hausmutter (-mütter) *nf*

matter – wichtig sein* *v irreg*
  It does not matter (to me) – Es macht (mir) nichts aus
  What is the matter? – Was ist los?

mattress – Matratze (-n) *nf*

mauve – lila *adj inv*

maximum – Höchst~ *pref*

maximum speed – Höchstgeschwindigkeit (-en) *nf*

maximum temperature – Höchsttemperatur (-en) *nf*

May – Mai *nm*
  in May – im Mai

may – (be allowed to) dürfen *v irreg*

may – (be able) können *v irreg*

maybe – vielleicht *adv*

mayonnaise – Mayonnaise *nf*

mayor – Bürgermeister (-) *nm*

mayoress – Bürgermeisterin (-nen) *nf*

me – mich *pron acc,* mir *pron dat*

meadow – Wiese (-n) *nf*

meal – Mahlzeit (-en) *nf*
  evening meal – Abendessen (-) *nnt*
  midday meal – Mittagessen (-) *nnt*

mean – bedeuten *v reg* †
  What does ... mean? – Was bedeutet ...?

mean – (nasty) gemein *adj*

mean – (money) geizig *adj*

meanwhile – inzwischen *adv*

measure – messen *v irreg*

meat – Fleisch *nnt*
  type of meat – Fleischsorte (-n) *nf*

mechanic – (male) Mechaniker (-) *nm*

mechanic – (female) Mechanikerin (-nen) *nf*

---

medal – Medaille (-n) *nf*
  gold medal – Goldmedaille *nf*
  silver medal – Silbermedaille *nf*
  bronze medal – Bronzemedaille *nf*
media – Medien *npl*
medicine – (science) Medizin *nf*
medicine – (remedy) Medikament (-e) *nnt*
medieval – mittelalterlich *adj*
Mediterranean – Mittelmeer *nnt*
medium – Mittel~ *pref*
medium length – mittellang *adj*
medium size – mittelgroß *adj*
meet – (arranged) sich treffen *v irreg refl*
meet – (chance) begegnen* (+ dat) *v reg* †
meet – (get to know) kennen lernen *v reg*
meet – (fetch) abholen *v reg sep*
meeting – Treffen (-) *nnt*
melon – Melone (-n) *nf*
member – Mitglied (-er) *nnt*
membership card – Mitgliedskarte (-n) *nf*
memory – Gedächtnis (-se) *nnt*
memory – (computer) Speicher (-) *nm*
mend – reparieren *v reg* †
  have mended – reparieren lassen *v irreg*
Men's toilets – Herren
menu – Speisekarte (-n) *nf*
  fixed price menu – Menü (-s) *nnt*
menu of the day – Tageskarte (-n) *nf*
merchandise – Ware (-n) *nf*
merry – fröhlich *adj*
  Merry Christmas! – Fröhliche Weihnachten! *excl*
mess – Durcheinander *nnt*
  in a mess – durcheinander *adv*
mess about – herumalbern *v reg sep*
message – Mitteilung (-en) *nf*
messy – unordentlich *adj*

metal – Metall (-e) *nnt*
method – Methode (-n) *nf*
metre – Meter *nm*
microchip – Mikrochip (-s) *nm*
micro-computer – Mikrocomputer (-) *nm*
microphone – Mikrofon (-e) *nnt*
microscope – Mikroskop (-e) *nnt*
microwave oven – Mikrowellenherd (-e) *nm*
midday – Mittag *nm*
  at midday – um Mittag
midday meal – Mittagessen *nnt*
  have midday meal – zu Mittag essen *v irreg*
middle – Mitte *nf*
  in the middle of – in der Mitte von (+ dat)
middle aged – mittleren Alters
Midlands – Mittelengland *nnt*
midnight – Mitternacht *nf*
  at midnight – um Mitternacht
might – könnte *see* **können**
mild – mild *adj*
mile – Meile (-n) *nf*
milk – Milch *nf*
milkman – Milchmann (-männer) *nm*
milk shake – Milkshake *nm*
millennium – Jahrtausend *nnt*
million – Million (-en) *nf*
mince – Hackfleisch *nnt*
mind – (look after) aufpassen auf (+ acc) *v reg sep*
  make up one's mind – sich entschließen *v irreg refl*
  I don't mind – Das macht mir nichts aus
  Mind the step! – Vorsicht Stufe!
  Never mind – Es macht nichts
mine – mein *poss adj*
  It's mine – Es gehört mir
  a friend of mine – ein Freund/eine Freundin von mir

---

adj - adjective	*v reg* - verb regular	*v sep* - verb separable	† - see verb info
prep - preposition	*v irreg* - verb irregular	*v refl* - verb reflexive	* - takes sein

miner – Bergarbeiter (-) *nm*
mineral water – Mineralwasser *nnt*
minibus – Kleinbus (-se) *nm*
minimum – Minimum (Minima) *nnt*
minimum – Mindest~ *pref*
minimum temperature –
Mindesttemperatur (-en) *nf*
minor – minderjährig *adj*
minor – (under 18) Minderjährige *nmf* ‡
mint – Pfefferminzbonbon (-s) *nnt*
mint tea – Pfefferminztee *nm*
minus – (maths) minus *prep*
minute – Minute (-n) *nf*
mirror – Spiegel (-) *nm*
miserable – unglücklich *adj*
misfortune – Unglück *nnt*
Miss – Fräulein (-) *nnt*
miss – (person) vermissen *v reg* †
miss – (train, etc) verpassen *v reg* †
mist – Nebel (-) *nm*
mistake – Fehler (-) *nm*
misty – nebelig *adj*
misunderstanding –
Missverständnis (-se) *nnt*
mix – mischen *v reg*
mixed – gemischt *adj*
mixed cold meats – Aufschnitt *nm*
mixed salad – gemischter Salat *nm*
moan – stöhnen *v reg*
moan about – (complain) sich
beklagen über (+ acc) *v reg refl* †
model – (fashion) Mannequin (-s) *nnt*
model – Modell (-e) *nnt*
a scale model – ein
maßstabgerechtes Modell *nnt*
do model-making – basteln *v reg*
modem – Modem (-s) *nnt*
moderate – mäßig *adj*
modern – modern *adj*
modern languages – Neusprachen
npl
moment – Augenblick (-e) *nm*

at the moment – zurzeit
at this moment – im Augenblick
in a moment – gleich *adv*
Monday – Montag (-e) *nm*
on Monday – am Montag
money – Geld *nnt*
change money – Geld wechseln
v reg
monkey – Affe (-n) *nm wk*
monster – Ungeheuer (-) *nnt*
month – Monat (-e) *nm*
per month – im Monat
monthly – monatlich *adj*
monument – Denkmal (-mäler) *nnt*
mood – Laune (-n) *nf*
in a bad mood – schlechter Laune
in a good mood – guter Laune
moon – Mond (-e) *nm*
moped – Moped (-s) *nnt*
more – mehr *adv*
more and more – immer mehr *adv*
more or less – mehr oder weniger
adv
more than – mehr als
There is no more – Es ist nichts
mehr da
morning – Morgen (-) *nm*
next morning – am nächsten
Morgen
tomorrow morning – morgen
früh
Moselle – Mosel *nf*
mosque – Moschee (-n) *nf*
mosquito – Moskito (-s) *nm*
most – am meisten *adv*
most – (people) die meisten
MOT – TÜV *nm*
mother – Mutter (Mütter) *nf*
mother-in-law – Schwiegermutter
(-mütter) *nf*
motherly – mütterlich *adj*
motor – Motor (-en) *nm*
motorbike – Motorrad (-räder) *nnt*

---

nm - noun masculine   *nf* - noun feminine   *nnt* - noun neuter   *npl* - noun plural
nom- nominative   *acc* - accusative   *gen* - genitive   *dat* - dative

motor boat – Motorboot (-e) *nnt*
motorcyclist – (male) Motorradfahrer (-) *nm*
motorcyclist – (female) Motorradfahrerin (-nen) *nf*
motor home – Campingbus (-se) *nm*
motorist – (male) Autofahrer (-) *nm*
motorist – (female) Autofahrerin (-nen) *nf*
motorway – Autobahn (-en) *nf*
mountain – Berg (-e) *nm*
mountain bike – Mountainbike (-s) *nnt*, Bergrad (-räder) *nnt*
mountain climbing – Bergsteigen *nnt*
mountaineer – (male) Bergsteiger (-) *nm*
mountaineer – (female) Bergsteigerin (-nen) *nf*
mountain range – Gebirge *nnt*
mouse – Maus (Mäuse) *nf*
moustache – Oberlippenbart (-bärte) *nm*
mouth – Mund (Münder) *nm*
mouthful – Mundvoll (-) *nm*
mouth organ – Mundharmonika (-harmoniken) *nf*
move – bewegen *v reg* †
move house – umziehen* *v irreg sep*
movement – Bewegung (-en) *nf*
mow the lawn – den Rasen mähen *v reg*
Mr, Sir – Herr
Mrs, Ms – Frau
much – viel *adv*
  so much – so viel *adv*
mud – Schlamm *nm*
muddy – schlammig *adj*

muddy shoes – schmutzige Schuhe *npl*
mug – (cup) Becher (-) *nm*
mug – (attack) überfallen *v irreg insep*
multi-coloured – bunt *adj*
multiple crash – Karambolage (-n) *nf*
multi-storey car park – Parkhaus (-häuser) *nnt*
mum(my) – Mutti (-s) *nf*
Munich – München
museum – Museum (Museen) *nnt*
mushroom – Pilz (-e) *nm*
music – Musik *nf*
  pop music – Popmusik *nf*
music centre – Stereoanlage (-n) *nf*
music department – Musikabteilung (-en) *nf*
music room – Musikraum (räume) *nm*
musician – (male) Musiker (-) *nm*
musician – (female) Musikerin (-nen) *nf*
Muslim – mohammedanisch *adj*
Muslim – (male) Mohammedaner (-) *nm*
Muslim – (female) Mohammedanerin (-nen) *nf*
must – *see* müssen
must not – *see* dürfen
mustard – Senf *nm*
mutton – Hammelfleisch *nnt*
my – mein *poss adj*
myself – mich *pron acc*, mir *pron dat*
mysterious – geheimnisvoll *adj*
mystery – Geheimnis (-se) *nnt*
myth – Märchen (-) *nnt*

N

nail – Nagel (Nägel) *nm*
naked – nackt *adj*
name – Name (-n) *nm wk*
 in the name (of) – im Namen
 (+ gen)
 My name is – Ich heiße
 What is your name? – Wie heißt
 du?/Wie heißen Sie?
name – nennen *v irreg*
nanny – Kindermädchen (-) *nnt*
narrow – eng *adj*
nasty – unangenehm *adj*
nation – Volk (Völker) *nnt*
national – national *adj*
national – (German) Bundes- *pref*
nationalist – nationalistisch *adj*
nationality – Staatsangehörigkeit
 (-en) *nf*
native – gebürtig *adj*
native language – Muttersprache *nf*
native town – Heimatstadt *nf*
natural – natürlich *adj*
natural gas – Erdgas *nnt*
natural history – Naturkunde *nf*
natural sciences –
 Naturwissenschaften *npl*
naturally – natürlich *adv*
nature – Natur *nf*
nature reserve – Naturschutzgebiet
 (-e) *nnt*
naughty – unartig *adj*
navy – Kriegsmarine (-n) *nf*
navy blue – marineblau *adj*
near (to) – in der Nähe (von + dat)
nearby – in der Nähe
nearest – nächst *adj*
nearly – fast *adv*
near sighted – kurzsichtig *adj*
neat – ordentlich *adj*
necessary – nötig, notwendig *adj*

necessity – Notwendigkeit (-en) *nf*
neck – (throat) Hals (Hälse) *nm*
 back of neck – Nacken (-) *nm*
necklace – Halskette (-n) *nf*
nectarine – Nektarine (-n) *nf*
need – brauchen *v reg*
 I need to do it – Ich muss es tun
needle – Nadel (-n) *nf*
needlework – Handarbeit *nf*
negative – negativ *adj*
neglect – vernachlässigen *v reg* †
neglected – vernachlässigt *adj*
neighbour – (male) Nachbar (-en) *nm
wk*
neighbour – (female) Nachbarin
 (-nen) *nf*
neighbourhood – Nachbarschaft
 (-en) *nf*
neighbouring – benachbart *adj*
neither – auch nicht *adv*
neither ... nor – weder ... noch *adv*
nephew – Neffe (-n) *nm wk*
nervous – nervös *adj*
netball – Korbball *nm*
Netherlands – Niederlande *npl*
neuter – Neutrum *nnt*
never – nie *adv*
never mind – es macht nichts
nevertheless – trotzdem *adv*
new – neu *adj*
New Year – Neujahr (-e) *nnt*
New Year's Day – Neujahrstag (-e)
 nm
New Year's Eve – Silvester *nnt*
New Zealand – Neuseeland *nnt*
news – (radio, TV) Nachrichten *npl*
newsagent – (male) Zeitungshändler
 (-) *nm*
newsagent – (female)
 Zeitungshändlerin (-nen) *nf*

---

nm - noun masculine *nf* - noun feminine *nnt* - noun neuter *npl* - noun plural
nom- nominative *acc* - accusative *gen* - genitive *dat* - dative

newspaper – Zeitung (-en) *nf*
next – nächst *adj*
   Who's next? – Wer ist dran?
next – dann *adv*
next door – nebenan *adv*
next to – neben (+ acc/dat) *prep*
next week – nächste Woche
next year – nächstes Jahr
nice – (person) nett *adj*
nice – (weather) schön *adj*
nice-looking – gut aussehend *adj*
nickname – Spitzname (-n) *nm wk*
niece – Nichte (-n) *nf*
night – Nacht (Nächte) *nf*
   Good night! – Gute Nacht! *excl*
night club – Nachtklub (-s) *nm*
last night – gestern Abend
nightdress – Nachthemd (-en) *nnt*
nightmare – Alptraum (-träume) *nm*
nil – null *adj*
   two - nil (2:0) – zwei zu null
nine – neun *adj*
nineteen – neunzehn *adj*
ninety – neunzig *adj*
ninety-one – einundneunzig *adj*
ninth – neunte *adj*
no – nein *adv*
no – kein *adj*
   no thank you – (nein) danke
   no entry – (on foot) kein Zutritt
   no entry – (vehicles) keine Einfahrt
   no good at – nicht gut in (+ dat)
   no longer – nicht länger
   no more – nicht mehr
   no-one – niemand *pron*
   no-one else – sonst niemand
   no parking – Parken verboten
   no smoking – Rauchen verboten
   no vacancies – belegt *adj*
nobody – niemand *pron*
noise – (quiet) Geräusch (-e) *nnt*
noise – (loud) Lärm *nm*

noisy – laut *adj*
non-drinking water – kein Trinkwasser
non-smoking – Nichtraucher
none the less – nichtsdestoweniger *adv*
nonsense – Unsinn *nm,* Blödsinn *nm*
noodles – Nudeln *npl*
noon – Mittag (-e) *nm*
normal – normal *adj*
normally – normalerweise *adv*
north – Nord- *pref*
north – Norden *nm*
North America – Nordamerika *nnt*
northerly – nördlich *adj*
Northern Ireland – Nordirland *nnt*
Northern Irish – nordirisch *adj*
Northern Irishman – Nordire (-n) *nm wk*
Northern Irishwoman – Nordirin (-nen) *nf*
north Germany – Norddeutschland *nnt*
north of – nördlich von (+ dat) *adj*
North Sea – Nordsee *nf*
Norway – Norwegen *nnt*
Norwegian – norwegisch *adj*
nose – Nase (-n) *nf*
nosebleed – Nasenbluten (-) *nnt*
nosy – neugierig *adj*
not – nicht
   He's not German – Er ist kein Deutscher
   not allowed – nicht erlaubt
   not any – kein *adj*
   not at all – gar nicht
   not far from here – nicht weit von hier
   not included – nicht inbegriffen
   not likely – auf keinen Fall
   not much – nicht viel
   not only – nicht nur
   not yet – noch nicht

---

note – (money) Schein (-e) *nm*
 50 mark note –
 Fünfzigmarkschein (-e) *nm*
note – (message) Zettel (-) *nm*
note – (message) Notiz (-en) *nf*
notebook – Notizbuch (-bücher) *nnt*
note down – notieren *v reg* †
notepad – Notizblock (-blöcke) *nm*
note paper – Briefpapier (-e) *nnt*
nothing – nichts
 nothing at all – gar nichts
 nothing else – nichts anderes
 nothing much – nicht viel
 nothing new – nichts Neues
notice – (information)
 Bekanntmachung (-en) *nf*
notice – (dismissal) Kündigung (-en)
 nf
notice – bemerken *v reg* †
noticeable – bemerkbar *adj*
notice board – Anschlagbrett (-er)
 nnt, das schwarze Brett
nought – Null *nf*

noun – Substantiv (-e) *nnt*
novel – Roman (-e) *nm*
 detective novel – Krimi (-s) *nm coll*
November – November *nm*
 in November – im November
now – jetzt *adv*
nowadays – heutzutage *adv*
nowhere – nirgendwo *adv*
nuclear power – Kernenergie *nf*
number – (house, etc) Nummer (-n) *nf*
number – (numeral) Zahl (-en) *nf*
 page number – Seite (-n) *nf*
number plate – Kennzeichen (-) *nnt*
numerous – zahlreich *adj*
nurse – (female) Krankenschwester
 (-n) *nf*
nurse – (male) Krankenpfleger (-) *nm*
nursery school – Kindergarten
 (-gärten) *nm*
nut (edible) – Nuss (Nüsse) *nf*
nylon – Nylon *nnt·*
 made of nylon – aus Nylon

O

oak tree – Eiche (-n) *nf*
OAP – (male) Rentner (-) *nm*
OAP – (female) Rentnerin (-nen) *nf*
obedient – gehorsam *adj*
obey – gehorchen (+ dat) *v reg* †
object – Gegenstand (-stände) *nm*
obligatory – obligatorisch *adj*
obliged – verpflichtet *adj*
oboe – Oboe (-n) *nf*
observe – bemerken *v reg* †
obstacle – Hindernis (-se) *nnt*
obstinate – stur *adj*
obtain – bekommen *v irreg*
obtain – kriegen *v reg coll*

obvious – offensichtlich *adj*
occasion – Gelegenheit (-en) *nf*
occasion – (special) Ereignis (-se) *nnt*
occasion – (time) Mal (-e) *nnt*
occasional – gelegentlich *adj*
occasionally – hin und wieder *adv*
occupant – (male) Bewohner (-) *nm*
occupant – (female) Bewohnerin
 (-nen) *nf*
occupation – Beruf (-e) *nm*
 What is your occupation? –
 Was sind Sie von Beruf?
occupational – Berufs~ *pref*
occupied – (busy) beschäftigt *adj*
occupied – (table, seat) besetzt *adj*

---

nm - noun masculine	*nf* - noun feminine	*nnt* - noun neuter	*npl* - noun plural
nom- nominative	*acc* - accusative	*gen* - genitive	*dat* - dative

ocean – Ozean (-e) *nm*
o'clock – Uhr
at six o'clock – um sechs Uhr
October – Oktober *nm*
in October – im Oktober
odd – (strange) seltsam *adj*
odd – (number) ungerade
odd jobs – Gelegenheitsarbeiten *npl*
do odd jobs –
Gelegenheitsarbeiten verrichten
v reg †
of – von (+ dat) *prep*
of – (made of) aus (+ dat) *prep*
a pot of tea – ein Kännchen Tee
a bottle of wine – eine Flasche
Wein
a pound of cheese – ein Pfund
Käse
two kilos of apples – zwei Kilo
Äpfel
12th of November – (letter
heading) den 12. November
of course – natürlich *adv*
off – (bad food) schlecht *adj*
off – (electrical) aus *adv*
off – (not here) weg *adv*
off – (tap) zu *adv*
get off the bus – aus dem Bus
aussteigen* *v irreg sep*
10% off – 10% Ermäßigung
offence – Straftat (-en) *nf*
commit an offence – ein
Verbrechen begehen *v irreg*
offend – (insult) beleidigen *v reg* †
offended – beleidigt *adj*
offer – Angebot (-e) *nnt*
special offer – Sonderangebot (-e)
nnt
offer – bieten *v irreg*, anbieten *v irreg*
sep
office – Büro (-s) *nnt*
official – offiziell *adj*
official – (male) Beamte *nm* ‡

official – (female) Beamtin (-nen) *nf*
often – oft *adv*
how often? – wie oft?
Oh! – Ach! *excl*
oil – Öl *nnt*
oil painting – Ölgemälde *nnt*
OK! – in Ordnung! *excl*
old – alt *adj*
How old are you? – Wie alt sind
Sie/Wie alt bist du?
I am 16 years old – Ich bin 16
Jahre alt
old age – Alter (-) *nnt*
old fashioned – altmodisch *adj*
olive oil – Olivenöl *nnt*
the Olympic games – die
Olympischen Spiele *npl*
omelette – Omelett (-s) *nnt*
on – (horizontal) auf (+ acc/dat) *prep*
on – (vertical) an (+ acc/dat) *prep*
on and off – (occasionally) ab und zu
adv
on behalf of – im Auftrag von (+ dat)
on board – an Bord *adv*
on foot – zu Fuß *adv*
on Friday – am Freitag *adv*
on Fridays – freitags *adv*
on purpose – absichtlich *adv*
on the bus – im Bus
get on the bus – in den Bus
einsteigen* *v irreg sep*
go on the bus – mit dem Bus
fahren* *v irreg*
on the ground floor – im
Erdgeschoss
on the left – links *adv*
on the left hand side – auf der
linken Seite
on the other side – auf der anderen
Seite
on the point of – im Begriff sein*
v irreg

---

adj - adjective | *v reg* - verb regular | *v sep* - verb separable | † - see verb info
prep - preposition | *v irreg* - verb irregular | *v refl* - verb reflexive | * - takes sein

he was on the point of phoning – er wollte gerade anrufen

on the Rhine – (afloat) auf dem Rhein

on the right – rechts *adv*

on the Thames – (afloat) auf der Themse

on the top floor – im obersten Geschoss

on the train – im Zug

on time – pünktlich *adj*

on top of – oben auf (+ dat) *adv*

and so on – und so weiter (usw.)

later on – später *adv*

What's on? – (cinema) Was läuft?

once – einmal *adv*

once more – noch einmal *adv*

one – ein *indef art m, nt*

one – eine *indef art f*

one off – einmalig *adj*

one way ticket – einfache Fahrkarte

one way street – Einbahnstraße (-n) *nf*

oneself – selbst *pron*

oneself – sich *pron refl*

onion – Zwiebel (-n) *nf*

only – einzig *adj*

only – nur *adv*

only – (time) erst *adv*

only child – Einzelkind (-er) *nnt*

onwards – vorwärts *adv*

open – offen *adj*, geöffnet *adj*

in the open air – im Freien

open air swimming pool – Freibad (-bäder) *nnt*

open – öffnen *v reg* †, aufmachen *v reg sep*

opening – Öffnung (-en) *nf*

opening hours – Öffnungszeiten *npl*

opera – Oper (-n) *nf*

opera house – Opernhaus (-häuser) *nnt*

operation – Operation (-en) *nf*

have an operation – sich operieren lassen *v irreg refl*

opinion – Meinung (-en) *nf*

in my opinion – meiner Meinung nach

opinion poll – Meinungsumfrage (-n) *nf*

opportunity – Gelegenheit (-en) *nf*

opposite – gegenüber (+ dat) *prep*

opposite – Gegenteil (-e) *nnt*

opt for – sich entscheiden für (+ acc) *v irreg refl*

optician – (male) Optiker (-) *nm*

optician – (female) Optikerin (-nen) *nf*

optimist – Optimist (-en) *nm wk*

optimistic – optimistisch *adj*

optional – auf Wunsch

optional subject – Wahlfach (-fächer) *nnt*

or – oder *coord conj*

oral – mündlich *adj*

oral question – mündliche Frage (-n) *nf*

oral test – mündliche Prüfung (-en) *nf*

orange – orange *adj inv*

orange – Apfelsine (-n) *nf*

orange juice – Orangensaft *nm*

orchestra – Orchester (-) *nnt*

order – (command) Befehl (-e) *nm*

order – (restaurant) Bestellung (-en) *nf*

order – (sequence) Folge (-n) *nf*

order – (tidiness) Ordnung (-en) *nf*

in alphabetical order – in alphabetischer Reihenfolge

in order to – um ... zu *conj*

order – (command) befehlen *v irreg*

order – (restaurant) bestellen *v reg* †

orderly – ordentlich *adj*

ordinal number – Ordinalzahl (-en) *nf*

ordinary – normal *adj*, gewöhnlich *adj*

organise – organisieren *v reg* †

---

nm - noun masculine   *nf* - noun feminine   *nnt* - noun neuter   *npl* - noun plural
nom- nominative   *acc* - accusative   *gen* - genitive   *dat* - dative

organised – organisiert *adj*
original – original *adj*
orphan – Waise (-n) *nf*
other – andere *adj*
   the other day – neulich *adv*
otherwise – sonst *adv*
Ouch! Ow! – Autsch! *excl*
ought – sollen *v irreg*
   I ought to do it – Ich sollte es tun
our – unser *poss adj*
ourselves – uns *pron refl*
out – (finished) zu Ende
   School's out – Die Schule ist aus
   The light is out – Das Licht ist aus
out – (outside) draußen *adv*
outdoors – draußen *adv*, im Freien
out of – aus (+ dat) *prep*
   six out of ten – sechs von zehn
out of breath – atemlos *adj*
out of date – altmodisch *adj*
out of order – (not working) außer
   Betrieb
out of season – außerhalb der Saison
outfit – (clothes) Kleidung (-en) *nf*
outside – draußen *adv*
   outside the door – draußen vor
   der Tür
outside – außerhalb von (+ dat) *prep*
outside – Außenseite (-n) *nf*
outskirts – Rand (Ränder) *nm*
outstanding – (very good)
   hervorragend *adj*
oval – oval *adj*
oven – Herd (-e) *nm*

microwave oven –
   Mikrowellenherd (-e) *nm*
over – (across, away from speaker)
   hinüber *adv*
over – (across, towards speaker)
   herüber *adv*
over – (finished) vorbei *adv*
over – (left) übrig *adv*
over – (above) über (+ acc/dat) *prep*
all over – (everywhere) überall *adv*
over and over – (again) immer
   wieder *adv*
over there – da drüben *adv*
overalls – Overall (-s) *nm*
overcoat – Mantel (Mäntel) *nm*
overdose – Überdosis (-dosen) *nf*
overhead projector –
   Tageslichtprojektor (-en) *nm*
overnight stay – Übernachtung (-en)
   nf
overseas – Übersee~ *pref*
overtake – überholen *v reg insep*
overturn – (boat) umkippen[*] *v reg*
   sep
overturn – (car) sich überschlagen
   v irreg refl insep
owe – (money) schulden *v reg* †
owe s.o. sthg – (thanks) jdm etwas
   verdanken *v reg* †
own – eigen *adj*
own – besitzen *v irreg*
owner – (male) Besitzer (-) *nm*
owner – (female) Besitzerin (-nen) *nf*
oxygen – Sauerstoff *nm*
ozone layer – Ozonschicht (-en) *nf*

P

pack – (case) packen *v reg*
pack of cards – Spiel (e) *nnt*
package – Paket (-e) *nnt*
package tour – Pauschalreise (-n) *nf*
packed lunch – Lunchpaket (-e) *nnt*
pad – (writing) Schreibblock (-blöcke) *nm*
paddock – Koppel (-n) *nf*
page – Seite (-n) *nf*
  at the bottom of the page – unten auf der Seite
  on page 51 – auf Seite 51
paid – bezahlt *adj*
pain – Schmerz (-en) *nm*
  be in pain – Schmerzen haben *v irreg*
painful – schmerzhaft *adj*
paint – (art) malen *v reg*
  paint the wall – die Wand streichen *v irreg*
painter – (male) Maler (-) *nm*
painter – (female) Malerin (-nen) *nf*
painter – (decorator) Anstreicher (-) *nm*
pair (of) – Paar *nnt*
  a pair of jeans – Jeans *nf*
  a pair of pyjamas – Schlafanzug *nm*
  a pair of shoes – ein Paar Schuhe
  a pair of shorts – eine kurze Hose *nf*
  a pair of trousers – eine Hose *nf*
Pakistan – Pakistan *nnt*
Pakistani – pakistanisch *adj*
Pakistani person – (male) Pakistaner (-) *nm*
Pakistani person – (female) Pakistanerin (-nen) *nf*
palace – Schloss (Schlösser) *nnt*
pale – (complexion) blass *adj*
pale – hell~ *pref*

pale blue – hellblau *adj*
pan – (cooking) Topf (Töpfe) *nm*
pancake – Pfannkuchen (-) *nm*
pants – (male) Unterhose (-n) *nf*
pants – (female) Slip (-s) *nm*
paper – Papier (-e) *nnt*
  made of paper – aus Papier
paper – (exam) Testbogen (-bögen) *nm*
  newspaper – Zeitung (-en) *nf*
paperback – Taschenbuch (-bücher) *nnt*
paperclip – Büroklammer (-n) *nf*
papers – (ID) Ausweis (-e) *nm*
paragraph – Absatz (-sätze) *nm*
parcel – Paket (-e) *nnt*
parents – Eltern *npl*
park – Park (-s) *nm*
park – parken *v reg*
parking – Parken *nnt*
parking lot – Parkplatz (-plätze) *nm*
parking meter – Parkuhr (-en) *nf*
parking space – Abstellplatz (-plätze) *nm*
parking ticket – Strafzettel (-) *nm*
parliament – (national) Parlament (-e) *nnt*
parliament – (regional) Landtag (-e) *nm*
parrot – Papagei (-en) *nm*
part – Teil (-e) *nm*
  spare part – Ersatzteil (-e) *nnt*
part – (acting) Rolle (-n) *nf*
  for the most part – meistens *adv*
  part of town – Stadtteil (-e) *nm*
  part-time – Teilzeit~ *pref*
  take part in – teilnehmen an (+ dat) *v irreg sep*
participate – teilnehmen *v irreg sep*
participle – Partizip (-ien) *nnt*
particular – besondere *adj*

---

nm - noun masculine   *nf* - noun feminine   *nnt* - noun neuter   *npl* - noun plural
nom- nominative   *acc* - accusative   *gen* - genitive   *dat* - dative

particularly – besonders *adv*
partner – (male) Partner (-) *nm*
partner – (female) Partnerin (-nen) *nf*
party – (celebration) Party (-s) *nf*
party – (political) Partei (-en) *nf*
pass – (an exam) bestehen *v irreg*
pass – (at table) reichen *v reg*
pass – (in car) vorbeifahren* an (+ dat) *v irreg sep*
pass – (on foot) vorbeigehen* an (+ dat) *v irreg sep*
pass – (overtake) überholen *v reg insep*
pass – (time) verbringen *v irreg*
passage – (book) Stelle (-n) *nf*
passage – (corridor) Gang (Gänge) *nm*
passenger – (male) Passagier (-e) *nm*
passenger – (female) Passagierin (-nen) *nf*
passer-by – (male) Passant (-en) *nm wk*
passer-by – (female) Passantin (-nen) *nf*
Passover – Passahfest (-e) *nnt*
passport – Pass (Pässe) *nm*
past – (beyond) hinter (+ acc/dat) *prep*
past – (time) nach (+ dat) *prep*
 five past four – fünf nach vier
 half past six – halb sieben
 quarter past three – Viertel nach drei
past – (travelling) an (+ dat) vorbei *prep*
 I'm going past school – Ich gehe an der Schule vorbei
pasta – Nudeln *npl*
paste – (glue) kleben *v reg*
pastime – Zeitvertreib (-e) *nm*
pastry – Teig (-e) *nm*
past tense – Vergangenheit (-en) *nf*
pâté – Pastete (-n) *nf*
path – Weg (-e) *nm*
pathetic – erbärmlich *adj*
patience – Geduld *nf*
patient – geduldig *adj*

patient – (male) Patient (-en) *nm wk*
patient – (female) Patientin (-nen) *nf*
patio – Terrasse (-n) *nf*
pause – Pause (-n) *nf*
pavement – Bürgersteig (-e) *nm*
paw – Pfote (-n) *nf*
pay – (salary) Gehalt (Gehälter) *nnt*
pay – (wages) Lohn (Löhne) *nm*
pay (for) – bezahlen *v reg* †
pay attention (to) – achten (auf + acc) *v reg* †
pay a visit to – (people) besuchen *v reg* †
pay a visit to – (sights) besichtigen *v reg* †
payment – Bezahlung (-en) *nf*
pay phone – Münzfernsprecher (-) *nm*
pay rise – Gehaltserhöhung (-en) *nf*
PC (computer) – PC (-s) *nm*
PE – Sport *nm*
peace – Frieden (-) *nm*
 Leave me in peace! – Lass mich in Ruhe! *excl*
peaceful – friedlich *adj*
peach – Pfirsich (-e) *nm*
peanut – Erdnuss (nüsse) *nf*
pear – Birne (-n) *nf*
pea – Erbse (-n) *nf*
peculiar – seltsam *adj*
pedestrian – (male) Fußgänger (-) *nm*
pedestrian – (female) Fußgängerin (-nen) *nf*
pedestrian crossing – Fußgängerüberweg (-e) *nm*
pedestrian precinct – Fußgängerzone (-n) *nf*
peel – schälen *v reg*
pen – (fountain) Füller (-) *nm*
pen – (ballpoint) Kuli (-s) *nm*, Kugelschreiber (-) *nm*
pencil – Bleistift (-e) *nm*
pencil case – Federmäppchen (-) *nnt*

---

adj - adjective	*v reg* - verb regular	*v sep* - verb separable	† - see verb info
prep - preposition	*v irreg* - verb irregular	*v refl* - verb reflexive	* - takes sein

pencil sharpener – Bleistiftspitzer (-) *nm*

pendant – Anhänger (-) *nm*

pen-friend – (male) Brieffreund (-e) *nm*

pen-friend – (female) Brieffreundin (-nen) *nf*

penknife – Taschenmesser (-) *nnt*

pensioner – (male) Rentner (-) *nm*

pensioner – (female) Rentnerin (-nen) *nf*

people – Leute *npl*

pepper – (spice) Pfeffer *nm*

pepper – (vegetable) Paprika (-s) *nm*

per – pro (+ acc) *prep*

  per cent – Prozent *nnt*

  per day – pro Tag

  per hour – pro Stunde

  per kilo – pro Kilo

  per month – pro Monat

  per person – pro Person

  per week – pro Woche

percussion instrument – Schlagzeug (-e) *nnt*

perfect – perfekt *adj*

performance – (drama) Vorstellung (-en) *nf*

performance – (sport, etc) Leistung (-en) *nf*

performer – (male) Künstler (-) *nm*

performer – (female) Künstlerin (-nen) *nf*

performing arts – (school) Theaterkunde *nf*

perfume – Parfüm *nnt*

perhaps – vielleicht *adv*

period – (lesson) Stunde (-n) *nf*

period – (time) Zeit (-en) *nf*

period – (in time) Zeitpunkt (-e) *nm*

period – (menstrual) Tage *npl*, Periode (-n) *nf*

  I've got my period – Ich habe meine Tage

permission – Erlaubnis (-se) *nf*

permit – erlauben *v reg* †

permitted – gestattet, erlaubt *adj*

person – (male or female) Person (-en) *nf*

  in person – persönlich *adv*

personal – persönlich *adj*

personal stereo – Walkman® (Walkmen) *nm*

persuade – überreden *v reg insep* †

pet – Haustier (-e) *nnt*

petrol – Benzin *nnt*

  4-star leaded petrol – Super verbleit *nnt*

  unleaded petrol – bleifrei *adj*

petrol pump – Zapfsäule (n) *nf*

petrol pump attendant – Tankwart (-e) *nm*

petrol station – Tankstelle (-n) *nf*

pharmacy – Apotheke (-n) *nf*

phone – Telefon (-e) *nnt*

  on the phone – am Telefon

phone – anrufen *v irreg sep,* telefonieren mit (+ dat) *v reg* †

phone book – Telefonbuch (-bücher) *nnt*

phone box – Telefonzelle (-n) *nf*

phone call – Anruf (-e) *nm*

phone card – Telefonkarte (-n) *nf*

phone number – Telefonnummer (-n) *nf*

photo – Foto (-s) *nnt*

  take a photo – fotografieren *v reg* †

photocopy – Fotokopie (-n) *nf*

photocopier – Fotokopiergerät(-e) *nnt*

photocopy – fotokopieren *v reg* †

photograph – Foto (-s) *nnt*

photographer – (male) Fotograf (-en) *nm wk*

photographer – (female) Fotografin (-nen) *nf*

photography – Fotografie *nf*

physical – körperlich *adj*

physical education – Sport *nm*

physics – Physik *nf*
physiotherapist – (male)
Physiotherapeut (-en) *nm wk*
physiotherapist – (female)
Physiotherapeutin (-nen) *nf*
piano – (upright) Klavier *nnt*
piano – (grand) Flügel (-) *nm*
I play the piano – ich spiele
Klavier
pick (out) – (choose) auswählen *v reg*
sep
pickpocket – Taschendieb (-e) *nm*
pick up – (collect) abholen *v reg sep*
pick up – (lift) aufheben *v irreg sep*
pick up phone – den Hörer
abnehmen *v irreg sep*
picnic – Picknick (-s) *nnt*
picnic – picknicken *v reg*
picnic area – Rastplatz (-plätze) *nm*
picture – Bild (-er) *nnt*
picturesque – malerisch *adj*
pie chart – Kreisdiagramm (-e) *nnt*
piece (of) – Stück (-) *nnt*
a piece of chocolate – ein Stück
Schokolade
piece of information – Auskunft *nf*
pig – Schwein (-e) *nnt*
piggy bank – Sparschwein (-e) *nnt*
pile – Haufen (-) *nm*
pill – Tablette (-n) *nf*
pill – (contraceptive) Pille (-n) *nf*
pillow – Kopfkissen (-) *nnt*
pillowcase – Kissenbezug (-züge) *nm*
pilot – (air) Pilot (-en) *nm wk*
pineapple – Ananas (-) *nf*
pink – rosa *adj inv*
pipe – (for tobacco) Pfeife (-n) *nf*
Pisces – (horoscope) Fische
pitch – Platz (Plätze) *nm*
pitch the tent – das Zelt aufbauen
v reg sep
pity – schade

What a pity! – Wie schade! *excl*
pizza – Pizza (-s) *nf*
placard – Plakat (-e) *nnt*
place – (spot) Stelle (-n) *nf*
place – (square) Platz (Plätze) *nm*
place – (town, etc) Ort (-e) *nm*
place of birth – Geburtsort (-e) *nm*
take place – stattfinden *v irreg sep*
at my place – bei mir
place – (vertical) stellen *v reg*
place – (horizontal) legen *v reg*
place – (insert) stecken *v reg*
place on – setzen auf (+ acc) *v reg*
plain – (no pattern) uni *adj inv*
plait – Zopf (Zöpfe) *nm*
plan – Plan (Pläne) *nm*
career plans – Berufspläne *npl*
future plans – Zukunftspläne *npl*
holiday plans – Urlaubspläne *npl*
plan – planen *v reg*
as planned – wie geplant
plan sthg – (intend) etwas vorhaben
v irreg sep
plane – Flugzeug (-e) *nnt*
by plane – mit dem Flugzeug
plant – Pflanze (-n) *nf*
plant – pflanzen *v reg*
plaster – (sticking) Pflaster *nnt*
plaster – (broken arm) Gips (-e) *nm*
plastic – Kunststoff (-e) *nm*
made of plastic – aus Kunststoff
plastic bag – Plastiktüte (-n) *nf*
plate – Teller (-) *nm*
platform – Bahnsteig (-e) *nm*
from platform 8 – auf Gleis 8
play – Theaterstück (-e) *nnt*
play – spielen *v reg*
play a trick on – veräppeln *v reg* †
play chess – Schach spielen *v reg*
play football – Fußball spielen
v reg

---

adj - adjective	*v reg* - verb regular	*v sep* - verb separable	† - see verb info
prep - preposition	*v irreg* - verb irregular	*v refl* - verb reflexive	* - takes sein

play the guitar – Gitarre spielen *v reg*	**Poland** – Polen *nnt*
player – (male) Spieler (-) *nm*	**police** – Polizei *nf*
player – (female) Spielerin (-nen) *nf*	**policeman** – Polizist (-en) *nm wk*
playground – Spielplatz (-plätze) *nm*	**police station** – Polizeiwache (-n) *nf*
playing card – Spielkarte (-n) *nf*	**police woman** – Polizistin (-nen) *nf*
playing field – Sportplatz (plätze) *nm*	**policy** – Politik *nf*
pleasant – angenehm *adj*	**polish** – polieren *v reg* †
please – bitte *adv*	**polite** – höflich *adj*
please do not ... – bitte nicht ...	**politeness** – Höflichkeit (-en) *nf*
pleased – (satisfied) zufrieden *adj*	**politician** – (male) Politiker (-) *nm*
be pleased about – sich freuen über (+ acc) *v reg refl*	**politician** – (female) Politikerin (-nen) *nf*
Pleased to meet you! – Angenehm! *excl*	**polluted** – verschmutzt *adj*
pleasure – Freude (-n) *nf*, Vergnügen *nnt*	**pollution** – Umweltschmutz *nm*, Umweltverschmutzung *nf*
It's a pleasure! – Bitte sehr! Gern geschehen! *excl*	**pond** – Teich (-e) *nm*
with pleasure – mit Vergnügen	**pony** – Pony (-s) *nnt*
pluck – pflücken *v reg*	**pony tail** – Pferdeschwanz (-schwänze) *nm*
plug – (electric) Stecker (-) *nm*	**poodle** – Pudel (-) *nm*
plug – (bath) Stöpsel (-) *nm*	**pool** – Schwimmbad (-bäder) *nnt*
plug in – anschließen *v irreg sep*	**pool** – (open air) Freibad (-bäder) *nnt*
plum – Pflaume (-n) *nf*	**pool** – (indoor) Hallenbad (-bäder) *nnt*
plumber – (male) Klempner (-) *nm*	**poor** – (bad) schlecht *adj*
plumber – (female) Klempnerin (-nen) *nf*	**poor** – (not rich) arm *adj*
plump – mollig *adj*	**poorly** – (ill) krank *adj*
pluperfect – Plusquamperfekt *nnt*	**pop music** – Popmusik *nf*
plural – Plural (-e) *nm*	**popular** – beliebt *adj*
in the plural – im Plural	**pork** – Schweinefleisch *nnt*
p.m. – nachmittags *adv*	**roast pork** – Schweinebraten *nm*
pocket – Tasche (-n) *nf*	**pork chop** – Schweinekotelett (-s) *nnt*
pocket money – Taschengeld *nnt*	**port** – Hafen (Häfen) *nm*
point – Punkt (-e) *nm*	**portion** – Portion (-en) *nf*
There's no point – Es hat keinen Zweck	**Portugal** – Portugal *nnt*
pointed – spitz *adj*	**Portuguese** – portugiesisch *adj*
pointless – zwecklos *adj*	**Portuguese person** – (male) Portugiese (-n) *nm wk*
poison – Gift (-e) *nnt*	**Portuguese person** – (female) Portugiesin (-nen) *nf*
poisonous – giftig *adj*	**posh** – vornehm *adj*
	position – Lage (-n) *nf*
	positive – positiv *adj*

---

nm - noun masculine	*nf* - noun feminine	*nnt* - noun neuter	*npl* - noun plural
nom- nominative	*acc* - accusative	*gen* - genitive	*dat* - dative

possess – besitzen *v irreg*
possibility – Möglichkeit (-en) *nf*
possible – möglich *adj*
possibly – möglicherweise *adv*
post – einwerfen *v irreg sep*
  post a letter – einen Brief
  einwerfen *v irreg sep*
postage stamp – Briefmarke (-n) *nf*
postal order – Postanweisung (-en) *nf*
postcard – Postkarte (-n) *nf*
post code – Postleitzahl (-en) *nf*
poster – Poster (-) *nnt*
post office – Post *nf*
postman – Briefträger (-) *nm*
postpone – verschieben *v irreg*
postwoman – Briefträgerin (-nen) *nf*
pot – (cooking) Topf (Töpfe) *nm*
  a pot of coffee – ein Kännchen
  Kaffee *nnt*
potato – Kartoffel (-n) *nf*
pot plant – Topfpflanze (-n) *nf*
pottery – (workshop) Töpferei (-en) *nf*
poultry – Geflügel *nnt*
pound – Pfund *nnt*
pour a drink – einschenken *v reg sep*
powder – Pulver (-) *nnt*
powder – (cosmetic) Puder (-) *nm*
power – Kraft (Kräfte) *nf*
powerful – mächtig *adj*
power point – Steckdose (-n) *nf*
practical – praktisch *adj*
practical work – praktische Arbeit *nf*
practice – Übung (-en) *nf*
  practice makes perfect – Übung
  macht den Meister
practice – (doctor) Praxis (Praxen) *nf*
practise – üben *v reg*
praise – loben *v reg*
precaution – Vorsichtsmaßnahme
  (-n) *nf*
precious – wertvoll *adj*
precise – genau *adj*

prefer – vorziehen *v irreg sep*
  I prefer tea to coffee – Ich trinke
  lieber Tee als Kaffee
prep – (homework) Hausaufgaben *npl*
preparation – Vorbereitung (-en) *nf*
preparatory – Vor~ *pref*
prep(aratory) school – private
  Grundschule (-n) *nf*
prepare – vorbereiten *v reg sep* †
prescribe – verschreiben *v irreg*
prescription – Rezept (-) *nnt*
presence – Anwesenheit (-en) *nf*
present – (not absent) anwesend *adj*
present – (current) gegenwärtig,
  im Moment *adj*
present – (gift) Geschenk (-e) *nnt*
  give as a present – schenken
  v reg
present – (tense) Präsens *nnt*
present – (introduce) vorstellen *v reg*
  sep
present – (radio, TV) moderieren
  v reg †
presenter – (TV) (male) Moderator
  (-en) *nm wk*
presenter – (TV) (female)
  Moderatorin (-nen) *nf*
press – (media) Presse *nf*
press – drücken *v reg*
press on – (continue) weitermachen
  v reg sep
pretend – tun so, als ob *v irreg*
pretty – hübsch *adj*
prevent – verhindern *v reg* †
previous – vorig, ehemalig *adj*
previously – früher *adv*
price – Preis (-e) *nm*
price list – Preisliste (-n) *nf*
priest – (RC) Priester (-) *nm*
primary school – Grundschule (-n) *nf*
primary school teacher – (male)
  Grundschullehrer (-) *nm*

| *adj* - adjective | *v reg* - verb regular | *v sep* - verb separable | † - see verb info |
| *prep* - preposition | *v irreg* - verb irregular | *v refl* - verb reflexive | * - takes sein |

primary school teacher – (female) Grundschullehrerin (-nen) *nf*

principal – (male) Direktor (-) *nm*

principal – (female) Direktorin (-nen) *nf*

principle – Prinzip (-ien) *nnt*

print – drucken *v reg*

printed – gedruckt *adj*

printer – Drucker (-) *nm*

priority – (traffic) Vorfahrt

prison – Gefängnis (-se) *nnt*

private – privat *adj*

private school – Privatschule (-n) *nf*

prize – Preis (-e) *nm*

probable – vermutlich *adj*

probably – wahrscheinlich *adv*

problem – Problem (-e) *nnt*

process – Prozess (-e) *nm*
  be in the process of – gerade dabei sein* *v irreg*

procession – Zug (Züge) *nm*

product – Produkt (-e) *nnt*

profession – Beruf (-e) *nm*
  What's your profession? – Was sind Sie von Beruf?

programme – (TV) Sendung (-en) *nf*

programme – Programm (-e) *nnt*

programmer – (male) Programmierer (-) *nm*

programmer – (female) Programmiererin (-nen) *nf*

progress – Fortschritt (-e) *nm*
  make progress – Fortschritte machen *v reg*

project – Projekt (-e) *nnt*

promise – Versprechen (-) *nnt*

promise s.o. sthg – jdm etwas versprechen *v irreg*

pronoun – Pronomen (-) *nnt*

pronounce – aussprechen *v irreg sep*

proper – (correct) richtig *adj*

proper – (decent) anständig *adj*

proper noun – Eigenname (-n) *nm wk*

propose – (suggest) vorschlagen *v irreg sep*

protect from – schützen vor (+ dat) *v reg*

protection – Schutz (-e) *nm*

protest – protestieren *v reg* †

Protestant – evangelisch *adj*

Protestant – Protestant (-en) *nm wk*

Protestant – Protestantin (-nen) *nf*

proud (of) – stolz (auf + acc) *adj*

prove – beweisen *v irreg*

province – Provinz (-en) *nf*

PSE – Lebenskunde *nf*

PTO – bitte wenden (b.w.)

pub – Kneipe (-n) *nf*

public – öffentlich *adj*

public holiday – Feiertag (-e) *nm*

public school – (UK) Privatschule (-n) *nf*

public transport – öffentliche Verkehrsmittel *npl*

publicity – Werbung (-en) *nf*

pudding – (dessert) Nachtisch (-e) *nm*

pull – ziehen *v irreg*

pull a face – ein Gesicht ziehen *v irreg*

pullover – Pullover (-) *nm*

pump up tyres – aufpumpen *v reg sep*

pun – Wortspiel (-e) *nnt*

punctual – pünktlich *adj*

punctuation – Zeichensetzung (-en) *nf*

puncture – Reifenpanne (-n) *nf*

punish – bestrafen *v reg* †

punishment – Strafe (-n) *nf*

pupil – (male) Schüler (-) *nm*

pupil – (female) Schülerin (-nen) *nf*

puppy – ein junger Hund *nm*

purchase – Kauf (Käufe) *nm*

purchase – kaufen *v reg*

purple – purpur *adj inv*

purpose – Zweck (-e) *nm*, Absicht (-en) *nf*
  on purpose – absichtlich *adv*

---

nm - noun masculine	*nf* - noun feminine	*nnt* - noun neuter	*npl* - noun plural
nom - nominative	*acc* - accusative	*gen* - genitive	*dat* - dative

purr – schnurren *v reg*
purse – Portemonnaie (-s) *nnt*
push – (a car) schieben *v irreg*
push – (door) drücken *v reg*
put – (horizontal) legen *v reg*
put – (insert) stecken *v reg*
put – (vertical) stellen *v reg*
put away – weglegen *v reg sep*
put back – zurückstellen *v reg sep*, zurücklegen *v reg sep*
put down – (vertical) hinstellen *v reg sep*
put down – (horizontal) hinlegen *v reg sep*

put in the right order – ordnen *v reg* †
put on – (clothes) anziehen *v irreg sep*
put on headlights – die Scheinwerfer einschalten *v reg sep* †
put on light – das Licht anmachen *v reg sep*
put on make-up – sich schminken *v reg refl*
put on – (play) aufführen *v reg sep*
put out – (light) ausmachen *v reg sep*
put up – (guest) unterbringen *v irreg sep*
put up with – aushalten *v irreg sep*
pyjamas – Schlafanzug (-züge) *nm*
puzzle – Rätsel (-) *nnt*

Q

qualification – Qualifikation (-en) *nf*
quality – Qualität (-en) *nf*
   good quality – guter Qualität
   poor quality – schlechter Qualität
quantity – Menge (-n) *nf*
quarrel – Streit (-e) *nm*
quarrel – sich streiten *v irreg refl*
quarry – Steinbruch (-brüche) *nm*
quarter – Viertel (-) *nnt*
   quarter of an hour – eine Viertelstunde *nf*
   quarter past one – Viertel nach eins
   quarter to two – Viertel vor zwei
   three quarters – drei viertel
   three quarters of an hour – Dreiviertelstunde (-n) *nf*
quarter – (town) Stadtteil (-e) *nm*
quay – Kai (-s) *nm*
queen – Königin (-nen) *nf*
question – Frage (-n) *nf*

ask a question – eine Frage stellen *v reg*
out of the question – das kommt nicht in Frage
question mark (?) – Fragezeichen *nnt*
question – fragen *v reg*
question s.o. – befragen *v reg* †
queue – Schlange (-n) *nf*
queue up – Schlange stehen *v irreg*
quick – schnell *adj*
   be quick – sich beeilen *v reg refl* †
quiet – (peaceful) still, ruhig *adj*
quiet – (without noise) leise *adj*
quilt – Steppdecke (-n) *nf*
quite – (fairly) ziemlich *adv*
quite – (totally) ganz *adv*
quiz – Quiz (-) *nnt*
quotation – Zitat (-e) *nnt*
quote – zitieren *v reg* †

R

rabbit – Kaninchen (-) *nnt*
race – (nationality) Rasse (-n) *nf*
race – (sport) Rennen (-) *nnt*
races – Pferderennen *nnt*
racket – (tennis) Schläger (-) *nm*
radiator – (in building) Heizkörper (-) *nm*
radiator – (in car) Kühler (-) *nm*
radio – Radio (-s) *nnt*
   be on the radio – im Radio sein* *v irreg*
radio cassette player – Radiokassettenrekorder (-) *nm*
railway – Eisenbahn (-en) *nf,* Bahn (-en) *nf*
railway carriage – Wagon (-s) *nm*
railway station – Bahnhof (-höfe) *nm*
   main railway station – Hauptbahnhof (-höfe) *nm*
rain – Regen *nm*
   in the rain – im Regen
rain – regnen *v reg* †
   It is raining – Es regnet
   It was raining – Es regnete
   It will rain – Es wird regnen
   It rained – Es hat geregnet
rainbow – Regenbogen (-bögen) *nm*
raincoat – Regenmantel (-mäntel) *nm*
rainy – regnerisch *adj*
Ramadan – Ramadan *nm*
rapid – schnell *adj*
rare – selten *adj*
raspberry – Himbeere (-n) *nf*
   raspberry tart – Himbeertorte (-n) *nf*
rat – Ratte (-n) *nf*
rate of exchange – Wechselkurs (-e) *nm*
rather – (fairly) ziemlich *adv*

I'd rather play tennis – Ich würde lieber Tennis spielen
raw – roh *adj*
razor – Rasierapparat (-e) *nm*
RE – Religion (-en) *nf*
reach – erreichen *v reg* †
read – lesen *v irreg*
reader – (male) Leser (-) *nm*
reader – (female) Leserin (-nen) *nf*
reading – Lesen *nnt*
reading matter – Lektüre *nf*
ready – fertig *adj*
   ready-made meal – Fertiggericht (-e) *nnt*
ready – (willing) bereit *adj*
real – (genuine) echt *adj*
real – (true) wirklich *adj*
realise – merken *v reg*
reality – Wirklichkeit (-en) *nf*
really – wirklich *adv*
reason – Grund (Gründe) *nm*
receipt – Quittung (-en) *nf*
receive – bekommen *v irreg,* erhalten *v irreg*
recent – neu *adj*
recently – neulich *adv*
reception – Empfang (Empfänge) *nm*
reception desk – (hotel) Rezeption *nf*
receptionist – Empfangsdame (-n) *nf*
recipe – Rezept (-e) *nnt*
reckon – (calculate) rechnen *v reg* †
reckon – (judge) meinen *v reg*
reckon – (think) denken *v irreg*
recognise – erkennen *v irreg*
recommend – empfehlen *v irreg*
recommended – empfohlen *adj*
record – (sport, etc) Rekord (-e) *nm*
record – (pop, etc) Schallplatte (-n) *nf*

---

record – (on tape) aufnehmen *v irreg sep*
recorder – (flute) Blockflöte (-n) *nf*
record player – Plattenspieler (-) *nm*
recount – erzählen *v reg* †
recover – (get back) zurückbekommen *v irreg sep*
recover – (get better) sich erholen *v reg refl* †
rectangular – viereckig *adj*
recycle – recyceln *v reg* †
red – rot *adj*
redcurrant – rote Johannisbeere (-n) *nf*
red haired – rothaarig *adj*
red wine – Rotwein (-e) *nm*
re-do – wiederholen *v reg insep* †
reduce – reduzieren *v reg* †
reduced – reduziert *adj*
reduction – (price) Ermäßigung (-en) *nf*
reel – (spool) Rolle (-n) *nf*
referee – (male) Schiedsrichter (-) *nm*
referee – (female) Schiedsrichterin (-nen) *nf*
refill – auffüllen *v reg sep*
reflexive verb – Reflexivverbum (-verben) *nnt*
refreshment bar – Imbissstube (-n) *nf*
refreshments – Erfrischungen *npl*
refuse – (rubbish) Müll *nm*
refuse – (to do sthg) sich weigern *v reg refl*
refuse – (permission) verweigern *v reg* †
region – Region (-en) *nf*
registered letter – Einschreibebrief (-e) *nm*
registration number – (car) Kennzeichen (-) *nnt*
regret – bedauern *v reg* †
regular – regelmäßig *adj*
rehearsal – Probe (-n) *nf*
relationship – Verhältnis (-se) *nnt*

relative – Verwandte *nmf* ‡
relatively – relativ *adv*
relax – sich entspannen *v reg refl* †
relaxation – Entspannung *nf*
relaxed – entspannt *adj*
reliable – zuverlässig *adj*
religion – Religion (-en) *nf*
remain – (stay) bleiben* *v irreg*
remain – (left over) übrig bleiben* *v irreg*
remainder – Rest *nm*
remarkable – merkwürdig *adj*
remedy for – Mittel gegen (+ acc) *nnt*
remember – sich erinnern an (+ acc) *v reg refl* †
remind of – erinnern an (+ acc) *v reg* †
remote control – (TV) Fernbedienung *nf*
removal van – Möbelwagen (-) *nm*
remove – entfernen *v reg* †
renew – erneuern *v reg* †
rent – Miete (-n) *nf*
rent – mieten *v reg* †
renting – Vermietung (-en) *nf*
repair – Reparatur (-en) *nf*
repair – reparieren *v reg* †
I have had my camera repaired – Ich habe meinen Fotoapparat reparieren lassen
repeat – wiederholen *v reg insep* †
repeat a year – (at school) sitzen bleiben* *v irreg*
replace – ersetzen *v reg* †
reply – antworten *v reg* †
reply to s.o. – beantworten *v reg* †
report – Bericht (-e) *nm*
report – (school) Zeugnis (-se) *nnt*
mid-year report – Halbjahreszeugnis (-se) *nnt*
reporter – (male) Reporter (-) *nm*
reporter – (female) Reporterin (-nen) *nf*
represent – vertreten *v irreg*

---

representative – (male) Vertreter (-) *nm*

representative – (female) Vertreterin (-nen) *nf*

reputation – Ruf (-e) *nm*

request – Bitte (-n) *nf*

rescue – retten *v reg* †

resemble – ähneln (+ dat) *v reg*

reservation – Reservierung (-en) *nf*

reserve – reservieren *v reg* †

reserved – reserviert *adj*

resident – (male) Einwohner (-) *nm*

resident – (female) Einwohnerin (-nen) *nf*

resit exam – eine Prüfung wiederholen *v reg insep* †

respect – Respekt *nm*

respectable – anständig *adj*

responsibility – Verantwortung *nf*

responsible – verantwortlich *adj*

rest – sich ausruhen *v reg refl sep*
  have a rest – Pause machen *v reg*
  the rest – Rest *nm*

restaurant – Restaurant (-s) *nnt*

restrict – einschränken *v reg sep*

result – Ergebnis (-se) *nnt*

retire – in den Ruhestand treten* *v irreg*

retired – im Ruhestand

retired person – (male) Rentner (-) *nm*

retired person – (female) Rentnerin (-nen) *nf*

return – zurückkommen* *v irreg sep*

return journey – Rückfahrt (-en) *nf*

return ticket – Rückfahrkarte (-n) *nf*
  A return ticket to Dresden –
    Einmal nach Dresden, hin und zurück
  Many happy returns! –
    Herzlichen Glückwunsch zum
    Geburtstag! *excl*

reunification – Wiedervereinigung *nf*

reverse – (car) rückwärts fahren* *v irreg*

revolver – Revolver (-) *nm*

reward – Belohnung (-en) *nf*

Rhine – Rhein *nm*

rhinoceros – Nashorn (-hörner) *nnt*

rib – Rippe (-n) *nf*

rice – Reis *nm*

rich – reich *adj*

ride – (bike) Rad fahren* *v irreg*

ride – (horse) reiten (*) *v irreg*

ridiculous – lächerlich *adj*

riding hat – Reitkappe (-n) *nf*

right – (not wrong) richtig *adj*
  be right – Recht haben *v irreg*
  That's right – Das stimmt
  the right answer – die richtige Antwort
  You are right – Du hast Recht

right! – also! *excl*

right – rechts *adv*
  keep to the right – rechts fahren* *v irreg*
  on the right – auf der rechten Seite
  to the right – rechts *adv*

right-handed – rechtshändig *adj*

right now – sofort *adv*

right winger – (sport) Rechtsaußen (-) *nm*

ring – Ring (-e) *nm*

ring – (bell) klingeln *v reg*
  ring the doorbell – klingeln *v reg*

ring binder – Ordner (-) *nm*

ring road – Umgehungsstraße (-n) *nf*

ring up – (phone) anrufen *v irreg sep*

rink – (skating) Eisbahn (-en) *nf*

rip – (clothes) zerreißen *v irreg*

ripe – reif *adj*

rise – (get up) aufstehen* *v irreg sep*

rise – (mountain) sich erheben *v irreg refl*

rise – (sun) aufgehen* *v irreg sep*

risk – Risiko (Risiken) *nnt*

river – Fluss (Flüsse) *nm*

road – Straße (-n) *nf*

country road – Landstraße (-n) *nf*
major road – Bundesstraße (-n) *nf*
road map – Straßenkarte (-n) *nf*
road sign – Straßenschild (-er) *nnt*
road user – (male)
Verkehrsteilnehmer (-) *nm*
road user – (female)
Verkehrsteilnehmerin (-nen) *nf*
roadworks – Baustelle (-n) *nf*
roast – braten *v irreg*
roast – Braten (-) *nm*
roast beef – Rinderbraten (-) *nm*
roast chicken – Brathähnchen (-) *nnt*
roast pork – Schweinebraten (-) *nm*
roast potatoes – Bratkartoffeln *npl*
rock climbing – Bergsteigen *nnt*
rocking chair – Schaukelstuhl
(-stühle) *nm*
rock music – Rockmusik *nf*
rock – schaukeln *v reg*
role – Rolle (-n) *nf*
role play – Rollenspiel (-e) *nnt*
roll – (bread) Brötchen (-) *nnt*, Semmel
(-n) *nf*
roller blades – Inliner *npl*
rollercoaster – Achterbahn (-en) *nf*
roller skate – Rollschuh fahren*
v irreg
roller skates – Rollschuhe *npl*
romantic – romantisch *adj*
roof – Dach (Dächer) *nnt*
room – Zimmer (-) *nnt*
double room – Doppelzimmer (-)
nnt
room with twin beds –
Zweibettzimmer (-) *nnt*
rose – Rose (-n) *nf*
rosé wine – Roséwein (-e) *nm*
Rosh Hashanah – das jüdische
Neujahr *nnt*
rotten – (awful) mies *adj coll*
rotten – (food) faul *adj*
rough book – Schmierheft (-e) *nnt*

rough draft – Entwurf (Entwürfe) *nm*
round – rund *adj*
go round a corner – um die Ecke
gehen* *v irreg*
go round to a friend's house –
einen Freund/eine Freundin
besuchen *v reg* †
round about – um ... herum (+ acc)
prep
roundabout – (fair) Karussell (-s) *nnt*
roundabout – (traffic)
Verkehrskreisel (-) *nm*
round here – hier in der Gegend
route – (bus) Linie (-n) *nf*
routine – Routine (-n) *nf*
row – (argument) Streit *nm*
row – (cinema) Rang (Ränge) *nm*
row – (loud noise) Krach *nm*
row – (argue) sich streiten *v irreg refl*
row – (boat) rudern *v reg*
rowdy – laut *adj*
royal blue – königsblau *adj*
RS – Religion *nf*
rub – reiben *v irreg*
rubber – (eraser) Radiergummi (-s) *nm*
rubber band – Gummiband
(-bänder) *nnt*
rubbish – Müll *nm*, Abfall *nm*
rubbish bin – Abfalleimer (-) *nm*
rucksack – Rucksack (-säcke) *nm*
rude – (impolite) unhöflich *adj*
rude – (very) ungezogen *adj*
rug – Teppich (-e) *nm*
rugby – Rugby *nnt*
ruin – kaputt machen *v reg*
rule – Regel (-n) *nf*
as a rule – in der Regel
ruler – Lineal (-e) *nnt*
run – laufen* *v irreg*
run away – weglaufen* *v irreg sep*
run down – hinunterlaufen* *v irreg sep*

---

adj - adjective   *v reg* - verb regular   *v sep* - verb separable   † - see verb info
prep - preposition   *v irreg* - verb irregular   *v refl* - verb reflexive   * - takes sein

She ran down the street – Sie ist die Straße hinuntergelaufen

run into – (meet) begegnen* (+ dat) *v reg* †

run into – (car) zusammenstoßen* mit (+ dat) *v irreg sep*

run out of – (building) hinauslaufen* aus (+ dat) *v irreg sep*

run out of petrol – eine Benzinpanne haben *v irreg*

We've run out of sugar – Der Zucker ist alle

I have run out of time – Ich habe keine Zeit mehr

run over – (accident) überfahren *v irreg insep*

run up – hinauflaufen* *v irreg sep*

He ran up the stairs – Er ist die Treppe hinaufgelaufen

runner up – (sport) Zweite *nmf* ‡

runway – Startbahn (-en) *nf*

rural – ländlich *adj*

rush – sich beeilen *v reg refl* †

I am in a rush – Ich habe es eilig

rush hour – Hauptverkehrszeit (-en) *nf*

Russia – Russland *nnt*

Russian – russisch *adj*

Russian person – (male) Russe (-n) *nm wk*

Russian person – (female) Russin (-nen) *nf*

S

sack – Sack (Säcke) *nm*

sad – traurig *adj*

saddle – Sattel (Sättel) *nm*

sadly – leider *adv*

sadness – Traurigkeit *nf*

safe – sicher *adj*

safe – Tresor (-e) *nm*

safety – Sicherheit *nf*

safety belt – Sicherheitsgurt (-e) *nm*

Sagittarius – Schütze

said – *see sagen*

sail – Segel (-) *nnt*

sail – segeln *v reg*

sailboard – Surfbrett (-er) *nnt*

sailing dinghy – Segelboot (-e) *nnt*

sailing ship – Segelschiff (-e) *nnt*

sailor – (civilian) Seemann (-männer) *nm*

sailor – (navy) Matrose (-n) *nm wk*

saint – Sankt *adj inv*

saint – Heilige *nmf* ‡

salad – Salat (-e) *nm*

salad – (green) grüner Salat *nm*

salad – (mixed) gemischter Salat *nm*

salad – (potato) Kartoffelsalat *nm*

salad – (tomato) Tomatensalat *nm*

salami – Salami *nf*

salary – Gehalt (Gehälter) *nnt*

sale – Verkauf (Verkäufe) *nm*

for sale – zu verkaufen

on sale – zu verkaufen

sale – Schlussverkauf (-verkäufe) *nm*

in the sales – im Schlussverkauf

sales assistant – (male) Verkäufer (-) *nm*

sales assistant – (female) Verkäuferin (-nen) *nf*

salmon – Lachs (-e) *nm*

salt – Salz *nnt*

salty – salzig *adj*

same – gleich *adj*

at the same time – gleichzeitig *adv*

---

nm - noun masculine	*nf* - noun feminine	*nnt* - noun neuter	*npl* - noun plural
nom - nominative	*acc* - accusative	*gen* - genitive	*dat* - dative

sand – Sand *nm*
sandal – Sandale (-n) *nf*
sand castle – Sandburg (-en) *nf*
sandwich – Butterbrot (-e) *nnt*
 an open sandwich – ein belegtes
 Brot
sanitary towel – Damenbinde (-n) *nf*
Santa Claus – Weihnachtsmann *nm*
sardine – Sardine (-n) *nf*
satellite – Satellit (-en) *nm wk*
satellite dish – Satellitenschüssel (-n)
 nf
satisfactory – befriedigend *adj*
satisfied – zufrieden *adj*
satisfy – befriedigen *v reg* †
Saturday – Samstag (-e) *nm,*
 Sonnabend (-e) *nm*
 on Saturday – am Samstag
 See you on Saturday! –
 Bis Samstag!
sauce – Soße (-n) *nf*
saucepan – Topf (Töpfe) *nm*
saucer – Untertasse (-n) *nf*
sausage – Wurst (Würste) *nf*
 boiled sausage – Bockwurst
 fried sausage – Bratwurst
save – retten *v reg* †
save – (computer) speichern *v reg*
save money – Geld sparen *v reg*
save up for – sparen für (+ acc) *v reg*
savings – Ersparnisse *npl*
saxophone – Saxophon (-e) *nnt*
say – sagen *v reg*
say goodbye – sich verabschieden
 v reg †
scarcely – kaum *adv*
scarf – (long) Schal (-s) *nm*
scarf – (square) Tuch (Tücher) *nnt*
scary – beängstigend *adj*
scene – (crime) Tatort (-e) *nm*
scene – (play) Szene (-n) *nf*
scenery – Landschaft (-en) *nf*

scenic – landschaftlich *adj*
school – Schule (-n) *nf*
 in school – in der Schule
 I walk to school – Ich gehe zu
 Fuß zur Schule
school – (boarding) Internat (-e) *nnt*
school – (comprehensive)
 Gesamtschule (-n) *nf*
 I go to a comprehensive school
 – Ich besuche eine Gesamtschule
school – (grammar) Gymnasium
 (Gymnasien) *nnt*
school – (nursery) Kindergarten
 (-gärten) *nm*
school – (primary) Grundschule (-n) *nf*
school – (private) Privatschule (-n) *nf*
school – (secondary modern)
 Realschule (-n) *nf*
school – (secondary modern)
 Hauptschule (-n) *nf*
school bag – Schultasche (-n) *nf*
school bus – Schulbus (-busse) *nm*
schoolboy – Schüler (-) *nm*
schoolgirl – Schülerin (-nen) *nf*
school holidays – Schulferien *npl*
school report – Zeugnis (-se) *nnt*
school rule – Schulregel (-n) *nf*
school student – (male) Schüler (-) *nm*
school student – (female) Schülerin
 (-nen) *nf*
school trip – Klassenfahrt (-en) *nf*
school uniform – Schuluniform (-en)
 nf
school year – Schuljahr (-e) *nnt*
science – Naturwissenschaft (-en) *nf*
science fiction – Sciencefiction *nf*
science fiction film – Sciencefiction
 Film (-e) *nm*
science fiction story –
 Sciencefiction Roman (-e) *nm*
scientific – wissenschaftlich *adj*
scientist – (male) Wissenschaftler (-)
 nm

---

adj - adjective	*v reg* - verb regular	*v sep* - verb separable	† - see verb info
prep - preposition	*v irreg* - verb irregular	*v refl* - verb reflexive	* - takes sein

scientist – (female) Wissenschaftlerin (-nen) *nf*

scissors – (pair of) Schere (-n) *nf*

scold – ausschimpfen *v reg sep*

scooter – Roller (-) *nm*

score a goal – ein Tor schießen *v irreg*

score a point – einen Punkt gewinnen *v irreg*

Scorpio – (horoscope) Skorpion

Scotland – Schottland *nnt*

Scotsman – Schotte (-n) *nm wk*

Scotswoman – Schottin (-nen) *nf*

Scottish – schottisch *adj*

scout – Pfadfinder (-) *nm*

scream – schreien *v irreg*

screen – (cinema) Leinwand (-wände) *nf*

screen – (TV) Bildschirm (-e) *nm*

screwdriver – Schraubenzieher (-) *nm*

scrum – Gedränge *nnt*

scuba diving – Tiefseetauchen *nnt*

sea – Meer (-e) *nnt,* See (-n) *nf*
 at the seaside – an der Küste
 by the sea – an der Küste

seafood – Meeresfrüchte *npl*

seagull – Möwe (-n) *nf*

seasick – seekrank *adj*

search – durchsuchen *v reg insep*

seaside resort – Badeort (-e) *nm*

season – (of year) Jahreszeit (-en) *nf*

season – (football, etc) Saison (-s) *nf*
 out of season – außerhalb der Saison

season ticket – Dauerkarte (-n) *nf*

seat – (train) Platz (Plätze) *nm*

seat belt – Sicherheitsgurt (-e) *nm*

second – zweite *adj*

second – (time) Sekunde (-n) *nf*

secondary school – *see school*

second class – (ticket) zweiter Klasse

second-hand – aus zweiter Hand, gebraucht

secret – geheim *adj*

secret – Geheimnis (-se) *nnt*

secretary – (male) Sekretär (-e) *nm*

secretary – (female) Sekretärin (-nen) *nf*

security – Sicherheit *nf*

see – sehen *v irreg*
 see again – wiedersehen *v irreg sep*
 see over – bitte wenden (b.w.)
 See you later! – Bis später!
 See you on Saturday! – Bis Samstag!
 See you soon! – Bis bald!
 See you this evening! – Bis heute Abend!
 See you tomorrow! – Bis morgen!

seem – scheinen *v irreg*

seize – ergreifen *v irreg*

seldom – selten *adv*

select – wählen *v reg*

selection – Auswahl *nf*

self-confident – selbstbewusst *adj*

self-employed – selbstständig *adj*

selfish – egoistisch *adj*

self-service – SB (Selbstbedienung) *nf*

self-service restaurant – Selbstbedienungsrestaurant (-s) *nnt*

sell – verkaufen *v reg* †

sellotape® – Tesafilm® *nm*

semi-colon (;) – Semikolon (-s) *nnt*

semi-detached house – Doppelhaus (-häuser) *nnt*

semi-final – Halbfinale (-n) *nnt*

send – schicken *v reg*
 send for the doctor – den Arzt kommen lassen *v irreg*

senior citizen – (male) Rentner (-) *nm*

senior citizen – (female) Rentnerin (-nen) *nf*

sensational – sensationell *adj*

sensible – (practical) praktisch *adj*

sensible – (wise) vernünftig *adj*

---

sensitive – sensibel *adj*

sentence – Satz (Sätze) *nm*

a separable verb – ein trennbares Verb *nnt*

separate – sich trennen *v reg*

separated – getrennt *adj*

separately – getrennt *adv*
   Do you want to pay separately? – Geht das getrennt oder zusammen?

separation – Trennung (-en) *nf*

September – September *nm*
   in September – im September

serial – Serie (-n) *nf*

serious – ernst *adj*
   it's not serious – es ist nichts Ernstes

serve – bedienen *v reg* †

serve oneself – sich bedienen *v reg refl* †

service – (maintenance) Dienst (-e) *nm*
   in the services – (army) beim Militär

service – (restaurant) Bedienung *nf*
   service (not) included – Bedienung (nicht) inklusive

service – (tennis) Aufschlag (-schläge) *nm*

service area – Raststätte (-n) *nf*

serviette – Serviette (-n) *nf*

session – (film) Vorführung (-en) *nf*

set – (put) setzen *v reg*

set – (school) Leistungsgruppe (-n) *nf*

set off – losfahren* *v irreg sep*

set out – sich auf den Weg machen *v reg refl*

set price menu – Menü (-s) *nnt*

set the alarm clock – den Wecker stellen *v reg*

set the table – den Tisch decken *v reg*

settee – Sofa (-s) *nnt*

settle – (bill) zahlen *v reg*

settle down – sich einleben *v reg refl sep*

seven – sieben *adj*

seventeen – siebzehn *adj*

seventh – siebte *adj*

seventy – siebzig *adj*

seventy-one – einundsiebzig *adj*

several – mehrere *adj*

severe – (injury) schwer *adj*

sew – nähen *v reg*

sewing – Nähen *nnt*

sewing machine – Nähmaschine (-n) *nf*

sexist – sexistisch *adj*

shade – Schatten (-) *nm*
   in the shade – im Schatten

shake – (tremble) zittern *v reg*

shake hands with s.o. – jdm die Hand geben *v irreg*

Shall we go? – Gehen wir?

shame – schade
   What a shame! – Wie schade! *excl*

shameful – beschämend *adj*

shampoo – Shampoo (-s) *nm*

shampoo one's hair – sich die Haare waschen *v irreg dat refl*

shape – Form (-en) *nf*

share – teilen *v reg*

sharp – scharf *adj*

shave – sich rasieren *v reg refl* †

she – sie *pron nom*

shed – Gartenhäuschen (-) *nnt*

sheep – Schaf (-e) *nnt*

sheet – (bed) Laken (-) *nnt*

sheet of paper – Blatt Papier *nnt*

shelf – Regal (-e) *nnt*

shellfish – Meeresfrüchte *npl*

shelter – Schutz *nm*

sheltered from – geschützt von (+ dat) *adj*

sherry – Sherry (-s) *nm*

shine – scheinen *v irreg*

shiny – glänzend *adj*

ship – Schiff (-e) *nnt*
shirt – Hemd (-en) *nnt*
shiver – zittern *v reg*
shoe – Schuh (-e) *nm*
  a pair of shoes – ein Paar Schuhe *nnt*
shoe shop – Schuhgeschäft (-e) *nnt*
shoe size – Schuhgröße (-n) *nf*
shoot – schießen *v irreg*
shoot dead – erschießen *v irreg*
shooting – Schießen *nnt*
shop – Geschäft (-e) *nnt*, Laden (Läden) *nm*, Handlung (-en) *nf*
  go round the shops – einen Einkaufsbummel machen *v reg*
shop assistant – (male) Verkäufer (-) *nm*
shop assistant – (female) Verkäuferin (-nen) *nf*
shopkeeper – Händler (-) *nm*
shoplifter – Ladendieb (-e) *nm*
shopping – Einkaufen *nnt*
  do the shopping – einkaufen gehen* *v irreg*
  go window shopping – einen Schaufensterbummel machen *v reg*
shopping bag – Einkaufstasche (-n) *nf*
shopping centre – Einkaufszentrum (-zentren) *nnt*
shopping list – Einkaufsliste (-n) *nf*
shop window – Schaufenster (-) *nnt*
short – (not long) kurz *adj*
short – (not tall) klein *adj*
shortly – bald *adv*
short-sighted – kurzsichtig *adj*
shorts – Shorts *npl*
  a pair of shorts – eine kurze Hose
should – sollte *see sollen*
shoulder – Schulter (-n) *nf*
shout – Schrei (-e) *nm*
shout – (scream) schreien *v irreg*
shout – (call) rufen *v irreg*

show – Aufführung (-en) *nf*
show – (variety/TV) Show (-s) *nf*
show – zeigen *v reg*
shower – Dusche (-n) *nf*
  have a shower – sich duschen *v reg refl*
shower – (rain) Regenschauer (-) *nm*
  There will be showers – Es wird Schauer geben
showing – (film) Vorführung (-en) *nf*
show-off – (male) Angeber (-) *nm*
show-off – (female) Angeberin (-nen) *nf*
show off – angeben *v irreg sep*
shrewd – schlau *adj*
shrimp – Krabbe (-n) *nf*
Shrove Tuesday – Faschingsdienstag *nm*
shut – schließen *v irreg*
shut in – einschließen *v irreg sep*
shutter – Rollladen (Rollläden) *nm*
shy – schüchtern *adj*
sick bay – (school) Lazarett (-e) *nnt*
sick person – Kranke *nmf* ‡
  feel sick – sich übel fühlen *v reg refl*
  I feel sick – Mir ist übel
side – Seite (-n) *nf*
  on the other side – auf der anderen Seite
side – (team) Mannschaft (-en) *nf*
sideboard – Anrichte (-n) *nf*
side by side – nebeneinander *adv*
sight – (view) Blick (-e) *nm*
sight – (tourist) Sehenswürdigkeit (-en) *nf*
sight – (visibility) Sicht *nf*
  in sight – in Sicht
  out of sight – außer Sicht
sightseeing – Tourismus *nm*
sign – Schild (-er) *nnt*
sign – (post) Wegweiser (-) *nm*
sign – unterschreiben *v irreg insep*
signal – Signal (-e) *nnt*

---

nm - noun masculine	*nf* - noun feminine	*nnt* - noun neuter	*npl* - noun plural
nom- nominative	*acc* - accusative	*gen* - genitive	*dat* - dative

signature – Unterschrift (-en) *nf*
signpost – Wegweiser (-) *nm*
silence – Stille (-n) *nf*
silent – still *adj*
  be silent – schweigen *v irreg*
silently – leise *adv*
silk – Seide (-n) *nf*
  made of silk – aus Seide
silly – dumm *adj*
  silly mistake – Dummheit (-en) *nf*
silver – silbern *adj*
silver – Silber *nnt*
similar – ähnlich *adj*
simple – einfach *adj*
since – seit (+ dat) *prep*
since – seitdem, da *sub conj*
sincere – herzlich *adj*
  Yours sincerely – mit
  freundlichen Grüßen
since then – seither *adv*
sing – singen *v irreg*
singer – (male) Sänger (-) *nm*
singer – (female) Sängerin (-nen) *nf*
single – (one/only) einzig *adj*
single – (unmarried) unverheiratet *adj*
single – Einzel‑ *pref*
single parent – Alleinerziehende *nmf* ‡
single person – (male) Junggeselle
  (-n) *nm wk*
single person – (female) Ledige *nf* ‡
single room – Einzelzimmer (-) *nnt*
single ticket – einfache Fahrkarte *nf*
A single to Hamburg – Einmal
  einfach nach Hamburg
singular – (grammar) Singular *nm*
  in the singular – im Singular
sink – Spülbecken (-) *nnt*
Sir – mein Herr
sister – Schwester (-n) *nf*
sister-in-law – Schwägerin (-nen) *nf*
sit – sitzen *v irreg*
sit down – sich hinsetzen *v reg refl sep*

Sit down! – (informal) Setz dich!
Sit down! – (formal) Setzen Sie sich!
sit down at table – zu Tisch
  kommen* *v irreg*
site – (camp) Platz (Plätze) *nm*
site – (building) Baustelle (-n) *nf*
sitting room – Wohnzimmer (-) *nnt*
situated – gelegen *adj*
  Malvern is situated in the
  Midlands – Malvern liegt in
  Mittelengland
situation – Situation (-en) *nf*
situation – (case) Fall (Fälle) *nm*
six – sechs *adj*
sixteen – sechzehn *adj*
sixteenth – sechzehnte *adj*
sixth – sechste *adj*
sixth form college –
  Oberstufenkolleg (-kollegien) *nnt*
sixth form student – (male)
  Abiturient (-en) *nm wk*
sixth form student – (female)
  Abiturientin (-nen) *nf*
sixty – sechzig *adj*
sixty-one – einundsechzig *adj*
size – Größe (-n) *nf*
size – (shoes) Schuhgröße (-n) *nf*
skate – Schlittschuh (-e) *nm*
skate – Schlittschuh laufen* *v irreg*
skateboard – Rollbrett (-er) *nnt*
skateboard – Rollbrett fahren*
  v irreg
skating rink – Eisbahn (-en) *nf*
ski – Ski fahren* *v irreg*
ski – Ski (-er) *nm*
ski boot – Skistiefel (-) *nm*
skid – ins Schleudern geraten* *v irreg*
ski lift – Skilift (-s) *nm*
ski-run – Piste (-n) *nf*
skiing – Skilaufen *nnt*
skilfully – geschickt *adv*
skilled – geschickt *adj*
skin – Haut *nf*

---

adj - adjective   *v reg* - verb regular   *v sep* - verb separable   † - see verb info
prep - preposition   *v irreg* - verb irregular   *v refl* - verb reflexive   * - takes sein

skinny – dünn *adj*
skirt – Rock (Röcke) *nm*
skive – schwänzen *v reg*
sky – Himmel (-) *nm*
sky blue – himmelblau *adj*
skyscraper – Wolkenkratzer (-) *nm*
sledge – Schlitten (-) *nm*
sleep – schlafen *v irreg*
  fall asleep – einschlafen* *v irreg sep*
sleep – Schlaf *nm*
sleeper car – Schlafwagen (-) *nm*
sleep in – ausschlafen *v irreg sep*
sleeping bag – Schlafsack (-säcke) *nm*
sleepy – schläfrig *adj*
sleeve – Ärmel (-) *nm*
slice – Scheibe (-n) *nf*
slice – schneiden *v irreg*
slicing sausage – Wurst (Würste) *nf*
slide – ausrutschen* *v reg sep*
slide – (playground) Rutschbahn (-en) *nf*
slide – (transparency) Dia (-s) *nnt*
slightly – ein bisschen
slim – schlank *adj*
slim – abnehmen *v irreg sep*
slip – ausrutschen* *v reg sep*
- **slip of paper** – Zettel (-) *nm*
slipper – Hausschuh (-e) *nm*,
  Pantoffel (-n) *nm*
slippery – glitschig *adj*
slope – Hang (Hänge) *nm*
sloping – schräg *adj*
slot machine – Automat (-en) *nm wk*
slot machine – Münzautomat (-en)
  nm wk
slow – langsam *adj*
slow down – langsamer werden*
  v irreg
slow train – Personenzug (-züge) *nm*,
  Bummelzug (-züge) *nm coll*
small – klein *adj*
small ad – Kleinanzeige (-n) *nf*
small change – Kleingeld *nnt*

small shop – Tante-Emma-Laden
  (-Läden) *nm*
smart – (clever) intelligent *adj*
smart – (fashionable) modisch *adj*
smart card – Chipkarte (-n) *nf*
smell – Geruch (Gerüche) *nm*
smell – (stink) stinken *v irreg*
smell (of) – riechen (nach + dat) *v irreg*
smelly – stinkig *adj*
smile – Lächeln (-) *nnt*
smile – lächeln *v reg*
smiling – lächelnd *adj*
smoke – Rauch *nm*
smoke – rauchen *v reg*
smoker – (male) Raucher (-) *nm*
smoker – (female) Raucherin (-nen) *nf*
smoking – (area) Raucher~ *pref*
  non smoking – (area)
  Nichtraucher~ *pref*
smooth – glatt *adj*
snack – Imbiss (-e) *nm*
snack bar – Imbissstube (-n) *nf*,
  Schnellimbiss *nm*
snail – Schnecke (-n) *nf*
sneeze – niesen *v reg*
snobbish – eingebildet *adj*
snooker – Snooker *nnt*
snore – schnarchen *v reg*
snow – schneien *v reg*
snow – Schnee *nm*
snowball – Schneeball (-bälle) *nm*
snowfall – Schneefall (-fälle) *nm*
snowman – Schneemann (-männer) *nm*
snowstorm – Schneesturm (-stürme) *nm*
snuggle – schnuggeln *v reg*
so – (therefore) also *adv*
so many – so viele
so much – so viel
So what? – Na und?
soaked – durchnässt *adj*
  soaked to the skin – völlig
  durchnässt *adj*

| *nm* - noun masculine | *nf* - noun feminine | *nnt* - noun neuter | *npl* - noun plural |
| *nom* - nominative | *acc* - accusative | *gen* - genitive | *dat* - dative |

soap – Seife (-n) *nf*
soap opera – Seifenoper (-n) *nf*
social studies – Sozialkunde *nf*
soccer – Fußball *nm*
society – Gesellschaft (-en) *nf*
sock – Socke (-n) *nf*
socket – Steckdose (-n) *nf*
sofa – Sofa (-s) *nnt*
soft – weich *adj*
  a soft drink – ein alkoholfreies
  Getränk *nnt*
software – Software *nf*
sold – verkauft *adj*
  sold out – ausverkauft *adj*
soldier – Soldat (-en) *nm wk*
solemn – feierlich *adj*
solicitor – (male) Rechtsanwalt
  (-anwälte) *nm*
solicitor – (female) Rechtsanwältin
  (-nen) *nf*
solid – solide *adj*
solution – Lösung (-en) *nf*
solve – lösen *v reg*
some – (countable) einige *adj*
some – (uncountable) etwas *adj inv*
some – (unspecified) irgend~ *pref*
somebody – jemand *pron nom, acc*
somebody – jemandem *pron dat*
some day – eines Tages
somehow – irgendwie
some ideas – ein paar Ideen
someone else – jemand anders *pron*
something – etwas
something bad – etwas Schlechtes
something else – etwas anderes
something good – etwas Gutes
sometime – irgendwann *adv*
sometimes – manchmal *adv*
somewhere – irgendwo *adv*
somewhere else – irgendwo anders
son – Sohn (Söhne) *nm*

son-in-law – Schwiegersohn (-söhne)
  nm
song – Lied (-er) *nnt*
soon – bald *adv*
  as soon as possible – so bald wie
  möglich
sore throat – Halsschmerzen *npl*
Sorry! – Entschuldigung!
  I'm sorry! – Es tut mir Leid!
sort – Sorte (-n) *nf*
sort of – Art (-en) *nf*
  What sort? – Welche Sorten?
  What sort of...? – Was für (+ acc)
sound – (excellent) prima *adj*
sound – (loud) Lärm *nm*
sound – (quiet) Geräusch (-e) *nnt*
soup – Suppe (-n) *nf*
sour – sauer *adj*
source – Quelle (-n) *nf*
south – Süden *nm*
  in South Germany – in
  Süddeutschland
  in the south – im Süden
South Africa – Südafrika *nnt*
South America – Südamerika *nnt*
southern – südlich *adj*
south of – südlich von (+ dat)
souvenir – Andenken (-) *nnt,*
  Souvenir (-s) *nnt*
soya – Soja~ *pref*
space – (universe) All *nnt*
space – (room) Platz (Plätze) *nm*
spade – Spaten (-) *nm*
spaghetti – Spaghetti *nf*
Spain – Spanien *nnt*
Spaniard – (male) Spanier (-) *nm*
Spaniard – (female) Spanierin (-nen) *nf*
Spanish – spanisch *adj*
Spanish – (language) Spanisch *nnt*
spare part – Ersatzteil (-e) *nnt*
spare time – Freizeit *nf*
spare wheel – Ersatzrad (-räder) *nnt*

---

adj - adjective	*v reg* - verb regular	*v sep* - verb separable	† - see verb info
prep - preposition	*v irreg* - verb irregular	*v refl* - verb reflexive	* - takes sein

sparkling wine – Schaumwein (-e) *nm*	**spend one's holiday** – die Ferien verbringen *v irreg*
sparkling water – Sprudel (-) *nm*	**spider** – Spinne (-n) *nf*
speak – sprechen *v irreg*	**spinach** – Spinat *nm*
speak German – Deutsch sprechen *v irreg*	**spirits** – (alcohol) Spirituosen *npl*

sparkling wine – Schaumwein (-e) *nm*
sparkling water – Sprudel (-) *nm*
speak – sprechen *v irreg*
speak German – Deutsch sprechen *v irreg*
speak German fluently – fließend deutsch sprechen *v irreg*
speaking test – mündliche Prüfung (-en) *nf*
speak loudly – laut sprechen *v irreg*
speak to s.o. – jdm sprechen *v irreg*
special – besondere *adj*
specialist – (doctor, male) Facharzt (-ärzte) *nm*
specialist – (doctor, female) Fachärztin (-nen) *nf*
speciality – Spezialität (-en) *nf*
specially – besonders *adv*
special offer – Sonderangebot (-e) *nnt*
special price – Sonderpreis (-e) *nm*
spectacle – (show) Aufführung (-en) *nf*
spectacles – (pair of glasses) Brille (-n) *nf*
spectacular – einmalig *adj*
spectator – (male) Zuschauer (-) *nm*
spectator – (female) Zuschauerin (-nen) *nf*
speech – (in public) Rede (-n) *nf*
speechless – sprachlos *adj*
speech marks („ ... ") – Anführungszeichen *npl*
speed – Geschwindigkeit (-en) *nf*
at high speed – mit hoher Geschwindigkeit
speed limit – Geschwindigkeitsbegrenzung (-en) *nf*
speedboat – Rennboot (-e) *nnt*
spell – buchstabieren *v reg* †
How do you spell that? – Wie schreibt man das?
spelling – Rechtschreibung *nf*
spend – (money) ausgeben *v irreg sep*
spend – (time) verbringen *v irreg*

spend one's holiday – die Ferien verbringen *v irreg*
spider – Spinne (-n) *nf*
spinach – Spinat *nm*
spirits – (alcohol) Spirituosen *npl*
spiteful – gehässig *adj*
splendid – großartig *adj*
spoil – kaputt machen *v reg*
spoil – (child) verwöhnen *v reg* †
spoilt – (child) verwöhnt *adj*
sponge – Schwamm (Schwämme) *nm*
spoon – Löffel (-) *nm*
spoonful – Löffel (-) *nm*
sport – Sport (Sportarten) *nm*
do sport – Sport treiben *v irreg*
sports car – Sportwagen (-) *nm*
sports centre – Sportzentrum (-zentren) *nnt*
sports club – Sportverein (-e) *nm*
sports facilities – Sportmöglichkeiten *npl*
sports ground – Sportplatz (-plätze) *nm*
sporty – sportlich *adj*
spot – (place) Stelle (-n) *nf*
spot – (zit) Pickel (-) *nm*
spotless – blitzsauber *adj*
spotty – (zits) pickelig *adj*
spotty – (fabric) gepunktet *adj*
sprain one's ankle – sich das Fußgelenk verstauchen *v reg dat refl* †
spray – (can) Sprühdose (-n) *nf*
spray – spritzen *v reg*
spread – (with butter, etc) schmieren *v reg*, buttern *v reg*
spring – Frühling *nm*
in spring – im Frühling
springboard – Sprungbrett (-er) *nnt*
sprout – Rosenkohl *nm, no pl*
spy – (male) Spion (-e) *nm*
spy – (female) Spionin (-nen) *nf*
spy film – Spionagefilm (-e) *nm*

spying – Spionage *nf*
spy story – Spionagegeschichte (-n) *nf*
square – (in town) Platz (Plätze) *nm*
square – (on paper) Feld (-er) *nnt*
square – (shape) viereckig *adj*
squash – (drink) Saft (Säfte) *nm*
squash – (sport) Squash *nnt*
squash – zerquetschen *v reg* †
squeeze – quetschen *v reg*
stable – Pferdestall (-ställe) *nm*
stadium – Stadion (Stadien) *nnt*
staff room – Lehrerzimmer (-) *nnt*
stage – Bühne (-n) *nf*
  be on the stage – auf der Bühne
  sein* *v irreg*
stain – Fleck (-en) *nm*
stain – beflecken *v reg* †
stairs – (staircase) Treppe (-n) *nf*
stall – Stand (Stände) *nm*
stalls – (theatre) Parkett *nnt*
stamp – Briefmarke (-n) *nf*
  collect stamps – Briefmarken
  sammeln *v reg*
stand – (on feet) stehen (*) *v irreg*
stand – (put up with) ertragen *v irreg*
  I can't stand her – Ich kann sie
  nicht ausstehen
stand up – aufstehen* *v irreg sep*
standard – (school achievement)
  Niveau *nnt*
standard lamp – Stehlampe (-n) *nf*
standard of living – Lebensstandard
  nm
staple – Heftklammer (-n) *nf*
stapler – Heftmaschine (-n) *nf*
star – (show business) Star (-s) *nm*
star – (sky) Stern (-e) *nm*
start – (beginning) Beginn *nm*
  at the start – am Anfang
start – beginnen *v irreg*, anfangen
  v irreg sep
start – (vehicle) anspringen* *v irreg sep*

start of school year –
  Schuljahresanfang (-anfänge) *nm*
start up – (turn key) anlassen *v irreg*
  sep
starter – (food) Vorspeise (-n) *nf*
startled – erschrocken *adj*
startling – erschreckend *adj*
state – (nation) Staat (-en) *nm*
stately home – Schloss (Schlösser) *nnt*
statement – Aussage (-n) *nf*
station – Bahnhof (-höfe) *nm*
  bus station – Busbahnhof (-höfe) *nm*
stationer's shop –
  Schreibwarenhandlung (-en) *nf*
stay – bleiben* *v irreg*
stay – Aufenthalt (-e) *nm*
stay – (hotel) Übernachtung (-en) *nf*
stay at a hotel – in einem Hotel
  übernachten *v reg insep* †
stay at home – zu Hause bleiben*
  v irreg
steady – (job) fest *adj*
  I have a steady
  boyfriend/girlfriend – Ich habe
  einen festen Freund/eine feste
  Freundin
steak – Steak (-s) *nnt*
steal – stehlen *v irreg,* klauen *v reg*
  coll
steam – Dampf *nm*
steamer – Dampfer (-) *nm*
steep – (hill) steil *adj*
steering wheel – Lenkrad (-räder) *nnt*
step – Schritt (-e) *nm*
step – (on stairs) Stufe (-n) *nf*
stepbrother – Stiefbruder (-brüder) *nm*
stepdaughter – Stieftochter (-töchter)
  nf
stepfather – Stiefvater (-väter) *nm*
stepmother – Stiefmutter (-mütter) *nf*
stepsister – Stiefschwester (-n) *nf*
stepson – Stiefsohn (-söhne) *nm*
stereo – Stereoanlage (-n) *nf*

---

personal stereo – Walkman®
(Walkmen) *nm*
stew – Eintopf *nm*
stewardess – Stewardess (-en) *nf*
stick – Stock (Stöcke) *nm*
stick – (glue) kleben *v reg*
sticker – Aufkleber (-) *nm*
sticky tape – Tesafilm® *nm*
stiff – steif *adj*
still – (not moving) still *adj*
 stand still – stillstehen *v irreg sep*
still – (yet) noch *adv*
sting – Stich (-e) *nm*
sting – stechen *v irreg*
stocking – Strumpf (Strümpfe) *nm*
stocky – untersetzt *adj*
stomach – Bauch (Bäuche) *nm*,
 Magen (-) *nm*
stomach ache – Magenschmerzen
 npl, Bauchschmerzen *npl*
stone – Stein (-e) *nm*
 built of stone – aus Stein
stool – Hocker (-) *nm*
stop – Haltestelle (-n) *nf*
 bus stop – Bushaltestelle (-n) *nf*
stop – (doing sthg) aufhören *v reg sep*
stop – (halt) anhalten* *v irreg sep*
stop – (prevent) verhüten *v reg* †
stop smoking –zu rauchen aufhören
 v reg sep
storey – Stockwerk (-e) *nnt*
 on the fifth storey – im fünften
 Stock
storm – Sturm (Stürme) *nm*
stormy – stürmisch *adj*
story – Geschichte (-n) *nf*
 horror story – Horrorgeschichte
 (-n) *nf*
 science fiction story –
 Sciencefiction Roman (-e) *nm*
storyteller – (male) Erzähler (-) *nm*
storyteller – (female) Erzählerin
 (-nen) *nf*

stove – (hob) Herd (-e) *nm*
stove – (oven) Ofen (Öfen) *nm*
straight – gerade, direkt *adj*
straight – (hair) glatt *adj*
straightaway – sofort *adv*
straight on – geradeaus *adv*
strange – seltsam *adj*
stranger – Fremde *nmf* ‡
strangle – erdrosseln *v reg* †
strawberry – Erdbeere (-n) *nf*
stream – Bach (Bäche) *nm*
street – Straße (-n) *nf*
 along the street – die Straße entlang
 at the corner of street – an der
 Straßenecke
 in the street – auf der Straße
stressed out – gestresst *adj*
stressful – stressig *adj coll*
strict – streng *adj*
strike – (hit) schlagen *v irreg*
strike – (walk-out) Streik (-s) *nm*
strike – streiken *v reg*
striker – (on strike) Streikende *nmf* ‡
striker – (football) Stürmer (-) *nm*
string – (piece of) Schnur (Schnüre) *nf*
string – (violin, racket) Saite (-n) *nf*
stringed instrument – (with bow)
 Streichinstrument (-e) *nnt*
string orchestra – Streichorchester (-)
 nnt
striped – gestreift *adj*
stroll – schlendern* *v reg*
strong – stark *adj*
stubborn – stur *adj*
student – (male) Student (-en) *nm wk*
student – (female) Studentin (-nen) *nf*
 sixth form student – (male)
 Abiturient (-en) *nm wk*
 sixth form student – (female)
 Abiturientin (-nen) *nf*

---

studies – Studium (Studien) *nnt*
studio – (workshop) Atelier (-s) *nnt*
studio – (TV) Studio (-s) *nnt*
studious – fleißig *adj*
study – (room) Arbeitszimmer (-) *nnt*
study – (at school) lernen *v reg*
study – (at university) studieren *v reg* †
stupid – dumm, blöd *adj*
   do something stupid – eine
   Dummheit begehen *v irreg*
sturdy – stark *adj*
style – Stil (-e) *nm*
sub~ – unter~ *pref*
subject – (school) Fach (Fächer) *nnt*
   A Level subject – Leistungsfach
   (-fächer) *nnt*
   compulsory subject – Pflichtfach
   (-fächer) *nnt*
   optional subject – Wahlfach
   (-fächer) *nnt*
subscription – Abonnement (-s) *nnt*
substitute – Ersatz *nm*
subtitled – mit Untertiteln
suburb – Vorort (-e) *nm*
   in a suburb – in einem Vorort
subway – (under road) Unterführung
   (-en) *nf*
succeed – gelingen* *v irreg*
   I've succeeded – Es ist mir
   gelungen
success – Erfolg (-e) *nm*
successful – erfolgreich *adj*
such – solche
   such a – ein solcher
sudden – plötzlich *adj*
suddenly – plötzlich *adv*
suede – Wildleder *nnt*
suffer – leiden *v irreg*
sugar – Zucker *nm*
suggest – vorschlagen *v irreg sep*
suit – (man's) Anzug (-züge) *nm*
suit – (woman's) Kostüm (-e) *nnt*

suit – stehen *v irreg*
   It suits me – Es steht mir
suitable – passend *adj*
suitcase – Koffer (-) *nm*
sulk – schmollen *v reg*
sum – (arithmetic) Rechnung (-en) *nf*
summer – Sommer *nm*
   in summer – im Sommer
summer holidays – Sommerferien
   npl
summery – sommerlich *adj*
summit – Gipfel (-) *nm*
sun – Sonne (-n) *nf*
sunbathe – sich sonnen *v reg refl*
sunburn – Sonnenbrand *nm*
sun cream – Sonnencreme (-n) *nf*
sun-glasses – (pair) Sonnenbrille (-n)
   nf
sunshine – Sonnenschein *nm*
sun-stroke – Sonnenstich *nm*
sun-tanned – gebräunt *adj*
sun-tan oil – Sonnenöl *nnt*
Sunday – Sonntag *nm*
   on Sunday – am Sonntag
sunny – sonnig *adj*
sunrise – Sonnenaufgang (-gänge) *nm*
sunset – Sonnenuntergang (-gänge) *nm*
sunshade – Sonnenschirm (-e) *nm*
super – super *adj inv*
superior – überlegen *adj*
supermarket – Supermarkt (-märkte)
   nm
super unleaded petrol – Super
   bleifrei *nm*
supervise – überwachen *v reg insep*
supper – (cold) Abendbrot (-e) *nnt*
supper – (hot) Abendessen (-) *nnt*
   eat supper – zu Abend essen *v irreg*
support – unterstützen *v reg insep*
sure – sicher *adj*
surely – sicherlich *adv*
surfboard – Surfbrett (-er) *nnt*

---

surfing – Surfen (-) *nnt*
surf – Brandung *nf*
surf the net – das Internet benutzen *v reg* †
surgery – (time) Sprechstunde (-n) *nf*
surgery – (doctor's) Praxis (Praxen) *nf*
surname – Familienname (-n) *nm wk*
surprise – Überraschung (-en) *nf*
surprise – überraschen *v reg insep*
surprised – überrascht *adj*
surprising – überraschend *adj*
surrounded by – umgeben von (+ dat) *adj*
surroundings – Umgebung *nf*
survey – Meinungsumfrage (-n) *nf*
suspect – verdächtigen *v reg* †
suspicion – Verdacht *nm*
swallow – (bird) Schwalbe (-n) *nf*
swallow – verschlucken *v reg* †
swap – tauschen *v reg*
sweater – Pullover (-) *nm*
sweatshirt – Sweatshirt (-s) *nnt*
Sweden – Schweden *nnt*
Swedish – schwedisch *adj*
Swedish person – (male) Schwede (-n) *nm wk*
Swedish person – (female) Schwedin (-nen) *nf*
sweep – kehren *v reg*
sweet – Bonbon (-s) *nnt*
sweet – (cute) niedlich *adj*
sweet – (nice) nett *adj*

sweet – (tasting) süß *adj*
sweet shop – Konditorei (-en) *nf*
sweet-smelling – wohlriechend *adj*
swiftness – Geschwindigkeit (-en) *nf*
swim – schwimmen (*) *v irreg*
swimming – Schwimmen *nnt*
swimming pool – Schwimmbad (-bäder) *nnt*
   indoor pool – Hallenbad (-bäder) *nnt*
   outdoor pool – Freibad (-bäder) *nnt*
swimsuit – Badeanzug (-züge) *nm*
swing – schaukeln *v reg*
swing – (child's) Schaukel (-n) *nf*
Swiss – schweizerisch *adj*
Swiss person – (male) Schweizer (-) *nm*
Swiss person – (female) Schweizerin (-nen) *nf*
switch off – ausschalten *v reg sep* †
switch on – (light, radio) einschalten *v reg sep* †
switch on – (gas) anzünden *v reg sep* †
Switzerland – Schweiz *nf*
   in Switzerland – in der Schweiz
swollen – geschwollen *adj*
swot – (male) Streber (-) *nm coll*
swot – (female) Streberin (-nen) *nf coll*
swot – pauken *v reg*, büffeln *v reg coll*
synagogue – Synagoge (-n) *nf*
syrup – (medicine) Saft (Säfte) *nm*
system – System (-e) *nnt*

---

table 193 **technical**

T

table – Tisch (-e) *nm*
  to lay the table – den Tisch
  decken *v reg*
tablecloth – Tischdecke (-n) *nf*
tablet – Tablette (-n) *nf*
table tennis – Tischtennis *nnt*
table wine – Tafelwein (-e) *nm*
tactful – taktvoll *adj*
tactless – taktlos *adj*
tail – Schwanz (Schwänze) *nm*
tailor – (male) Schneider (-) *nm*
tailor – (female) Schneiderin (-nen) *nf*
take – nehmen *v irreg*
take – (person) bringen *v irreg*
take an exam – eine Prüfung machen
  v reg
take away – mitnehmen *v irreg sep*
take away – (food) zum Mitnehmen
take back – zurücknehmen *v irreg sep*
take drugs – Drogen nehmen *v irreg*
take hold of – greifen *v irreg*
take notes – Notizen machen *v reg*
take off – (aircraft) starten* *v reg* †
take off – (coat, etc) ausziehen *v irreg*
  sep
take one's driving test – den
  Führerschein machen *v reg*
take one's place – Platz nehmen
  v irreg
take part in – teilnehmen an (+ dat)
  v irreg sep
take photos – Fotos machen *v reg*
take place – stattfinden *v irreg sep*
take the dog for a walk – mit dem
  Hund spazieren gehen* *v irreg*
Take the first on the left! –
  Nehmen Sie die erste Straße links!
talk – sprechen *v irreg*
talk to – sich unterhalten mit (+ dat)
  v irreg refl insep

talkative – gesprächig *adj*
tall – groß *adj*
tame – zahm *adj*
tampon – Tampon (-s) *nm*
tanned – gebräunt *adj*
tap – Wasserhahn (-hähne) *nm*
tape – Kassette (-n) *nf*
tape – (record) aufnehmen *v irreg sep*
tape recorder – Kassettenrekorder
  (-) *nm*
tart – (cake) Kuchen (-) *nm*
tartan – Schottenmuster *nnt*
task – Aufgabe (-) *nf*
taste – Geschmack (Geschmäcke) *nm*
taste – probieren *v reg* †
  It tastes good – Es schmeckt
Taurus – (horoscope) Stier
tax – Steuer (-n) *nf*
taxi – Taxi (-s) *nnt*
taxi driver – (male) Taxifahrer (-)*nm*
taxi driver – (female) Taxifahrerin
  (-nen) *nm*
taxi rank – Taxistand (-stände) *nm*
tea – Tee *nm*
  lemon tea – Zitronentee *nm*
tea – (meal, cold) Abendbrot(-e) *nnt*
tea – (meal, hot) Abendessen (-) *nnt*
teabag – Teebeutel (-) *nm*
teach – unterrichten *v reg insep* †
teacher – (male) Lehrer (-) *nm*
teacher – (female) Lehrerin (-nen) *nf*
teaching – (lesson) Unterricht *nm*
tea cup – Teetasse (-n) *nf*
team – Mannschaft (-en) *nf*
teapot – Teekanne (-n) *nf*
tease – necken *v reg*
teaspoon – Kaffeelöffel (-) *nm*
tea towel – Geschirrtuch (-tücher) *nnt*
technical – technisch *adj*

---

adj - adjective   *v reg* - verb regular   *v sep* - verb separable   † - see verb info
prep - preposition   *v irreg* - verb irregular   *v refl* - verb reflexive   * - takes sein

technical drawing – technisches Zeichnen *nnt*
technical secondary school – Realschule (-n) *nf*
technician – (male) Techniker (-) *nm*
technician – (female) Technikerin (-nen) *nf*
technology – Technologie (-n) *nf*
teddy bear – Teddybär (-en) *nm wk*
teenager – Jugendliche *nmf* ‡
telegram – Telegramm (-e) *nnt*
telephone – Telefon (-e) *nnt*
by telephone – telefonisch
telephone s.o. – telefonieren mit (+ dat) *v reg* †
telephone – anrufen *v irreg sep*
telephone box – Telefonzelle (-n) *nf*
telephone directory – Telefonbuch (-bücher) *nnt*
telephone number – Telefonnummer (-n) *nf*
television – Fernsehen *nnt*
television set – Fernseher (-) *nm*
on television – im Fernsehen
watch television – fernsehen *v irreg sep*
tell – jdm sagen *v reg*
tell lies – lügen *v irreg*
tell off – ausschimpfen *v reg sep*
telly – Glotze *nf coll*
temperature – Temperatur (-en) *nf*
maximum temperature – Höchsttemperatur (-en) *nf*
minimum temperature – Tiefsttemperatur (-en) *nf*
have a high temperature – Fieber haben *v irreg*
ten – zehn *adj*
ten out of ten – zehn Punkte haben *v irreg*
tenant – (male) Mieter (-) *nm*
tenant – (female) Mieterin (-nen) *nf*
tender – zart *adj*

tennis – Tennis *nnt*
game of tennis – Tennisspiel (-e) *nnt*
tennis ball – Tennisball (-bälle) *nm*
tennis court – Tennisplatz (-plätze) *nm*
tennis racket – Tennisschläger (-) *nm*
tennis shoe – Tennisschuh (-e) *nm*
tense – nervös *adj*
tent – Zelt (-e) *nnt*
pitch a tent – ein Zelt aufbauen *v reg sep*
take down a tent – ein Zelt abbauen *v reg sep*
tenth – zehnte *adj*
term – (school) Trimester (-) *nnt*
term – (university) Semester (-) *nnt*
autumn half-term holiday – Herbstferien *npl*
February half-term holiday – Halbjahresferien *npl*
summer half-term holiday – Pfingstferien *npl*
terminus – Endstation (-en) *nf*
terrace – Terrasse (-n) *nf*
terraced house – Reihenhaus (-häuser) *nnt*
terrible – schrecklich, furchtbar *adj*
terrific – wunderbar *adj*
terrify – erschrecken *v irreg*
be terrified – große Angst haben *v irreg*
test – Test (-s) *nm*
driving test – Fahrprüfung (-en) *nf*
speaking test – mündliche Prüfung (-en) *nf*
text book – Schulbuch (-bücher) *nnt*
Thames – Themse *nf*
by the Thames – an der Themse
on the Thames – (afloat) auf der Themse
than – als *sub conj*
less ... than – weniger ... als

more ... than – mehr ... als
thank – danken (+ dat) *v reg*
thank s.o. – sich bedanken *v reg refl* †
thank you – danke *adv*
thank you very much – vielen Dank
no thank you – (nein) danke *adv*
thanks to – dank (+ gen/dat) *prep*
that – dass *subord conj*
that – jener *dem pron*
that – das *pron*
That comes to ten marks – Das macht zehn Mark
That depends – Es kommt darauf an
That is to say – Das heißt
That's all – Das wär's
That's enough – Das reicht
That's right – Das stimmt
thatched roof – Strohdach (-dächer) *nnt*
that one – dieser *dem pron*
the – der, die, das, die, etc *pron*
theatre – Theater (-) *nnt*
theft – Diebstahl *nm*
their – ihr *poss adj*
 It's theirs – Das gehört ihnen
them – sie *pron acc*
them, to them – ihnen *pron dat*
themselves – sich *pron refl*
then – dann, danach, darauf *adv*
there – (motion) dahin *adv*
 I am going there – Ich gehe dahin
there – (position towards) dort *adv*
there are, there is – es gibt (+ acc)
 There are no ... – Es gibt keine ...
 There is no ... – Es gibt keinen/keine/kein ...
 There was, there were – Es gab
 There will be – Es wird ... geben
 There would be – Es gäbe
therefore – also, deshalb *adv*
thermometer – Thermometer (-) *nnt*

thermometer – (medical) Fieberthermometer (-) *nnt*
these – diese *dem pron*
they – sie *pron nom*
they – (people in general) man *pron nom sing*
thick – (not clever) dumm *adj*
thick – (not thin) dick *adj*
thief – (male) Dieb (-e) *nm*
thief – (female) Diebin (-nen) *nf*
thigh – Schenkel (-) *nm*
thin – dünn *adj*
thing – Ding (-e) *nnt*, Sache (-n) *nf*
thingamajig – Dingsbums *nnt*
think – denken *v irreg*, glauben *v reg*
think – (have opinion) meinen *v reg*
think about – nachdenken über (+ acc) *v irreg sep*
think of – denken an (+ acc) *v irreg*
third – (fraction) Drittel (-) *nnt*
third – (in order) dritte *adj*
thirst – Durst *nm*
 be thirsty – Durst haben *v irreg*
 I am thirsty – Ich habe Durst
thirteen – dreizehn *adj*
thirtieth – dreißigste *adj*
thirty – dreißig *adj*
this – dieser *dem pron*
This is Anne speaking – Anne am Apparat
this way – hier entlang *adv*
those – jene *dem pron*
thought – Gedanke (-n) *nm wk*
thousand – tausend *adj*
thousands of – Tausende von (+ dat)
threaten – bedrohen *v reg* †
three – drei
throat – Hals (Hälse) *nm*
 have a sore throat – Halsschmerzen haben *v irreg*
throat pastille – Halstablette (-n) *nf*

---

adj - adjective	*v reg* - verb regular	*v sep* - verb separable	† - see verb info
prep - preposition	*v irreg* - verb irregular	*v refl* - verb reflexive	* - takes sein

through – durch (+ acc) *prep*	**till** – bis (+ acc) *prep*
through train – Durchgangszug (-züge) *nm,* D-Zug (-Züge) *nm*	**time** – (occasion) Mal (-e) *nnt*
throw – werfen *v irreg*	**time** – Zeit (-en) *nf*
thumb – Daumen (-) *nm*	**dinner time** – (school) Mittagspause (-n) *nf*
thunder – Donner *nm*	**free time** – Freizeit *nf*
thunder – donnern *v reg*	**a long time ago** – vor vielen Jahren

through – durch (+ acc) *prep*
through train – Durchgangszug (-züge) *nm,* D-Zug (-Züge) *nm*
throw – werfen *v irreg*
thumb – Daumen (-) *nm*
thunder – Donner *nm*
thunder – donnern *v reg*
thunderstorm – Gewitter (-) *nnt*
  There will be thunderstorms – Es wird Gewitter geben
Thursday – Donnerstag *nm*
  on Thursday – am Donnerstag
tick – (✓) ankreuzen *v reg sep*
ticket – (bus, train) Fahrkarte (-n) *nf*
ticket – (plane) Ticket (-s) *nnt*
  book of tickets – Streifenkarte (-n) *nf*
  return ticket – Rückfahrkarte (-n) *nf*
  single ticket – einfache Fahrkarte (-n) *nf*
  weekly ticket – Wochenkarte (-n) *nf*
ticket inspector – (male) Schaffner (-) *nm*
ticket inspector – (female) Schaffnerin (-nen) *nf*
ticket machine – Fahrkartenautomat (-en) *nm wk*
ticket office – Schalter (-) *nm*
  at the ticket office – am Schalter
tide – (high) Flut (-en) *nf*
  at high tide – bei Hochwasser
tide – (low) Ebbe (-n) *nf*
  at low tide – bei Tiefwasser
tidy – ordentlich *adj*
tidy up – aufräumen *v reg sep*
tie – Krawatte (-n) *nf,* Schlips (-e) *nm*
tie – anbinden *v irreg sep*
tiger – Tiger (-) *nm*
tight – eng *adj*
tights – (pair of) Strumpfhose (-n) *nf*
till – (cash) Kasse (-n) *nf*

till – bis (+ acc) *prep*
time – (occasion) Mal (-e) *nnt*
time – Zeit (-en) *nf*
  dinner time – (school) Mittagspause (-n) *nf*
  free time – Freizeit *nf*
  a long time ago – vor vielen Jahren
  every time – jedes Mal
  for a long time – für eine lange Zeit
  for the first time – zum ersten Mal
  for the last time – zum letzten Mal
  from time to time – ab und zu *adv,* dann und wann *adv*
  have a good time – sich amüsieren *v reg refl* †
  Have a good time! – Viel Spaß! *excl*
  many, many times – sehr oft
  on time – pünktlich *adv*
  three times – dreimal *adv*
time – (by clock) Uhr
  At what time? – Um wie viel Uhr?
  What time is it? – Wie spät ist es?
time – (on clock) Uhrzeit (-en) *nf*
time off – (work) Urlaub *nm*
time off – (leisure) Freizeit *nf*
timetable – (school) Stundenplan (-pläne) *nm*
timetable – (transport) Fahrplan (-pläne) *nm*
tin – Dose (-n) *nf*
tin opener – Dosenöffner (-) *nm*
tiny – winzig *adj*
tip – (end) Ende (-n) *nnt*
tip – (hint) Tipp (-s) *nm*
tip – (money) Trinkgeld (-er) *nnt*
tip – (rubbish) Müllhalde (-n) *nf*
tip – (summit) Gipfel (-) *nm*
tired – müde *adj*
tiring – ermüdend *adj*

---

tissue – Papiertaschentuch (-tücher) *nnt*
title – (homework) Überschrift (-en) *nf*
title – (book, play) Titel (-) *nm*
to – (in order to) um ... zu *conj*
to – in (+ acc) *prep*
  to the cinema – ins Kino
  to the church – in die Kirche
  to the hotel – ins Hotel
to – nach (+ dat) *prep*
  to Berlin – nach Berlin
to – zu (+ dat) *prep*
  to the post office – zur Post
  to the shops – zu den Geschäften
  to the school – zur Schule
  to the station – zum Bahnhof
  from 4th to 10th July – vom vierten bis zum zehnten Juli
to – (clock time) vor (+ dat) *prep*
  It's quarter to four – Es ist Viertel vor vier
  at quarter to four – um Viertel vor vier
toast – (bread) Toast *nm*
tobacco – Tabak (-e) *nm*
tobacconist – (male) Tabakhändler (-) *nm*
tobacconist – (female) Tabakhändlerin (-nen) *nf*
tobacconist's shop – Tabakhandlung (-en) *nf*
today – heute *adv*
today – (nowadays) heutzutage *adv*
toe – Zeh (-en) *nm*
together – zusammen *adv*
toilet – Toilette (-n) *nf*
toilet block – Sanitäranlage (-n) *nf*
toilet paper – Toilettenpapier *nnt*
token – Münze (-n) *nf*
told – gesagt *see* sagen
tolerate – tolerieren *v reg* †
toll – Zoll *nm*
tomato – Tomate (-n) *nf*

tomorrow – morgen *adv*
day after tomorrow – übermorgen *adv*
from tomorrow – ab morgen
See you tomorrow! – Bis morgen! *excl*
tomorrow evening – morgen Abend
tomorrow morning – morgen früh
ton – Tonne (-n) *nf*
tone – Ton (Töne) *nm*
tone – (on phone) Signal (-e) *nnt*
tongue – Zunge (-n) *nf*
mother tongue – Muttersprache (-n) *nf*
tonight – (evening) heute Abend
tonight – (night-time) heute Nacht
too – (as well) auch *adv*
too – (excessively) zu *adv*
Too bad – Pech!
too many – zu viele
too many people – zu viele Leute
too much – zu viel
tool – Werkzeug (-e) *nnt*
tooth – Zahn (Zähne) *nm*
toothache – Zahnschmerzen *npl*
  have toothache – Zahnschmerzen haben *v irreg*
toothbrush – Zahnbürste (-n) *nf*
toothpaste – Zahnpasta *nf*
top – (summit) Gipfel (-) *nm*
top – oben *adv*
  at the top – oben *adv*
  at the top of the page – oben auf der Seite *prep*
topic – Thema (Themen) *nnt*
torch – Taschenlampe (-n) *nf*
torn – zerrissen *v irreg*
tortoise – Schildkröte (-n) *nf*
total – Endsumme (-n) *nf*
totally – total *adv*
touch – berühren *v reg* †

---

adj - adjective	*v reg* - verb regular	*v sep* - verb separable	† - see verb info
prep - preposition	*v irreg* - verb irregular	*v refl* - verb reflexive	* - takes sein

tough – (meat) zäh *adj*
tough – (resilient) widerstandsfähig *adj*
Tough luck! – Pech! *excl*
tour – Tour (-en) *nf*
tourism – Tourismus *nm*
tourist – (male) Tourist (-en) *nm wk*
tourist – (female) Touristin (-nen) *nf*
tourist centre – Touristenstadt (-städte) *nf*
tourist information office – Informationsbüro (-s) *nnt*
tourist office – Verkehrsamt (-ämter) *nnt*
tournament – Tournier (-e) *nnt*
tow – schleppen *v reg*
towards – (time) gegen (+ acc) *prep*
towards midday – gegen Mittag
towards – (place) in Richtung
towards Berlin – in Richtung Berlin
towards – (in relation to) gegenüber (+ dat) *prep*
towards – entgegen *adv*
towel – (bath) Badetuch (-tücher) *nnt*
towel – (hand) Handtuch (-tücher) *nnt*
tower – Turm (Türme) *nm*
tower block – Wohnblock (-s) *nm*
town – Stadt (Städte) *nf*
  into town –in die Stadt
  in town – in der Stadt
town centre – Stadtmitte (-n) *nf*
  in the town centre – in der Stadtmitte
town hall – Rathaus (-häuser) *nnt*
town plan – Stadtplan (-pläne) *nm*
toy – Spielzeug (-e) *nnt*
track – Bahn (-en) *nf*
tracksuit – Trainingsanzug (-anzüge) *nm*
tractor – Traktor (-en) *nm*
trade – (profession) Beruf (-e) *nm*
trade – (business) Handel *nm*

tradition – Tradition (-en) *nf*
traditional – traditionell *adj*
traffic – (drugs) Handel *nm*
traffic – (vehicles) Verkehr *nm*
traffic jam – Stau (-s) *nm*
traffic lights – Ampel (-n) *nf*
trailer – Anhänger (-) *nm*
train – Zug (Züge) *nm*
  by train – mit dem Zug
  catch the train – den Zug nehmen *v irreg*
  get on the train – in den Zug einsteigen* *v irreg sep*
  get off the train – aus dem Zug aussteigen* *v irreg sep*
  through train – Durchgangszug (-züge) *nm*
train – (animal) dressieren *v reg* †
train – (sport) trainieren *v reg* †
trainer – (person) Trainer (-) *nm*
trainer – (shoe) Turnschuh (-e) *nm*
training – (vocational) Ausbildung (-en) *nf*
tram – Straßenbahn (-en) *nf*
trampoline – Trampolin (-e) *nnt*
trampoline – Trampolin springen* *v irreg*
transform – verwandeln *v reg* †
transistor – (radio) Kofferradio (-s) *nnt*
translate – (in writing) übersetzen *v reg insep*
translate – (interpret) dolmetschen *v reg*
translation – Übersetzung (-en) *nf*
transport – Transportmittel (-) *nnt*
travel – fahren* *v irreg*, reisen* *v reg*
travel agency – Reisebüro (-s) *nnt*
travel by bus – mit dem Bus fahren* *v irreg*
travel by car – mit dem Wagen fahren* *v irreg*
travel by coach – mit dem Reisebus fahren* *v irreg*

---

travel by train – mit dem Zug fahren* *v irreg*

traveller – Reisende *nmf* ‡

travellers' cheque – Reisescheck (-s) *nm*

tray – Tablett (-s) *nnt*

treasure – Schatz (Schätze) *nm*

treat – (medical) behandeln *v reg* †

treatment – Behandlung (-en) *nf*

trend – Tendenz (-en) *nf,* Trend (-s) *nm*

tree – Baum (Bäume) *nm*
  fruit tree – Obstbaum (-bäume) *nm*

tremble – zittern *v reg*

trembling – zitternd *adj*

tremendously – furchtbar *adv*

trendy – in *adj inv*

triangle – Dreieck (-e) *nnt*

trip – (outing) Ausflug (Ausflüge) *nm*

trip – (journey) Reise (-n) *nf*

trip over – (fall) hinfallen* *v irreg sep*

trolley – (supermarket) Einkaufswagen (-) *nm*

trolley – (luggage) Kofferkuli (-s) *nm*

trombone – Posaune (-n) *nf*

trouble – Problem (-e) *nnt*
  be in trouble – Probleme haben *v irreg*

trousers – (pair of) Hose (-n) *nf*

trout – Forelle (-n) *nf*

truant – schwänzen *v reg coll*

truck – Lastwagen (-) *nm*

true – richtig, wahr *adj*

trumpet – Trompete (-n) *nf*

trunk road – Bundesstraße (-n) *nf*

trunks – (swimming) Badehose (-n) *nf*

trust – Vertrauen *nnt*

trust – trauern *v reg*

truth – Wahrheit (-en) *nf*

try – versuchen *v reg* †

try – (food) probieren *v reg* †

try on – (clothes) anprobieren *v reg sep* †

try to – versuchen *v reg* †
  I tried to phone – Ich habe versucht anzurufen

T-Shirt – T-Shirt (-s) *nnt*

tube – (toothpaste, etc) Tube (-n) *nf*

tube – (London) U-Bahn *nf*

tube station – U-Bahnstation (-en) *nf*

Tuesday – Dienstag *nm*
  on Tuesday – am Dienstag

tulip – Tulpe (-n) *nf*

tumble drier – Wäschetrockner (-) *nm*

tuna – Thunfisch (-e) *nm*

tune – (music) Melodie (-n) *nf*

tune – (instrument) stimmen *v reg*

tunnel – Tunnel (-) *nm*
  Channel Tunnel – Kanaltunnel *nm*

turkey – Truthahn (-hähne) *nm*

Turkey – die Türkei *nf*

turn – drehen *v reg*

turn – (off road) abbiegen *v irreg sep*

turn off – (light) ausschalten *v reg sep* †

turn off – (tap) zudrehen *v reg sep*

turn on – (light) anmachen *v reg sep*

turn on – (tap) andrehen *v reg sep*

turn pale – blass werden* *v irreg*

turn round – sich umdrehen *v reg refl sep*

turquoise – türkis *adj inv*

TV news – Nachrichten *npl*

twelfth – zwölfte *adj*

twelve – zwölf *adj*

twelve o'clock – (mid-day) Mittag *nm*

twelve o'clock – (midnight) Mitternacht *nf*

twentieth – zwanzigste *adj*

twenty – zwanzig *adj*

twenty-one – einundzwanzig *adj*

---

adj - adjective	*v reg* - verb regular	*v sep* - verb separable	† - see verb info
prep - preposition	*v irreg* - verb irregular	*v refl* - verb reflexive	* - takes sein

twenty-first – einundzwanzigste *adj*
twice – zweimal *adv*
twins – Zwillinge *npl*
twin brother – Zwillingsbruder (-brüder) *nm*
twin sister – Zwillingsschwester (-n) *nf*
twin town – Partnerstadt (-städte) *nf*
twist an ankle – sich das Fußgelenk verrenken *v reg dat refl* †
two – zwei *adj*
type – (sort) Art (-en) *nf*
type – Typ (-en) *nm*

type – tippen *v reg*
typewriter – Schreibmaschine (-n) *nf*
typical – typisch *adj*
typist – (male) Stenotypist (-en) *nm wk*
typist – (female) Stenotypistin (-nen) *nf*
tyre – Reifen (-) *nm*
  to have a flat tyre – eine Reifenpanne haben *v irreg*
tyre pressure – Reifendruck *nm*
  check the tyre pressure – den Reifendruck kontrollieren *v reg* †

U

ugly – hässlich *adj*
UK – das Vereinigte Königreich *nnt*
umbrella – Regenschirm (-e) *nm*
un~ – un~ *pref*
unaccustomed – ungewohnt *adj*
unavoidable – unvermeidlich *adj*
unbearable – unerträglich *adj*
unbelievable – unglaublich *adj*
uncertain – ungewiss *adj*
uncle – Onkel (-) *nm*
uncomfortable – unbequem *adj*
unconscious – bewusstlos *adj*
under – unter (+ acc/dat) *prep*
underclothes – Unterwäsche *nf, no pl*
underground – U-Bahn (-en) *nf*
underground station – U-Bahnstation (-en) *nf*
underground ticket – U-Bahnfahrkarte (-n) *nf*
underline – unterstreichen *v irreg insep*
underneath – unter (+ acc/dat) *prep*
underpants – (pair of) Unterhose (-n) *nf*

understand – verstehen *v irreg*
understanding – verständnisvoll *adj*
understanding – Verständnis (-se) *nnt*
understood – verstanden *adj*
  I have not understood – ich habe nicht verstanden
undertake – unternehmen *v irreg insep*
underwear – Unterwäsche *nf, no pl*
undress – sich ausziehen *v irreg refl sep*
unemployed – arbeitslos *adj*
unemployed person – Arbeitslose *nmf* ‡
unemployment – Arbeitslosigkeit *nf*
uneven – ungleich *adj*
unexpected – unerwartet *adj*
unfair – unfair *adj*
unfavourable – ungünstig *adj*
unfit – unfit *adj*
unfold – entfalten *v reg* †
unforgettable – unvergesslich *adj*
unfortunate – unglücklich *adj*

---

nm - noun masculine	*nf* - noun feminine	*nnt* - noun neuter	*npl* - noun plural
nom- nominative	*acc* - accusative	*gen* - genitive	*dat* - dative

unfortunately – leider, unglücklicherweise *adv*
unfriendly – unfreundlich *adj*
ungrateful – undankbar *adj*
unhappy – unglücklich *adj*
unhurt – unverletzt *adj*
unification – Vereinigung *nf*
uniform – Uniform (-en) *nf*
unify – vereinigen *v reg* †
unimportant – unwichtig *adj*
unique – einmalig *adj*
unit – Einheit (-en) *nf*
    the Day of German Unity – der Tag der Deutschen Einheit *nm*
United Kingdom – das Vereinigte Königreich *nnt*
universal – allgemein *adj*
universal – Universal– *pref*
universe – Universum (Universen) *nnt*
university – Universität (-en) *nf*
unjust – ungerecht *adj*
unknown – unbekannt *adj*
unleaded – bleifrei *adj*
unleaded petrol – bleifreies Benzin *nnt*
unlucky – unglücklich *adj*
unmarried – ledig *adj*
unnecessary – unnötig *adj*
unpack – auspacken *v reg sep*
unpleasant – unangenehm *adj*
untidy – unordentlich *adj*
until – bis (+ acc) *prep*
    until Sunday – bis Sonntag
    not until Sunday – erst am Sonntag

untruthful – unehrlich *adj*
unusual – ungewöhnlich *adj*
unwell – krank, unwohl *adj*
    I am unwell – Mir ist unwohl
up – oben *adv*
    be up – (out of bed) aufgestanden sein* *v irreg*
uphill – bergauf *adv*
up there – dort oben *adv*
upon – auf (+ acc/dat) *prep*
upper – ober– *pref*
upside down – auf den Kopf gestellt *adj*
upstairs – oben *adv*
    go upstairs – nach oben gehen* *v irreg*
urban – städtisch *adj*
urgency – Dringlichkeit *nf*
urgent – dringend *adj*
us – uns *pers pron acc/dat*
USA – die Vereinigten Staaten *npl*
use – (custom) Brauch (Bräuche) *nm*
use – Gebrauch *nm, no pl*
use – Benutzung *nf*
use – (make use of) benutzen *v reg* †
use – (need) brauchen *v reg*
useful – nützlich *adj*
useless – nutzlos *adj*
user – (male) Benutzer (-) *nm*
user – (female) Benutzerin (-nen) *nf*
usherette – Platzanweiserin (-nen) *nf*
usual – normal, gewöhnlich *adj*
    as usual – wie gewöhnlich *adv*
usually – normalerweise *adv*

---

adj - adjective   *v reg* - verb regular   *v sep* - verb separable   † - see verb info
prep - preposition   *v irreg* - verb irregular   *v refl* - verb reflexive   * - takes sein

V

vacancies – Zimmer frei
  no vacancies – belegt *adj*
vacuum cleaner – Staubsauger (-) *nm*
vacuum – staubsaugen *v reg*
vague – ungenau *adj*
vain – (conceited) eitel *adj*
  in vain – vergebens *adv*
valid – gültig *adj*
valley – Tal (Täler) *nnt*
valuable – wertvoll, kostbar *adj*
valuables – Wertsachen *npl*
value – Wert (-e) *nm*
van – Lieferwagen (-) *nm*
vanilla – Vanille *nf*
vanilla ice cream – Vanilleeis *nnt,*
  no pl
vanish – verschwinden* *v irreg*
vanity – Eitelkeit (-en) *nf*
varied – verschieden *adj*
vary – verschieden sein* *v irreg*
VAT – MWSt (Mehrwertsteuer) *nf*
VCR – Videokassettenrekorder (-) *nm*
veal – Kalbfleisch *nnt*
vegan – vegan *adj*
vegan – (male) Veganer (-) *nm*
vegan – (female) Veganerin (-nen) *nf*
vegetable – Gemüse *nnt no pl*
vegetarian – vegetarisch *adj*
vegetarian – (male) Vegetarier (-) *nm*
vegetarian – (female) Vegetarierin
  (-nen) *nf*
vehicle – Fahrzeug (-e) *nnt*
velvet – Samt *nm*
verb – Verb (-en) *nnt*
version – Ausführung (-en) *nf*
  in the original version –
  (soundtrack) im Originalton
very – sehr *adv*
vest – Unterhemd (-en) *nnt*

vet – (male) Tierarzt (-ärzte) *nm*
vet – (female) Tierärztin (-nen) *nf*
vicar – (protestant, male) Pastor (-en)
  nm
vicar – (protestant, female) Pastorin
  (-nen) *nf*
victim – Opfer (-) *nnt*
victorious – siegreich *adj*
victory – Sieg (-e) *nm*
video – Video~ *pref*
video camera – Videokamera (-s) *nf*
video cassette – Videokassette (-n) *nf*
video game – Videospiel (-e) *nnt*
video recorder –
  Videokassettenrekorder (-) *nm*
video – auf Video aufnehmen *v irreg*
  sep
Vienna – Wien
view – Blick (-e) *nm*, Aussicht (-en) *nf*
viewer – (male) Zuschauer (-) *nm*
viewer – (female) Zuschauerin (-nen)
  nf
vigorous – lebhaft *adj*
vile – (person) ekelhaft *adj*
vile – (weather) scheußlich *adj*
village – Dorf (Dörfer) *nnt*
vine – Rebstock *nm*
vinegar – Essig *nm*
vine grower – (male) Weinbauer (-n)
  nm wk
vine grower – (female) Weinbäuerin
  (-nen) *nf*
vineyard – Weinberg (-e) *nm*
viola – Bratsche (-n) *nf*
violence – Gewalt *nf*
violent – (person) gewalttätig *adj*
violent – (storm) gewaltig *adj*
violin – Geige (-n) *nf,* Violine (-n) *nf*
Virgo – Jungfrau
visa – Visum (Visen) *nnt*

---

visibility – Sicht *nf, no pl*
visible – sichtbar *adj*
visit – Besuch (-e) *nm*
visit – (person) besuchen *v reg* †
visit – (tourist attraction) besichtigen
  v reg †
visitor – (guest) Gast (Gäste) *nm*
  We have visitors – Wir haben
  Besuch
visitor – (tourist, male) Besucher (-)
  nm
visitor – (tourist, female) Besucherin
  (-nen) *nf*

vital – unbedingt notwendig *adj*
vocabulary – (individual items)
  Vokabel (-n) *nf*
vocabulary – (complete list)
  Wortschatz *nm*
voice – Stimme (-n) *nf*
volleyball – Volleyball *nm*
voluntary – freiwillig *adj*
volunteer – Freiwillige *nmf* ‡
vomit – sich erbrechen *v irreg refl,*
  sich übergeben *v irreg insep,* kotzen
  v reg coll
voyage – Reise (-n) *nf*

W

waffle – (edible) Waffel (-n) *nf*
wages – Lohn (Löhne) *nm*
waist(line) – Taille (-n) *nf*
waistcoat – Weste (-n) *nf*
wait – warten *v reg* †
wait (for) – warten auf (+ acc) *v reg* †
waiter – Kellner (-) *nm*
Waiter! – Herr Ober! *excl*
waiting room – Wartesaal (-säle) *nm*
waitress – Kellnerin (-nen) *nf*
Waitress! – Fräulein! *excl*
wake s.o. – wecken *v reg*
wake up – aufwachen* *v reg sep*
Wales – Wales *nnt*
walk – gehen* *v irreg*
walk – (stroll) Spaziergang (-gänge)
  nm
walk the dog – den Hund ausführen
  v reg sep
  go for a walk – spazieren gehen*
  v irreg
walkman® – Walkman® (Walkmen)
  nm
wall – (exterior) Mauer (-n) *nf*
wall – (interior) Wand (Wände) *nf*

wallet – Brieftasche (-n) *nf*
wallpaper – Tapete (-n) *nf*
wallpaper – tapezieren *v reg* †
want – wollen *v irreg*
war – Krieg (-e) *nm*
warden – (youth hostel, male)
  Herbergsvater (-väter) *nm*
warden – (youth hostel, female)
  Herbergsmutter (-mütter) *nf*
warden – (traffic, male) Hilfspolizist
  (-en) *nm wk*
warden – (traffic, female) Politesse
  (-n) *nf*
wardrobe – Kleiderschrank
  (schränke) *nm*
warm – warm *adj*
  I am warm – Mir ist warm
  It is warm – (weather) Es ist warm
warm up – sich aufwärmen *v reg refl*
  sep
warn about – warnen vor (+ dat)
  v reg
warning – Warnung (-en) *nf*
was – war *see sein**
  It was – Es war

| *adj* - adjective | *v reg* - verb regular | *v sep* - verb separable | † - see verb info |
| *prep* - preposition | *v irreg* - verb irregular | *v refl* - verb reflexive | * - takes sein |

was able to – konnte *see können*
was obliged to – musste *see müssen*
wash – (clothes etc) waschen *v irreg*
  have a wash – sich waschen
  v irreg refl
  I have washed – Ich habe mich
  gewaschen
wash basin – Waschbecken (-) *nnt*
wash one's hair – sich die Haare
  waschen *v irreg dat refl*
  I'm washing my hair – Ich
  wasche mir die Haare
washing – (clothes) Wäsche *nf*
  do the washing – die Wäsche
  machen *v reg*
washing machine – Waschmaschine
  (-n) *nf*
washing powder – Waschpulver *nnt*
washing up liquid – Spülmittel *nnt*
  do the washing up – spülen *v reg*
wasp – Wespe (-n) *nf*
waste – verschwenden *v reg* †
  a waste of time –
  Zeitverschwendung *nf, no pl*
wasted – (useless) nutzlos *adj*
wasted – (time, effort) verloren *adj*
wasteful – verschwenderisch *adj*
waste paper basket – Papierkorb
  (-körbe) *nm*
watch – Armbanduhr (-en) *nf*
watch – zusehen *v irreg sep*, zuschauen
  v reg sep, gucken *v reg coll*
watch TV – fernsehen *v irreg sep*
water – Wasser *nnt, no pl*
water – (plants) begießen *v irreg*
waterproof – wasserdicht *adj*
water sports – Wassersport *nm*
  do watersports – Wassersport
  treiben *v irreg*
water skiing – Wasserskifahren *nnt*
water-ski – Wasserski laufen* *v irreg*
wave – (hand) winken *v reg*
wave – (sea) Welle (-n) *nf*

way – (method) Art (-en) *nf*
way – (route) Weg (-e) *nm*
  a long way off – weit weg
  by the way – übrigens
  in this way – auf diese Weise
  on the way – unterwegs *adv*
  the right way – der richtige Weg
way in – (on foot) Eingang (-gänge) *nm*
way in – (by car) Einfahrt (-en) *nf*
way out – (on foot) Ausgang (-gänge)
  nm
way out – (by car) Ausfahrt (-en) *nf*
WC – WC (-s) *nnt*
we – wir *pers pron*
weak – schwach *adj*
wear – tragen *v irreg*
wear out – verschleißen *v irreg*
weather – Wetter *nnt, no pl*
  in bad weather – bei schlechtem
  Wetter
  in good weather – bei gutem
  Wetter
weather forecast –
  Wettervorhersage (-n) *nf*
wedding – Hochzeit (-en) *nf*
wedding dress – Hochzeitskleid (-er)
  nnt
Wednesday – Mittwoch *nm*
  on Wednesday – am Mittwoch
weeds – Unkraut *nnt, no pl*
week – Woche (-n) *nf*
  during the week – in der Woche
  last week – letzte Woche
  next week – nächste Woche
  per week – pro Woche
weekdays – wochentags *adv*
weekend – Wochenende (-n) *nnt*
weekly – wöchentlich *adj*
weep – weinen *v reg*
weigh – wiegen *v irreg*
weight – Gewicht (-e) *nnt*
welcome – willkommen *adj*
Welcome! – Herzlich willkommen!

You're welcome! – Nichts zu danken!

welcome – willkommen heißen *v irreg*

welcoming – freundlich *adj*

well – (water) Brunnen (-) *nm*

well – gut *adv*
  all is well – alles geht bestens
  as well – auch *adv*
  I am well – Mir geht es gut
  Get well soon! – Gute Besserung!

well-behaved – artig *adj*

well brought up – guterzogen *adj*

well-built – (person) stark gebaut *adj*

well-cooked – (steak) gut durchgebraten *adj*

Well done! – Gut gemacht! *excl*

well-known – bekannt *adj*

well-paid – gut bezahlt *adj*

Welsh – walisisch *adj*

Welsh – (language) Walisisch *nnt*

Welshman – Waliser (-) *nm*

Welsh woman – Waliserin (-nen) *nf*

went – *see gehen**

west – Westen *nm*
  in the west – im Westen
  west of – westlich von (+ dat)

western – (film) Western (-) *nm*

West Indian – westindisch *adj*

West Indian – (male) Westinder (-) *nm*

West Indian – (female) Westinderin (-nen) *nf*

the West Indies – die Westindischen Inseln *npl*

wet – nass *adj*

wet paint – frisch gestrichen

wet through – durchnässt *adj*

what? – was? *adv*

What is that? – Was ist das?

What did you say? – Was hast du gesagt?

What's going on? – Was ist los?

What's the matter? – Was ist los?

What else? – Was sonst?

What's new? – Was gibt's neues?

what – was *sub conj*

what? – (how) wie? *adv*

What is ... like? – Wie ist ...? *adv*

What is your name? – Wie heißt du? Wie heißen Sie?

What (did you say)? – Wie bitte?

What does ... mean? – Wie heißt ..?

What is the time? – Wie spät ist es?

What is it in German? – Wie heißt das auf Deutsch?

What is the way to ...? – (+ town name) Wie kommt man nach ...?

What is the best way to ...? – (+ building) Wie kommt man am besten zum/zur ...?

what? – (which?) welche? *adj*

What colour? – Welche Farbe?

What a pity! – Schade! *excl*

What is it about? – Worum handelt es sich?

whatsit – Dingsbums *nnt coll*

wheel – Rad (Räder) *nnt*

wheelbarrow – Schubkarre (-n) *nf*

wheelchair – Rollstuhl (-stühle) *nm*

when – (in past) als *sub conj*

when – (whenever) wenn *sub conj*

when? – (question) wann? *adv*

where – wo *sub conj*

where? – wo? *adv*

where (from)? – woher *adv*

Where do you come from? – Woher kommst du?

(to) where? – wohin *adv*

Where are you going (to)? – Wohin gehst du?

whether – ob *sub conj*

which – der, die, das *rel pron*

which? – welche? *adj*

while – während *sub conj*
  a long while – lange *adv*

---

whilst – während *sub conj*
whipped cream – Schlagsahne (-n) *nf*
whisky – Whisky *nm, no pl*
whisper – flüstern *v reg*
whistle – pfeifen *v irreg*
white – weiß *adj*
  white coffee – Kaffee mit Sahne
  white wine – Weißwein (-e) *nm*
Whitsun – Pfingsten *npl*
who? – wer?
Who is coming with us? – Wer
  kommt mit?
Who(m) did you see? – Wen hast
  du gesehen?
Who did you give the book to? –
  Wem hast du das Buch gegeben?
whose – wessen *rel pron*
whose? – wessen?
whole – ganz *adj*
  on the whole – im Großen und
  Ganzen
  the whole time – die ganze Zeit
wholemeal bread – Vollkornbrot (-e)
  nnt
why? – warum? *adv*
wide – breit *adj*
widely known – weit verbreitet *adj*
widow – Witwe (-n) *nf*
widowed – verwitwet *adj*
widower – Witwer (-) *nm*
width – Breite (-n) *nf*
wife – Frau (-en) *nf*
wild – wild *adj*
will – *see future tenses*
will – (want to) wollen *v irreg*
win – gewinnen *v irreg*
wind – Wind (-e) *nm*
windy – windig *adj*
window – Fenster (-) *nnt*
window – (shop) Schaufenster (-) *nnt*
window shopping – einen
  Schaufensterbummel machen *v reg*

windscreen – Windschutzscheibe (-n)
  nf
windscreen wiper –
  Scheibenwischer (-) *nm*
windsurf – windsurfen *v reg*
  I went windsurfing – Ich bin
  windsurfen gegangen
wine – Wein (-e) *nm*
wine bar – Weinstube (-n) *nf*
wine list – Getränkekarte (-n) *nf*
winger – (sport) Außen (-) *nm*
winner – (male) Sieger (-) *nm*
winner – (female) Siegerin (-nen) *nf*
winter – Winter *nm*
  in winter – im Winter
winter sports – Wintersport *nm,*
  no pl
wipe – wischen *v reg*
wise – weise *adj*
wish – Wunsch (Wünsche) *nm*
wish – wünschen *v reg*
  Best wishes – alles Gute *excl*
wish (to) – wollen *v irreg*
wish to – Lust haben zu *v irreg*
with – mit (+ dat) *prep*
  With best wishes from – (male,
  formal) Ihr *poss adj*
  With best wishes from – (male,
  informal) dein *poss adj*
  With best wishes from –
  (female, formal) Ihre *poss adj*
  With best wishes from –
  (female, informal) deine *poss adj*
  with pleasure – mit Vergnügen
  with success – mit Erfolg
without – ohne (+ acc) *prep*
without doubt – zweifellos *adv*
witness – (male) Zeuge (-n) *nm wk*
witness – (female) Zeugin (-nen) *nf*
woman – Frau (-en) *nf*
wonder – sich fragen *v reg refl*
wonderful – wunderbar,
  wunderschön *adj*

---

wood – Holz *nnt*
wooden – aus Holz
woodwork – Werken *nnt*
wool – Wolle (-n) *nf*
woollen – aus Wolle
word – Wort (Worte) *nnt*
word processing – Textverarbeitung *nf*
word processing program – Textverarbeitungsprogramm (-e) *nnt*
work – Arbeit (-en) *nf*
  on working days – werktags
  out of work – arbeitslos *adj*
  part-time work – Teilzeitarbeit (-en) *nf*
work – (person) arbeiten *v reg* †
  work hard – fleißig arbeiten *v reg* †
  work part-time – halbtags arbeiten *v reg* †
work – (machine) funktionieren *v reg* †
worker – (male) Arbeiter (-) *nm*
worker – (female) Arbeiterin (-nen) *nf*
work experience – Berufspraktikum (-praktika) *nnt*
workshop – Werkstatt (-stätten) *nf*
world – Welt (-en) *nf*
world championship – Weltmeisterschaft (-en) *nf*
worldwide – weltweit *adj*
worm – Wurm (Würmer) *nm*
worn out – verschlissen *adj*
worried – ängstlich *adj*
worry – sich Sorgen machen (über + acc) *v reg dat refl*
  Don't worry! – Keine Angst! *excl*

worse – schlimmer *adj*
worse and worse – immer schlimmer *adv*
worth – Wert (-e) *nm*
  It's worth DM 2,000 – Es ist DM 2 000 wert
  It's not worth it – Es lohnt sich nicht
worthless – wertlos *adj*
worth seeing – sehenswert *adj*
worthwhile – sinnvoll *adj*
wound – Wunde (-n) *nf*
wrap up – (present) einpacken *v reg sep*
wrist – Handgelenk (-e) *nnt*
wrist watch – Armbanduhr (-en) *nf*
write – schreiben *v irreg*
write back – beantworten *v reg* †
write down – aufschreiben *v irreg sep*
write to – schreiben an (+ acc) *v irreg*
writer – (male) Schriftsteller (-) *nm*
writer – (female) Schriftstellerin (-nen) *nf*
writing paper – Schreibpapier *nnt*
  in writing – schriftlich *adj*
written test – schriftliche Prüfung *nf*
wrong – falsch *adj*
  be wrong – unrecht haben *v irreg*
  I am wrong – Ich habe Unrecht
  What's wrong? – Was ist los?
wrong number – falsch verbunden
wrong side – Kehrseite (-n) *nf*
wrong way round – falsch 'rum

X

Xmas – Weihnachten *npl*
X-ray – Röntgenbild *nnt*
X-ray – röntgen *v reg*

to be X-rayed – sich röntgen lassen *v irreg refl*

---

adj - adjective	*v reg* - verb regular	*v sep* - verb separable	† - see verb info
prep - preposition	*v irreg* - verb irregular	*v refl* - verb reflexive	* - takes sein

Y

yacht – Jacht (-en) *nf*
yacht marina – Jachthafen (-häfen) *nm*
yard – (place) Hof (Höfe) *nm*
yawn – gähnen *v reg*
year – Jahr (-e) *nnt*
  be X years old – X Jahre alt sein*
  in Year 7 – im sechsten Schuljahr
  in Year 8 – im siebten Schuljahr
  in Year 9 – im achten Schuljahr
  in Year 10 – im neunten Schuljahr
  in Year 11 – im zehnten Schuljahr
  in Year 12 – in der Oberstufe
  in Year 13 – (male) Abiturient
  in Year 13 – (female) Abiturientin
  last year – letztes Jahr
  next year – nächstes Jahr
  school year – Schuljahr (-e) *nnt*
yearly – jährlich *adj*
yell – grölen *v reg coll*
yellow – gelb *adj*
yes – ja *adv*
yes, really – doch *adv*
yesterday – gestern *adv*
  the day before yesterday –
  vorgestern *adv*
yesterday evening – gestern Abend *adv*
yet – noch *adv*
  not yet – noch nicht *adv*
yoga – Joga *nm, no pl*
yoghurt – Joghurt (-s) *nm*

you – (informal) du *pron nom sing*
you – (informal) dich *pron acc sing*
you – (informal) dir *pron dat sing*
you – (formal) Sie *pron nom/acc sing or pl*
you – (formal) Ihnen *pron dat sing or pl*
you – (informal) ihr *pron nom pl*
you – (informal) euch *pron acc/dat pl*
you – (persons unspecified) man *pron nom sing*
you – (persons unspecified) einen *pron acc sing*
you – (persons unspecified) einem *pron dat sing*
young – jung *adj*
young people – Jugend *nf, no pl*
young person – Jugendliche *nmf ‡*
younger – jünger *adj*
youngest – jüngste *adj*
your – (formal) Ihr *poss adj*
your – (informal sing) dein *poss adj*
your – (informal pl) euer *poss adj*
yourself – selbst *adv*
Yours – (informal) Alles Gute
Yours faithfully – (very formal) Hochachtungsvoll *adv*
Yours sincerely – (formal) mit freundlichen Grüßen
youth – Jugend *nf, no pl*
youth club – Jugendklub (-s) *nm*
youth hostel – Jugendherberge (-n) *nf*

---

nm - noun masculine   *nf* - noun feminine   *nnt* - noun neuter   *npl* - noun plural
nom- nominative   *acc* - accusative   *gen* - genitive   *dat* - dative

Z

zebra – Zebra (-s) *nnt*
zebra crossing – Zebrastreifen *nm*
zero – Null (-en) *nf*
zip – Reißverschluss (-verschlüsse) *nm*
zit – Pickel (-) *nm*
zither – Zither (-n) *nf*
zone – Zone (-n) *nf*

industrial zone – Industriegebiet (-e) *nnt*
pedestrian zone – Fußgängerzone (-n) *nf*
zoo – Zoo (-s) *nm,* Tiergarten (-gärten) *nm*

---

adj - adjective
prep - preposition

v reg - verb regular
v irreg - verb irregular

v sep - verb separable
v refl - verb reflexive

† - see verb info
* - takes sein

Verb table

Verbs with separable or inseparable prefixes and with the prefixes *be-*, *ent-*, *er-*, *ge-* and *ver-* should be looked up without their prefix. * denotes verb with *sein* in perfect and other compound tenses.

Infinitive	3rd Person Present	Imperfect	Perfect	Meaning
backen	**bäckt**	backte	gebacken	to bake
befehlen	**befiehlt**	befahl	befohlen	to command
begießen	begießt	begoss	begossen	to water (plants)
beginnen	beginnt	begann	begonnen	to begin
beißen	beißt	biss	gebissen	to bite
bersten	**birst**	barst	geborsten*	to burst
beschließen	beschließt	beschloss	beschlossen	to decide
beschreiben	beschreibt	beschrieb	beschrieben	to describe
biegen	biegt	bog	gebogen	to bend
bieten	**bietet**	bot	geboten	to offer
binden	**bindet**	band	gebunden	to fasten
bitten (um)	**bittet (um)**	bat (um)	gebeten	to ask (for)
blasen	**bläst**	blies	geblasen	to blow
bleiben	bleibt	blieb	geblieben*	to stay
braten	**brät**	briet	gebraten	to roast
brechen	**bricht**	brach	gebrochen	to break
brennen	brennt	brannte	gebrannt	to burn
bringen	bringt	brachte	gebracht	to bring

Infinitive	3rd Person Present	Imperfect	Perfect	Meaning
denken	denkt	dachte	gedacht	to think
dürfen	**darf**	durfte		to be allowed to
empfehlen	**empfiehlt**	empfahl	empfohlen	to recommend
erschrecken	**erschrickt**	erschrak	erschrocken	to terrify
essen	**isst**	aß	gegessen	to eat
fahren	**fährt**	fuhr	gefahren*	to travel
fallen	**fällt**	fiel	gefallen*	to fall
fangen	**fängt**	fing	gefangen	to catch
finden	**findet**	fand	gefunden	to find
fliegen	fliegt	flog	geflogen*	to fly
frieren	friert	fror	gefroren	to freeze
geben	**gibt**	gab	gegeben	to give
gehen	geht	ging	gegangen*	to go
gelingen	gelingt	gelang	gelungen*	to succeed
genießen	genießt	genoss	genossen	to enjoy
geschehen	**geschieht**	geschah	geschehen*	to happen
gewinnen	gewinnt	gewann	gewonnen	to win
greifen	greift	griff	gegriffen	to grasp
haben	**hat**	hatte	gehabt	to have
halten	**hält**	hielt	gehalten	to stop, to hold
hängen	hängt	hing	gehangen	to hang

Infinitive	3rd Person Present	Imperfect	Perfect	Meaning
heben	hebt	hob	gehoben	to lift
heißen	heißt	hieß	geheißen	to be called
helfen	**hilft**	half	geholfen	to help
kennen	kennt	kannte	gekannt	to know
kommen	kommt	kam	gekommen*	to come
können	**kann**	konnte		to be able to
laden	**lädt**	lud	geladen	to load
lassen	**lässt**	ließ	gelassen	to leave
laufen	**läuft**	lief	gelaufen*	to run
leiden	**leidet**	litt	gelitten	to suffer
leihen	leiht	lieh	geliehen	to lend
lesen	**liest**	las	gelesen	to read
liegen	liegt	lag	gelegen	to lie
liegen lassen	lässt liegen	ließ liegen	liegen lassen	to leave lying around
messen	**misst**	maß	gemessen	to measure
mögen	**mag**	mochte		to like to
müssen	**muss**	musste		to have to
nehmen	**nimmt**	nahm	genommen	to take
nennen	nennt	nannte	genannt	to name
pfeifen	pfeift	pfiff	gepfiffen	to whistle
raten	**rät**	riet	geraten	to guess

Infinitive	3rd Person Present	Imperfect	Perfect	Meaning
reiben	reibt	rieb	gerieben	to rub
reißen	reißt	riss	gerissen	to tear
reiten	**reitet**	ritt	geritten*	to ride
riechen	riecht	roch	gerochen	to smell
rufen	ruft	rief	gerufen	to call
scheiden	**scheidet**	schied	geschieden	to part
scheinen	scheint	schien	geschienen	to shine, to seem
schießen	schießt	schoss	geschossen	to shoot
schieben	schiebt	schob	geschoben	to push
schlafen	**schläft**	schlief	geschlafen	to sleep
schlagen	**schlägt**	schlug	geschlagen	to hit
schleichen	schleicht	schlich	geschlichen*	to creep
schließen	schließt	schloss	geschlossen	to shut
schneiden	**schneidet**	schnitt	geschnitten	to cut
schreiben	schreibt	schrieb	geschrieben	to write
schreien	schreit	schrie	geschrieen	to shout
schweigen	schweigt	schwieg	geschwiegen	to be silent
schwimmen	schwimmt	schwamm	geschwommen(*)	to swim
sehen	**sieht**	sah	gesehen	to see
sein	**ist**	war	gewesen*	to be
singen	singt	sang	gesungen	to sing

Infinitive	3rd Person Present	Imperfect	Perfect	Meaning
sinken	sinkt	sank	gesunken*	to sink
sitzen	sitzt	saß	gesessen	to sit
sollen	**soll**	sollte		to be supposed to, to ought to
sprechen	**spricht**	sprach	gesprochen	to speak
springen	springt	sprang	gesprungen*	to jump
stechen	**sticht**	stoch	gestochen	to sting
stehen	steht	stand	gestanden	to stand
stehlen	**stiehlt**	stahl	gestohlen	to steal
sterben	**stirbt**	starb	gestorben*	to die
steigen	steigt	stieg	gestiegen*	to climb
stinken	stinkt	stank	gestunken	to smell
stoßen	**stößt**	stieß	gestoßen*	to bump
streichen	streicht	strich	gestrichen	to cancel
sich streiten	**streitet**	stritt	gestritten	to argue
tragen	**trägt**	trug	getragen	to carry, to wear
treffen	**trifft**	traf	getroffen	to meet, to hit
treiben	treibt	trieb	getrieben	to do (sport)
treten	**tritt**	trat	getreten*	to step
trinken	trinkt	trank	getrunken	to drink
tun	tut	tat	getan	to do

Infinitive	3rd Person Present	Imperfect	Perfect	Meaning
verbringen	verbringt	verbrachte	verbracht	to spend time
vergessen	**vergisst**	vergaß	vergessen	to forget
vergleichen	vergleicht	verglich	verglichen	to compare
verlassen	**verlässt**	verließ	verlassen	to leave
verlieren	verliert	verlor	verloren	to lose
vermeiden	**vermeidet**	vermied	vermieden	to avoid
verschleißen	verschleißt	verschliss	verschlissen	to wear out
verschwinden	**verschwindet**	verschwand	verschwunden*	to disappear
versprechen	**verspricht**	versprach	versprochen	to promise
wachsen	**wächst**	wuchs	gewachsen*	to grow
waschen	**wäscht**	wusch	gewaschen	to wash
weisen	weist	wies	gewiesen	to show
werben	wirbt	warb	geworben	to attract, to advertise
werden	**wird**	wurde	geworden*	to become
werfen	**wirft**	warf	geworfen	to throw
wiegen	wiegt	wog	gewogen	to weigh
wissen	**weiß**	wusste	gewusst	to know
wollen	**will**	wollte		to want to
ziehen	zieht	zog	gezogen	to pull
zwingen	zwingt	zwang	gezwungen	to force

GRAMMAR INFORMATION

ADJECTIVES

Adjectives followed by a noun

Adjectives followed by a noun agree with ("match") the noun by taking an ending which depends on four factors:

- (a) the article (determiner) or lack of one in front of the adjective
- (b) the gender of the noun - masculine, feminine, or neuter
- (c) the case of the noun - nominative, accusative, genitive or dative
- (d) whether the noun is singular or plural

There are three tables (sets) of adjective endings. The one to use depends on which article (determiner) is used:

Table 1:

After *der/die/das, etc* (the); *dieser* (this); *jener* (that); *jeder* (each); *welcher* (which); *solcher* (such a), *mancher* (many a) and *alle* (all, which is, of course, plural)

	Masculine Singular	Feminine Singular	Neuter Singular	Plural (all genders)
Nom:	der kleine Mann	die kleine Frau	das kleine Kind	die kleinen Leute
Acc:	den kleinen Mann	die kleine Frau	das kleine Kind	die kleinen Leute
Gen:	des kleinen Mannes	der kleinen Frau	des kleinen Kindes	der kleinen Leute
Dat:	dem kleinen Mann	der kleinen Frau	dem kleinen Kind	den kleinen Leuten

Remember:

- All Genitive and Dative Singular and all Plural endings are *-en.*
- Masculine and Neuter nouns in the Genitive singular have *-es* or *-s* added. If they are single syllable nouns they usually add *-es.*
- You need to add *-n* to nouns which do not already have one in the Dative Plural of all genders.

Table 2:

After *ein/eine/ein* (a), kein (no), *and the Possessive Adjectives, mein* (my), *dein* (your, familiar singular), *sein* (his/its), *ihr* (her/its), *unser* (our), *euer* (your, familiar plural), *Ihr* (your, polite singular or plural) and *ihr* (their) the adjective has the following endings:

	Masculine Singular	Feminine Singular	Neuter Singular	Plural](all genders)
Nom:	ein kleiner Mann	eine kleine Frau	ein kleines Kind	keine kleinen Leute
Acc:	einen kleinen Mann	eine kleine Frau	ein kleines Kind	keine kleinen Leute
Gen:	eines kleinen Mannes	einer kleinen Frau	eines kleinen Kindes	keiner kleinen Leute
Dat:	einem kleinen Mann	einer kleinen Frau	einem kleinen Kind	keinen kleinen Leuten

Remember:
- For reasons of logic, *ein* itself has no plural. If "a" is plural (i.e. "some"), adjectives follow the plural pattern for Table 3 given below.
- All Genitive and Dative Singular and all Plural endings are *-en*.
- Masculine and Neuter nouns in the Genitive singular have *-es* or *-s* added. If they are single syllable nouns they usually add *-es*.
- You need to add *-n* to nouns which do not already have one in the Dative Plural of all genders.

Table 3:
Adjectives which are used alone before the noun have the following endings:

	Masculine Singular	Feminine Singular	Neuter Singular	Plural (all genders*)
Nom:	guter Wein	gute Milch	gutes Bier	gute Getränke
Acc:	guten Wein	gute Milch	gutes Bier	gute Getränke
Gen:	guten Weins	guter Milch	guten Biers	guter Getränke
Dat:	gutem Wein	guter Milch	gutem Bier	guten Getränken

(*also after non-specific numbers: *viele* (many), *mehrere* (several), *einige* (a few), *ein paar* (a few) and numbers)

Remember:
- Masculine and Neuter nouns in the Genitive singular have or *-s* added. If they are single syllable nouns they usually add *-es*.
- You need to add *-n* to nouns which do not already have one in the Dative Plural of all genders.

Adjectives not followed by a noun

Adjectives which stand alone - usually after *sein, werden* and *scheinen* - do not have an adjective ending.

Example:	Der Mann ist klein	*The man is small*

CASES

The four cases in German can seem difficult to understand. In fact, the rules for their use are relatively straightforward.

Nominative

The Nominative case is used:

1. for the subject of a verb

Example:	Heute scheint **die Sonne**	*Today the sun is shining*

Remember: The subject is not always the first idea in a sentence. (see **word order**)

2. after the verbs *sein, werden, bleiben, heißen* and *scheinen*

Accusative

The Accusative case is used:

1. for the direct object (the thing that suffers the action of the verb) of most verbs.

Example:	Ich habe **einen Kuli** gekauft	*I bought a biro*

2. after certain prepositions. (See **prepositions**).

Dative

The Dative case is used:

1. after certain prepositions. (See **prepositions**)

2. after certain verbs which always take the Dative.

The most frequent are *helfen (to help), folgen (to follow)* and *danken (to thank)*.

Example: Ich helfe **meinem Vater** in der Küche
              I help my father in the kitchen

3. for the indirect object of a verb
   Example: Er gibt **seiner** Mutter das Buch
                 He gives the book to his mother

Genitive

The Genitive case is used:

1. to show "of" or possession. You may find it easier to use von + Dative.

   Example: ein Foto **meiner Schwester**   *a photo of my sister*
                 ein Foto **von meinem Bruder**   *a photo of my brother*

2. An alternative form similar to English usage (but with no apostrophe) is used with the names of people, towns or countries.

   Example: Barbaras Kuli   *Barbara's biro*

3. after certain prepositions. (See **prepositions).**

CONJUNCTIONS

Conjunctions are words which join two clauses, such as "and", "but", "because" and "while". There are two kinds of conjunction in German, known as co-ordinating conjunctions and subordinating conjunctions.

Co-ordinating conjunctions

These join two clauses which could otherwise stand as two German sentences in their own right without any changes being made to them. Most of them can also link single words or phrases in lists. There are five common ones.

They have NO effect on word-order. They are:

   und *and*   aber *but*   oder *or*   sondern *but not*   denn *for*

   Example: Er wohnt in Lübeck **und** er hat dort viele Freunde
                 He lives in Lübeck and has many friends there

Subordinating conjunctions

These are conjunctions which add a subordinate clause (i.e. one which could not stand on its own as a German sentence without any changes being made to it) on to a main clause. They affect the word order by sending the verb to the end of the clause.

Example: **Wenn** es heute regnet, bleibe ich zu Hause
Ich bleibe zu Hause, **wenn** es heute regnet
I shall stay at home if it rains today

If a separable verb is the last word in the clause it does not separate.

Example: Wenn er heute **ankommt**, bleibe ich zu Hause
If he arrives today I shall stay at home

The common subordinating conjunctions are listed below:

als	*when (single occasion in* past)
nachdem	*after (she had done* that)
ob	*whether*
weil	*because*
wenn	*if, when, whenever (repeated* occasion)

NOUNS

German nouns always start with a capital letter.

All German nouns belong to one of three grammatical genders, masculine (der), feminine (die), or neuter (das).

Plural forms are difficult in German, and the only way to make real headway in learning plural forms is to learn them with each new word.

Singular: der Stadtplan *map*   die Schule *school*   das Buch *book*
Plural: die Stadtpläne *maps*   die Schulen *schools*   die Bücher *books*

Adjectival nouns ‡

All adjectives and participles can be used as nouns in German. They are then written with a capital letter.

Example: Deutsche *nmf* ‡   *German person*

Adjectival nouns take the same endings as they would if they were followed by a noun of the appropriate gender.

Like Table 1:

	Masculine Singular	Feminine Singular	Plural
Nom:	der Deutsche	die Deutsche	die Deutschen
Acc:	den Deutschen	die Deutsche	die Deutschen
Gen:	des Deutschen	der Deutschen	der Deutschen
Dat:	dem Deutschen	der Deutschen	den Deutschen

Like Table 2:

	Masculine Singular	Feminine Singular	Plural (Like Table 3)
Nom:	ein Deutscher	eine Deutsche	Deutsche
Acc:	einen Deutschen	eine Deutsche	Deutsche
Gen:	eines Deutschen	einer Deutschen	Deutscher
Dat:	einem Deutschen	einer Deutschen	Deutschen

Weak nouns *nm wk, nnt wk*

These nouns are slightly irregular. They are **masculine** with the exception of *das Herz*.

The majority have *-en* throughout the plural and in all cases of the singular except the Nominative. They do not usually have an *-s* in the Genitive singular. However, the following **do** add an *-s* in the Genitive singular: *der Name, der Buchstabe, der Gedanke* and *das Herz*.

Example:	Singular	Plural
Nominative:	der Franzose	die Franzosen
Accusative:	den Franzosen	die Franzosen
Genitive:	des Franzosen	der Franzosen
Dative:	dem Franzosen	den Franzosen
Nominative:	der Mensch	die Menschen
Accusative:	den Menschen	die Menschen
Genitive:	des Menschen	der Menschen
Dative:	dem Menschen	den Menschen

PREPOSITIONS

Prepositions are words which are used to show a relationship between one noun and another. This word often shows the position of one thing in relation to another. Prepositions in German are followed by different cases.

Prepositions which take the Accusative

bis	*as far as; until*	ohne	*without*
durch	*through*	um	*at + clock times, about*
für	*for*	pro	*per*
gegen	*against*	wider	*against*

Example:	**für** meinen Vater	*for my father*
	durch die Aula	*through the school hall*

Prepositions which take the Dative

aus	*out of, made of*
außer	*except for*
bei	*at the house of*
gegenüber*	*opposite*
mit	*with, by*
nach	*to, after + time*
seit	*since, for*
von	*from, of*
zu	*to, at, at + price*

* may come before or after the noun

Example: **mit** meinem Freund   *with my (boy)friend*
            seit zwei Jahren   *for two years*
            der Kirche **gegenüber** *opposite the church*

Remember:
- Even though *aus* and *zu* imply motion, they **ALWAYS** take the Dative.
- Most nouns add an -*n* in the Dative plural if they do not already have one. This is often forgotten.

Example: Ich sehe meine alten Freunde mit meinen neuen Freunden
            I see my old friends with my new friends

Prepositions which take either Dative or Accusative
Nine common prepositions can take either Accusative or Dative. These can best be learnt in related groups.

in	*in, inside*
an	*on (the side of), at, of*
auf	*on (top of), at, in*
hinter*	*behind*
vor*	*in front of, before*
über	*over*
unter*	*under*
neben*	*next to*
zwischen*	*between*

* usually with Dative

Remember:
If the preposition is about position, then the Dative is used. If it is about motion towards, then the Accusative is used.

Example: Ich gehe **in die** Schule   (in + Accusative - motion)
I go to **school**
Ich arbeite **in der** Schule   (in + Dative - position)
I work in school

Prepositions which take the Genitive
These are listed with the three most common ones first, then related pairs.

trotz	*despite, in spite of*
während	*during*
wegen	*because of*
außerhalb	*outside (of)*
innerhalb	*within*
anstatt	*instead of*
statt	*instead of*

Example: **während** der Ferien   *during the holidays*
trotz der Hitze   *despite the heat*

Tip: Remember that masculine and neuter nouns add an *-s* in the Genitive singular.

Example: **wegen** des schlechten Wetters
because of the bad weather

PERSONAL PRONOUNS AND POSSESSIVES

Nominative	Accusative	Dative	Possessive
ich	mich	mir	mein
du	dich	dir	dein
Sie	Sie	Ihnen	Ihr
er	ihn	ihm	sein
sie	sie	ihr	ihr
es	es	ihm	sein
wir	uns	uns	unser
ihr	euch	euch	euer (eure)
Sie	Sie	Ihnen	Ihr
sie	sie	ihnen	ihr

Sie or du?

Germans are very concerned to use the correct form for "you". Getting it wrong is impolite. The following are the main rules concerning choice of "you":

1. *du/dich/dir/dein* is used for speaking to a child (up to about 15) or an animal, and between children, students, relatives and close friends.

2. *ihr/euch/euch/euer* is used to address a group of two or more people in which at least some would be addressed as *"du"*.

3. *Sie/Sie/Ihnen/Ihr* is used in all other instances, particularly if addressing one or more strangers.

Er, sie and es

Remember that "it" may refer to a masculine or feminine noun in German, and that *er* or *sie, ihn* or *sie, ihm* or *ihr* may be needed in preference to *es,* which is reserved for neuter nouns. *Er* and *sie* do not refer solely to biological gender.

Example: Hier ist die Tasche. Ich habe **sie** gestern gekauft
             Here is the bag. I bought it yesterday
             Hier ist der neue Stuhl. Ich habe **ihn** gestern bekommen
             Here is the new chair. I got it yesterday.

Man

The word *man* takes third person singular endings and means literally in English 'one'.

Example: **Man** muss die Hausaufgaben machen
             One must do the homework

WORD ORDER

1. In a simple sentence, the verb is the second idea. It may come after the subject, after another idea, or after a subordinate clause.

   In compound tenses such as the perfect tense, the auxiliary (*haben* or *sein*) occupies the position of second idea in the sentence, while the past participle is at the end of the sentence. The rest of the sentence is sandwiched between the two. In the same way the main part of a separable verb occupies the position of the second idea in the sentence and the prefix is at the end of the sentence.

   A modal verb takes the second position in the sentence. If there is an infinitive it goes to the end of the sentence.

   Our preference is to call this rule the "1 - 2 - 3 rule".

	VERB		
1st idea	**2nd idea**	**3rd idea**	
Ich	**gehe**	heute in die Stadt	
Heute	**gehe**	ich in die Stadt	
In die Stadt	**gehe**	ich heute	
Wenn es sonnig ist,	**gehe**	ich in die Stadt	
Ich	**bin**	in die Stadt	gegangen
Ich	**habe**	ein Buch	gekauft
Der Bus	**kommt**	um neun Uhr	an
Ich	**will**	eine Banane	essen
Er	**muss**	ins Bett	gehen

2. Adverbs in German are usually in the order Time - Manner - Place.

Time	Manner	Place
Ich fahre heute	mit dem Bus	nach Worcester

3. If two sentences are joined by a co-ordinating conjunction such as *und, aber,* or *oder,* the conjunction does NOT count in the word order for the 1 - 2 - 3 rule and has no effect on it.

   Example: Ich **mag** Mathe aber ich **mag** lieber Chemie
   I like Maths but I prefer Chemistry

4. If a clause is joined to the rest of the sentence by a subordinating conjunction, the verb (or the auxiliary) goes to the end of that clause. The past participle comes before the auxiliary.

   Example: Ich fahre mit dem Bus zur Schule, wenn es um 8 Uhr **regnet**
   I travel to school by bus if it is raining at 8 o'clock
   Renate weiß, dass sie zu spät abgefahren **ist**
   Renate knows that she has set off too late

VERBS

When a verb is listed in a dictionary or word list, it is given in the **Infinitive**.

Example: wohnen   *live*

gehen   *go, walk*

The infinitive will normally be the starting point in describing how tenses are formed.

Regular and irregular verbs

There are two main sorts of verbs in German:

Regular which follow a rule. Regular verbs are often called **weak** verbs in German (because they do not have a "mind of their own"). They are marked *v reg*. Some regular verbs have minor variations. They are marked *v reg†*. See page 229.

Irregular which do not always follow a rule and therefore have to be learnt. Irregular German verbs are often called **strong** verbs (because they are "strong-minded").
They are marked *v irreg*.

Both regular and irregular verbs can fall into the following categories:

Reflexive marked *v reg refl* or *v irreg refl*.
If the reflexive pronoun is dative, they are marked *v reg dat refl* or *v irreg dat refl*.

Separable with prefixes which separate and go to the end of the clause. They are marked *v reg sep* or *v irreg sep*.

Inseparable with prefixes which do not separate. They are marked *v reg insep* or *v irreg insep*.

Regular Verbs *v reg*

Infinitive/ Command	Present	Perfect
spielen	ich spiele	ich habe gespielt
to play	du spielst	du hast gespielt
	Sie spielen	Sie haben gespielt
Spiel!	er/sie/es spielt	er/sie/es hat gespielt
Spielt!	wir spielen	wir haben gespielt
Spielen Sie!	ihr spielt	ihr habt gespielt
	Sie spielen	Sie haben gespielt
	sie spielen	sie haben gespielt

Irregular Verbs *v irreg*

Infinitive/ Command	Present	Perfect
sehen	ich sehe	ich habe gesehen
to see	du siehst	du hast gesehen
	Sie sehen	Sie haben gesehen
Sieh!	er/sie/es sieht	er/sie/es hat gesehen
Seht!	wir sehen	wir haben gesehen
Sehen Sie!	ihr seht	ihr habt gesehen
	Sie sehen	Sie haben gesehen
	sie sehen	sie haben gesehen

Irregular Verbs with 'sein' *v irreg*

Infinitive/ Command	Present	Perfect
gehen*	ich gehe	ich bin gegangen
to go	du gehst	du bist gegangen
	Sie gehen	Sie sind gegangen
Geh!	er/sie/es geht	er/sie/es ist gegangen
Geht!	wir gehen	wir sind gegangen
Gehen Sie!	ihr geht	ihr seid gegangen
	Sie gehen	Sie sind gegangen
	sie gehen	sie sind gegangen

Reflexive Verbs *v refl*

Infinitive/ Command	Present	Perfect
sich waschen *to wash (oneself)* Wasch dich! Wascht euch! Waschen Sie sich!	ich wasche mich du wäschst dich Sie waschen sich er/sie/es wäscht sich wir waschen uns ihr wascht euch Sie waschen sich sie waschen sich	ich habe mich gewaschen du hast dich gewaschen Sie haben sich gewaschen er/sie/es hat sich gewaschen wir haben uns gewaschen ihr habt euch gewaschen Sie haben sich gewaschen sie haben sich gewaschen

Separable Verbs *sep*

Infinitive/ Command	Present	Perfect
aufstehen* *to get up, to stand up* Steh auf! Steht auf! Stehen Sie auf!	ich stehe auf du stehst auf Sie stehen auf er/sie/es steht auf wir stehen auf ihr steht auf Sie stehen auf sie stehen auf	ich bin aufgestanden du bist aufgestanden Sie sind aufgestanden er/sie/es ist aufgestanden wir sind aufgestanden ihr seid aufgestanden Sie sind aufgestanden sie sind aufgestanden

Haben or sein?

The choice of *haben* or *sein* as auxiliary in the perfect tense can cause some difficulty. In this dictionary verbs which require *sein* are marked with *.
A simple rule of thumb is:

Verbs of motion, plus *bleiben*, *sein* and *werden* require *sein* as an auxiliary.

sein	*to be*	haben	*to have*
ich bin	*I am*	ich habe	*I have*
du bist	*you are*	du hast	*you have*
Sie sind	*you are*	Sie haben	*you have*
er/sie/es ist	*he/she/it is*	er/sie/es hat	*he/she/it has*
wir sind	*we are*	wir haben	*we have*
ihr seid	*you are*	ihr habt	*you have*
sie sind	*they are*	sie haben	*they have*
Sie sind	*you are*	Sie haben	*you have*

Modal Verbs

The Plural forms follow the pattern of the regular verbs. Note, however, the singular forms:

können *to be able to*	wollen *to want to*	müssen *to have to*	mögen *to like*	dürfen *to be allowed to*	sollen *ought to, to be supposed to*
ich kann	ich will	ich muss	ich mag	ich darf	ich soll
du kannst	du willst	du musst	du magst	du darfst	du sollst
er/sie/es kann	er/sie/es will	er/sie/es muss	er/sie/es mag	er/sie/es darf	er/sie/es soll
wir können	wir wollen	wir müssen	wir mögen	wir dürfen	wir sollen
ihr könnt	ihr wollt	ihr müsst	ihr mögt	ihr dürft	ihr sollt
sie können	sie wollen	sie müssen	sie mögen	sie dürfen	sie sollen
Sie können	Sie wollen	Sie müssen	Sie mögen	Sie dürfen	Sie sollen

The modal verbs are often followed by another verb. This second verb will be in the infinitive form and will be the last word in a main sentence.

Ich will heute Abend ins Kino **gehen** aber ich muss die Hausaufgaben **machen**
I want to go to the cinema tonight, but I have to do my homework

Imperfect

The Imperfect is the past tense most commonly used in formal writing such as books and newspapers. Here are some common imperfect forms you might meet:

ich war	*I was*	ich kaufte	*I bought*
ich hatte	*I had*	es regnete	*it rained*
ich ging	*I went*	es schneite	*it snowed*
ich fuhr	*I went*		

Regular verbs with variations †

Some regular verbs have minor variations. They are marked *v reg*†.

1. Verbs ending in *-ieren* (except *schmieren*) do not have a *ge-* on the front of the past participle in the perfect and other compound tenses.

   Example: kopieren   ich habe kopiert

Verbs in this category include:

addieren, adoptieren, akzeptieren, sich amüsieren, anprobieren, arrangieren, blockieren, buchstabieren, dekorieren, demonstrieren, diskutieren, dressieren, existieren, fotografieren, fotokopieren, funktionieren, gratulieren, identifizieren, informatisieren, informieren, installieren, sich interessieren, kontrollieren, kopieren, korrigieren, moderieren, notieren, organisieren, passieren*, polieren, probieren, protestieren, sich rasieren, reduzieren, reparieren, reservieren, schikanieren, studieren, tapezieren, telefonieren, tolerieren, trainieren, zitieren

2. Verbs starting with *be-, emp-, ent-, er-, ge-, ver-* and *zer-* do not add a *ge*-on the front of the past participle in the perfect and other compound tenses.

    Example: beenden   ich habe ... beendet

Verbs in this category include:

sich bedanken, bedauern, bedeuten, (sich) bedienen, bedrohen, sich beeilen, beenden, beflecken, befragen, befriedigen, begegnen*, begleiten, begrüßen, behandeln, sich beklagen, beleidigen, bemerken, beneiden, benutzen, beobachten, sich beruhigen, berühren, sich beschweren, besichtigen, bestätigen, bestellen, bestrafen, besuchen, bewegen, bewundern, bezahlen, empören, entdecken, entführen, sich entschuldigen, sich entspannen, entwickeln, erforschen, sich erholen, (sich) erinnern, sich erkälten, erklären, sich erkundigen, erlauben, ermutigen, erneuern, erreichen, ersetzen, erstaunen, erwähnen, erwarten, erzählen, gehorchen, gehören, sich gewöhnen, veräppeln, verdächtigen, verdanken, verdienen, vereinigen, verfaulen, verhaften, verhindern, verhüten, verkaufen, verlangen, (sich) verletzen, verleugnen, vermieten, vernachlässigen, verpassen, verrenken, verrichten, verschlucken, verschwenden, versichern, verspäten, verstauchen, (sich) verstecken, versuchen, verursachen, verwandeln, verweigern, verwöhnen, zerquetschen, zerstören

3. Verbs whose infinitives end in *-den, -men, -nen* and *-ten* have the endings *-test* in the *du* form and *-tet* in the *er* and *ihr* forms of the present tense. In the imperfect tense, they add an extra e before the imperfect endings are added. In the perfect tense, they add an extra e before the final *-t* of the past participle.

    Example: arbeiten   du arbei**test**, er arbei**tet**; ich arbei**te**te, etc;
                                       ich habe gear**beitet**

Verbs in this category include:

abtrocknen, achten, antworten, anzünden, arbeiten, atmen, ausrichten, ausschalten, (sich) baden, beantworten, bluten, bürsten, einschalten, entfalten, entfernen, falten, flirten, husten, kosten, landen*, (sich) leisten, mieten, öffnen, ordnen, rechnen, retten, schalten, schulden, senden, starten*, töten, trocknen, übernachten, unterrichten, vollenden, vorbereiten, warten, sich wenden, wetten, zelten, züchten

WRITING LETTERS AND POSTCARDS

Pupils are often asked to write a letter or a postcard in German. It is particularly important to **carry out the tasks set in the question.** In other words, you should not write a pre-prepared letter which has only a vague resemblance to the question.

Postcards are nearly always to friends. Letters can be to friends and family (informal letters) or to businesses, hotels or public offices (formal letters).

Informal letters and postcards

Letter envelope

When you write an envelope or a card to an address in Germany:-

Write *Herrn, Frau* or *Familie* first on a line on its own.
Sometimes the surname is written next, followed by the first name.
The street name comes before the house number.
Leave a line space before writing the 5-figure postcode.
It is written before the name of the town, on the same line.
The town is usually written in capital letters.

The name and address of the sender are normally written on the back of the envelope, after the word *Absender:* or *Abs:* (Sender).

Informal Letters

Town and date   It is usual just to write the name of the town and the date.
Put this information in the **top right-hand corner** of the page.

Dear ...

Lieber Robert,	(male)
Liebe Anne,	(female)
Lieber Robert, liebe Anne,	(more than one person)
Liebe Freunde,	(plural, all male, male and female)
Liebe Freundinnen,	(plural, all female)

Punctuation   Nowadays a comma is frequently used after *Liebe(r)* ...,
The first word of the letter should start with a lower case letter
unless it requires a capital letter (because it is a noun or *Sie*).
If an exclamation mark is used after *Liebe(r)* ...! then the first word
of the letter should begin with a capital letter.

du or Sie?   Informal letters and postcards to one person are usually written in
the **du** form. Since the 1998 spelling reform, **du, dich, dir** and
dein are no longer written with a capital letter in informal letters.
If you are writing to more than one person, use **ihr, euch** and
euer, again without capitals.

Closing   Useful phrases include:

Das ist alles für heute.	*That's all for today.*
Jetzt muss ich meine	*Now I'm going to*
Hausaufgaben machen	*do my homework.*
Ich hoffe, bald	*I hope to hear*
von dir zu hören.	*from you soon.*
Schreib bald.	*Write soon.*
Bis später.	*See you soon.*

Signing off   Use one of these phrases:

Alles Gute
Mit besten Grüßen

Follow it with one of these expressions:

dein Brieffreund	(if you are male)
deine Brieffreundin	(if you are female)
dein	(if you are male)
deine	(if you are female)

Finally, sign your name.

Formal letters

Your address   In the **top right-hand corner** of the page write your own address.

Recipient's Address

In the **top left-hand corner** of the page put the name and address of the person or firm you are writing to.

Date   Write the date under your address.

Dear ...

Lieber Herr Kohl,	*Dear + name*
Liebe Frau Kohl,	*Dear + name*
Sehr geehrter Herr,	*Dear Sir*
Sehr geehrte Dame,	*Dear Madam*
Sehr geehrte Damen und Herren,	*Dear Sirs*

Punctuation   Nowadays a comma is frequently used after *Liebe(r)* ...,
The first word of the letter should start with a lower case letter unless it requires a capital letter (because it is a noun or *Sie*).
If an exclamation mark is used after *Liebe(r)* ...! then the first word of the letter should begin with a capital letter.

du or Sie?   Formal letters are always written in the **Sie** form. Use **Sie, Ihnen** and **Ihr.** Don't forget the capital letters.

Signing off   Business letters in German usually end with

mit freundlichen Grüßen

which is the equivalent of *Yours sincerely* or *Yours faithfully*.

Hochachtungsvoll

is used nowadays only in very formal letters.

Finally, sign your name.

The envelope   Your name and address are normally written on the back of the envelope, after *Absender/Abs*. (See page 231).

Sample informal letter

Malvern, den 6.Mai 1999

Lieber Klaus,

vielen Dank für deinen Brief, der gestern hier angekommen
ist ...

Schreib bald wieder
dein Brieffreund

Paul

Sample formal letter

John WHITE
32 New Street
OLDTOWN
OT6 7XY
GB

Städtisches Informationsbüro
Hauptstraße 26
64720 ERBACH
Germany   den 14. November 1999

Sehr geehrte Damen und Herren,

mit diesem Brief bitte ich Sie um einige Informationen über ...

Vielen Dank für Ihre Mühe.

mit freundlichen Grüßen

John WHITE

INSTRUCTIONS

Note: These instructions have been given in the **du** form, which is the one used by most text books. Versions of the most frequently used command words in the **Sie** form can be found at the end of this section on page 239.

All four skills: Listening, Reading, Speaking, Writing
Sequence words

zuerst	*first*
jetzt	*now*
dann	*then*

Questions

um wie viel Uhr?	*at what time?*
wann?	*when?*
warum?	*why?*
was?	*what?*
was heißt ...?	*what does ... mean?*
was kostet ...?	*how much does ... cost?*
was kostet das?	*how much is it?*
welchen ziehst du vor?	*which one do you prefer?*
wer hat Recht?	*who is right?*
wie?	*how?*
wie ist er/sie/es?	*what is he/it like?*
wo?	*where?*
wo ist ...?	*where is ...?*
wo sind ...?	*where are ...?*

Information

auf Deutsch	*in German*
auf Englisch	*in English*
bitte wenden	*turn over the page*
deiner Meinung nach	*in your opinion*
du wirst nicht alle Buchstaben brauchen	*you will not need all the letters*
einige Fragen	*some questions*
einige Sätze	*some sentences*
er spricht über	*he is talking about*
es wird zwei Pausen im Ausschnitt geben	*there will be two pauses in the extract*
es wird zwei Pausen in der Ansage geben	*there will be two pauses in the announcement*

falsch	*false, wrong*
folgende Antworten	*the following answers*
für jede Frage/für jede Person	*for each question/for each person*
für jeden Kunden	*for each customer*
hier ist ein Beispiel	*here is an example*
in Ziffern	*in numbers*
richtig	*true*
sie spricht mit ...	*she is speaking to ...*
sie spricht über ...	*she is talking about ...*
zwischen zwei Personen	*between two people*

Listening and Reading

beantworte auf Deutsch	*answer in German*
beantworte auf Deutsch oder kreuze die Kästchen an	*answer in German or tick the boxes*
beantworte die Fragen	*answer the questions*
bitte wenden	*turn the page, turn over*
du darfst ein Wörterbuch benutzen, wenn du willst	*you may use a dictionary if you wish*
du findest Information über...	*you will find information on...*
du wirst eine Mitteilung/einen Dialog/eine Sendung/ein Interview hören	*you are going to hear a message/a dialogue/a programme/an interview*
du wirst einige Dialoge zweimal hören	*you will hear twice some short dialogues*
entscheide	*Decide*
ergänze die Sätze	*complete the sentences*
erkläre, wie/erkläre, warum	*explain how/explain why*
finde das Symbol, das dem Wort entspricht	*find the symbol which matches the word*
finde den entsprechenden Satz für jedes Foto	*find the sentence which matches each photo*
finde den Fehler	*find the mistake*
finde den Text, der jedem Bild/Titel entspricht	*find the text which matches each picture/title*
finde die richtige Antwort auf jede Frage	*choose the right answer to each question*
finde die Worte, die Redewendungen	*find the words, the phrases*
finde X auf dem Plan	*find X on the plan*
fülle die Einzelheiten aus	*complete the details*
fülle die Liste/die Tabelle aus	*complete the list/table/grid*
fülle die Lücken aus	*fill in the blanks*
fülle die Vergleiche aus	*complete the comparisons*

höre das Beispiel an	*listen to the example*
höre gut zu	*listen carefully*
korrigiere die Aussage	*correct the statement*
korrigiere die Fehler	*correct the mistakes*
kreuze das Kästchen an	*tick the box*
kreuze den richtigen Satz an	*tick the appropriate sentence*
kreuze die richtigen Kästchen an	*tick the (appropriate) boxes*
kreuze nur 5 Kästchen an	*tick 5 boxes only*
lies den Artikel, den Text, die Geschichte	*read the article, the text, the story*
lies den Brief	*read the letter*
lies die Anweisungen	*read the instructions*
lies die Anzeigen	*read the adverts*
lies die Fragen	*read the questions*
lies die Information	*read the information*
lies die Liste/lies die Notizen	*read the list/look at the notes*
lies einen Ausschnitt aus einer Zeitung	*read the extract from a newspaper*
lies folgende Sätze	*read the following sentences*
lies sorgfältig	*read carefully*
mach Notizen	*make notes*
notiere die Einzelheiten	*note down the details*
ordne die Bilder richtig ein	*put the pictures into the correct order*
ordne die Wörter richtig ein	*arrange the words in the correct order*
schau dir die Tabelle an	*look at the grid*
schau dir die Bilder an	*look at the drawings*
schreibe auf Englisch	*write the equivalent in English*
schreibe das Wort, das zu den anderen nicht passt	*write the odd word out*
schreibe den Buchstaben	*write the letter*
schreibe den entsprechenden Buchstaben	*write the letter which matches*
schreibe den richtigen Buchstaben ins Kästchen	*put the correct letter in the box*
schreibe die Antworten	*write the answers*
schreibe die Nummer	*write the number*
schreibe im Kästchen die Nummer des entsprechenden Bildes	*write the number of the illustration in the box*
schreibe Notizen	*make notes*
schreibe die entsprechenden Nummern	*write the numbers which match*
sind die Sätze richtig oder falsch?	*are the sentences true or false?*
unterstreiche/verbinde	*underline/match up*
wähle die passendste Beschreibung	*choose the description which best fits*
wähle die richtige Antwort	*choose the correct answer*
wähle ja oder nein	*circle yes or no*

wenn der Satz richtig ist, kreuze das Kästchen **richtig** an	*if the sentence is true, tick the **true** box*
wenn der Satz falsch ist, kreuze das Kästchen **falsch** an	*if the sentence is false, tick the **false** box*
wenn die Aussage falsch ist, korrigiere sie	*if the statement is incorrect, write a correct one*
wenn die Aussage richtig ist, kreuze das Kästchen **richtig** an	*if the statement is true, tick the **true** box*
wenn die Aussage falsch ist, kreuze das Kästchen **falsch** an	*if the statement is true, tick the **false** box*
zeichne ein Pfeil, um zu zeigen, welches Bild sich auf welches Bild bezieht	*draw an arrow to show which picture goes with which sign*
zeig auf dem Plan/auf der Karte	*mark on the plan/map*

Speaking

beantworte diese Fragen	*answer these questions*
bedanke dich beim Ladenbesitzer	*thank the shopkeeper*
beende die Unterhaltung höflich	*end the conversation politely*
begrüße den Prüfer	*greet the examiner*
benutze die Symbole, um einen Dialog zu erfinden	*use the symbols to make up a dialogue*
beschreibe das Bild	*describe the picture*
bitte um folgende Information	*ask for the following information*
sag, was du gemacht hast	*say what you did*
schau dir dir Bilder an	*look at the pictures, the photos*
sprich	*speak*
stelle Fragen	*ask questions*

Writing

ändere	*change*
beantworte den Brief	*reply to the letter*
beantworte die Fragen, die im Brief stehen	*answer the questions asked in the letter*
bereite folgende Aufgaben auf Deutsch vor	*prepare the following tasks in German*
beschreibe	*describe/write a description of*
du darfst ein Wörterbuch benutzen	*you can use a dictionary*
erfinde eine Broschüre, ein Poster	*prepare a brochure, a poster*
erkläre, wie .../ erkläre, warum ...	*explain how ... /explain why ...*
erwähne	*mention*
erzähle, was du gemacht hast	*say what you did*
frage nach folgenden Einzelheiten	*ask for the following details*

frage um Rat	*ask for advice*
fülle das Formular aus	*fill in the form*
gib Auskunft	*give information*
gib deine Eindrücke	*give your impressions*
gib deine Meinung und sage warum	*write your opinion and the reasons for it*
in deinem Brief sollst du ...	*in your letter you should ...*
sag, was du gemacht hast	*say what you did*
schreibe die Einzelheiten	*write the details*
schreibe eine Antwort	*write a reply*
schreibe eine Kurzfassung	*summarise*
schreibe eine Liste	*write a list*
schreibe eine Postkarte/einen Brief	*write a postcard/a letter*
schreibe einen Artikel	*write an article*
schreibe etwa 100 Worte	*write about 100 words*
stelle dich vor	*introduce yourself*
stelle dir vor, dass ...	*imagine that...*
vergleiche	*make a comparison*
wähle Thema 1 oder Thema 2	*choose title 1 or title 2*

Common commands in the Sie form

antworten Sie	*reply*	machen Sie einen Kreis um	*circle*
beenden Sie	*finish*		
begrüßen	*greet*	notieren Sie	*note*
benutzen Sie	*use*	ordnen Sie	*arrange*
bereiten Sie ... vor	*prepare*	schauen Sie sich ... an	*look at*
beschreiben Sie	*describe*	schreiben Sie	*write*
entscheiden Sie	*decide*	setzen Sie ein	*put*
ergänzen Sie	*complete*	Sie können	*you can*
erklären Sie	*explain*	sprechen Sie (über)	*speak (about)*
erwähnen Sie	*mention*		
erzählen Sie	*tell (a story)*	stellen Sie sich vor	*imagine*
finden Sie	*find*		
fragen Sie	*ask*	unterstreichen Sie	*underline*
fragen Sie	*ask (questions)*		
füllen Sie ... aus	*fill in*	verbessern Sie	*correct*
geben Sie	*give*	wählen Sie	*choose*
hören Sie ... zu	*listen to*	wenden Sie	*turn*
kreuzen Sie an	*tick*	zeichnen Sie	*draw*
lesen Sie	*read*	zeigen Sie	*indicate*
machen Sie	*make*		

Mitteleuropa

Nordsee

Ostsee

Oder

• Bremen   • Hamburg

Weser   *Elbe*

• Berlin

• Hannover

• Düsseldorf   • Leipzig
• Köln   Dresden •
• Bonn

Deutschland

Mosel   • Frankfurt   *Main*

• Nürnberg

• Stuttgart

Donau

Rhein   • München
Bodensee   • Salzburg
• Basel   • Wien

Österreich

• Zürich   • Innsbruck

• Bern

die Schweiz

• Genf

Dange | Wzzy | Lean on me
stand by me